CLOUD COMPUTING 2018

The Ninth International Conference on Cloud Computing, GRIDs, and Virtualization

February 18 - 22, 2018

Barcelona, Spain

CLOUD COMPUTING 2018 Editors

Bob Duncan, University of Aberdeen, UK

Yong Woo Lee, University of Seoul, Korea

Aspen Olmsted, College of Charleston, USA

Printed from e-media with permission by:

Curran Associates, Inc.
57 Morehouse Lane
Red Hook, NY 12571

Some format issues inherent in the e-media version may also appear in this print version.

Printed by Curran Associates, Inc. (2018)

International Academy, Research, and Industry Association (IARIA)
412 Derby Way
Wilmington, DE 19810

Phone: (408) 893-6407
Fax: (408) 527-6351

petre@iaria.org

Additional copies of this publication are available from:

Curran Associates, Inc.
57 Morehouse Lane
Red Hook, NY 12571 USA
Phone: 845-758-0400
Fax: 845-758-2633
Email: curran@proceedings.com
Web: www.proceedings.com

CLOUD COMPUTING 2018

Forward

The Ninth International Conference on Cloud Computing, GRIDs, and Virtualization (CLOUD COMPUTING 2018), held between February 18 - 22, 2018 - Barcelona, Spain, continued a series of events targeted to prospect the applications supported by the new paradigm and validate the techniques and the mechanisms. A complementary target was to identify the open issues and the challenges to fix them, especially on security, privacy, and inter- and intra-clouds protocols.

Cloud computing is a normal evolution of distributed computing combined with Service-oriented architecture, leveraging most of the GRID features and Virtualization merits. The technology foundations for cloud computing led to a new approach of reusing what was achieved in GRID computing with support from virtualization.

The conference had the following tracks:

- Cloud computing
- Computing in virtualization-based environments
- Platforms, infrastructures and applications
- Challenging features

Similar to the previous edition, this event attracted excellent contributions and active participation from all over the world. We were very pleased to receive top quality contributions.

We take here the opportunity to warmly thank all the members of the CLOUD COMPUTING 2018 technical program committee, as well as the numerous reviewers. The creation of such a high quality conference program would not have been possible without their involvement. We also kindly thank all the authors that dedicated much of their time and effort to contribute to CLOUD COMPUTING 2018. We truly believe that, thanks to all these efforts, the final conference program consisted of top quality contributions.

Also, this event could not have been a reality without the support of many individuals, organizations and sponsors. We also gratefully thank the members of the CLOUD COMPUTING 2018 organizing committee for their help in handling the logistics and for their work that made this professional meeting a success.

We hope that CLOUD COMPUTING 2018 was a successful international forum for the exchange of ideas and results between academia and industry and to promote further progress in the area of cloud computing, GRIDs and virtualization. We also hope that Barcelona provided a pleasant environment during the conference and everyone saved some time for exploring this beautiful city.

CLOUD COMPUTING 2018 Chairs

CLOUD COMPUTING 2018 Steering Committee

Carlos Becker Westphall, Federal University of Santa Catarina, Brazil
Yong Woo Lee, University of Seoul, Korea
Christoph Reich, Furtwangen University, Germany
Hong Zhu, Oxford Brookes University, UK
Bob Duncan, University of Aberdeen, UK
Aspen Olmsted, College of Charleston, USA
Alex Sim, Lawrence Berkeley National Laboratory, USA

CLOUD COMPUTING 2018 Industry/Research Advisory Committee

Antonin Chazalet, Orange, France
Sören Frey, Daimler TSS GmbH, Germany
Mohamed Mohamed, IBM, Almaden Research Center, USA
Raul Valin Ferreiro, Fujitsu Laboratories of Europe, Spain
Uwe Hohenstein, Siemens AG, Germany
Bill Karakostas, VLTN gcv, Antwerp, Belgium
Matthias Olzmann, noventum consulting GmbH - Münster, Germany
Ze Yu, Google Inc, USA

CLOUD COMPUTING 2018

Committee

CLOUD COMPUTING 2018 Steering Committee

Carlos Becker Westphall, Federal University of Santa Catarina, Brazil
Yong Woo Lee, University of Seoul, Korea
Christoph Reich, Furtwangen University, Germany
Hong Zhu, Oxford Brookes University, UK
Bob Duncan, University of Aberdeen, UK
Aspen Olmsted, College of Charleston, USA
Alex Sim, Lawrence Berkeley National Laboratory, USA

CLOUD COMPUTING 2018 Industry/Research Advisory Committee

Antonin Chazalet, Orange, France
Sören Frey, Daimler TSS GmbH, Germany
Mohamed Mohamed, IBM, Almaden Research Center, USA
Raul Valin Ferreiro, Fujitsu Laboratories of Europe, Spain
Uwe Hohenstein, Siemens AG, Germany
Bill Karakostas, VLTN gcv, Antwerp, Belgium
Matthias Olzmann, noventum consulting GmbH - Münster, Germany
Ze Yu, Google Inc, USA

CLOUD COMPUTING 2018 Technical Program Committee

Saeid Abolfazli, YTL Communications and Xchanging, Malaysia
Maruf Ahmed, The University of Sydney, Australia
Onur Alparslan, Osaka University, Japan
Abdulelah Alwabel, PSA University, KSA
Er. Annappa, National Institute of Technology Karnataka, India
Sergio Antonio Andrade de Freitas, University of Brasilia, Brazil
Atakan Aral, Vienna University of Technology, Austria
Filipe Araujo, University of Coimbra, Portugal
Pattakou Argyro, University of the Aegean, Greece
Irina Astrova, Tallinn University of Technology, Estonia
José Aznar, i2CAT Foundation, Spain
Jorge Barbosa, Universidade do Porto, Portugal
Ali Kashif Bashir, Osaka University, Japan
Luis Eduardo Bautista Villalpando, Autonomous University of Aguascalientes, Mexico
Thais Batista, UFRN - CCET - DIMAp, Brazil
Carlos Becker Westphall, Federal University of Santa Catarina, Brazil
Ali Beklen, HotelRunner, Turkey

Andreas Berl, Technische Hochschule Deggendorf, Germany
Simona Bernardi, Centro Universitario de la Defensa - Academia General Militar, Spain
Peter Bloodsworth, University of Oxford, UK
Rodrigo N. Calheiros, Western Sydney University, Australia
Paolo Campegiani, Università Roma Tor Vergata, Italy
Juan-Vicente Capella-Hernández, Universitat Politècnica de València, Spain
Mª del Carmen Carrión Espinosa, University of Castilla-La Mancha, Spain
Eddy Caron, ENS de Lyon, France
K. Chandrasekaran, N.I.T.K, India
Hsi-Ya Chang, National Center for High-Performance Computing, Taiwan
Ruay-Shiung Chang, National Taipei University of Business, Taipei, Taiwan
Kyle Chard, University of Chicago and Argonne National Laboratory, USA
Nadeem Chaudhary, University of Warwick, UK
Antonin Chazalet, Orange, France
Claudia-Melania Chituc, Eindhoven University of Technology, The Netherlands
Enrique Chirivella Perez, University of the West of Scotland, UK
Lawrence Chung, The University of Texas at Dallas, USA
Antonio Corradi, Università di Bologna, Italy
Fabio M. Costa, Federal University of Goiás, Brazil
Noel De Palma, University Grenoble Alpes, France
Chen (Cherie) Ding, Ryerson University, Canada
Ioanna Dionysiou, University of Nicosia, Cyprus
Rim Drira, National School of Computer Science, Tunisia
Bob Duncan, University of Aberdeen, UK
Nabil El Ioini, Free University of Bozen-Bolzano, Italy
Kaoutar El Maghraoui, IBM T.J. Watson Research Center, New York, USA
Islam Elgedawy, Middle East Technical University, Northern Cyprus Campus, Turkey
Khalil El-Khatib, University of Ontario Institute of Technology, Canada
José Enrique Armendáriz-Íñigo, Public University of Navarre, Spain
Javier Fabra, Universidad de Zaragoza, Spain
Fairouz Fakhfakh, University of Sfax, Tunisia
Qiang Fan, New Jersey Institute of Technology, USA
Sonja Filiposka, Ss. Cyril and Methodius University - Skopje, Macedonia
Sören Frey, Daimler TSS GmbH, Germany
Somchart Fugkeaw, University of Tokyo, Japan
Javier García Blas, Universidad Carlos III De Madrid, Spain
Filippo Gaudenzi, Università Degli Studi di Milano, Italy
Sandra Gesing, University of Notre Dame, USA
Zakaria Gheid, Ecole nationale supérieure d'informatique, Algeria
Rahul Ghosh, American Express Big Data Labs, Bangalore, India
Katja Gilly, Miguel Hernandez University, Spain
Spyridon Gogouvitis, Siemens AG, Germany
Nils Gruschka, Kiel University of Applied Science, Germany
Jordi Guitart, Universitat Politècnica de Catalunya - Barcelona Supercomputing Center, Spain
Aayush Gupta, IBM Research, USA
Biruk Habtemariam, IBM, Canada
Jung Hae Sun, The University of Seoul, South Korea
Rui Han, Institute of Computing Technology - Chinese Academy of Sciences, China

Ronny Hans, Technische Universität Darmstadt, Germany
Ragib Hasan, University of Alabama at Birmingham, USA
Sergio Hernández, University of Zaragoza, Spain
Herodotos Herodotou, Cyprus University of Technology, Cyprus
Uwe Hohenstein, Siemens AG, Germany
Chih-Cheng Hung, Kennesaw State University, USA
Luigi Lo Iacono, TH Köln, Germany
Anca Daniela Ionita, University Politehnica of Bucharest, Romania
Saba Jamalian, kCura LLC, Chicago, USA
Eugene John, The University of Texas at San Antonio, USA
Carlos Juiz, University of the Balearic Islands, Spain
Dae-Ki Kang, Dongseo University, South Korea
Verena Kantere, University of Geneva, Switzerland
Bill Karakostas, VLTN gcv, Antwerp, Belgium
Sokratis Katsikas, Norwegian University of Science and Technology, Norway / University of Piraeus, Greece
Zaheer Khan, University of the West of England, Bristol, UK
Peter Kilpatrick, Queen's University Belfast, UK
Nikos Komninos, City University London, UK
Nane Kratzke, Lübeck University of Applied Sciences, Germany
Heinz Kredel, Universität Mannheim, Germany
Yu Kuang, University of Nevada, Las Vegas, USA
Alex MH Kuo, University of Victoria, Canada
Romain Laborde, University Paul Sabatier (Toulouse III), France
Yong Woo Lee, University of Seoul, Korea
Anna Levin, IBM Research, Israel
Tonglin Li, Oak Ridge National Laboratory, USA /
Dan Lin, Missouri University of Science and Technology, USA
Panos Linos, Butler University, USA
Xiaodong Liu, Edinburgh Napier University, UK
Jay Lofstead, Sandia National Laboratories, USA
Kerry S. Long, IARPA, USA
Glenn Luecke, Iowa State University, USA
Min Luo, Huawei Technologies, USA
Yutao Ma, Wuhan University, China
Shikharesh Majumdar, Carleton University, Canada
Zoltan Mann, University of Duisburg-Essen, Germany
Ming Mao, University of Virginia, USA
Olivier Markowitch, Universite Libre de Bruxelles, Belgium
Attila Csaba Marosi, Institute for Computer Science and Control - Hungarian Academy of Sciences, Hungary
Keith Martin, Royal Holloway - University of London, UK
Goran Martinovic, J.J. Strossmayer University of Osijek, Croatia
Fanjing Meng, IBM Research, China
Philippe Merle, Inria, France
Anastas Mishev, University Ss Cyril and Methodius in Skopje, Macedonia
Mohamed Mohamed, IBM, Almaden Research Center, USA
Patrice Moreaux, LISTIC - Polytech Annecy-Chambéry - University Savoie Mont Blanc, France

Hassnaa Moustafa, Intel Corporation, USA
Francesc D. Muñoz-Escoí, Universitat Politècnica de València, Spain
Amina Ahmed Nacer, University of Bejaia, Algeria / University of Lorraine, France
Adel Nadjaran Toosi, University of Melbourne, Australia
Hidemoto Nakada, National Institute of Advanced Industrial Science and Technology (AIST), Japan
Susanta Nanda, Symantec Research Labs, USA
Joan Navarro, La Salle - Universitat Ramon Llull, Spain
Richard Neill, RN Technologies, USA
Paolo Nesi, University of Florence, Italy
Marco Netto, IBM Research, Brazil
Bogdan Nicolae, IBM Research, Ireland
Aspen Olmsted, College of Charleston, USA
Matthias Olzmann, noventum consulting GmbH - Münster, Germany
Aida Omerovic, SINTEF, Norway
Brajendra Panda, University of Arkansas, USA
Alexander Papaspyrou, Technische Universität Dortmund, Germany
David Paul, University of New England, Australia
Giovanna Petrone, Universita' di Torino, Italy
Dimitrios Pezaros, University of Glasgow, UK
Agostino Poggi, DII - University of Parma, Italy
Thomas E. Potok, Oak Ridge National Laboratory, USA
Walter Priesnitz Filho, Federal University of Santa Maria, Rio Grande do Sul, Brazil
Abena Primo, Huston-Tillotson University, USA
Francesco Quaglia, Sapienza Universita' di Roma, Italy
Danda B. Rawat, Howard University, USA
Daniel A. Reed, University of Iowa, USA
Damir Regvart, Croatian Academic and Research Network - CARNet, Croatia
Christoph Reich, Furtwangen University, Germany
Sebastian Rieger, Fulda University of Applied Sciences, Germany
Sashko Ristov, University of Innsbruck, Austria
Takfarinas Saber, University College Dublin, Ireland
Valentina Salapura, IBM Watson Health, USA
Mohsen Amini Salehi, University of Louisiana Lafayette, USA
Elena Sánchez-Nielsen, Universidad de La Laguna, Spain
Lutz Schubert, University of Ulm, Germany
Wael Sellami, Higher Institute of Computer Sciences of Mahdia, Tunisia
Alireza Shameli-Sendi, Ericsson security research, Montreal, Canada
Jianchen Shan, New Jersey Institute of Technology, USA
Mohammad Shojafar, Sapienza University of Rome, Italy
Altino Manuel Silva Sampaio, Escola Superior de Tecnologia e Gestão | Instituto Politécnico do Porto, Portugal
Alex Sim, Lawrence Berkeley National Laboratory, USA
Mukesh Singhal, University of California, Merced, USA
George Spanoudakis, University of London, UK
Cristian Stanciu, University Politehnica of Bucharest, Romania
Vlado Stankovski, University of Ljubljana, Slovenia
Yuqiong Sun, Symantec Research Labs, USA
Kwa-Sur Tam, Virginia Tech, USA

Copyright Information

Table of Contents

Can EU General Data Protection Regulation Compliance be Achieved When Using Cloud Computing?

Bob Duncan
Business School
University of Aberdeen, UK
Email: bobduncan@abdn.ac.uk

***Abstract*—The forthcoming EU General Data Protection Regulation (GDPR) will come into effect across the EU on 25th May 2018. It will certainly be the case that a great many companies will be inadequately prepared for this significant event. While a great many companies who use traditional in-house distributed systems are likely to have a hard enough job trying to comply with this new regulation, but those businesses who use any form of cloud computing face a particularly difficult additional challenge, namely the Cloud Forensic Problem. It is not enough that cloud use presents a far more challenging environment, but that the cloud forensic problem presents a far more difficult barrier to compliance. This problem arises due to the fact that all computing systems are constantly under serious attack, but once an attacker gains a foothold in a cloud system and becomes an intruder, there is very little to prevent the intruder from helping themselves to any manner of data covered by the GDPR, either by viewing it, modifying it, deleting it or ex-filtrating it from the victim system. Worse, there is nothing to prevent the intruder from gaining sufficient privileges to then completely delete all trace of their incursion, possibly deleting far more records than they need to in the process. We address exactly what the requirements of EU GDPR compliance are, consider whether this can be done without resolving the Cloud Forensic Problem, and propose some approaches to mitigate this problem, and possibly the massive potential fines that could then be levied.**

Keywords–EU GDPR; Compliance; Cloud computing; cloud forensic problem.

I. INTRODUCTION

The forthcoming EU General Data Protection Regulation (GDPR) [1], is likely to present one of the greatest compliance challenges faced by companies across the globe. Every company that trades anywhere on earth, should they deal with even a single EU resident, must ensure they are compliant with the EU GDPR. If that company suffers a security breach and the records of any EU citizen are compromised, then the jurisdiction of the GDPR will extend globally, and that company may be pursued and fined significant sums of money.

Achieving information security is a big enough challenge for companies who use conventional distributed network systems, but once companies start using cloud systems, the challenge increases exponentially. There are many reasons for this, mostly arising from the complexity of the additional relationships, and agendas, of different participant companies involved in cloud systems. Much research has been carried out to attempt to resolve these problems e.g., [2], [3], [4], [5], [6].

The most challenging, and as yet, unresolved issue is the cloud forensic problem, otherwise known as "The elephant in the room." Pretty much everyone knows about it, yet nobody is prepared to discuss it, let along try to resolve the problem, due to the difficulty of the challenge it presents. The forthcoming implementation of the EU GDPR means that heads can no longer be left in the sand. This will not present an acceptable defence.

If any company using cloud is unable to resolve the cloud forensic problem, we suggest this will present such a fundamental issue that it will be impossible for that company to comply with this new regulation. As far back as 2011 and in subsequent years [7], [8], [9], [10], a great deal of research was focussed on trying to resolve this issue, yet it is clear from looking at regulatory fines for breaches that the message is not getting though.

In 2012, Verizon estimated that a total of 174 million data records were compromised [11]. By 2017, this had increased to an estimated 2 billion records lost or compromised in the first half of 2017 alone [12]. Yahoo disclosed a 1 billion compromised account breach in the 2013 attacks, yet when Verizon took over Yahoo last year, it turned out that **ALL 3 billion accounts** had been compromised [13].

In Section II, we take a look at the implications of non-compliance for any company that falls under the jurisdiction of the forthcoming EU GDPR. In Section III, we identify what the Cloud Forensic Problem is, and address why it is such a challenging problem to overcome. In Section IV, we ask whether it is possible to attain compliance without addressing the cloud forensic problem. In Section V, we address the minimum requirements required necessary to achieve compliance. In Section VI, we look at what achieving the minimum requirements will allow us to do. In Section VII, we consider the limitations of this work, and in Section VIII, we discuss our conclusions.

II. THE EU GENERAL DATA PROTECTION REGULATION

Why should companies be concerned about compliance with the forthcoming EU GDPR [14]? Perhaps the maximum fine for being non-compliant, and suffering a serious cyber breach of the greater of €20million or 4% of global turnover might serve to grab their attention. We should therefore take a closer look at the detail of the regulation.

The Article 29 Working Party [15]was set up by the European Commission under the terms of Article 29 of the Data Protection Directive in 1996, and its main stated missions are to:

- Provide expert advice to the States regarding data protection;
- Promote the consistent application of the Data Protection Directive in all EU state members, as well as Norway, Liechtenstein and Iceland;
- Give to the Commission an opinion on community laws (first pillar) affecting the right to protection of personal data;
- Make recommendations to the public on matters relating to the protection of persons with regard to the processing of personal data and privacy in the European Community.

During the time it has been active, the Article 29 Working Party has overseen the evolution of the GDPR, and has seen thousands of amendments proposed. One of the best proposals was the requirement to report all breaches "... within 72 hours of the breach occurring", which would have had the impact of ensuring that all organisations would give security top priority in order to achieve compliance. However, following much lobbying, this was watered down to ". . . within 72 hours of discovery of a breach." This rather takes the urgency away from organisations.

On the other hand, another key amendment involved broadening the scope of the regulation, from all organisations anywhere in the EU, to any organisation anywhere in the globe, which stores privately identifiable information relating to any individual resident anywhere in the EU. This will certainly get the attention of far more organisations than would have been the case had it been an EU only requirement.

In the next three subsections, we have a look at how the GDPR seeks to streamline activities for both organisations and data subjects; how the GDPR will use enforcement mechanisms to ensure compliance; and what happens in the event of a data breach.

A. The Streamlining Goals of the GDPR

1) For Organisations: The idea for organisations is to streamline compliance by providing:

A single set of rules which would apply anywhere in the EU and by using the One Stop Shop approach, covered by Articles 46 to 55 of the GDPR, this would make for a streamlined approach for all organisations, whether based inside or outside the EU.

2) For Data Subjects: The idea for data subjects is to make the whole process for them much simpler by providing:

- Right of Access (under Article 15) - which gives data subjects the right to access their personal data held by any company subject to compliance with the GDPR;
- Right to Erasure (under Article 17) - which gives data subjects the right to have erasure carried out on certain data held by organisations about the data subject on any one of a number of grounds including non-compliance with article 6.1 (lawfulness) that includes a case (f) where the legitimate interests of the controller is overridden by the interests or fundamental rights and freedoms of the data subject;
- Data Portability (under Article 20) - data subjects have certain rights to data portability (particularly in the case of social media accounts), whereby a person shall be able to transfer their personal data from one electronic processing system to and into another, without being prevented from doing so by the data controller;
- Data Protection by Design and by Default (under Article 25) - seeks to ensure that all data subjects can expect privacy by design and by default, that has been designed into the development of business processes for products and services. This requires that privacy settings must be set at a high level by default and that technical and procedural measures should be taken care of by the controller in order to make sure that the processing, throughout the whole processing lifecycle, complies with the regulation. A report by the European Union Agency for Network and Information Security (ENISA) [16], elaborates on what needs to be done to achieve privacy and data protection by design. It specifies that encryption and decryption operations must be carried out locally, not by remote service, because both keys and data must remain in the power of the data owner if any privacy is to be achieved. Furthermore, it specifies that outsourced data storage on remote clouds is practical and relatively safe, as long as only the data owner, not the cloud service, holds the decryption keys;
- Consent by Data Subjects - data subjects must have given their consent for data about them to be processed, thus providing a lawful basis for processing.

3) A Lawful Basis for Processing: The data subject must have given consent which must be explicit for data collected and the purposes data is used for (Article 7; defined in Article 4). Data controllers must be able to prove "consent" (opt-in) and consent may be withdrawn. Consent for children must be given by the child's parent or custodian, and must be verifiable (Article 8). Such consent to the processing of his, her or their personal data for one or more specific processing purposes, must be:

- necessary for the performance of a contract to which the data subject is party or in order to take steps at the request of the data subject prior to entering into a contract;
- necessary for compliance with a legal obligation to which the controller is subject;
- necessary in order to protect the vital interests of the data subject or of another natural person;
- necessary for the performance of a task carried out in the public interest or in the exercise of official authority vested in the controller;
- necessary for the purposes of the legitimate interests pursued by the controller or by a third party, except where such interests are overridden by the interests or fundamental rights and freedoms of the data subject which require protection of personal data, in particular where the data subject is a child.

B. Enforcement Mechanisms

- Appointing a Data Protection Officer - this person would be required for all data processor organisations, and a person with expert knowledge of data protection law and practices should assist the controller or processor to monitor internal compliance with this Regulation. The appointment of a DPO within a large organization will be a challenge for the Board as well as for the individual concerned, due to the myriad governance and human factor issues that organisations and companies will need to address given the scope and nature of the appointment. In addition, the post holder will need to create their own support team and will also be responsible for their own continuing professional development as they need to be independent of the organization that employs them, effectively as a "mini-regulator";

- Ensuring Compliance with the GDPR, by checking that all the correct mechanisms are properly defined and in place, mainly through compliance demonstration, e.g, the data controller should implement measures which meet the principles of data protection by design and data protection by default. Such measures include the process of pseudonymising (Recital 78), i.e., by means of encryption, which process should be completed as soon as is practically possible.
- The GDPR seeks to provide Responsibility and Accountability by all parties involved in data processing, with expanded notice requirements covering retention time for personal data, and contact information for data controller and data protection officer. Automated decision-making for individuals, including algorithmic means of profiling (Article 22), which is regarded as contestable, similar to the Data Protection Directive (Article 15), receive particular attention. The expectation is that all actors involved in the whole process of data processing will behave responsibly and will be fully accountable for their actions. Data Protection Impact Assessments (Article 35) have to be conducted when specific risks occur to the rights and freedoms of data subjects. Risk assessment and mitigation is required and prior approval of the Data Protection Authorities (DPA) is required for high risks. Data Protection Officers (Articles 3739) are to ensure compliance within organizations.

C. *In the event of a Data Breach*

In the event of a data breach, under the GDPR, the Data Controller will be under a legal obligation to notify the Supervisory Authority without undue delay. The reporting of a data breach is not subject to any *de minimis* standard and must be reported to the Supervisory Authority within 72 hours after having become aware of the data breach (Article 33). Individuals have to be notified if adverse impact is determined (under Article 34), unless the data was encrypted. In addition, the data processor will have to notify the controller without undue delay after becoming aware of a personal data breach (under Article 33).

1) Sanctions: The following sanctions can be imposed:

- a warning in writing in cases of first and non-intentional non-compliance;
- regular periodic data protection audits;
- a fine of up to €10million or up to 2% of the annual worldwide turnover of the preceding financial year in case of an enterprise, whichever is greater, where there has been an infringement of the following provisions (Article 83, Paragraph 4[18]):
  - the obligations of the controller and the processor pursuant to Articles 8, 11, 25 to 39 and 42 and 43;
  - the obligations of the certification body pursuant to Articles 42 and 43;
  - the obligations of the monitoring body pursuant to Article 41(4).
- a fine up to €20million or up to 4% of the annual worldwide turnover of the preceding financial year in case of an enterprise, whichever is greater, where there has been an infringement of the following provisions: (Article 83, Paragraph 5 & 6[18]):
  - the basic principles for processing, including conditions for consent, pursuant to Articles 5, 6, 7 and 9;
  - the data subjects' rights pursuant to Articles 12 to 22;
  - the transfers of personal data to a recipient in a third country or an international organisation pursuant to Articles 44 to 49;
  - any obligations pursuant to Member State law adopted under Chapter IX;
  - non-compliance with an order or a temporary or definitive limitation on processing or the suspension of data flows by the supervisory authority pursuant to Article 58(2) or failure to provide access in violation of Article 58(1).

The above details provide the essence of what we need to know in order to understand what information will be required to be delivered in the event of breach, in order for the data processor to be compliant with the GDPR. In the next section, we will take a look at the Cloud Forensic Problem, and why it is such a difficult problem, not only from the security perspective, but also from the GDPR compliance problem.

III. The Cloud Forensic Problem (and Why it is Such a Difficult Problem)

As we have already stated, all computing systems are constantly under serious attack, but once an attacker gains a foothold in a cloud system and becomes an intruder, there is little to prevent the intruder from helping themselves to any amount of data covered by the GDPR, either by viewing it, modifying it, deleting it or ex-filtrating it from the victim system [17], [18], [19]. Worse, there is nothing to prevent the intruder from gaining sufficient privileges to then completely delete all trace of their incursion, possibly deleting far more records than they need to in the process, leading to further problems for business continuity.

This is often known as "The elephant in the room" in cloud circles. Pretty much everyone knows about it, yet nobody is prepared to discuss it, let alone try to resolve the problem, due to the difficulty of the challenge it presents. Make no mistake, this is a serious challenge to defend against, let alone overcome. However, not only is it a serious challenge for organisations using cloud, it also presents a major obstacle to compliance with the GDPR.

Once all trace of the intrusion has been deleted, there will be very little forensic trail left to follow, meaning many companies will be totally unaware that the intrusion has taken place, let alone understand what records have been accessed, modified, deleted or stolen. All too often, companies will believe they have retained a full forensic trail in their running instance, but often forget that without special measures being taken to save these records off-site [2], they will vanish when the instance is shut down.

Currently, in any cloud based system, there must be a complete and intact audit trail in order for the breached organisation to be able to tell which records have been accessed, modified, deleted or stolen. Where the audit trail and all forensic records have been deleted, there remains no physical means for any organisation to be able to tell which records have been accessed, modified, deleted or stolen, putting these organisations immediately in multiple breaches of the GDPR.

IV. Is it Possible to Achieve Compliance with the EU GDPR without Addressing the Cloud Forensic Problem?

The short answer is, of course, it is not! For the reasons outlined in the previous section, we can see that there is indeed nothing to prevent an intruder from destroying every scrap of forensic proof of their incursion into any current cloud system. It is clear that any form of forensic record or audit trail can not therefore be safely stored on any running cloud instance.

This means that the only safe method of storage of forensic data will be somewhere off-site from the running cloud instances. Clearly, the off-site storage must be highly secure, preferably stored in an append-only database, and should especially be held in encrypted format, with all encryption keys held elsewhere.

Doubtless some will say that as long as they are not breached, then they will not be in breach of the GDPR. While that may very well be true, how will they be able to tell whether they have not been breached, against the circumstance where they have been breached, and the breach has been very well covered up. They will have no means of knowing, let alone proving the point.

Let us suppose that a complaint is made to the regulator, the organisation will have no means of proving that the data has not been tampered with. Equally, if the breach has been extremely well covered up, they will neither have the means of complying with the requirement to: a) report the breach within 72 hours, nor b) have any means of determining which records have been accessed, modified, deleted or stolen. Let us now suppose that the conversion of private data has yet to be encrypted, and worse, that the encryption and decryption keys are held on the cloud instance "for convenience". If we were to receive a request from any users whose data had just been compromised, we would be unable to comply with the request, meaning we would now be looking at multiple breaches, thus causing the fine level to escalate to the higher level, as outlined in Subsubsection II-C1.

V. The Minimum Requirements to Achieve Compliance with the GDPR

We have seen that to do nothing would not be a viable option as far as GDPR compliance is concerned. Attacks will continue unabated. We must therefore be prepared and armed with whatever tools we can develop to ensure we achieve as high a level of compliance as we possibly can.

We therefore need to consider what the absolute minimum technical requirement might be to attain our objective of GDPR compliance. We know that under the GDPR the organisation must be able to:

- provide a Right of Access (under Article 15) to personal data by data subject, if requested;
- provide the means to comply with a Right to Erasure (under Article 17) by data subject, subject to the appropriate grounds being met;
- provide privacy by design;
- in the event of a data breach, report the breach to the Supervisory Authority within 72 hours after having become aware of the data breach (Article 33). The breach must also be reported to the controller without undue delay after becoming aware of a personal data breach;
- in the event of a data breach, notify the data subject if adverse impact is determined (under Article 34), unless the data was encrypted;

In the case of the first requirement, we would require to ensure the provenance and veracity of the contents of the database. In the case of the second requirement, if appropriate, the same provision would apply.

In the case of the third requirement, the cloud system must be designed in accordance with the recommendations of the Article 29 Working Party [20], which suggests the reports produced by ENISA should be followed. This report [21] specifies that encryption and decryption operations must be carried out locally, not by remote service, because both keys and data must remain in the power of the data owner if any privacy is to be achieved. Furthermore, it specifies that outsourced data storage on remote clouds is practical and relatively safe, as long as only the data owner, not the cloud service, holds the decryption keys. ENISA have also produced a stream of other relevant reports, including a Cloud Risk report in 2009 [22], and recommendations for certification in 2017 [23].

In the case of the fourth requirement, we would require to ensure the provenance and veracity of the contents of the database. In the case of the fifth requirement, where the data is not yet encrypted, the same provision would also apply. However, it should be stressed that it will always be preferable to ensure data is encrypted before it leaves the control of the data owner.

It is clear that where no steps have been taken to ensure the cloud forensic problem has been mitigated, the organisation will fail on every count. Thus, as a minimum, we need to ensure the following steps are taken:

- all personal data should be encrypted, and this should be performed locally;
- the encryption and decryption keys should not be maintained on the cloud instance;
- a full audit trail of the entire database must be maintained off-site;

- full forensic records of all users having accessed the database and carried out any commands on the database must be collected and stored off-site.

VI. What Will the Minimum Requirements Allow us to do?

Let us now assume that we have completed the minimum requirements. Can we now be sure that we can be compliant with the provisions of the GDPR? We must therefore look at each of the five reporting requirements in turn to establish whether we will be able to meet these requirements.

1) First, if a data subject serves us with a Right of Access request, can we respond in the affirmative? We are now sure that we hold the subject's data securely, in encrypted format in our database. Further we can prove that the data has only been accessed by duly authorised persons, and that the data records have neither been modified, stolen nor deleted. We are therefore compliant on the first requirement;
2) Next, if a data subject serves us with a right to Erasure notice, can we comply with that request. Assuming the request can be legitimately carried out and is not prohibited by statute, then since we can correctly identify the private data held about the data subject, then there is no reason why we would be unable to delete the appropriate data as requested. Accordingly, we would be compliant on the second requirement;
3) Next, can we provide privacy by design? Since we can comply with the first two requirements, this is a clear indication that we are potentially capable of supplying privacy by design;
4) In the event of a data breach, can we report the breach to the Supervisory Authority within 72 hours of discovery? In the case of a data breach, we will not only be able to notify the breach within 72 hours of discovery, we will actually be able to notify within 72 hours of the occurrence of the breach. In addition, since we will retain full forensic data and audit trails for the system, we will also be able to provide very precise details of which records were accessed and read, which might have been modified, with full details of what modifications were made, which records were deleted, and which records were exfiltrated from the system. Not only that, but we will be able to provide full details of how the perpetrators got into the system and where they forwarded any stolen records, which means we can identify precisely which records were compromised, thus ensuring we would be beyond fully compliant;
5) In the event of a data breach, would we be able to notify the data subject if adverse impact is determined (under Article 34)? In the event of a data breach, we would be able to identify every single record attacked, and identify every single data subject affected. Since the full records would already be encrypted, we would not be required to notify the data subjects, but would be fully capable of so doing. This would mean we would again be beyond fully compliant.

Thus, we can reasonably claim that we would be in a position to be fully compliant with all the requirements of the GDPR, thus providing an exceptionally high level of privacy on behalf of all data subjects. Thus, the level of exposure of data subjects would be extremely minimised, thus ensuring compliance with the regulation, and therefore the likelihood that we would be able to fully mitigate any penalty that would otherwise be applied by the regulator.

Contrast this position with the case where cloud users do not take these mitigatory steps. In every requirement - they would be non-compliant, thus exposing the enterprise to the full extent of penalties allowed, namely the greater of €20million or 4% of global turnover.

VII. Limitations and Discussion

There are two very important tasks that must be performed in order not to limit the effectiveness of this approach. Since persistent storage in the cloud instance cannot retain data beyond its currently running lifetime [2], we must also make sure that all necessary logs and data is stored securely elsewhere. And as the default settings for virtually all database software involves logging being turned off [17], we must ensure this function is turned on in all running cloud instances, again, with the data being stored securely elsewhere.

This prompts the question of what data we require to keep. In order to meet our regulatory compliance requirement, we need to understand the 5 W's — namely: Who is accessing our system? Where have they come from? What are they looking for? When is this happening? From this data, we should be able to infer the Why? Are they authorised to be in the system, to enter the system the way they have, to look at the data they are trying to access, and at the time they are trying to access it? Deducing the Why can give an indicator of anomalous behaviour.

Many database software offers additional full audit trail capabilities. Each additional capability will require more and more storage resources. A balance will need to be found between the minimum requirement consistent with maintaining performance and a cost effective level of storage. The risk in not utilising all that is on offer, would be that this might compromise security, reducing the ability of achieve compliance.

However, it is clear that a sensible precaution to mitigate this risk would be to encrypt all the data being held on all databases maintained within the system, ensuring that encryption/decryption keys are not stored on the cloud instances. While encryption is not mandatory, in the event of a breach where encryption is not used, the fine levied by the regulator is likely to be much higher as a consequence.

VIII. Conclusion

The forthcoming GDPR will certainly present a serious wake up call to a great many companies operating around the globe if they find themselves falling under the jurisdiction of this new regulation. In this paper, we have considered whether it is possible to achieve regulatory compliance where any organisation is using cloud computing. Again, we reiterate that without suitable precautions being put in place, the answer is a resounding "No!".

We have outlined the key requirements from the regulation to which all organisations falling under its jurisdiction must comply. We have identified the currently unresolved "Cloud Forensic Problem" as presenting the largest obstacle to achieving compliance.

We have proposed how this challenging problem may be approached to ensure that cloud users can be fully compliant with this new regulation, with little more than being sensibly organised. Clearly, additional cost will require to be incurred, and there may be a small impact on latency, but these costs could significantly mitigate the possibility of a huge regulatory fine in the event of a breach. It is also likely that this approach will ensure faster discovery of the occurrence of a breach, thus minimising the potential impact on business continuity.

REFERENCES

[1] EU, "EU General Data Protection Regulation (GDPR)," 2017. [Online]. Available: http://www.eugdpr.org/ [Last accessed: 22 December 2017]

[2] R. K. L. Ko, P. Jagadpramana, M. Mowbray, S. Pearson, M. Kirchberg, B. S. Lee, and Q. Liang, "TrustCloud: A Framework for Accountability and Trust in Cloud Computing," Perspective, 2011, pp. 1–9.

[3] R. K. L. Ko, B. S. Lee, and S. Pearson, "Towards achieving accountability, auditability and trust in cloud computing," Commun. Comput. Inf. Sci., vol. 193 CCIS, 2011, pp. 432–444.

[4] N. Papanikolaou, S. Pearson, and M. C. Mont, "Towards Natural-Language Understanding and Automated Enforcement of Privacy Rules and Regulations in the Cloud: Survey and Bibliography," Analysis, 2011, pp. 1–9.

[5] S. Pearson, "Taking Account of Privacy when Designing Cloud Computing Services," Current, 2009, pp. 44–52.

[6] S. Pearson, "Toward accountability in the cloud," IEEE Internet Comput., vol. 15, no. 4, jul 2011, pp. 64–69. [Online]. Available: http://ieeexplore.ieee.org/lpdocs/epic03/wrapper.htm?arnumber=5934852

[7] N. Papanikolaou, S. Pearson, M. C. Mont, and R. Ko, "A Toolkit for Automating Compliance in Cloud Computing Services," Int. J. Cloud Comput., vol. x, no. x, 2014, pp. 45–68.

[8] J. Singh and J. M. Bacon, "On middleware for emerging health services," J. Internet Serv. Appl., vol. 5, no. 1, 2014, p. 6.

[9] J. Singh, J. Bacon, and D. Eyers, "Policy Enforcement Within Emerging Distributed, Event-based Systems," Proc. 8th ACM Int. Conf. Distrib. Event-Based Syst. - DEBS '14, 2014, pp. 246–255.

[10] J. Singh, J. Powles, T. Pasquier, and J. Bacon, "Seeing through the clouds: Management, control and compliance for cloud computing," Cloud Comput., 2015, pp. 1–12.

[11] Verizon, "2012 Data Breach Investigation Report: A study conducted by the Verizon RISK Team in cooperation with the United States Secret Service and Others," Tech. Rep., 2012. [Online]. Available: http://www.verizonenterprise.com/resources/reports/rp_data-breach-investigations-report-2012_en_xg.pdf [Last accessed: 22 December 2017]

[12] Verizon, "Verizon Security Breach Report 2017," Tech. Rep., 2017.

[13] S. Khandelwal, "Its 3 Billion! Yes, Every Single Yahoo Account Was Hacked In 2013 Data Breach," 2017. [Online]. Available: https://thehackernews.com/2017/10/yahoo-email-hacked.html [Last accessed: 22 December 2017]

[14] The European Parliament and The European Council, "General Data Protection Regulation," Off. J. Eur. Union, vol. 2014, no. October 1995, 2016, pp. 20–30.

[15] EU, "Opinion 05/2012 on Cloud Computing (Data Protection)," 2012.

[16] G. Danezis, J. Domingo-Ferrer, M. Hansen, J.-H. Hoepman, D. L. Metayer, R. Tirtea, and S. Schiffner, Privacy and Data Protection by Design - from policy to engineering, 2015, no. December.

[17] B. Duncan and M. Whittington, "Enhancing Cloud Security and Privacy: The Power and the Weakness of the Audit Trail," in Cloud Comput. 2016 Seventh Int. Conf. Cloud Comput. GRIDs, Virtualization, no. April.Rome: IEEE, 2016, pp. 125–130.

[18] G. Weir, A. Aßmuth, M. Whittington, and B. Duncan, "Cloud Accounting Systems, the Audit Trail, Forensics and the EU GDPR: How Hard Can It Be?" in Br. Account. Financ. Assoc. Scottish Area Gr. Annu. Conf.Aberdeen: BAFA, 2017, p. 6.

[19] P. Tobin, M. McKeever, J. Blackledge, M. Whittington, and B. Duncan, "UK Financial Institutions Stand to Lose Billions in GDPR Fines: How can They Mitigate This?" in Br. Account. Financ. Assoc. Scottish Area Gr. Annu. Conf., BAFA, Ed., Aberdeen, 2017, p. 6.

[20] EU, "Unleashing the Potential of Cloud Computing in Europe," 2012. [Online]. Available: http://eur-lex.europa.eu/LexUriServ/LexUriServ.do?uri=SWD:2012:0271:FIN:EN:PDF [Last accessed: 22 December 2017]

[21] ENISA, "Article 4 Technical Report," ENISA, Tech. Rep., 2011.

[22] ENISA, "Cloud Risk," ENISA, Tech. Rep., 2009. [Online]. Available: https://www.enisa.europa.eu/publications/cloud-computing-risk-assessment [Last accessed: 22 December 2017]

[23] ENISA, "Recommendations on European Data Protection Certification," Tech. Rep., 2017.

A Study into Smart Grid Consumer-User Profiling for Security Applications

Mutinta Mwansa, William Hurst, Carl Chalmers, Yuanyuan Shen, Aaron Boddy
Department of Computer Science
Liverpool John Moores University
Byrom Street
Liverpool, L3 3AF, UK
Email: M.Mwansa@2017.ljmu.ac.uk, {W.Hurst, C.Chalmers, Y.Shen}@ljmu.ac.uk, A.Boddy@2011.ljmu.ac.uk

Abstract— **A smart meter measures energy consumption with more granular detail than conventional analogue meters. The Advanced Metering Infrastructure (AMI) facilitates real-time two-way communication between the consumer and the rest of the energy grid. Information concerning electricity consumption, demand and response and home energy generation is communicated back to the local utility for monitoring and billing purposes. However, the detailed electricity usage patterns and trends can also be used to understand daily consumer habits and their routines. The collection and analysis of such data raises significant security and ethical concerns which must be adequately addressed. This paper focuses on the data collected from the residential smart grid using its default reading frequency of 30 minutes. The research demonstrates how the information can be exploited to remotely profile users and detect abnormal user behaviours using cloud-based analytics. Security implications are outlined and a case study is put forward as a demonstration of information that can be obtained through consumer profiling.**

Keywords- Smart meters; Profiling; Advanced Metering Infrastructure, Data Classification, Data Analysis.

I. INTRODUCTION

Smart meters are a core component of the smart grid, which is a complex dynamic network of interconnected devices. This infrastructure provides mechanisms for information exchange, decision making and actuation. Smart grid systems include producers, consumers and actors to ensure a resource saving and economically efficient electrical network. Typically, they reduce financial losses, operational costs and enable the suppliers to forecast their customers' demands [1]. As a result, smart meters are being implemented on a global scale. Many countries such as the UK, USA, Australia and Italy are already advanced in their smart meter implementation. The UK alone is aiming to install over 50 million gas and electricity smart meters by 2020 [2].

The smart grid represents a technological era of resilience, performance and efficiency across the entire power industry; from generation all the way to consumption. While the benefits of the smart grid are clear, it also introduces a number of different risks and challenges. The complexity and interoperability of the smart grid mean that it is exposed to a series of digital threats from invasion of privacy to a sabotage of a critical national infrastructure [3]. As the smart grid is highly interconnected, security attacks can originate from various points. As a result, electric industries invest heavily in cyber-threat mitigation [4]. In particular, the acquired data from the smart metering infrastructure poses a significant risk to both the grid and its stakeholders if a security breach occurs. The research composure in this paper demonstrates the type of sensitive information which can be constructed from smart meter data using its default reading frequency of 30 minutes. Here detailed routines of the occupant can be exposed using different profiling techniques and data analytics.

The data used in this paper is collated from a smart meter trial deployed in 75,000 homes. The remainder of the paper is as follows. A background research on smart grid systems and associated technologies is put forward in Section 2. Subsequently, typically section 3 presents a sample of the data collected from our smart meter case study. Both data visualisations and statistical analysis of the data is undertaken. Section 4 discusses the methodology and techniques used for profiling users and highlighting the benefits of cloud computing for data processing within the wider smart grid. The paper is concluded in Section 5 where a discussion of the results is presented. In particular, this paper focuses on the smart meter and investigates the novel approaches for consumer profiling and for the consumers to monitoring energy usage in real time.

II. BACKGROUND RESEARCH

A smart meter is an electronic device that records consumption of utility services (such as electricity and gas) at fixed intervals. It replaces existing analogue meters where energy usage readings are collected manually usually over a longer period. The system automatically communicates consumption information using a predefined schedule, to the Meter Data Management System (MDMS).

A. *Smart Meters*

Typically, the main aim of the smart meter is to facilitate real time energy usage readings at granular intervals, to both the consumer and smart grid stakeholders [5]. In order to achieve this aim, load information is obtained from consumer electrical devices while measuring the total aggregated energy consumption for the given property. Additional information, such as home generated electricity is provided to the utility company and/or system operator for enhanced monitoring and accurate billing. Some of these roles and benefits include:

- Accurate recording, transmitting and storing of information for defined time periods (to a minimum of 10 seconds). All UK smart meters must store energy usage readings for a maximum of 13 months providing a unique insight into energy consumption.
- Offer two way communications to and from the meter so that, for example, suppliers can read meters remotely [6], facilitate demand and response and upgrade tariff information.
- Support future management of energy supply to help distribution companies manage supply and demand across their networks [7]. This is achieved automatically through previously agreed Demand Response (DR) actions.

A significant amount of research exists on how the data collected from the smart meters can be used to detect energy usage patterns in residential homes via user profiling [8] However, investigations into the security behind the security of smart meter analytics, is still a challenging and prevalent area of research [9].

The collector of the device retrieves the data and may process it or simply pass it on for processing upstream. Data is transmitted via a Wide Area Network (WAN) to the utilities central collection point for processing and use by business applications. Since the communications path is two way, signals or commands can be sent directly to the meters, customer premise or distribution device. The combination of the electronic meters with two-way communications technology for information, monitor and control is commonly referred to as the AMI.

B. *The AMI*

The AMI facilitates the bidirectional communication between the consumer and the rest of the smart grid stake holders. It reduces the traditional need for energy usage readings to be collected manually [10]. The smart meter is able to communicate with a gateway through a Home Area Network (HAN), Wide Area Network (WAN) or a Neighbourhood Area Network (NAN), which is outlined as follows in Figure 1:

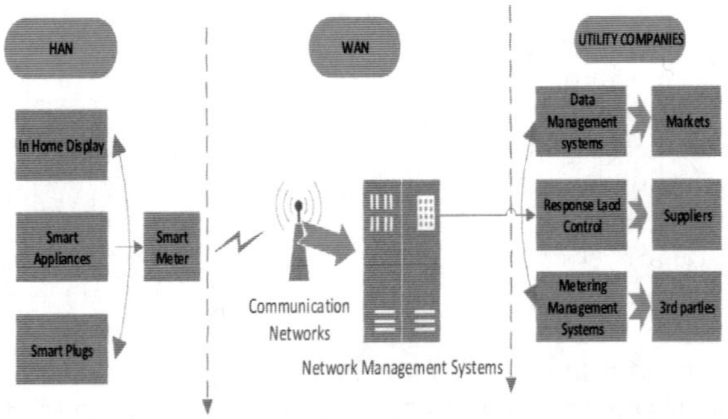

Figure 1. Advanced Metering Infrastructure

The HAN is housed inside the consumer premises and is made up of different devices e.g., Meters, Thermostats, Electric storage devices, ZigBee transmitters. The HAN contains both the electrical and gas smart meter, which generates detailed consumption data. The data generated is transmitted in NANs and WANs and eventually to the control station for power corrective measure [11]. The HAN is responsible for providing communication between electrical devices and the access points. The WAN handles the communication between the utility companies and the HAN. The WAN is responsible for sending all meter data to the utility, using a robust backhaul network, such as carrier Ethernet, GSM, CDMA or 3G [12].

All of the acquired data is sent to the Meter Data Management System (MDMS), which is responsible for storing, managing and analysing the data [13]. The MDMS sits within the data and communications layer of the AMI. This component is an advanced software platform, which deploys data analytics while facilitating the various AMI applications and objectives. These applications include: managing metered consumption data, outage management, demand and response, remote connect / disconnect, and smart meter events and billing [14]. This information can be shared with consumers, partners, market operators and regulators.

C. *Smart Grid Challenges concerning User Profiling*

The major concern for profiling users is the privacy of the consumer. As demonstrated in Section 4, smart meters enable detailed profiling of consumers, their energy usage and the household activities. This information can be used by others, either maliciously or inadvertently to ascertain an insight into an individual's home life. For example, activities or occupancies of a home for specific periods of time can be determined. In a general sense, analysis of granular smart meter energy data could result in 1) invasion of privacy; 2) unwanted publicity and embarrassment (e.g., public disclosure of private facts or the publication of facts which place a person in a false light); 3) endangering of the physical security of life. The security policies governing the reliability of the smart grid depend on appropriate connectivity protocols and the national institute of standards and technology being the reference model proposed. [15]. Behaviour profiling and confidentiality of security for the consumers as it is inextricably linked to their privacy. This research is devoted to presenting ways of ensuring confidentiality and privacy within the smart home/smart grid communication interoperability.

D. *Cloud Computing and the Smart Grid*

Cloud computing is currently used to mitigate the data processing challenges that are associated with the smart gird implementation. The data generated from the smart grid means that cloud processing platforms are now required to process and extract meaning from the acquired data while ensuring a robust energy delivery network. There are numerous advantages that are associated with cloud computing platforms, which can be applied to the smart metering infrastructure to support its various objectives [16]. Cloud computing is an ever developing computational platform, which combines hardware, storage and high bandwidth networking to provide scalable solutions to third party organisations. The smart grid requires a fault tolerant, efficient data processing and communications infrastructure in order to deliver a reliable and affordable power distribution network [17]. The emergence of smart grids brings many benefits but also various challenges in terms of data management and integration. The smart grid by its very nature is a complex platform with vast storage, communication and computational requirements. To facilitate these requirements smart grids can leverage the following cloud computing benefits:

- Cloud computing is flexible and scalable. This ensures adequate resource allocation and provisioning [18]. As smart grid components are deployed on a large scale, cloud computing can be used to overcome scalability problems by provisioning additional resources as required.
- Cloud services maintain the underlying computational hardware and software. Smart grids are regarded as a critical infrastructure, which supplies essential utilities to the consumer. Any down time in services can have a detrimental impact on service users. As most cloud components are virtualised, guests can be migrated from one host to another while maintenance is undertaken. This removes the need for downtime and minimises service disruption [19].
- Many cloud providers are geographically distributed, which not only ensures low latency but also provides service replication. Essentially, services are mirrored in one or more additional data centres to prevent service disruption in the event of an outage.

III. CASE STUDY

The project outlined in this paper theorises that the detailed electricity usage patterns generated by smart meters describes the vast amount of data collected within the smart grid. In order to process and analyse large volumes of data, we propose the use of cloud computing because of its high performance computing resources and the high capacity storage devices [20].

The amount of data required to process transactions of two million customers reaches upwards of 22 gigabytes per day [21]. It is a significant challenge to manage this data; which may include the selection, deployment, monitoring, and analysis processes. A real-time information processing is usually required in the smart grid to meet the needs of smart grid condition monitoring based on the smart grid condition monitoring with cloud computing [22]. Any delay may cause a serious consequence in the whole system, which has to be avoided as much as possible. As such, the methodology put forward in this paper makes use of a cloud platform for data processing

By the end of 2020, the UK government plans to have smart meters installed in every household and commercial business. Providers are able to use this resource by integrating their own software frameworks through an agreed communication standard. Smart meters utilise the ZigBee Smart Energy profile, which can be used to pair Consumer Access Devices CAD's using the ZigBee protocol. ZigBee has an operating range up to 70 meters with a data transmission speed of 250kbs. In addition, the UK DECC have declared SMETS2, which cites the use of ZigBee Smart Energy 1.x. This facilities access to smart meter data for both consumers and other 3rd parties.

A. *Data Study*

In this sub-section, a demonstration of the data that is collected from smart meters and how it can be analysed to model user behaviour is demonstrated. Table 1 below demonstrates a sample of smart meter data collected over a period of one month (January) for a single home occupant. The general supply of energy used on a daily basis (the energy delivered) is measured in KWH and can be described as what is used to bill the customer. Figure II shows an example of energy reading of an individual household meter. Data is being collected over a 30 min time interval period and the "energy delivered" in KWH. The customer key is the primary key used to identify the consumer while the End Date Time highlights the time and date of the acquired reading. Both the general supply and off peak supply are recorded based on the specified tariff.

TABLE 1. INDIVIDUAL READING SHOWING A MONTH USAGE PERIOD.

1	CUSTOMER_KEY	End Datetime	General Supply KWH	Off Peak KWH	Year
2	8410148	1/1/2013 0:29	0.081	0	2013
3	8410148	1/1/2013 0:59	0.079	0	2013
4	8410148	1/1/2013 1:29	0.082	0	2013
5	8410148	1/1/2013 1:59	0.085	0	2013
6	8410148	1/1/2013 2:29	0.073	0	2013
7	8410148	1/1/2013 2:59	0.07	0	2013
8	8410148	1/1/2013 3:29	0.07	0	2013
9	8410148	1/1/2013 3:59	0.072	0	2013
10	8410148	1/1/2013 4:29	0.071	0	2013
11	8410148	1/1/2013 4:59	0.074	0	2013

In order to visualise and analyse the energy usage patterns the smart meter data was extracted, transformed and loaded into a data model. The software used for this task was Microsoft Power BI. The platform facilitates the aggregation of data from multiple sources including both on premise and cloud infrastructure. Fig. 2 presents an example of 70K household meter readings showing the energy usage and the behaviour trend over a period of 12 months. Here we can see the general distribution of energy readings highlighting the energy requirements for different households. This type of data visualisation could give suggestion to the number of occupants living in a given premise. Houses with increased energy usage are more liking to have an increased number of occupants.

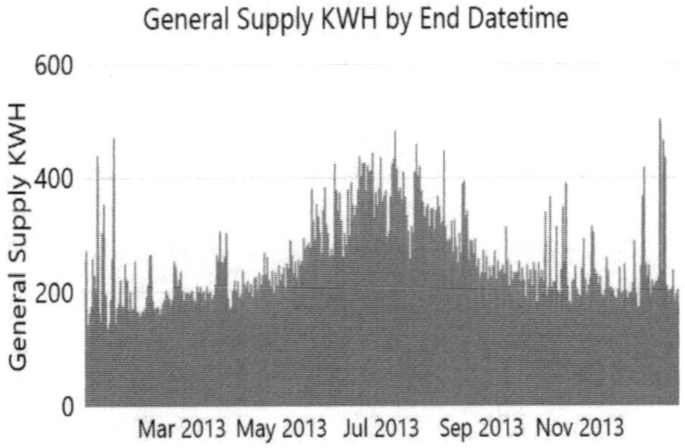

Figure 2. A Meter reading showing 12 months usage.

Fig. 3 highlights numerous meter readings taken over a 7 month period to demonstrate what effects a seasonal change has on energy usage.

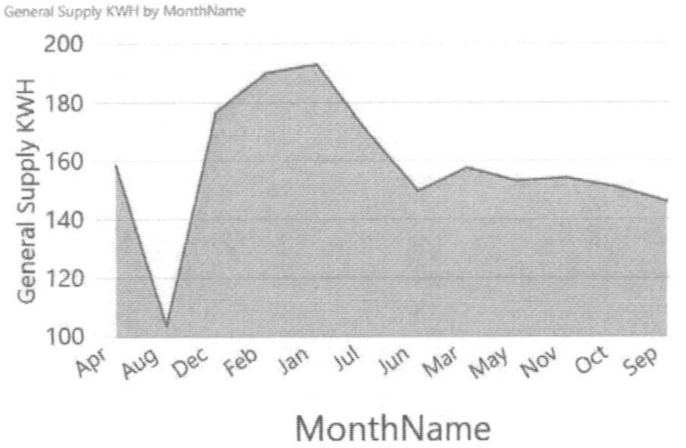

Figure 3. A Meter reading showing several months usage.

The data shows the trend of which period during the year consumers in residential homes use energy less. The high peaks indicate the energy is mostly used probably because of the winter when there is drastic drop in temperatures. As the data shows, it is very much possible to identify electrical device behaviour from smart meter data collection.

B. Stastical Annalysis

A Smart-frame cloud computing, is a flexible, scalable, and secure information management framework for smart grids based on cloud computing technology. Our idea is to build the framework at three hierarchical levels: top, regional, and end user levels in which the first two levels consist of cloud computing centres while the last level contains end-user smart devices. The top cloud computing centre takes responsibility of managing general devices and accumulation of data across the regional cloud computing centres which are placed in the lower level in the hierarchy. The regional cloud computing centres are in turn responsible for managing intelligent devices, which have lower hierarchical level than the regional cloud computing centres in specific regions (e.g., with in a city), and processing data of these devices. The figures below show and compare two users one with normal behaviour and one with abnormal behaviour energy usage patterns. Figure 4 presents a scatter graph for one smart meter in the trail. Here the results show that the consumer does not use electricity with any repeatability in behaviour.

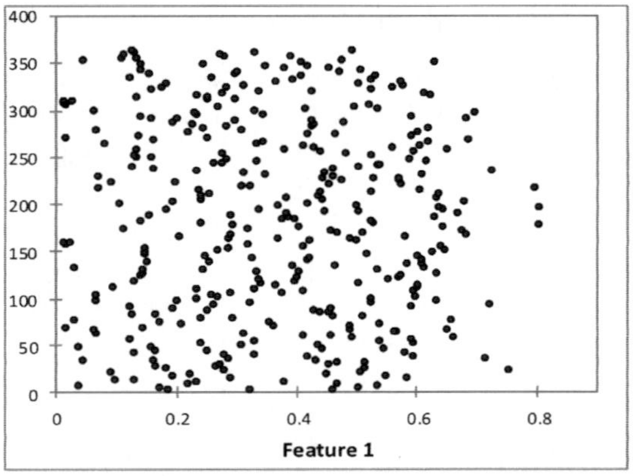

Figure 4. A Meter reading showing abnormal energy usage.

Fig. 5 presents a scatter graph for the second smart meter. Here, the consumer shows clear repeatability in patterns of behaviour while aspects of abnormal behaviour can be observed in the outliners.

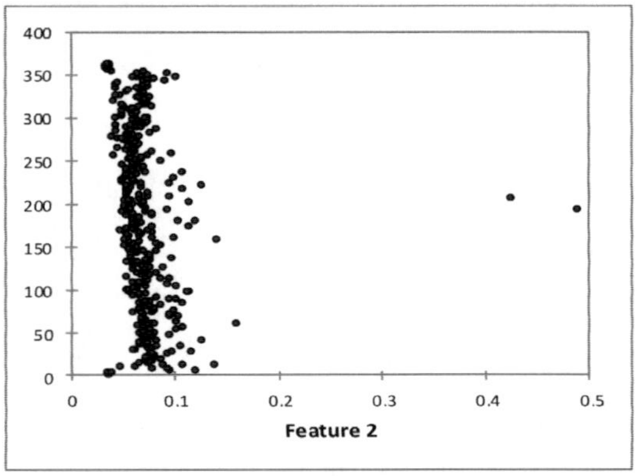

Figure 5. A Meter reading showing normal energy usage.

IV. METHODOLOGY

In the following section, we propose a novel system to facilitate the handling and analysis of smart meter data.

The solution proposed below will help network operators to identify, control and manage security risks in smart grid infrastructures and also to establish a detailed correlation between energy usage, weather conditions and other events as well as data management solutions.

Clear deviations can be seen from the above two energy users from their behaviour; the patterns reflect an individual's unique behavioural characteristics. Figure VI shows how much a meter can process a vast amount of data in a short period and if we have a number of such users then data storage is extreme and hence proposal of the cloud computing framework below.

A. *System Design*

A cloud computing based framework for big data information management in smart grids provides not only flexibility and scalability but also security. As displayed in Figure 6, the chosen topology to be implemented in this project is discussed as follows:

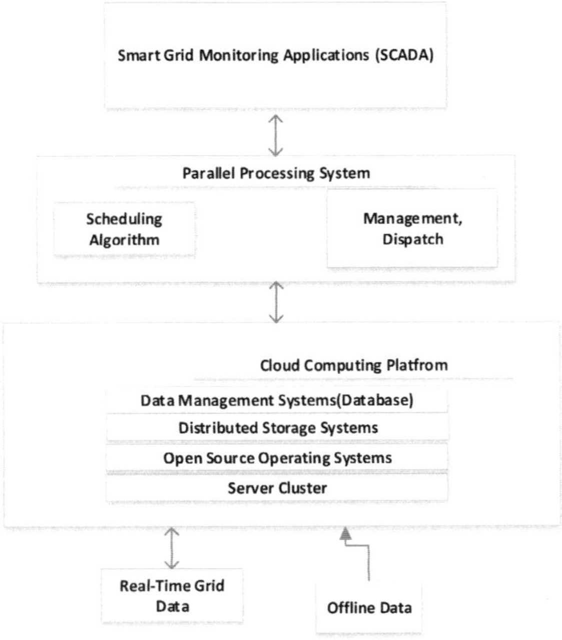

Figure 6. Cloud Computing framework for Smart Grid Monitoring Application

Smart grid monitoring application (SCADA): It is an application layer to monitor the status of the main power feeders, branch circuits, electrical equipment's, distributed generation units, energy storage units and the different parts of the smart grid to determine the real time online.

Parallel processing system: The amount of data collected on the smart grid is massive, distributed and complex. The parallel processing system enables the system to use a parallel computing to utilise the in demand computational and storage resource of cloud computing.

Cloud computing platform: In this architecture, cloud computing offers web based resizable computing capacity in the cloud, massive data management systems and distributed storage systems. Cloud platforms can play an important role in software architectures that allow more effective use of smart grid applications.

V. CONCLUSION

In this paper, the security implications of the smart meter installation are outlined. The electronic meters for electricity (smart meters) are undergoing an increasing deployment in private homes all over the world. As a consequence, an ever growing physical communication network, made up of millions of local meters, has been established. Likewise a complex data processing infrastructure has emerged which exploits numerous technologies and services to deliver an automated smart metering system.

The benefits of the smart meter implementation are vast. However, many of the considerable advantages are so far in favour primarily, if not solely, of the energy distributors. They provide a simplified, more efficient, and less costly transaction with customers, e.g., for meter reading, billing, and energy supply administration. The detail and granularity of the data collected can be used in many ways by utility companies. Some examples include forecasting energy usage, demand and response and consumer profiling. However there are future challenges facing the smart gird implementation.

Smart grids require an enormous pool of computing and massive data storage requirements are discussed. Cloud computing is proposed to overcome these demands by providing highly scalable computing resources to host smart grid applications. The details and granularity can be used to address many current and future challenges, which are faced by the grid. One of the main challenges is to meet the processing and storage of the vast data collected by the smart meter. The smart grid infrastructure will need information technology support to integrate data flow from numerous applications, to predict power usage and respond to events. Cloud computing services are ideally suited to support such data intensive always repeatedly. A significant issue surrounding security and data protection remain an ongoing challenge for smart grid operators. The data posed in this paper highlights how energy usage information can be used to profile both large numbers of households and individual consumers,

Our future work will be to implement coordinated fault protection mechanism with the help of cloud-based infrastructure in smart grid. In this infrastructure, different pieces of equipment are able to perform together efficiently to implement privacy preserving data collection techniques such as billing, and real time monitoring. The use of machine learning (specifically anomaly detection) will be integrated into our approach to facilitate the real time detection of abnormal behaviour within the smart metering infrastructure.

REFERENCES

[1] S.Florian, "Smart grid security, Innovative solutions for a modernized smart grid," 2015.

[2] J.Zheng, D.W. Gao, and L.Lin, " Smart meters in smart grid: An overview. In Green Technologies," Conference IEEE, pp. 57-64, April, 2013.

[3] E.D. Knapp, J.T. Longil, " Industrial Network Security: Securing Critical Infrastructure Networks and Smart Grid, SCADA and other Industrial Control Systems," Chapter, 12, 2015.

[4] B.Obama, "Taking the cyberattack threat seriously," Wall Street Journal, 19, 2012.

[5] W. Lingfeng, V. Devabhaktuni, N. Gudi, "Smart Meters for Power Grid – Challenges, Issues, Advantages and Status," IEEE/PES Power Systems Conference and Exposition, PSCE, pp. 1-7, March , 2011.

[6] C. Bennett, D. Highfill, "Networking AMI Smart Meters," November 2008, IEEE Energy2030.

[7] M. Anas, N. Javaid, A. Mahmood, S. M. Raza, U. Qasim and Z. A. Khan, "Minimizing Theft using Smart Meters in AMI," Seventh International Conference on P2P, Parallel, Grid, Cloud and Internet Computing, 2012.

[8] C. Chalmers, W. Hurst, W, M.Mackay, & P. Fergus, "Smart Meter Profiling For Health Applications. In the Proceedings of the International Joint Conference on Neural Networks," July, 2015

[9] K.K.R.Choo, "The cyber threat landscape: Challenges and future research directions: Computers & Security," vol. 30 no. 8, pp. 719-731, 2011.

[10] M.Popa, "Data Collecting from Smart Meters in an Advanced Metering Infrastructure, Proceedings of 15th International Conference on Intelligent Engineering Systems," 2011.

[11] R. Robinson, J. McDonald, B. Singletary, D. Highfill, N. Greenfield, M. Gilmore Advanced metering Security Threat Model .

[12] D. Niyato, P.Wang, "Cooperative transmission for meter data collection in smart grid," IEEE Communications Magazine, vol. 40, 2012.

[13] Y.T. Hoi, F.T. Kim , T.C. Kwok, C.T. Hoi, R.C. Hao, P.Gerhard, Hancke, F.M. Kim, "The Generic Design of a High-Traffic Advanced Metering Infrastructure Using ZigBee," vol. 10, pp. 836-844, 2014.

[14] B.Coalton, and H. Darren, "Networking AMI Smart Meters," IEEE Energy, vol. 2030, November, 2008.

[15] S.Bera, S.Misra, and J.J. Rodrigues, "Cloud computing applications for smart grid: A survey. IEEE Transactions on Parallel and Distributed Systems," vol .26, no. 5, pp.1477-1494, 2015.

[16] D.S.Markovic, D.Zivkovic, I. Branovic, R. Popovic, and D. Cvetkovic, "Smart power grid and cloud computing:Renewable and Sustainable Energy Reviews," vol. 24, pp.566-577, 2013

[17] A. Gupta, L.V. Kale, F. Gioachin, V. March, C.H. Suen, B.S. Lee, P. Faraboschi, R. Kaufmann, and D. Milojicic, "The who, what, why and how of high performance computing applications in the cloud. In Proceedings of the IEEE International Conference on Cloud Computing Technology and Science,", no.5,July,2013.

[18] M.Armbrust, A. Fox, A. Griffith, R. Joseph, A.D. Katz, R. Konwinski, A.Lee, G. Patterson, D. Rabkin, A. Stoica, and M.Zaharia, "A view of cloud computing. Communications of the ACM", vol.53, no.4, pp.50-58,2010.

[19] J.Baliga, R.W.Ayre, K. Hinton, and R.S.Tucker, "Green cloud computing: Balancing energy in processing, storage, and transport," Proceedings of the IEEE, vol. 99. No. 1, pp. 149-167,2011.

[20] B.Neenan, and R.C. Hemphill, "Societal benefits of smart metering investments. The electricity journal," vol. 21. No. 8. pp. 32-45,2008.

[21] J. Zheng, D.W. Gao, and L. Lin, "Smart meters in smart grid: An overview. In Green Technologies Conference," IEEE, pp. 57-64, April, 2013

[22] B.David "is a contributing editor at Scientific American, Is the U.S. grid better prepared to prevent a repeat of the 2003 blackout," Available from: [www.scientificamerican.com/article/us-electrical-grid-better-prepared-than-2003-blackout-ask-the-experts/], August, 2013.

Application of a Secure Cloud Based Learning Environment for Inclusive Practice in Mainstream Education: A Higher Education Case Study

Nigel Beacham
Computing Science
University of Aberdeen, UK
Email: n.beacham@abdn.ac.uk

Bob Duncan
Business School
University of Aberdeen, UK
Email: robert.duncan@abdn.ac.uk

Abstract—**In previous literature, an inclusive practice approach to counteract possible areas of concern regarding cloud-based security for virtual learning environments has been proposed. In this paper, the theoretical framework 'transformability theory' underpinning such a proposal is applied in the context of higher education. Practicalities and limitations applying to such an idealised approach in a real context are explored in the form of a case study. The case study includes both the multiple and mixed roles that learning analytics and usability play in cloud-based security. Whilst such roles provided by technology still rely on the need for a social and technical system approach based on a pedagogical focus aligned with educational beliefs, attitudes and practices, observations from the case study show that risks and threats can be managed on a perception and actual occurrence basis. Such encouraging findings from this pilot study support the need for a larger more substantial investigation into the theoretical approach. The proposal for this case study is very timely, due to the concerns surrounding both the cloud forensic problem and the potential impact of the provisions of the forthcoming EU General Data Protection Regulation. The case study will outline a workable approach to achieve high levels of both security and privacy, such that compliance with the new regulation can be achieved.**

Keywords–Inclusive education; security; privacy; cloud based systems; virtual learning environments; transformability theory.

I. Introduction

From a practical perspective, cloud presents an ideal basis for developing educational systems. It can be rapidly deployed, is eminently scalable, requires no massive capital outlay, and has no long lead time for delivery. Of course, no solution is ever completely perfect. The educational system will be running on someone else's hardware, and often software too. This means there will be additional concerns that will be necessary to contend with, such as security, privacy and accountability.

Of course, while it is sensible to deal with such issues, there is also the added concern and impact from legislation and regulation that will also have an impact. This means these issues must be dealt with rigorously. Legislation, such as the Data Protection Act [1], have substantial penalties that can be levied in the event of non-compliance. However, such penalties will pale into insignificance compared to the forthcoming EU General Data Protection Regulation (GDPR) [2], which comes into effect on 25th May 2018.

In the case of the GDPR, the maximum penalty, in the event of a significant breach where non-compliance of the responsible organisation is a contributory factor, can be the greater of €20 million or 4% of global turnover based on the previous year's accounts. This represents a serious amount of money, and in an area where budgets are already a big enough challenge, this would have a significant adverse impact on learning.

Human and social factors are important to consider when designing cloud-based security within education systems. As a consequence, there is a real lack of literature that has studied these factors and interventions from the perspective of inclusive social/technical systems. The realisation by others has led to an increased interest in researching systems to improve cyber-security [3]. One dilemma is the lack of theoretical rigour underpinning what amounts to a technological solution. Studies that have been conducted, whilst encouraging, nevertheless focus on the human factors of security systems [4] [5]. Such studies focus on the behavioural aspects using an experimental and empirical approach based upon behavioural psychology theories. Whilst these highlight strategies and provide insights into some of the key factors contributing towards the challenges of security, it remains to be seen whether in practice such strategies amount to real behavioural change and ultimately reduce security threats and risks in educational organisations.

In Section II, we discuss previous work in this area. In Section III, we next consider the security and privacy weaknesses in cloud systems, in order to understand the magnitude of the problem. In Section IV, we outline how we might approach we might take to attempt to find a way to try to resolve this problem. In Section V, we consider the technical strategies that ought to be deployed. In Section VI, we outline the manner in which the case study will be deployed. In Section VII, we consider and discuss the limitations of the work, and in Section VIII, we discuss our conclusions.

II. Previous Work

From an inclusive education perspective, much research exists on strategic and technological approaches to enhancing inclusion [7]–[9], but little if any account for the cybersecurity threats and risks. Some of the most interesting work has been undertaken by Young, which focuses on inclusive spaces. Young [10] explores how organisational spaces impact on the effectiveness of education strategies and practices. Whilst having a safe place to retreat to is an important factor, the research does not address security aspects and in particularly cybersecurity.

The same can be said from the perspective of adopting inclusive strategies and practices through ICT. There is a growing body of research studying education inclusion using Information and Commuications Technology (ICT), which show encouraging results [11]–[14]. Whilst many of the studies tend to focus on the benefits, there is also evidence that ICT can inhibit inclusive education; albeit not from the perspective of using cybersecurity technologies [15]. This highlights the issue that little if any research considers the cybersecurity aspects in terms of whether inclusive strategies reduce the risks and threats of cybersecurity or whether cybersecurity technologies can enhance or inhibit inclusion?

Based upon Beacham and Duncan's [3] theoretical framework for considering inclusive cloudbased security for education, and possible ways in which such a framework may manifest its self in the context of an inclusive learning environment, the following sections of this paper explores in more detail how such theory and inclusive pedagogies can be used in practice through pedagogical strategies to bring about real change and improvement in reducing risks and threats of cybersecurity.

Such insights will form the basis of a case study undertaken within Higher Education (HE). This case study will seek to highlight the difficulties in developing an experiment to measure the change in behaviour being encouraged. This case study will pilot the framework and obtain experimental and empirical evidence highlighting the benefits and challenges using such a framework in an authentic context. Lessons from the case study will be used to inform further investigations within real-world contexts.

III. Security and Privacy Weaknesses in Cloud Systems

All systems are the subject of serious penetration attempts by attackers. While resisting such attacks presents a huge challenge, where cloud is involved, the challenge is even greater. The attackers make no distinction between what kind of organisation, or individual they are attacking. They seek to get into the system, then dig themselves in, hiding themselves away to become a hidden intruder, with the goal of finding as much useful information as they can to extract for their own nefarious purposes.

This presents a serious challenge to defend an organisation properly from attack [16]–[19], but in the case of cloud, we also suffer from a fundamental, as yet unsolved, problem known as the cloud forensic problem. Once an attacker breaches a cloud system and becomes an intruder, there is nothing to then prevent them from escalating privileges until they are in a position to delete the forensic trail recording their ingress into the system, thus potentially turning them into an invisible intruder.

Once the intruder reaches this stage, they present a serious threat, since they are now in a position to help themselves to anything they want from the cloud system, and can also use this position as a springboard to attack other systems elsewhere within the organisation. They would also be in a position to completely shut down the running cloud instance, which would delete all data that had not been made persistent elsewhere. This could pose a serious challenge in trying to identify which information has been compromised, or stolen.

As if that were not bad enough, the forthcoming EU regulation, the GDPR [2], comes into effect on 25th May 2018. There is a requirement to report any breach within 72 hours of discovery. However, where forensic records have been destroyed, it may prove impossible to comply fully with this requirement. This would potentially expose the organisation to a fine, which in the worst case, could be the greater of €20million or 4% of global turnover, based on the previous year's accounts.

Duncan and Whittington [20] recently proposed a possible solution to this problem through the use of generating a full forensic and audit trail to be stored off site in an immutable database. We like this approach for its simplicity of application, there being nothing overly technical involved. Sadly, this will not be the only problem to contend with.

While there are a great many technical solutions, which have been developed to address technical issues [21]–[25], there are also other issues that need to be addressed. Many organisations forget that business architecture comprises a combination of people, process and technology, and not technology alone [26]. Thus, organisations who rely on technological solutions alone will be likely to fail to achieve a satisfactory level of security and privacy.

The weakest link of any organisation is usually the people involved in the organisation. Attackers have long recognised that people are very susceptible to attack via a wide range of social engineering attacks, malicious links in emails, spoof web sites, and a whole range of other attacks designed to target the weaknesses of the people of the organisation, rather than directly attacking the Information Technology (IT) systems of the organisation.

IV. The Approach

Whilst some general ways of enhancing the social and technical approaches to security and inclusion have been independently reported [3], this section highlights inclusive pedagogies and practices that can be used in computer science education. We selected computer science education because not only are students susceptible to the security threats and risk as students in general, but that these cohorts of students need to have knowledge and understanding about cyber-security if they are to engineer secure application systems in future.

Creating an authentic testbed in which to pilot such an investigation of this type is not without its difficulties. In the framework outlined by Beacham and Duncan [3], such systems would entail developing a socio technical system around an inclusive learning community involving pupils, teachers, parents, technicians, school management and administration, and staff within the local authority, to name but a few. Developing a socio-technical system for use within a real mainstream educational organisation such as a school or local authority would be fraught with educational and technical challenges; not to mention ethical and political issues.

For this reason, a smaller and more manageable system will be constructed, safe within the confines of a Higher Education Institution (HIE). The pilot system seeks to build a similar inclusive learning community but with a more manageable number of stakeholders. The inclusive learning community provides a framework in which to encourage inclusive strategies such as co-agency, everybody and trust,

TABLE I. DARE'S STRATEGIES [7]

Strategy to:	Co-agency	Everyone	Trust
Invite students to join different groups. Meeting the minds of learners to lift the limits posed by a security system.		X	X
Get to know each other. Find ways to connect with each other building on their strengths as opposed to differentiating tasks.		X	X
Avoid singling students out. Plan tasks to be open to all in learning community.		X	X
Help students with studying and finding solutions. Seek ways for tutors to learning from learners and building valued partnerships.	X	X	
Group sub-groups of students together or with buddies. Develop a community culture, which "not just facilitates access and engagement (to learning tasks) but to reinforce young peoples' active sense of their powers and competence as thinkers and learners that what they have to bring and contribute to their own learning is important, valued and welcome."		X	X
Use a problem based learning approach by dividing community into small and meaningful groups.		X	X
Insist on learners taking shared responsibility for **learning activities** and allow learners to make rules and decisions.	X	X	
Tutors focus is to "transform the context, the curriculum, and the conditions that sustain learning." In partnership with learners.	X	X	
Adopt security mechanisms that are accessible, afford well-being and achievement for all based on unity and solidarity learning.		X	X

but is formed and managed within the confines of a cohort studying within an HEI. This provides a more appropriate context and environment in which to undertake an initial pilot to empirically study the effectiveness of such a system.

A. *Inclusive strategies*

Before undertaking the pilot, it was important to ascertain what strategies increase inclusion within learning communities [6]. These strategies were then applied in the context of the case study with the intention of collecting evidence, which showed an inclusive learning community can reduce security threats and risks.

The strategies considered relate to the three principles of transformability theory. They consist of:

- Co-agency strategies that encourage tutors and students to work together and view each other as equal partners in the teaching and learning process;
- Everybody strategies that promote collaboration with stakeholders, such as parents, Local Authorities and education agencies;
- Trust strategies that seek to develop effective scaffolding for tutors and learners.

As shown in TABLE I, such principles were implemented by using the inclusive strategies listed in the table.

Such overlapping strategies underpin criteria, which will be used to evaluate the effectiveness of the intervention covered in the case study.

In the next section, we discuss the technical strategies that should be deployed in the framework.

V. TECHNICAL STRATEGIES

In order to construct a realistic learning environment, a closed prototype has been developed containing the following features:

- Authentication, by using access control, passwords or multi factor authentication;
- Monitoring/logging/reporting can be carried out in real-time, providing a transparent system;
- Auditing will be carried out using an independent, read-only closed system;
- Privacy will be achieved through a combination of actions/activity based focus and encryption.

In Figure 1, we outline how the various components of the system will fit together. We consider how each type of strategy addresses threats and risks outlined in the theoretical framework, mapping strategies to practice — this is the focus of the pilot study.

Thus, we require to include a simple mechanism whereby we collect ALL the forensic data and audit trail data that we are likely to need, in addition to what the cloud system can already collect, and store this into an "append-only" database. This immutable database must be stored off-site from the cloud instance in order to make it more difficult for the attacker to understand what is going on.

This immutable database must run on a server with no other function, other than to solely concentrate on the retention of the forensic data and the audit trail for the cloud instances it is designed to protect. We must remember that it will be necessary to actively provide a means of collecting both the forensic data and the full range of audit trail data we require, since as Duncan and Whittington note, many of these functions are switched off by default from a great many database systems [27] [20].

This data collection should include additional material to identify the specific cloud instance identifying number (ID), a timestamp to indicate generation time of the data collected, and if we want to take a paranoid approach, we could also serialise the data collected ID using a centrally generated number, which would assist in post hack event analysis. Indeed, the central ID generator could be monitored to seek out anomalous numbering sequences from which alerts could be generated to instantly warn of a developing situation.

This solution will provide us with the one fundamental means of being able to answer the big GDPR question in the event of a breach — namely we can identify which information, if any, that was compromised in the breach. While it is not a regulatory requirement, encryption of Personally Identifiable Information (PII) [2] will go a long way to help mitigate any liability in the event of a breach.

In the next section, we outline the rationale and methodology for the pilot case study.

VI. THE PILOT CASE STUDY

The socio component of the system involves the forming of a learning community. The community consists of students and

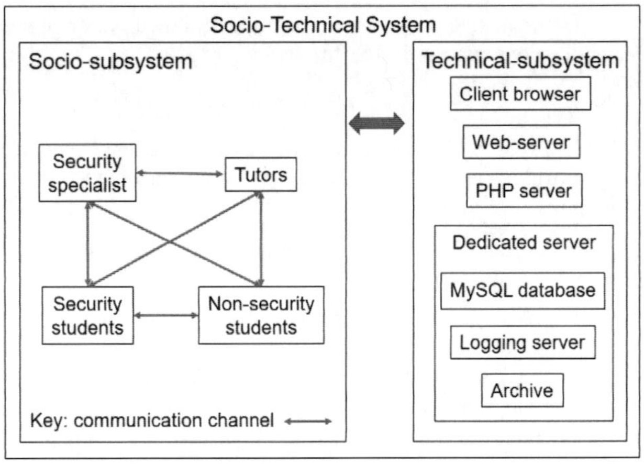

Figure 1. Socio-technical system approach to an inclusive cloud-based security learning environment.

tutors co-working together on achieving learning outcomes of a course studying Human Computer Interaction (HCI). Whilst the course covers conventional topics, it also includes the additional topic of usable security.

The students consist of two campus-based cohorts studying for a Master of Science (MSc) in Information Technology degree programme. One group of students form part of a September intake and have studied cyber-security in the previous term. The second group of students form part of a January intake beginning their programme.

Both cohorts of students are taught together on the HCI course. The course involves two one-hour lectures and one two-hour practical session. The lectures include materials that help students enhance their knowledge about usability with the aim of them understanding its relevance to usable security. In the practical sessions, they work in teams to complete tasks targeted at applying such knowledge and understanding. Students are also provided with additional materials and encouraged to undertake further reading and study around the usability aspects of security.

Although some of the students will have studied aspects of cyber-security, more broadly, students are not expected to know or understand the technicalities of cyber-security. For example, they do not need to know how to develop systems which require users to have a username and password, only that such process places usability constraints to use an application, such as having to recall authentication details.

The students are expected to use their knowledge and understanding to outline the types of data gathering approaches they would use as part of an Interface Design, and the types of evaluation approaches they would use to measure the usability of the security aspects of the user interface.

Regarding the technical component of the system, to attempt to make the case study authentic, students along with tutors develop and manage their groups own cloud-based learning environment. The cloud-based learning environment includes a small commercial system of a retail organisation. The students are tasked with reviewing this system and make recommendations for its usability.

In addition to students and tutors working together, for the socio-technical is to be effective, tutors are expected to work with cloud-based security specialist, and through student experts (who have studied a cybersecurity course) to implement technical aspects of the cloud-based security VLE. The mission for each student team involves the implementation of a user interface in the form of a low-fidelity prototype. Students are required to consider different ways to prevent social engineering and improve usability security. Students who have previously studied cybersecurity are expected to lead the practical sessions, helping the security specialist to share knowledge and expertise throughout the entail learning community.

A key aspect of the exercise involved tutors leaving students to drive agenda and facilitate the addressing of issues. Where possible consider the use of CSCW as opposed to independent standalone and individual practices. This includes each student team incorporating an ethical hacking approach by recruiting testers to attack their small commercial system, and conducting their own evaluation of the system. Students will have been given access to key components of the technical system such as the web server and database management system, but not the dedicated server. This server will be restricted to students but not tutors and the security specialist. Students will be introduced to ethical hacking and encouraged to test the usability and effectiveness of each teams solution. They will not be aware of the dedicated system.

Throughout the course tutors will assess the progress of the students and evaluate the performance of each teams security system. Tutors seek to address the following key questions based on students progress.

- How usability forms part of security; how it is integral to useable security.
- How technical strategies are realised within pilot.
- How social strategies are realised within pilot.
- How inclusive strategies realised within pilot.

Throughout, students are not made aware of the inclusive strategies taking centre stage. Tutors will be seeking evidence to what extent such strategies are present and being applied. Future work will seek to develop this aspect based upon findings.

In the course of the Pilot Study, students are asked to address the human weak link in security, and to explore ways of managing risks and threats within the provided cloud-based secure learning environment.

We outline below the main components of the Pilot Case Study to be implemented:

- Pilot Case Study to be implemented within HE;
- Aims and objectives of pilot case study:
    - To address the human weak link in security;
    - To enhance an inclusive security learning community, culture and environment;
    - To explore ways of managing risks and threats within a cloud-based secure learning environment.
- Targets MSc IT students studying the programme full time on campus:
    - September starts will have studied the first term of the programme;

  - January starts will have just started the programme.
- Rationale for target sample:
  - Students have various levels of knowledge and understanding of Information Security (IS);
  - Some students received course on IS;
  - Some students will not have received a course on IS.
- Cloud-based learning environment:
  - MyAberdeen / MyTimetable / MyCurriculum;
  - Email / Virtual Desktop Infrastructure (VDI) / Zend / PHPMYADMIN;
  - Bring Your Own Devices (BYOD)s — mobiles, tablets, laptops, PCs;
  - Personal storage space — University, external;
  - Social media — linkedin, facebook, twitter, youtube;
  - Integrated Development Environment (IDE)s — cloud9, Codio, Git/Github, SPM;
  - Other — Dropbox, milkthecow.
- How inclusive strategies are realised within pilot case study;
- How technical strategies are realised within pilot case study;
- Pilot case study forms part of a course on HCI; how to develop usable security.

Tutors and students develop and manage their own cloud-based learning environment as part of practical sessions. Practical sessions require students to apply content covered in HCI lectures and then consider its relevance to cloud-based security systems within HE. Additional two-hour voluntary weekly sessions introduced to provide space in the schedule for reflection and planning.

Tutors work with cloud-based experts, and through student experts (who have studied on the IS course) to implement technical aspects of the cloud-based security Virtual Learning Environment (VLE). The mission for each student group is to implement a course wiki in the form of a MySQL database with independent logging. Students are required to consider different ways to prevent social engineering and improve usability of security.

A key aspect of the exercise involved tutors leaving students to drive the agenda and facilitate the addressing of issues. Where possible, we considered the use of Computer Supported Co-operative Work (CSCW) as opposed to independent standalone and individual practices. This includes each student team incorporating an ethical hacking approach by recruiting testers to attack their small commercial system, and conducting their own evaluation of the system. Students will have been given access to key components of the technical system such as the web server and database management system, but not the dedicated server. This server will be restricted to students but not tutors and the security specialist. Students will be introduced to ethical hacking and encouraged to test the usability and effectiveness of each teams solution. They will not be aware of the dedicated system.

Throughout the course tutors will assess the progress of the students and evaluate the performance of each teams security system.

Tutors seek to address the following key questions based on students' progress:

- How usability forms part of security; how it is integral to use-able security;
- How technical strategies are realised within pilot;
- How social strategies are realised within pilot;
- How inclusive strategies realised within pilot.

Throughout, students are not made aware of the inclusive strategies taking centre stage. Tutors will be seeking evidence as to what extent such strategies are present and being applied. Future work will seek to develop this aspect based upon the findings. In the next section, we address some limitations of this work.

VII. Limitations and Discussion

There are a number of limitations in this work, which we will now discuss. Whilst the initial intentions are proving positive, this pilot case study involves small numbers of students who have had time to develop relationships as peers with fellow students and tutors. A key factor lacking is the heterogeneous nature of teams in learning environments. However, we plan to address this once the pilot case study concludes. Once the findings are fully analysed, we will incorporate the findings and implement the full case study starting from September, which will give us access to the impact of the full heterogeneous nature of teams in learning environments.

We hope to get the message across to all students that there needs to be serious consideration given to taking into account the potential impact of new legislation and regulation as it comes in to effect. Further education institutions need to be at the cutting edge so that once students leave with their qualifications, they will be ideally placed to ensure their future employers will be better able to improve policies, procedures and good working practices, to ensure they achieve adequate compliance with legislative and regulatory bodies. We also hope that students will achieve a better understanding of how to approach achieving a high level of usable security in their future employment.

VIII. Conclusion

This pilot case study forms part of a proof of concept for a longer term case study, which we hope to use to be able to ensure all students gain a better understanding of all the issues of security and privacy that must now be taken into account for all organisations who handle any form of PII. We anticipate being able to present the results of this pilot case study at the conference.

We believe the concept will help ensure that all students will be able to work in a secure and private environment, while learning how to safeguard themselves, their peers and their future employers. The proposed framework will be able to ensure that organisations can achieve compliance with the forthcoming EU GDPR, as well as achieving compliance with existing legislation on security and privacy. By ensuring that the framework can be resistant to the effects of the cloud forensic problem, this will ensure a robust capability to provide a high level of security and privacy.

Naturally, we accept that there will be a need for a more thorough and substantial investigation, and we will endeavour to achieve this with the next phase of the project, where we will be applying the framework to a full cohort of students, which will allow us to understand how those with different levels of experience can work together to ensure the safety of the whole educational environment.

REFERENCES

[1] Crown, "Data Protection Act 1998," 1998. [Online]. Available: http://www.legislation.gov.uk/ukpga/1998/29/contents [Retrieved: December 2017]

[2] EU, "EU General Data Protection Regulation (GDPR)," 2017. [Online]. Available: http://www.eugdpr.org/ [Retrieved: December 2017]

[3] N. Beacham and B. Duncan, "Development of a Secure Cloud Based Learning Environment for Inclusive Practice in Mainstream Education," in Cloud Comput. 2017 Eighth Int. Conf. Cloud Comput. GRIDs, Virtualization, Athens, 2017, pp. 1–4.

[4] J. M. Blythe, L. Coventry, and L. Little, "Unpacking security policy compliance : The motivators and barriers of employees ' security behaviors," Proceedings of the Eleventh Symposium On Usable Privacy and Security (SOUPS 2015), Ottawa, Canada, 2015, pp. 103–122.

[5] S. L. Pfleeger and D. D. Caputo, "Leveraging behavioral science to mitigate cyber security risk," Computers and Security, vol. 31, no. 4, 2012, pp. 597–611.

[6] D. Mitchell, " What really works in special and inclusive education: Using evidence-based teaching strategies." (2nd ed.). [Online] Available: http://ovidsp.ovid.com/ovidweb.cgi?T=JS&PAGE=reference&D=psyc11&NEWS=N&AN=2014-03315-000 [Retrieved December 2017]

[7] L. Dare and E. Nowicki, "Strategies for inclusion: Learning from students' perspectives on acceleration in inclusive education," Teaching and Teacher Education, vol. 69, 2018, pp. 243–252.

[8] H. Dong, "Strategies for teaching inclusive design," Journal of Engineering Design, vol. 21, no. 2-3, 2010, pp. 237–251.

[9] V. E. Mumford and J. P. Chandler, "Strategies for Supporting Inclusive Education for Students with Disabilities," Strategies, vol. 22, no. 5, 2009, pp. 10–15 Taylor & Francis Group.

[10] K. S. Young, "Institutional separation in schools of education: Understanding the functions of space in general and special education teacher preparation," Teaching and Teacher Education, vol. 27, no. 2, 2011, pp. 483–493

[11] L. Florian and J. Hegarty, ICT and Special Educational Needs: a tool for inclusion. McGraw-Hill Education (UK), 2004.

[12] A. Istenic Starcic and S. Bagon, "ICT-supported learning for inclusion of people with special needs: Review of seven educational technology journals, 1970-2011," British Journal of Educational Technology, vol. 45, no. 2, 2014, pp. 202–230.

[13] A. K. Yadav, "Supporting Inclusive Education Through ICT Implementation: An Intermediary Role," Educational Quest, vol. 5, no. 1, 2014, pp. 51–55.

[14] World Health Organisation, "Assistive Technology for Children with Disabilities: Creating Opportunities for Education, Inclusion and Participation A discussion paper," World Health Organization, 2015, p. 34.

[15] N. Beacham, "Developing NQTs e-pedagogies for inclusion," University of Aberdeen, Aberdeen, Tech. Rep. May, 2011. [Online]. Available: https://www.heacademy.ac.uk/system/files/8065_0.pdf [Retrieved: December 2017]

[16] N. Papanikolaou, S. Pearson, M. C. Mont, and R. Ko, "A Toolkit for Automating Compliance in Cloud Computing Services," Int. J. Cloud Comput., vol. x, no. x, 2014, pp. 45–68.

[17] J. Singh and J. M. Bacon, "On middleware for emerging health services," J. Internet Serv. Appl., vol. 5, no. 1, 2014, p. 6.

[18] J. Singh, J. Bacon, and D. Eyers, "Policy Enforcement Within Emerging Distributed, Event-based Systems," Proc. 8th ACM Int. Conf. Distrib. Event-Based Syst. - DEBS '14, 2014, pp. 246–255.

[19] J. Singh, J. Powles, T. Pasquier, and J. Bacon, "Seeing through the clouds: Management, control and compliance for cloud computing," Cloud Comput., 2015, pp. 1–12.

[20] B. Duncan and M. Whittington, "Creating and Configuring an Immutable Database for Secure Cloud Audit Trail and System Logging," Int. J. Adv. Secur., no. 3&4, 2017.

[21] R. K. L. Ko et al., "TrustCloud: A Framework for Accountability and Trust in Cloud Computing," Perspective, 2011, pp. 1–9.

[22] R. K. L. Ko, B. S. Lee, and S. Pearson, "Towards achieving accountability, auditability and trust in cloud computing," Commun. Comput. Inf. Sci., vol. 193 CCIS, 2011, pp. 432–444.

[23] N. Papanikolaou, S. Pearson, and M. C. Mont, "Towards Natural-Language Understanding and Automated Enforcement of Privacy Rules and Regulations in the Cloud: Survey and Bibliography," Analysis, 2011, pp. 1–9.

[24] S. Pearson, "Taking Account of Privacy when Designing Cloud Computing Services," Current, 2009, pp. 44–52.

[25] S. Pearson, "Toward accountability in the cloud," IEEE Internet Comput., vol. 15, no. 4, jul 2011, pp. 64–69.

[26] PWC, "UK Information Security Breaches Survey - Technical Report 2012," PWC2012, Tech. Rep. April, 2012.

[27] B. Duncan and M. Whittington, "Creating an Immutable Database for Secure Cloud Audit Trail and System Logging," in Cloud Comput. 2017 Eighth Int. Conf. Cloud Comput. GRIDs, Virtualization. Athens, Greece: IARIA, ISBN: 978-1-61208-529-6, 2017, pp. 54–59.

Providing Tamper-Resistant Audit Trails for Cloud Forensics with Distributed Ledger based Solutions

Mats Neovius
Department of Business Management and Analytics
Arcada University of Applied Sciences
Jan-Magnus Janssons plats 1, 00550 Helsinki, Finland
mats.neovius@arcada.fi

Magnus Westerlund
Department of Business Management and Analytics
Arcada University of Applied Sciences
Jan-Magnus Janssons plats 1, 00550 Helsinki, Finland
magnus.westerlund@arcada.fi

Jonny Karlsson
Department of Business Management and Analytics
Arcada University of Applied Sciences
Jan-Magnus Janssons plats 1, 00550 Helsinki, Finland
jonny.karlsson@arcada.fi

Göran Pulkkis
Department of Business Management and Analytics
Arcada University of Applied Sciences
Jan-Magnus Janssons plats 1, 00550 Helsinki, Finland
goran.pulkkis@arcada.fi

Abstract—**Network and information security are often more challenging in cloud computing than in onsite computing. Cloud computing resources are publicly accessible and thereby through this availability increase the risk of intrusion. The increase in the processing of sensitive data on cloud resources makes security challenges more noteworthy, particularly in light of legal issues around cross-border transfers and data protection. Technologies preventing intrusion are effective, yet not perfect. Once a system is compromised, the intruder frequently starts to delete and to modify audit trails and system log files for covering-up the intrusion. Complete and untampered audit trails and log files are essential for the legitimate owner of the cloud instance or service to estimate the losses, to reconstruct the data, to detect the origin of the intrusion attack, and eventually in a court of law be able to prosecute the attacker. Due to this, improved methods for performing forensics in the cloud domain are desperately needed. The baseline for any forensic investigation is assured data availability and integrity. In this position paper, we outline how the availability and integrity of this forensic data can be assured by applying distributed ledger based solutions for securely storing audit trails and log files in immutable databases. Given this approach, an attacker can neither delete, nor modify past trails or logs but merely stop generating new data into log files. The position presented here is novel, yet light enough for practical use.**

Keywords-forensics; cloud computing; distributed ledger; blockchain; security; privacy.

I. INTRODUCTION

The last decade has entailed a transition from onsite to cloud computing. Cloud computing provides access to a pool of interconnected resources enabled by the Internet. It abstracts the hardware from the client and has a "pay-per-use" business model. In cloud computing, the resources are elastically provisioned with storage space, service, computing platforms as virtual machines [1], and networking infrastructures obtained upon request [2] [3]. Hence, cloud computing is "a model for enabling ubiquitous, convenient, on-demand network access to a shared pool of configurable computing resources (e.g., networks, servers, storage, applications and services) that can be rapidly provisioned and released with minimal management effort or service provider interaction" [2]. Three basic cloud computing service models are Software as a Service (SaaS), Platform as a Service (PaaS), and Infrastructure as a Service (IaaS). Contemporary cloud-based software engineering directs towards Cloud Native Applications (CNA). A CNA is a service specifically designed to run in the cloud. CNAs are often deployed as self-contained units (containers) that are designed to scale horizontally. A CNA is often implemented as micro-services [4]. The technicalities are described in detail in [5]. In addition, the availability of cloud computing resources is augmented by the Intercloud initiative [6], envisioned as the "cloud of clouds". Hence, the Intercloud then provides virtually unlimited resources to any connected device. Connected devices include mobile devices, giving rise to the term Mobile Cloud Computing [7], and Internet-of-Things (IoT) devices [8]. Consequently, the end user's device running an application that utilizes cloud resources may be seen as the mere portal to the cloud relying on the service provider in administering the security and privacy of the data.

Academic research in network and computer forensics has a long history. Schneier and Kelsey [9] suggests a solution for keeping an audit log on insecure servers by offering a tamper-proof forensic scheme that stored and maintained log entries. However, with the shift to cloud computing the complexity and importance of keeping an audit trail has increased drastically. Cloud forensics has been defined as "the application of digital forensics in cloud computing as a subset of network forensics" [10] and as "to reconstruct past cloud computing events through identification, collection, preservation, examination, interpretation and reporting of digital evidence" [11]. As the former definition suggests forensics to be restricted to the

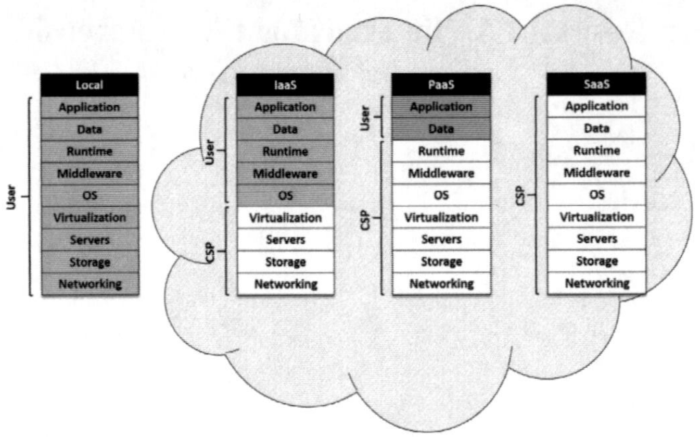

Figure 1. Access control to basic cloud service models in comparison to a local system.

network access, the latter definition includes the audit trail as a means to reconstruct events, as well as interpretation and reporting of evidence. Cloud forensics, therefore, requires audit trails to be stored in a manner with assured availability and integrity where no changes may occur.

A reasonable first choice for storage of audit trails for cloud forensics is an append-only (immutable) conventional database installation where read rights are assigned only to carefully selected set of agents. Existing implementations of immutable databases include configured conventional ones. In its most secure installation, it is hosted in-house with no means of external access and restricted physical access. Every access point (let these be logical or physical) weaken assurance of integrity. In-house installations are, however, not pragmatic for a cloud computing environments; nor are the cloud remote installations. On this challenge, purpose-built databases and filesystems are being developed, e.g., Datomic [12]. Implementation details of an immutable database for cloud audit trail are reported by Duncan and Whittington in [13]. Another attempt is the InterPlanetary File System (IFPS) [14]. The IPFS is fundamentally a protocol inspired by the Bitcoin blockchain protocol. It tries to make the web a digital resemblance to printed paper in documenting data, i.e., something that is permanent, unalterable and controllable.

Regardless of the technology, a distributed and replicated append-only storage provides stronger tamper resistance to a centralized one, specifically in relevance to nation-state-sponsored cyber-attacks. A distributed ledger is a replicated database, which is shared by nodes in a peer-to-peer network. Consensus algorithms are required to ensure replication and insertion across network nodes. In a truly distributed ledger, there is no central administrative node or centralized data storage. Thus, a distributed ledger storage for audit trails has stronger tamper resistance than any centralized immutable database implementation [15] [16].

This paper is a position paper that outlines an approach for storing the audit trail data using blockchain solutions. In the next Section, we discuss the current status of digital forensics in the cloud. In Section III, a tamper-resistant distributed ledger of the blockchain type that is based on protected storage of audit trails is presented. Finally, conclusions and proposals for future work are presented in Section IV. The distributed ledger technology is briefly described in an Appendix with the emphasis on the blockchain.

II. CLOUD FORENSICS AND AUDIT TRAILS

Audit trails for cloud forensics consist of collected log data of network traffic and data processing activities of computing devices. A generator of such data is the Intrusion Detection System (IDS) that extracts features from collected log data and analyzes these. The cloud service provider (CSP) is responsible for generating this IDS data. However, depending on the service model, the point of responsibility deviates.

Log data for audit trails can be scattered and stored in different locations due to the characteristics of the cloud. In the cloud, the level of access is divided between the cloud service user and the CSP. The level of access in the basic cloud service models is shown in Figure 1. This significantly complicates the data acquisition process. For example in the SaaS and PaaS models, only application related logs can be accessed by the cloud service user. Though in PaaS, a cloud service user can develop an application to be able to get some additional forensics data whereas, in SaaS, this is not possible. In the IaaS model, cloud service users can move to the operating system layer for acquiring forensic data. In all service models, the forensic investigators are dependent on the CSP to ensure that needed audit trail data has been collected. This is currently thus a trust issue since the availability and integrity of the data that may be affected are not transparent. Only when both parties are fully contributing to an immutable audit trail can it provide the required transparency needed for continued investigation and legal measures.

Verifiable audit trails are essential in forensic investigations to reconstruct and rigorously examine intrusions in the cloud. The reconstruction is central to find out what damage the intrusion has caused and discover sources and origins of intrusion attacks. When an attack has occurred, the cloud service user must engage a cloud forensics investigation to analyze the audit trail related to the attacked service in order to find forensic evidence. For this, the audit trail is fundamental in meeting with the EU General Data Protection Regulation (GDPR) [17], requiring enterprises to report security breaches within 72 hours after detection. Moreover, it should be possible for a CSP to present evidence on its own behalf that the source of the intrusion was external.

Traditionally, in digital forensics investigators take control of the affected physical device and perform forensic investigations on these by searching for evidence of malicious activity. For cloud computing being inherently dynamic, the methods traditionally used in digital forensics render themselves impractical [18]. Different cloud service users may virtually share physical resources through the hypervisor and thus, isolate the scene for forensics is next to impossible. This leads to issues that have to be addressed by the forensic investigation, namely, it must be proven that any data extracted is not mixed with some other customer's data and that the availability, privacy, and integrity of the other user's data must be maintained.

Cloud forensics challenges are mostly related to architectural, data collection, and legal issues [11] [19], as well as in composing provenance data. Provenance data is the "metadata that provides details of the origins (history) of a data object" [20]. That is, provenance data is metadata tracing the history of data objects starting from original source data [21]. Complete provenance of all data stored in the cloud, all distributed computations, all data exchanges, and all transactions would enable identification of exact sources of cloud intrusion attacks and detect insider attacks in forensic investigations [22].

III. PROTECTION SOLUTIONS FOR AUDIT TRAIL DATA

Audit trail data for cloud forensics requires secure protection since it is vulnerable to corruption by accidental faults and malicious forgery [23]. Protection must repel accidental corruption and all malicious anti-forensics attacks by ensuring both integrity and availability of the data. This Section discusses requirements for distributed ledger based protection solutions for audit trails in the cloud and presents some blockchain based solution proposals. Distributed ledger technology with the focus on blockchain technology is described in an Appendix.

A. *Requirements for Distributed Ledger based Solutions*

Usage of a distributed ledger for protection of cloud forensics data is possible only if three fundamental requirements are fulfilled. First, a sufficiently large network of nodes must be available for storing replicated copies of the distributed ledger. Secondly, each network node must have sufficient storage and processing resources for management of a distributed ledger replication. Thirdly, it must be possible to extend the distributed ledger with new data produced at the data rate needed (i.e. throughput).

B. *Existing Blockchain Based Solutions*

Applying the blockchain and distributed ledger technologies in various domains is currently a hot research and business development topic. These technologies have been proposed for many financial technology solutions with extensions assuring programmatical smart contracts, to preserve (and control) privacy and personal data, provide transparency on transactions, and in the industrial IoT to keep track of logistic chains. These are all very intriguing applications, but we concentrate on ones that are directly relevant to the distributed audit trail data. Further, we focus on forensic data in the cloud computing environment as we find this area to be among the most challenging problems for distributed ledgers.

The integrity of cloud forensics data can be ensured by Public Key Infrastructure (PKI) signatures which depend on a certificate authority. This is not a feasible solution in the cloud infrastructure which is inherently decentralized. An alternative to PKI signatures is keyless signatures implemented by a blockchain based distributed Keyless Signature Infrastructure [24] [25].

A blockchain based data provenance architecture, the ProvChain, is described and evaluated in [26]. ProvChain has been designed for collection and verification of cloud computing users' provenance data. ProvChain can use the global Bitcoin blockchain since the collected provenance data is restricted to metadata records of cloud service users' operations on data files stored in the cloud. Recorded metadata attributes are RecordID, Date and Time, UserID, Filename, AffectedUser, and FileOperation. A FileOperation is file creation, file modification, file copy, file share, or file delete. UserID attributes are hashed to protect cloud users' privacy. Provenance auditors can, therefore, access cloud users' provenance metadata but cannot correlate the metadata to users owning the metadata. Only the Cloud Service Provider (CSP) can relate provenance data to cloud service users owning the data. Provenance metadata records are published in blocks of a blockchain implemented by a blockchain network consisting of globally participating nodes. Several metadata records can be stored in one blockchain transaction. Each metadata record is extended with a hash and a Merkle hash tree [27], is constructed for the metadata records in a block. The Merkle root is stored as a block header attribute. ProvChain is built on the top of the open source cloud computing application ownCloud [28]. The Tierion Data API [29], is used to publish provenance metadata records in the blockchain. Tierion generates for each transaction a blockchain receipt based on the Chainpoint standard [30]. The Merkle hash tree included in this blockchain receipt proves that the provenance metadata records were recorded at a specific time. A provenance auditor can request a blockchain receipt via Tierion Data API, access the related blockchain block with Blockchain Explorer [31], and validate the provenance metadata records in the block with the Merkle hash tree in the receipt. Measured ProvChain overhead for retrieval of provenance metadata of one file operation is about 0.7...0.8 s in an ownCloud test application [26].

Blockchain-based tamper-resistant registration of provenance data related to accessing medical data records in cloud storage is outlined in [32] [33]. The provenance data stored in the blockchain is available for auditing and in forensic investigations to detect privacy violations of medical data record owners. The outlined solution for protection of provenance data is applicable also to other types of personal data records.

C. Proposed Distributed Ledger based Solutions

An ideal solution would be a global network of nodes fulfilling all three requirements in Section III A. The global Bitcoin blockchain fulfils the two first requirements, but this blockchain cannot be extended with new blocks at a rate needed. Computationally it is not possible that even for a small cloud computing environment all the audit trail data for forensic investigations would be stored in the Bitcoin blockchain. The reason is the current blockchain size in combination with the throughput constrained Proof-of-Work (PoW) consensus algorithm.

However, other possible solutions may be engineered that circumvent this issue. One possible solution is a network of distributed ledger nodes, for example, blockchain nodes maintained by a CSP or preferably by several cooperating CSPs. As of the second requirement in Section III A, all cloud computing users cannot be nodes in a distributed ledger network since also resource-constrained mobile devices and IoT devices can use cloud computing services. Moreover, a faster consensus algorithm than PoW must be implemented for the used distributed ledger.

Hashgraph is a distributed ledger technology with a Byzantine consensus algorithm using a gossip protocol [34] [35]. While Bitcoins PoW implementation limits the throughput 7 transaction/s, the Hashgraph consensus algorithm can process even tens of thousands transactions/s [36]. The Archive Database proposed in [13] to be used as an immutable database for cloud audit trails could be implemented by a network of Hashgraph nodes maintained by a CSP or several cooperating CSPs. Each time when the database audit trail plugin stores log data the same data is transmitted to a preferably randomly chosen Hashgraph node. Reception of the log data creates a signed time-stamped event including a transaction storing the log data. An immutable record of all stored events is - due to the high event processing rate of a Hashgraph network – almost immediately available in each Hashgraph node. The Hashgraph fulfils all requirements in Section III A. However, at the time of writing it is deployed in permissioned environments and is, therefore, a permissioned distributed ledger technology. Still, a federated decentralized installation maintained by several cooperating CSP or other service providers may offer an alternative to a public distributed ledger.

There are also other proposals that address the need for high throughput distributed ledgers. Off-chain state agreement solutions commonly referred to as state channel technology, have been developed for handling many small transactions. A use case for the development of state channel technology has been to handle micro-transactions, which in addition to needing a high throughput also require a minuscule transaction cost for the clearance of each transaction. [37]

IV. CONCLUSIONS

This is a position paper outlining novel ideas on applying distributed ledger based solutions for storing audit trails in the cloud and more specifically, for micro-service deployments. The security features of the distributed ledger assure the integrity of the audit trails which is essential for trustable cloud forensics. The challenge is timely as the EU GDPR becomes enforced from May 2018. Moreover, the recent advancements in distributed ledgers, blockchains (cryptocurrencies) and their various spinoffs set the scene for applying this new technology by novel means. This paper lay the ground for distributed ledger technology in terms of cloud forensics.

APPENDIX

A. Distributed Ledger Technology

The most deployed distributed ledger type is a blockchain, which extends the shared database with a sequence of blocks storing transactional data. Blocks are chronologically and cryptographically linked to each another. Other distributed ledger types are the Tangle Network and Hashgraph. For the Tangle network, a Directed Acyclic graph-based network is used instead of a replicated linked chain of blocks in blockchain network nodes [38].

A Hashgraph network consists of nodes, which create context dependent events and communicate with each other using a gossip protocol. An event is a timestamped and digitally signed data structure consisting of one or several transactions and two hashes. One hash is extracted from the latest event on the node from which the latest gossip was received and the other hash is extracted from the preceding event created on the same node. A created event is sent as gossip to another randomly selected Hashgraph node together with all events still not known by the selected node. As event creation and gossip transmission continue in all Hashgraph nodes, all created events are immutably stored in each Hashgraph node. A Byzantine consensus on the order of events is achieved with probability 1 using a virtual voting procedure if more than 2n/3 nodes are uncorrupt where n is the number of nodes in the Hashgraph network. The details of the gossip protocol, the virtual voting, and the Byzantine consensus algorithm are presented in [39] and [35].

The blockchain technology is at the time of writing the best-known solution for implementing distributed ledgers and we, therefore, choose to focus on it. Findings concerning distributed ledgers, in general, should be transferable to other solutions such as the hashgraph and the Tangle network, once they become widely validated as secure.

Nakamoto introduced in 2008 blockchain technology as the Bitcoin cryptocurrency platform [40]. A blockchain implements a distributed database in which a list of records called blocks is stored. New blocks can always be appended to the list but stored blocks are neither removed nor changed. The distributed database is replicated in nodes of a peer-to-

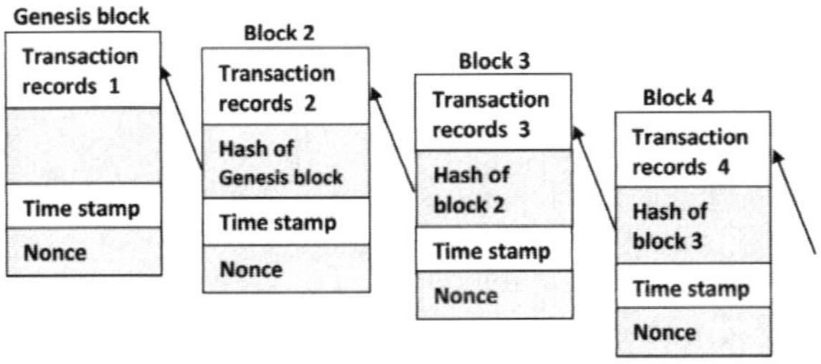

Figure 2. Basic blockchain structure.

peer blockchain network. A complete database copy is therefore stored in each network node. The blockchain topology is a chain, since after the first block each additional block contains a hash link to the preceding block, see Figure 2. The first block is called Genesis Block. Each block is also time stamped, however not necessarily to a universal time server.

A blockchain network node is owned by a blockchain user for execution of blockchain operations. A unique key pair of public key cryptography must also be owned by a blockchain user. The public key represents the identity of a blockchain user. A blockchain user executes a blockchain operation by initiating a transaction, which transfers some asset, for example, a cryptocurrency amount or a data object, to another blockchain user. A transaction creates a record, which is signed by the initiator of the transaction and transmitted to all nodes in the blockchain network. Each blockchain network node tries to validate a received transaction record with the transaction initiator's public key. A transaction record, which does not become validated by all blockchain network nodes, is discarded as invalid. Validated transaction records are collected by so-called mining nodes in the blockchain network and stored as lists in candidate blocks, which are time stamped. Each mining node executes a computation called mining on its candidate block. The candidate block of the mining node which first achieves a predefined mining goal is linked to the blockchain and all other mining nodes' candidate blocks are discarded. Several mining implementations for blockchains exist. Bitcoin blockchain mining uses PoW, where each mining node repeats hashing the concatenation of the last block in the blockchain and a new randomly chosen value. The mining goal is to create a hash of required difficulty.

There are public, permissioned, and private blockchains. A public blockchain, for example, Bitcoin, can be used by anyone. A public blockchain user copies the entire blockchain and installs the blockchain software on a personal node, which joins the blockchain network. Any blockchain user can also install the mining software on their own blockchain network node. Only a public blockchain can be trusted to fulfil the distributed ledger definition, as permission and private blockchains often maintain a centralized control node.

Recent blockchain implementations with extended functionality are denoted as Blockchain 2.0 for which an interesting feature is the smart contract introduced in [41]. A smart contract is a software component encompassing contractual terms and conditions enabling the verification, negotiation, or enforcement of a contract. A blockchain platform supporting smart contracts is Ethereum [42].

Blockchain security relies on the hash links between successive blocks combined with the replication of the entire blockchain to all blockchain network nodes. A public blockchain is therefore practically tamper-proof because a block cannot be changed without changing all the subsequent blocks and participation of all blockchain network nodes to validate and register the change. As the public blockchain is not managed by any centralized authority that could be a target of attacks it is less sensitive to some attack types such as DOS attacks, because full blockchain replicas are stored in many blockchain network nodes. However, an intrusion into a sufficient number of blockchain network nodes including some mining nodes can cause data losses and/or insertion of corrupt data in the attacked blockchain [43].

The tamper resistance of a blockchain does not exclude security vulnerabilities. Security attacks against blockchains are described and evaluated in [44] [45] [46] [47].

REFERENCES

[1] D. A. B. Fernandes, L. F. B. Soares, J. V. Gomes, M. M. Freire, and P. R. M. Inácio, "Security issues in cloud environments: a survey," International Journal of Information Security, vol. 13, iss. 2, pp. 113-170, Apr. 2014.

[2] P. Mell and T. Grance, "The NIST Definition of Cloud Computing," Special Publication 800-145, National Institute of Standards and Technology, U.S. Dept. Commerce, 2011.

[3] J. Köhler, K. Jünemann, and H. Hartenstein, "Confidential database-as-a-service approaches: taxonomy and survey," J. Cloud Computing: Advances, Systems and Applications, vol. 4, no. 1, 2015. doi:10.1186/s13677-014-0025-1

[4] N. Dragoni et al., "Microservices: yesterday, today, and tomorrow," April 2017. [Online]. Available from: https://arxiv.org/pdf/1606.04036.pdf

[5] N. Kratzke and P.-C. Quint, "Understanding cloud-native applications after 10 years of cloud computing - A systematic mapping study," J. Systems and Software, vol. 126, pp. 1-16, April 2017, https://doi.org/10.1016/j.jss.2017.01.001

[6] D. Bernstein, E. Ludvigson, K. Sankar, S Diamond, and M. Morrow, "Blueprint for the Intercloud - Protocols and Formats for Cloud Computing Interoperability," Proc. Fourth International Conference on Internet and Web Applications and Services (ICIW'09), IEEE Press, 2009, pp.328-336.

[7] M. Shiraz, A. Gani, R. H. Khokhar, and R. Buyya, "A review on distributed application processing frameworks in smart mobile devices for mobile cloud computing," IEEE Communications Surveys and Tutorials, vol. 15, no. 3, pp. 1294–1313, 2013.

[8] L. Jiang et al., "An IoT-Oriented Data Storage Framework in Cloud Computing Platform," IEEE Transactions on Industrial Informatics, Vol. 10, No. 2, pp. 1443-1451, May 2014.

[9] B. Schneier, and J. Kelsey, "Secure audit logs to support computer forensics," ACM Transactions on Information and System Security, vol. 1, no. 3, pp. 159-176, 1999.

[10] K. Ruan, J. Carthy, T. Kechadi, and M. Crosbie, "Cloud Forensics: An Overview," in Advances in Digital Forensics VII, pp. 35–46, 2011. [Online]. Available from: http://cloudforensicsresearch.org/publication/Cloud_Forensics_An_Overview_7th_IFIP.pdf

[11] P. Mell and T. Grance, "Nist cloud computing forensic science challenges," Draft NISTIR 8006, National Institute of Standards and Technology, U.S. Department of Commerce, June 2014. [Online]. Available from: https://csrc.nist.gov/csrc/media/publications/nistir/8006/draft/documents/draft_nistir_8006.pdf

[12] Cognitect, Inc. Datomic The fully transactional, cloud-ready, distributed database, 2016. [Online]. Available from: http://www.datomic.com/

[13] B. Duncan and M. Whittington, "Creating an Immutable Database for Secure Cloud Audit Trail and System Logging," Eighth International Conference on Cloud Computing, GRIDs, and Virtualization, Athens: IARIA, 2017, pp. 54–59.

[14] J. Benet, "IPFS – Content Addressed, Versioned, P2P File System (DRAFT 3)", 2017 [Online]. Available from: https://github.com/ipfs/ipfs/blob/master/papers/ipfs-cap2pfs/ipfs-p2p-file-system.pdf

[15] Distributed Ledger Technology: beyond blockchain, 2016. [Online]. Available from: https://www.gov.uk/government/uploads/system/uploads/attachment_data/file/492972/gs-16-1-distributed-ledger-technology.pdf

[16] D. Mills et al., "Distributed ledger technology in payments, clearing, and settlement," Finance and Economics Discussion Series 2016-095, 2016.

[17] EUR-Lex Regulation [EU] 2016/679. General Data Protection Regulation (GDPR). [Online]. Available from: http://eur-lex.europa.eu/eli/reg/2016/679/oj

[18] V. M. Katilu, V. N. L. Franqueira, and O. Angelopoulou, "Challenges of Data Provenance for Cloud Forensic Investigations," Proc. 10th Int. Conf. on Availability, Reliability and Security, IEEE Press, 2015, pp. 312-317.

[19] M. E. Alex and R. Kishore, "Forensics Framework for Cloud computing," J. Computers and Electrical Engineering, vol. 60, iss. C, pp. 193-205, May 2017.

[20] K.-K. Muniswamy-Reddy and M. Seltzer, "Provenance as first class cloud data," ACM SIGOPS Operating Systems Review, vol. 43, no. 4, pp. 11-16, Jan. 2009, doi:10.1145/1713254.1713258

[21] Y. L. Simmhan, B. Plale, and D. Gannon, "A survey of data provenance in e-science," ACM Sigmod Record, vol. 34, no. 3, pp. 31–36, 2005.

[22] D. K. Tosh et al., "Security Implications of Blockchain Cloud with Analysis of Block Withholding Attack," Proc. 17th IEEE/ACM International Symposium on Cluster, Cloud and Grid Computing, IEEE Press, 2017, pp. 458-467.

[23] B. Lee, A. Awad, and M. Awad, "Towards secure provenance in the cloud: A survey," Proc. 8th International Conference on Utility and Cloud Computing (UCC), IEEE Press, 2015, pp. 577–582.

[24] A. Buldas, A. Kroonmaa, R. Laanoja, "Keyless signatures infrastructure: How to build global distributed hash-trees," Nordic Conference on Secure IT Systems, Springer, 2013, pp. 313–320.

[25] Guardtime. Cloud Assurance with Blockchains, 2017. [Online]. Available from: https://guardtime.com/solutions/cloud

[26] X. Liang, et al., "ProvChain: A Blockchain-based Data Provenance Architecture in Cloud Environment with Enhanced Privacy and Availability," Proc. 17th IEEE/ACM International Symposium on Cluster, Cloud and Grid Computing, IEEE Press, 2017, pp. 468-477.

[27] R. C. Merkle, "A Digital Signature Based on a Conventional Encryption Function," in Advances in Cryptology - CRYPTO '87, LNCS 293, Springer, 1988.

[28] ownCloud, 2017. [Online]. Available from: https://owncloud.org/

[29] Tierion Documentation, 2017. [Online]. Available from: https://tierion.com/docs

[30] Chainpoint, 2017. [Online]. Available from: https://chainpoint.org/

[31] BTC.com, 2017. [Online]. Available from: https://btc.com/

[32] Q. Xia, E. B. Sifah, A. Smahi, S. Amofa, and X. Zhang, ''BBDS: Blockchain-based data sharing for electronic medical records in cloud environments,'' Information 2017, vol. 8, iss. 2, Apr. 2017, doi:10.3390/info8020044

[33] Q. Xia et al., "MeDShare: Trust-Less Medical Data Sharing Among Cloud Service Providers via Blockchain," IEEE Access, vol 5, pp. 14757-14767, July 2017.

[34] G. Kingslay, "Hashgraph vs. Blockchain Is the end of Bitcoin and Ethereum near?" [Online]. Available from: https://coincodex.com/article/1151/hashgraph-vs-blockchain-is-the-end-of-bitcoin-and-ethereum-near/

[35] L. Baird, The Swirlds Hashgraph Consensus Algorithm: Fair, Fast, Byzantine Fault Tolerance, Swirlds Tech Report Swirlds-TR-2016-01, May 31, 2016. [Online]. Available from: http://www.swirlds.com/downloads/SWIRLDS-TR-2016-01.pdf

[36] Blockchain Technologies Feature Analysis, 2016. [Online]. Available from: https://lists.w3.org/Archives/Public/public-blockchain/2016Oct/att-0004/BlockchainTechnologiesFeatureAnalysis.html

[37] Z. Hess, Y. Malahov, and J. Pettersson, "Æternity blockchain", 2017. [Online]. Available from: https://aeternity.com/aeternity-blockchain-whitepaper.pdf

[38] S. Popov, "The Tangle," White Paper, 2017. [Online]. Available from: https://iota.org/IOTA_Whitepaper.pdf

[39] L. Baird, "Hashgraph Consensus: Detailed Examples," Swirlds Tech Report Swirlds-TR-2016-02, Dec 11, 2016. [Online]. Available from: http://www.swirlds.com/downloads/SWIRLDS-TR-2016-02.pdf

[40] S. Nakamoto, "Bitcoin: A Peer-to-Peer Electronic Cash System," 2008. [Online]. Available from: https://bitcoin.org/bitcoin.pdf

[41] N. Szabo, "The Idea of Smart Contracts," 1997. [Online]. Available from: http://www.fon.hum.uva.nl/rob/Courses/InformationInSpeech/CDROM/Literature/LOTwinterschool2006/szabo.best.vwh.net/idea.html

[42] Ethereum Blockchain App Platform. [Online]. Available from: https://www.ethereum.org/

[43] M. Conoscenti, A. Vetro, J. C. de Martin, "Blockchain for the Internet of Things: a Systematic Literature Review," Proc. 13th International Conference on Computer Systems and Applications (AICCSA), IEEE Press, 2016, pp. 1-6.

[44] Eyal, I and E. G. Sirer, "Majority is not Enough: Bitcoin Mining is Vulnerable," arXiv:1311.0243v5 [cs.CR], Nov. 2013. [Online]. Available from: https://arxiv.org/pdf/1311.0243v5.pdf

[45] S. Barber, X. Boyen, E. Shi, and E. Uzun, "Bitter to Better – How to Make Bitcoin a Better Currency," in LNCS 7397, Switzerland: Springer, pp. 399-414, 2012.

[46] E. Heilman, A. Kendler, A. Zohar, and S. Goldberg., "Eclipse Attacks on Bitcoin's Peer-to-Peer Network," Proc. 24th USENIX Security Symposium, 2015, pp. 129-144.

[47] K. Nayak, S. Kumar, A. Miller, and E. Shi, "Stubborn mining: Generalizing selfish mining and combining with an eclipse attack," Proc. IEEE European Symposium on Security and Privacy (EuroS&P), IEEE Press, 2016, pp. 305-320.

A Management View of Security and Cloud Computing

Ndubuisi Anomelechi*, William Cooper†, Bob Duncan‡ John D. Lamb§
Business School, University of Aberdeen, UK
Emails: *n.anomelechi@abdn.ac.uk, †william.cooper@abdn.ac.uk, ‡robert.duncan@abdn.ac.uk, §j.d.lamb@abdn.ac.uk

Abstract—**Cloud security is often seen as a technical problem. We argue that its solution needs both technical and management input. We find that cloud computing offers reliability and flexibility and its low cost makes it attractive, particularly to small and medium sized enterprises. We note that security technology must be adopted universally and often promptly. It requires both an organisational commitment and an individual commitment, which is most readily obtained if the technology places a low knowledge burden on users: that is, it is transparent or adds only a few, often-repeated, tasks. We note that providers have already achieved this in many cloud services. Organisations need clarity of what security is provided and who is responsible for breaches. They also need cloud providers to help them identify and recover from breaches. We consider why breaches have now become a hot topic, and provide a suggestion of how to mitigate the impact of these whilst meeting our management objectives and complying with the forthcoming EU General Data Protection Regulation.**

Keywords–Management goals; cloud security; EU GDPR.

I. INTRODUCTION

It is generally considered good practice for business organisations to embrace innovation, which may include disruptive technologies where appropriate [1], thereby doing things in what might be argued to be smarter ways. Such approaches may be adopted by sole trader start-up businesses to large scale multi-national corporations. While this all sounds entirely laudable and appears to make good business sense, there are some issues that may not be getting the level of attention they merit. The pressures on businesses to be efficient and effective, aligned with the adoption of innovative technology, raises issues that previously may not have been considered problematic. The potential for conflicting interests and flawed reasoning [2], is clearly demonstrated when it comes to the arena of cyber security and the way in which the importance of such may be viewed by businesses. This may be argued to be particularly relevant to the Small and Medium sized Enterprises (SME) sector and to the adoption and use of cloud computing.

The central element of concern is that too little attention may be paid to ensuring an adequate level of security is in place when businesses make use of cloud computing. Even where security elements have been made available, these may be compromised by the behaviour of individuals accessing the systems concerned. It has long been recognised that elements of interface design and ease of use are important when it comes to people effectively using computing provision. Human behaviour has been recognised as requiring ease of use more generally, for example by Drucker [3], who advised that removing difficulties would increase the likelihood of desired behaviour. The central message here would be that, if we wish cloud computing facilities to be accessed securely, we also need to consider issues of human behaviour and ensure we facilitate ease of use by removing potential difficulties that might detract from successful implementation of security elements.

In Section II, we consider how cloud is used and how it will impact on SMEs, and in Section III, we consider cloud security weaknesses. In Section IV, we address adoption and diffusion of innovations, and in Section V, we discuss the limitations of our management goals. In Section VI, we ask whether that is it, and discover some major issues that must be addressed. In Section VII, we consider how we might find a quick solution to this problem, and in Section VIII, we consider whether our ideas can meet the management goals we have set ourselves. Finally, in Section IX, we discuss our conclusions and future work.

II. CLOUD COMPUTING

Cloud services and environments are variously defined. We note here the distinctions between Software as a Service (SaaS), Platform as a Service (PaaS) and Infrastructure as a Service (IaaS) [4] [5]. SaaS includes cloud file systems, web servers and database management. Any business user of cloud services is likely to use at least some of these. And businesses that use PaaS and IaaS may still use these separately for both convenience and security. We focus on these, because they are where cloud services must minimally provide security.

We note immediately that using a cloud system creates security issues that cannot be fully resolved by the enterprises served. When attackers breach a cloud system, there is nothing to stop them deleting the forensic trail. This means the enterprises cannot tell a regulator which files have been accessed, modified, deleted or exfiltrated. Secure encryption can mitigate this problem but still gives the enterprise no means to preserve data integrity other than keeping private backups of data. But this contradicts reasons for an SME choosing a Cloud Service Provider (CSP): to improve reliability without excessive cost.

We note that there may be further security responsibilities for both business users and CSPs. We focus on SMEs because they are most likely to choose cloud services without having the technical knowledge to deal with all the security issues that either a large entreprise or a CSP can.

A. Cloud Use: Advantages for SMEs

The potential gains for SMEs who choose to adopt cloud computing may be considered to include improvements in capacity, reliability and flexibility, reduced costs and faster time to market [6] [7]. The central benefits of the cloud approach may be considered to include low-cost availability, innovation power, expandability and environmental protection. Cloud computing enables the use of computing resources without the need to own them, which reduces the overhead costs for the businesses involved. This offers SMEs the potential for international capability, which would be likely to be more expensive using alternative means [8]. Cloud use would potentially allow SMEs to compete at levels that previously would have been considered the domain of larger businesses. Research indicates that adoption of cloud services by SMEs relates to the potential advantage offered and that cloud computing may be of particular benefit to entrepreneurial ventures within developing nations [9].

B. Cloud Use: Adoption by SMEs

The adoption of cloud computing by SMEs is an area that has been highlighted as requiring further research. Entrepreneurial factors have been identified as likely to influence adoption of innovative technology, such as cloud computing. On a commercial basis, such innovative technology may be regarded as risky [10]. While cloud technologies may facilitate the development of SMEs, it may also open them to increased threats [11]. The cloud option may be considered to offer personalised and inexpensive computing facility on-demand [12] and to offer scalable capabilities [13], which is likely to be attractive to many within the SME sector. The scalability and mobility offered by the cloud option may offer greater levels of control over costs.

It is hardly surprising that such an option would be considered as a business asset and that those businesses for whom the minimisation of overhead costs, whilst maintaining cutting edge capability, is particularly valuable, would seek to utilise this facility. This is likely to be of particular relevance to SMEs, as their available budgets are likely to be lower than those of larger businesses. Supplier support may also be considered to be influential in the decision to adopt, with small businesses being more likely to rely on such external support [14]. Business concerns regarding the use of cloud computing may be considered to include lock-in, privacy and security, each of which may have a negative impact on the adoption of cloud computing by SMEs. The ease of use aspect of cloud computing is considered likely to impact the adoption level in SMEs, as has competitive pressure and the importance of relative advantage [11]. Cloud vendor lock-in may be exacerbated by the likely effort involved in moving to alternate providers. SMEs may be argued to be particularly vulnerable in this regard as they are less likely to have bargaining power [15]. The importance of the privacy element and the related issues of security and trust have been highlighted as important in the adoption process, with early adopters and prospectors emerging as more inclined to trust service providers. Security and privacy fears relate to the potential for public disclosure of sensitive information [16].

C. Security Issues

A major potential risk with cloud computing is that of security, with such elements as protocols, authentication processes and specific security standards requiring to be addressed. Thus, factors of concern for CSPs implementing security may be more technical.

Factors of concern to business entities when (rather than if) breaches occur include loss of productivity, (intellectual) property and business share, besides impact on customer experience/relationship and cost of recovery from an attack. Of utmost concern however will be business continuity. SMEs are more vulnerable to these as they are arguably less able to absorb the impacts of them than larger organisations. Whilst we argue that the CSP should assume responsibility for data integrity and recovery from breaches, obligations relating to the business continuity costs above remain the responsibility of the enterprises.

Partly owing to vendors' and developers' marketing strategies, new technology is often adopted on the assumption of complete sufficiency and security. Very little consideration tends to be given to what might happen in the event of a failure or breach. This gives rise to numerous risks related to the factors of concern. Such risks cannot be mitigated without the adoption by each user organisation, including SMEs, of a robust system security and disaster recovery strategy.

The nature of cloud computing is such that the users data is stored in a relational data base using fixed schemata. This raises the likelihood of stability and security issues for users. These may relate to traditional security, availability and third party data control. Risks may be due to the cloud providers, law restrictions, hackers, or the equipment in use. Such issues may be addressed in a range of ways, including information-centric security, transparency regarding data transfer and disposal, and the use of encryption [8]. The concept of cloud security may be considered to encapsulate ways in which the infrastructure and the applications and data within it are protected. As with most situations interrelated elements are put at risk by the weakest link in their chain. With the use of cloud computing it may be argued that the cloud itself may be the weakest link, given that once this is penetrated the assailant may erase any traces of entry and proceed to access areas within the cloud at will. One of the central issues in relation to cloud security might be argued to be that of user behaviour. Perceived usefulness and perceived ease of use [17] may be considered important in relation to the use of technology and this may impact approaches taken to security provision and the effective use of such.

III. Cloud Security Weaknesses

From a technical and legal perspective, there are several aspects of security that businesses have to comply with. For much data there is a legal requirement to ensure privacy and confidentiality. From a business perspective availability, integrity and authenticity are important and corruption or misuse may create legal or professional problems, for example, with accounting systems. In addition there is an increasing requirement for businesses to be able to (i) detect and (ii) recover from breaches of security, in both cases as fast as possible.

We may note three features that are likely to be true of most ICT security technologies. First, to work, the technologies often need to be adopted by everyone within an organisation. Second, many of the people adopting the technology may see little reward from using it. Third, both managers and users may have limited understanding of the reasons for using it or even of what the technology does. This can be particularly problematic for SMEs who, in choosing to outsource security to a CSP, may employ no one with this understanding.

When enterprises, especially SMEs, use cloud computing we show that both enterprise and CSP will have to implement some aspects of security. Since no one security model will work in all cases, it is vital to pin down who is responsible for which aspects of security in the service level agreements.

A. Secure cloud computing

Arguably it is even more important to develop technologies for security that are also as transparent as possible. For example, where encryption or data integrity are required, ideally the implementation should be at the level of the file system (whether local, remote or cloud) and handled within the operating systems so that users can be minimally aware. For example, the file manager and applications should be able to open, close, modify and copy files without the user being aware, except perhaps if there is an opportunity to copy data from a secure system to an insecure one.

The first requirement, then, that we identify for secure cloud computing for enterprises is that what it provides must place as low a knowledge burden as possible on end users. In practice this usually means that CSPs need to offer security as part of the cloud service. Possibly a business could provide encryption before storing data on an insecure cloud service. But this is likely to be difficult without increasing the knowledge burden on users and so increasing risk. Better is if the CSP provides encryption software as part of the service. Better still is to provide both encryption software and encryption standard so that the business requires only keys and knowldge to decrypt its data, but is relieved of the knowledge burden by using the CSP. Maintaining data integrity, detecting breaches and recovering from them should be the responsibility of the CSP managing the data.

The second requirement is that CSPs should provide clarity on what security is being provided, why it is being provided and who is responsible for what aspects of security. We have found that enterprises, especially SMEs, often lack the technical knowledge to identify this for themselves. It is important, however, to identify whether the security provided includes each of encryption (and how secure), authentication and data integrity. It is important also to identify who is responsible for any security failure. It may be clear that a CSP is responsible for implementing encryption standards, providing software and maintaining data integrity. But it is important also to make sure enterprises, who seek a low knowledge burden, are aware of their responsibilities, for example in choosing passwords, preventing unauthorised use of secure keys and preventing release of information through, for example, email or usb memory devices. It is also important to identify who is legally and financially responsible for security breaches that are the fault of the CSP.

A third requirement is that enterprises need means of rapid recovery from security breaches. That is, they need to recognise that there is always a risk of security failure and they need (i) means to detect failure rapidly, (ii) methods to prevent further damage and (iii) means to recovery rapidly from failures. Typically, this requirement places burdens on both enterprise and CSP. The enterprise needs to have means to deal rapidly with problems arising because it failed in its responsibilities. CSPs need means such as those suggested in [5] of detecting, reporting and recovering from breaches in security or failures in data integrity in the CSP.

The human issue with cloud security, and the use of such by those in SMEs, may be argued to parallel the issues raised regarding the design of software and the design of the human-computer interface. There may be some conflict of interest in the design of software, which is attributable to the fact that those who build it are also those who design it. When this is related to customer expectations with regard to functionality, ease of use and the like we may find a noticeable mismatch. The way in which people interact with software may be argued to lie within the specialist domain of usability and if we look slightly deeper into the human-computer interaction, the domain of psychology Cooper ([18], p. 94) reminds us, "Successful interfaces are those that focus on the users goals ldots." If we consider the cloud security element from such a perspective we may conclude that the end user may in many instances be SMEs, for whom the primary motivation to use the cloud is that it offers business advantage at low cost. The likely expectation of such users might be considered to be that all security issues are taken care of for them within the package provided.

Essentially, the SME users may be considered in a similar way to most of those who drive cars. They wish to benefit from the independence and enhanced capability offered, but they are unlikely to wish to do all the required maintenance of the safety elements within the machine. However, while variations in capability and performance range may be considered acceptable, relative to the cost of purchase or lease, it is unlikely to be considered acceptable that safety should be compromised. The expectation is likely to be that those providing the artefact, which offers the enhanced capability, should take whatever steps are necessary to ensure safety is ensured on a fail-safe basis. For SMEs accessing cloud facilities this might be applied to security and the responsibility for dealing with any breaches of such in a fail-safe manner. For CSPs, the challenge might be to inform SME users that, like car drivers, they must take some responsibility.

IV. Adoption and Diffusion of Innovations

Getting users to adopt cloud services or to comply with security needs usually means persuading them to adopt some technology that implements these things. This is a management problem. There is management research going back 40 years or so on how technology gets adopted. None that we know of is on security; a little is on cloud adoption; much may be helpful.

Rogers [19] summarises much of the recent research on how technology diffusion occurs. The research identifies innovation as a process over a period of time. Usually it divides it into stages. For example, [20] identifies knowledge, persuasion, decision, implementation and confirmation stages while [21] identifies initiation, adoption, acceptance, routinisation and infusion. What matters here is not the particular stage model but that adoption takes place, usually individually, over time and various factors influence the speed and likelihood of transition between stages.

Davis et al [17] summarise two models that identify influencing factors. The first is a general theory of reasoned action model, which helps us identify intended behaviours. The second, the technology acceptance model adds the perceived usefulness and perceived ease of use. They find that perceived usefulness is the primary, and ease of use secondary the secondary, determinant in people's intention to use technology. Gallivan [21] looks at influencing factors when adoption is not voluntary and finds that strong and clear communication, high resource commitment and centralised planning and control contribute to better adoption, but, as usual, finds many individual factors also influence.

Walley and Amin [22] study customers rather than users and discuss their adoption of customer processing technology such as ATMs, petrol pumps and vending machines. They identify factors affecting customer choice to use the technology or not. The ones of interest are these. Customers adopt better if they repeat the use of the technology often. They prefer technology that presents a low variety of tasks. They are more likely to choose the technology if they value what it provides. They also discuss the extent to which customers find using the technology rewarding. The study is of interest because it identifies the factors likely to make voluntary adoption work.

In a review of organisational adoption of technology, Fichman [23] classifies types of technology by two dimensions. The first combines the extent of interdependency between users and the burden of knowledge required for adoption. The second looks at the locus: individual or organisational adoption. The examples of [22] are adopted individually and work best when knowledge burden is low. Most customer-processing technologies do not have interdependency between customers.

Security technology requires both the organisational locus of adoption and an individual locus: one user not adopting is enough for failure. So, we need at the same time high resource commitment and clear communication from management, and a choice of technology that users are very likely to adopt. Often the adoption is needed quickly and so factors slowing individual adoption are undesirable. It may be difficult, however, to make the technology rewarding to the user and many may fail to perceive its usefulness. That is, while the adoption is essentially organisational, it makes sense to regard users as like the customers of ATMs and petrol pumps. That is, organisations should prefer technology that requires little new knowledge and changes as little as possible, or even reduces, the tasks that the users must perform.

The ideal, then, is for managers to choose technologies that are transparent or nearly so. Applying this, we can see some of the reasons for the success and growth of cloud services. Not only do they meet organisational requirements for outsourced computing at a reasonable cost, but user adoption is ensured by making the services simple enough that users can be unaware they are using them. For example, when a CSP provides file storage, programs or database servers that are set up so that users cannot easily distinguish them from software on their computer, then adoption is easy and managing the process is largely limited to managers committing the resources to ensure staff computers are set up correctly.

V. Limitations and Discussion

These requirements presents challenges for managers. They must be able to identify competently what they need from cloud providers. And they must be willing to provide the resource for it.

The most challenging problems for enterprises will be those where users have to increase their burden of knowledge or where security is dependent on technology that has a high degree of interdependency among users, especially when the users are outside of the organisation.

Passwords are a good example of where there may be little choice but to increase the knowledge of users. Passwords should have high information entropy, but most users perceive little value in learning this. It is possible to remove some of the burden from the users by testing and reporting entropy at the time a password is set and by rejecting weak passwords. But it remains important to teach users good ways to remember strong passwords. It may be impossible to prevent users using a good password on a secure system and also using it on a less secure one, such as when they use their work password on their social-media account.

The most common applications where there is a high interdependency between users are email and web browsers. These technologies, like most computing applications, were developed long before security standards. What makes them difficult to replace is that all parties must implement more or less the same standards. Secure email requires the co-operation of both sender and recipient and is usually impractical between organisations. Secure email within an organisation is possible, though may be expensive to make transparent. It is possible to remove email attachments, but without incentive to coöperate, users can bypass this kind of transparent security measure, for example by using web-based email. Possibly a secure email standard, but it is likely to take decades to get enough users to use it.

Web browsers can be easier to manage, because the security threat is largely external. Here again, managers are best advised to try to use a web browser with security features that require little or no knowledge from the user. But, once again, they leave open the possibility of having an intruder undetected in the system. For SMEs in particular, this presents a challenge, because they are likely not to have the expertise to deal with this. PaaS, where the web browser is provided by the CSP can improve matters. But if it is not easier to use the cloud-based web browser users are likely to see little reward from it and so find it simpler to use a web browser on their own device, which is much harder to secure.

VI. Is That It?

Well, under normal circumstances, having made researchers aware of the management issues as we see them, we could perhaps relax and wait for researchers to deliver, were it not for two very pertinent dark clouds on the horizon. The first is the Cloud Forensic Problem and the second is the forthcoming EU General Data Protection Regulation (GDPR), which comes into effect on 25th May 2018.

The first dark cloud—the Cloud Forensic Problem, can be best described as the elephant in the room. Many are aware that it exists, but few are willing to talk about it. It concerns the fundamental weakness in cloud computing, namely, that although cloud cyber security research has progressed significantly during the past decade on strengthening cloud security, there is one major and important issue that has yet to be resolved, namely that once an attacker finally breaches cloud defences, and become embedded within the system, they become an intruder for as long or as little time as they wish. Their primary goal will be to escalate privileges until they can seek out the forensic trail and obliterate all evidence of their presence within the system and how they were able to get there. Their desire is often to obtain a permanent foothold within the system, so that they can return again and again in order to harvest whatever they can get their hands on. Worst of all, there is absolutely nothing that existing cloud systems can do to prevent this from happening.

The second dark cloud we need to consider is the question of why cloud cyber security is becoming such a hot topic?

While there are many other pieces of data protection around that need to be complied with, the real reason this is becoming such a hot topic is that once the forthcoming EU GDPR [24], comes into effect, any company that is breached will be required, on pain of potentially massive punitive fines, to report exactly which records were accessed, modified, deleted or ex-filtrated from the company system. By potentially massive, punitive fines, we consider the larger of €20 million or 4% of Global Turnover, for every breach, to be a serious amount for any company, whether large or small.

If the cloud forensic trails are purged, this will leave the breached company with a potentially impossible task for them to comply with the strict reporting requirements of the legislation, namely that they must report every breach within 72 hours of discovery of the breach. Without the existence of forensic log data, it is doubtful whether any such company would be able to meet even this simplified deadline. If we consider that five years ago, the global average time between breach and discovery was 6 months [25], and that by last year, this had only improved to three weeks [26], it is clear that no matter how quickly a breach is discovered, if the forensic trail has been completely wiped, then a company will likely be unable to understand which records may have been seen, modified, tampered with, deleted or ex-filtrated from the system.

Once a breach is spotted, if due to the deletion of some or all of the forensic data by the intruder, the company will be unlikely to understand which records must be reported under the regulation. This will render them liable to a much higher range of possible penalties under the regulation.

The answer then, is a resounding no. The EU GDPR will kick in within the next few months time, and those companies who are not ready will have no excuse. This means that something must be done NOW, not months after the GDPR kicks in.

VII. How do we Find a Quick Solution to This Problem?

Given the fact that the Cloud Forensic Problem has not been solved, it is clear that the solution cannot be run on the existing cloud server, otherwise it will be exposed to the same problem as everything else. A simple approach would be to use the Duncan and Whittington approach [27]–[30], whereby the audit trail, the forensic trail and a log of all database commands made are safely stored in an immutable database held on a system external to the main cloud system. All existing logging would continue to be carried out on the existing cloud servers to encourage those attackers who succeed in becoming intruders might be lulled into a false sense of security.

Obviously, these covert logging systems will themselves become a target for attackers, but if they are configured as ultra high security servers with no direct web access, no other software running on them, and highly restricted access, together with a serious Intrusion Detection and Monitoring System, they will be a little more difficult to breach. These, it turn, can also be protected by another similar system, or indeed a chain of them, to provide a continuous self protecting loop, preferably with each system running on a different CSP offering.

VIII. Will this Meet the Criteria we have Identified as being Important from a Management Perspective?

We have prepared a list of the management goals we have identified in the paper, which we consider essential to meet in order to ensure a high level of take up of security systems within an organisation.

TABLE I. How our proposed Solution will Impact on Management Goals

Management Goals Identified	Impact of our proposal
1. Management need reliability at reasonable cost and possibly scalability	No adverse impact
2. To avoid lock-in	No adverse impact
3. Very low knowledge burden to use secure computing	No adverse impact
4. Need to be able to protect data integrity, maintain privacy and detect breaches	Helps achieve goal
5. Need clarity about who is responsible legally and financially for security and what is provided by CSPs	Ability to retain forensic trail helps with legal recourse
6. Need to be able to recover rapidly from breaches of security or damage to data	Helps achieve goal
7. Require security technology that is readily adopted by the whole organisation	Helps achieve goal
8. Require a very low knowledge burden so that they get adoption by everyone individually	Helps achieve goal
9. Need high resource commitment and clear communication from management	Not expensive to implement

As we can see, the proposed method of implementing this security approach is likely to have a minimum adverse impact on our management goals, and therefore is likely to stand a much higher chance of successful implementation.

IX. Conclusion and Future Work

From a management perspective, we consider it is very important that any security system meet our management goals in order to ensure a high level of uptake. We can see from TABLE I that we can implement the proposed methods to ensure a high level of security in cloud systems is achieved, which we can do while fulfilling our identified management goals. A useful bonus is that we can also comply with the EU GDPR and will have a useful means of ensuring rapid turnaround of our business continuity plans.

This means that there will be a higher likelihood that such an approach will be successfully implemented, especially by SMEs. This will also ensure that in the event of a systems breach, it will be possible to fully comply with the GDPR reporting requirements. Also, the ability to fully recover from such an attack will enhance any business continuity plan, ensuring a faster and more full recovery than would otherwise be possible.

In future work, we propose the development of a use case model to test how well a company might recover from an attack whilst still remaining compliant with the GDPR. We believe this can provide a useful means of ensuring many SMEs, who would otherwise fall foul of the new regulation.

References

[1] J. Tidd, J. Bessant, and K. Pavitt, Managing innovation. Hoboken. NJ: Wiley, 2013.

[2] Y. Chen, V. Paxson, and R. H. Katz, "Handbook of Cloud Computing," Handbook of Cloud Computing, vol. 20, no. 2010, 2010, pp. 493–516.

[3] P. Drucker, Management Challenges for the 21st Century, ser. Management Challenges for the 21st Century. HarperCollins, 1999, no. pt. 794.

[4] P. Mell and T. Grance, "The NIST Definition of Cloud Computing," NIST, Tech. Rep., 2011. [Online]. Available: http://nvlpubs.nist.gov/nistpubs/Legacy/SP/nistspecialpublication800-145.pdf [Last accessed: November 2017]

[5] G. Weir and A. Aßmuth, "Strategies for Intrusion Monitoring in Cloud Services," Cloud Computing 2017: The Eighth International Conference on Cloud Computing, GRIDs, and Virtualization, 2017, pp. 1-5.

[6] M. Miller, Cloud Computing: Web-Based Applications That Change the Way You Work and Collaborate Online. Que Publishing, 2008.

[7] S. Marston, Z. Li, S. Bandyopadhyay, J. Zhang, and A. Ghalsasi, "Cloud computing - The business perspective," Decision Support Systems, vol. 51, no. 1, 2011, pp. 176–189.

[8] K. Gai and S. Li, "Towards Cloud Computing: A Literature Review on Cloud Computing and Its Development Trends," 2012 Fourth International Conference on Multimedia Information Networking and Security, 2012, pp. 142–146.

[9] S. Greengard, "Cloud computing and developing nations," Communications of the ACM, vol. 53, no. 5, 2010, pp. 18–20.

[10] V. Ratten, "Entrepreneurial and ethical adoption behaviour of cloud computing," Journal of High Technology Management Research, vol. 23, no. 2, 2012, pp. 155–164.

[11] Y. Alshamaila, S. Papagiannidis, and F. Li, "Cloud computing adoption by SMEs in the north east of England," Journal of Enterprise Information Management, vol. 26, no. 3, 2013, pp. 250–275.

[12] L. Wang, G. Von Laszewski, A. Younge, X. He, M. Kunze, J. Tao, and C. Fu, "Cloud computing: A perspective study," New Generation Computing, vol. 28, no. 2, 2010, pp. 137–146.

[13] D. C. Plummer, T. J. Bittman, T. Austin, D. W. Cearley, and D. M. Smith, "Cloud Computing : Defining and Describing an Emerging Phenomenon," Gartner Research, vol. G00156220, no. June, 2008, pp. 1–9.

[14] W. DeLone, "Determinants of Success for Computer Usage in Small Business," MIS Quarterly, vol. 12, no. 1, 1988, pp. 51–61.

[15] P. K. Ross and M. Blumenstein, "Cloud computing as a facilitator of SME entrepreneurship," Technology Analysis \& Strategic Management, vol. 27, no. 1, 2015, pp. 87–101.

[16] M. Stern-Peltz and J. Armitage, "IT Firms Lose billions after NSA Scandal Exposed by Whistleblower Edward Snowden," 2013. [Online]. Available: http://www.independent.co.uk/life-style/gadgets-and-tech/news/it-firms-lose-billions-after-nsa-scandal-exposed-by-whistleblower-\\edward-snowden-9028599.html [Last accessed: November 2017]

[17] F. D. Davis, R. P. Bagozzi, and P. R. Warshaw, "User Acceptance of Computer Technology: A Comparison of Two Theoretical Models Author," Management Science, vol. 35, no. 8, 1989, pp. 982–1003.

[18] A. Cooper, About Face: The Essentials of User Interface Design. IDG Books Worldwide, Inc., 1995.

[19] E. M. Rogers, Diffusion of Innovations, 5th ed. New York: Free Press, 2003.

[20] E. M. Rogers, Diffusion of Innovations, 3rd ed. London: The Free Press, 1983.

[21] M. J. Gallivan, "Organizational adoption and assimilation of complex technological innovations," ACM SIGMIS Database, vol. 32, no. 3, 2001, p. 51.

[22] P. Walley and V. Amin, "Automation in a Customer Contact Environment," International Journal of Operations & Production Management, vol. 14, no. 5, 1994, pp. 86–100.

[23] R. G. Fichman, "Information Technology Diffusion: A Review of Empirical Research," Proceedings of the Thirteenth International Conference on Information Systems ({ICIS} '92), 1992, pp. 195–206.

[24] EU, "EU General Data Protection Regulation," 2017. [Online]. Available: http://www.eugdpr.org/ [Last accessed: November 2017]

[25] Verizon, "2012 Data Breach Investigations Report," Verizon, Tech. Rep., 2012.

[26] Verizon, "2016 Verizon Data Breach Report," Tech. Rep., 2016.

[27] B. Duncan and M. Whittington, "Enhancing Cloud Security and Privacy: The Power and the Weakness of the Audit Trail," in Cloud Computing 2016: The Seventh International Conference on Cloud Computing, GRIDs, and Virtualization, no. April. Rome: IEEE, 2016, pp. 125–130.

[28] B. Duncan and M. Whittington, "Cloud cyber-security: Empowering the audit trail," International Journal on Advances in Security, vol. 9, no. 3 & 4, 2016, pp. 169–183.

[29] B. Duncan and M. Whittington, "Creating an Immutable Database for Secure Cloud Audit Trail and System Logging," in Cloud Computing 2017: The Eighth International Conference on Cloud Computing, GRIDs, and Virtualization. Athens, Greece: IARIA, ISBN: 978-1-61208-529-6, 2017, pp. 54–59.

[30] B. Duncan and M. Whittington, "Creating and Configuring an Immutable Database for Secure Cloud Audit Trail and System Logging," International Journal On Advances in Security, no. 3&4, 2017.

About an Immune System Understanding for Cloud-native Applications

Biology Inspired Thoughts to Immunize the Cloud Forensic Trail

Nane Kratzke
Lübeck University of Applied Sciences, Germany
Center of Excellence for Communication, Systems and Applications (CoSA)
Email: nane.kratzke@fh-luebeck.de

Abstract—**There is no such thing as an impenetrable system, although the penetration of systems does get harder from year to year. The median days that intruders remained undetected on victim systems dropped from 416 days in 2010 down to 99 in 2016. Perhaps because of that, a new trend in security breaches is to compromise the forensic trail to allow the intruder to remain undetected for longer in victim systems and to retain valuable footholds for as long as possible. This paper proposes an immune system inspired solution, which uses a more frequent regeneration of cloud application nodes to ensure that undetected compromised nodes can be purged. This makes it much harder for intruders to maintain a presence on victim systems. Basically, the biological concept of cell-regeneration is combined with the information systems concept of append-only logs. Evaluation experiments performed on popular cloud service infrastructures (Amazon Web Services, Google Compute Engine, Azure and OpenStack) have shown that between 6 and 40 nodes of elastic container platforms can be regenerated per hour. Even a large cluster of 400 nodes could be regenerated in somewhere between 9 and 66 hours. So, regeneration shows the potential to reduce the foothold of undetected intruders from months to just hours.**

***Keywords*–cloud computing; node regeneration; container platform; append-only log; forensic trail;**

I. Introduction

Cloud computing has become a great enabler for a variety of different IT-enabled business and service models. The ability to deploy new systems rapidly without concern for forward planning, accessing corporate budgets and the ability to scale up (or down) on demand has proved particularly attractive for a continuously rising number of companies and organizations. Many research studies and programs have been actively involved in trying to develop systems in a responsible way to ensure the security and privacy of users. But compliance with standards, audits and checklists, does not automatically equals security [1]. Furthermore, there is a fundamental issue remaining, which presents a serious challenge, and is of great concern. Once an attacker successfully breaches a cloud system and becomes an intruder, usually escalating privileges the longer they are in the system, there is nothing then to prevent them from deleting or modifying the forensic trail. Preventing this from happening presents a serious challenge, and in the light of forthcoming regulation from various countries, and of particular interest the forthcoming EU General Data Protection Regulation (GDPR), which has a regime of penalties which can rise up to the greater of €20 million or 4% of global turnover. The other challenging aspect of this legislation is that any security breach must be reported within 72 hours. While the original idea was to do this "within 72 hours of the occurrence of a breach", it has been somewhat watered down to read "within 72 hours of discovery of a breach". We believe this is a backward step, since there will be less incentive for firms to deal with the real problem, and instead will perhaps encourage some to delay "discovery" to suit their own agendas. For cloud users who are breached, particularly where the intruder deletes or modifies the forensic trail, the longer the intruder remains in the system, the more difficult it becomes to be able to properly report the full impact of the breach, which is also likely to lead to higher levels of fines.

In our recent research [2], we exploited successfully elastic container platforms and their "designed for failure" capabilities to realize transferability of cloud-native applications at runtime. By transferability, we mean that a cloud-native application can be moved from one (public or private) Infrastructure as a Service (IaaS) provider infrastructure to another without any downtime and therefore without being noticed by its users. These platforms are more and more used as distributed and elastic runtime environments for cloud-native applicatons [3].

Table I lists some elastic container platforms that gained a lot of interest in recent years. These platforms can be understood as a kind of cloud infrastructure unifying middleware for cloud-native applications [4]. These platforms can be even used to transfer cloud applications between different cloud service providers at runtime. We think that it should be possible to make use of the same features to immunize the forensic trail simply by moving an application within the same provider infrastructure. To move anything from A to A makes no sense at first glance. However, let us be paranoid and aware that with some probability and at a given time, an attacker will be successful and compromise at least one virtual machine. In these cases, a transfer from A to A would be an efficient counter measure – because the intruder immediately loses any hijacked machine that is moved. To understand that, the reader must know that our approach does not effectively move a machine, it regenerates it [2]. So, to move a machine means to launch a compensating machine unknown to the intruder and to terminate the former (hi-jacked) machine. So, whenever an application is moved (basically the hosting container platform is moved and not the application itself) all of its virtual machines are regenerated. And this would effectively eliminate undetected hi-jacked machines, as well as those which have not been compromised. The biological analogy of this strategy is called *"cell-regeneration"* and the attack on ill cells is coordinated by an immune system. This paper describes the first ideas for such a kind of immune system for cloud applications.

The paper will explain these basic and unconventional thoughts following this **outline**. To provide some context for the reader, Section II will explain the general lifecycle of a cyber attack and will show that two aspects have to be addressed to protect the forensic trail. First of all, it is assumed that every system can be penetrated due to unknown exploits [5]. Nevertheless, systems can be built which are capable of being able to regenerate penetrated nodes. That makes it harder for intruders to maintain a presence on penetrated systems over a longer time. Section III will summarize some of our recent research to explain how such systems can be built. However, even in a short amount of time, the forensic trail can be deleted or compromised. So, the task is to find a solution to store the forensic trail in such a way as to make it un-erasable and un-compromise-able. Section IV will propose a double logging architecture which exploits messaging systems like Kafka [6] to realize regenerating append-only logging systems which are recovering from penetrations. Section V shows some evaluation results measured from transferability experiments. These numbers are used to estimate possible regeneration intervals for systems of different sizes and to compare it with median dwell times reported by security companies over the last seven years (see Table II). The advantages and limitations of this proposal are related to other work in Section VI. We conclude our considerations in Section VII.

II. The Lifecycle of Cyber Attacks

Figure 1 shows the cyber attack life cycle model, which is used by the M-Trends reports [7] to report developments in cyber attacks over the years. According to this model an attacker passes through different stages to complete their mission. It starts with initial reconnaissance and compromising of access means (often using mobile phones or the desktop PCs of employees, who are generally not security experts). These steps are very often supported by social engineering methodologies [8] and phishing attacks [9]. The goal is to establish a foothold near the system of interest. All these steps are not covered by this paper, because the proposed technical solution is not able to harden the weakest point in security - the human being. We refer to corresponding research like [8] [9].

The following steps of this model are more interesting for this paper. According to the cyber attack life cycle model the attacker's goal is to escalate privileges to get access to the target system. Because this leaves trails on the system which could reveal a security breach, the attacker is motivated to compromise the forensic trail. According to the M-Trends 2017 report attackers make more and more use of counter-forensic measures to hide their presence and impair investigations. The report refers to batch scripts used by financial intruders to delete pre-fetch entries, clear Microsoft Windows event logs and securely delete arbitrary files. These batch scripts are run to hide the execution of malware that was scraping payment card information from memory. The technique is simple, but the intruders' knowledge of forensic artifacts demonstrate increased sophistication, as well as their intent to persist in the environment.

With a barely detectable foothold, the internal reconnaissance of the victim's network is carried out to allow the lateral movement to the target system. This is a complex and lengthy process and may even take weeks. So, infiltrated machines have worth for attackers and tend to be used for as long as possible, even after mission completion. Although the numbers are decreasing, Table II shows how astonishingly long a period on average an intruder has access to a victim system at the time of writing this paper. According to this reference model for cyber attacks two conclusions can be drawn.

(1) An undetected attacker should lose access to compromised nodes of the system as fast as possible. The Sections III and V will propose a solution on how the undetected days on a system can be reduced from months down to days, or even hours. Even if undetected days on systems can be reduced dramatically, it **(2) must be still impossible to compromise the forensic trail**. Otherwise intrusions might be short, but remain undetectable. Section IV will propose a solution on how to log the forensic trail using append-only logging systems (which could itself be compromised).

III. From Transferable to Regenerate-able Cloud Applications

Our recent research dealt with the question of how to design cloud-native applications that are transferable between different cloud service providers to reduce vendor lock-in situations. One aspect that can be learned from this is that there is no common understanding of what a cloud-native application really is. A kind of software that is *"intentionally designed for the cloud"* is an often heard but vacuous phrase. However, noteworthy similarities exist between various view points on *cloud-native applications* (CNA) [3]. A common approach is to define maturity levels in order to categorize different kinds of cloud applications. Table III shows a maturity model proposed by the *Open Data Center Alliance*. And common motivations for CNA architectures are fault isolation, fault tolerance, and automatic recovery to improve **safety**, and to enable horizontal (instead of vertical) application **scalability** [10]. Fehling et al. [11] proposed the IDEAL model for CNAs. A CNA should strive for an **isolated state**, is **distributed**, provides **elasticity** in a horizontal scaling way, and should be operated on **automated deployment machinery**. Finally, its components should be **loosely coupled**.

Balalaie et al. [13] stress that these properties are addressed by cloud-specific architecture and infrastructure approaches like **Microservices** [14], **API-based collaboration**, adaption of **cloud-focused patterns** [11], and **self-service elastic platforms** that are used to deploy and operate these microservices via self-contained deployment units (containers). These platforms provide additional operational capabilities on top of IaaS infrastructures like automated and on-demand scaling of

TABLE I. SOME POPULAR OPEN SOURCE ELASTIC PLATFORMS

Platform	Contributors	URL
Kubernetes	Cloud Native Found.	http://kubernetes.io (initiated by Google)
Swarm	Docker	https://docker.io
Mesos	Apache	http://mesos.apache.org/
Nomad	Hashicorp	https://nomadproject.io/

TABLE II. UNDETECTED DAYS ON VICTIM SYSTEMS [7]

Year	External notification	Internal discovery	Median
2010	-	-	416
2011	-	-	?
2012	-	-	243
2013	-	-	229
2014	-	-	205
2015	320	56	146
2016	107	80	99

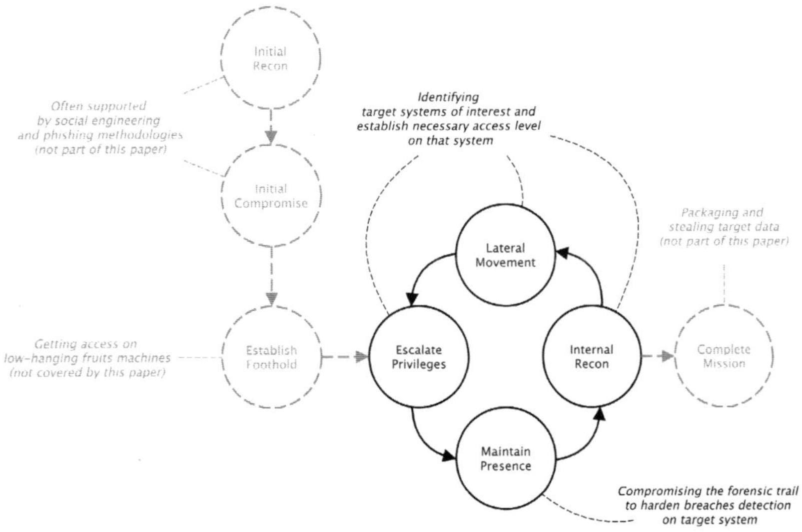

Figure 1. The cyber attack life cycle model. Adapted from the cyber attack lifecycle used by the M-Trends reports, see Table II

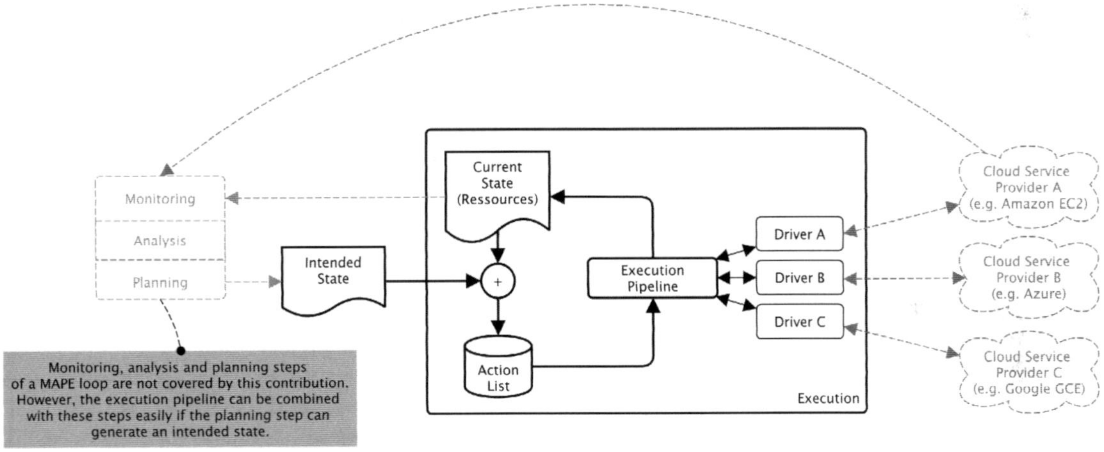

Figure 2. The execution loop and synchronized security group concept

application instances, application health management, dynamic routing and load balancing as well as aggregation of logs and metrics [3]. Some open source examples of such kinds of elastic platforms are listed in Table I.

If the reader understands the commonality that cloud-native applications are operated (more and more often) on elastic – often container-based – platforms, it is an obvious idea to delegate the responsibility for the forensic trail to these platforms. Furthermore, our recent research shows that the operation of these elastic container platforms and the design of applications running on-top should be handled as two completely different engineering problems. This often solves several issues in modern cloud-native application engineering [15]. And that is not just true for the transferability problem but might be an option for the forensic trail as well. These kinds of platforms are an essential part of the immune system of modern cloud-native applications.

Furthermore, **self-service elastic platforms** (see Table I) are really "bulletproofed" [10]. *Apache Mesos* [16] has been successfully operated for years by companies like Twitter or Netflix to consolidate hundreds of thousands of compute nodes. Peinl and Holzschuher [17] provide an excellent overview for interested readers. Elastic container platforms are **designed for failure** and provide self-healing capabilities via auto-placement, auto-restart, auto-replication and auto-scaling features. They will identify lost containers (for whatever reasons, e.g., process failure or node unavailability) and will restart containers and place them on remaining nodes. These features are absolutely necessary to operate large-scale distributed systems in a resilient way. However, these exact same features can be used intentionally to **realize transferability requirements** or to **purge "compromised nodes"**.

In recent research [2] [15] we demonstrated a software prototype that provides the control process shown in Figure 2. This process relies on an *intended state* ρ and a *current state* σ of a container cluster (attached nodes, existing security groups. If no multi-cloud settings are considered, security groups can be ignored almost completely. This is done by this paper for simplicity reasons. If the intended state differs from the current state ($\rho \neq \sigma$), necessary adaption actions are deduced (creation and attachment/detachment of nodes, creation and termination of security groups) and processed by an execution pipeline fully automatically (see Figure 3) to reach the *intended state* ρ, so that $\rho = \sigma'$ where σ' is the current state in time after σ.

With this kind of control process, a cluster can be simply resized by changing the intended state of the cluster (adding $\sigma = N \mapsto \sigma' = N+i$ or decreasing $\sigma = N \mapsto \sigma' = N-i$ the intended amount of nodes). If the cluster is shrinking and nodes have to be terminated, affected containers will be rescheduled to other available nodes. Migrations between different cloud service providers become possible as well. Let us assume a cluster with N nodes provided by *Amazon Web Services* (*AWS*) that shall be transferred to *Google Compute Engine* (*GCE*). So, the starting current state would be $\sigma = (N, 0)$. If we want to move from *AWS* to *GCE* we can transfer an elastic container platform in the following way. In a first step, we simply add the amount of nodes provisioned by *AWS* to the clusters intended state $\rho = (N, N)$ – but on *GCE*'s side, so we get $\sigma' = (N, N)$ after a cycle of the control process. In a second step, we shut down all nodes provided by *AWS* by removing them from the intended state $\rho = (0, N)$ and get $\sigma'' = (0, N)$ after another cycle. The cluster will observe node failures and trigger its self-healing features to reschedule lost containers accordingly. From an inner point of view of the platform, rescheduling operations are tasked due to node failures. From an outside point of view, it looks like (and in fact **is**) a migration from one provider to another provider at run-time. This should make the general idea clear – and the reader is referred to [2] [15] for more details.

It is essential to understand that a node is migrated by adding a new node to the cluster and delete the former node. Therefore, the intruder looses access to every migrated node, because this instance is terminated and replaced by a complete new node instantiated from a virtual machine image. This is mainly done to keep things simple for the above mentioned control process. A migration is no "live-migration" and keeps no user-related state on the affected machine during or after migration. The container platform will detect container unavailabilities due to node failures and will reschedule lost containers on other nodes. This is all handled by the container platform. For an intruder, the only way to keep a foothold in the system would be to inject malicious code into a virtual machine or container image that is used to launch nodes for the container platform or container on the platform. However, that is a completely different kind of attack, which is not covered by this paper.

TABLE III. CLOUD APPLICATION MATURITY MODEL [12]

Level	Maturity	Criteria
3	Cloud native	- A CNA can migrate across infrastructure providers at runtime and without interruption of service. - A CNA can automatically scale out/in based on stimuli.
2	Cloud resilient	- The application state is isolated in a minimum of services. - The application is unaffected by dependent service failures. - The application is infrastructure agnostic.
1	Cloud friendly	- The application is composed of loosely coupled services. - Application services are discoverable by name (not by IP). - Application components are designed using cloud patterns. - Application compute and storage are separated.
0	Cloud ready	- The application runs on virtualized infrastructure. - The application can be instantiated from image or script.

The downside of this approach is,that this will only work for level 2 (cloud resilient) or level 3 (cloud native) applications (see Table III) which by design, can tolerate dependent service failures (due to node failures and container rescheduling) which may occur for a limited amount of time. However, for that kind of level 2 or level 3 application, we can use the same control process to regenerate nodes of the container cluster. The reader shall consider a cluster with $\sigma = N$ nodes. If we want to regenerate one node, we change the intended state to $\rho = N + 1$ nodes which will add one new node to the cluster ($\sigma' = N + 1$). And in a second step, we will decrease the intended size of the cluster to $\rho' = N$ again, which has the effect that one node of the cluster is terminated ($\sigma'' = N$). So, we regenerated one node simply by adding one node and deleting one node. We could even regenerate the complete cluster by changing the cluster size in the following way: $\sigma = N \mapsto \sigma' = 2N \mapsto \sigma'' = N$. But, this would consume more resources because the cluster would double its size for a limited amount of time. A more resource efficient way would be to regenerate the cluster in N steps: $\sigma = N \mapsto \sigma' = N + 1 \mapsto \sigma'' = N \mapsto ... \mapsto \sigma^{2N-1} = N + 1 \mapsto \sigma^{2N} = N$.

Whenever such a regeneration is triggered, all (even undetected) hijacked machines would be terminated and replaced by other machines, but the applications running on-top of this platform would be unaffected. For an attacker, this means losing their foothold in the system completely. Imagine if this were to be done once a day or even more frequently? The question is whether it is possible to do it with these frequencies and this paper will return to this question in Section V.

IV. PROPOSAL OF AN IMMUNE SYSTEM ARCHITECTURE

Section III showed that it is possible for level 2 or level 3 cloud-native applications to be operated on a permanently regenerating platform that makes it hard for an intruder to maintain a foothold in the system. Yet the forensic trail can be deleted or compromised in only a short amount of time. So, there is the need to store the forensic trail in a way to be undeleteable and uncompromiseable. One obvious solution is to store the logs not on the same system but to consolidate them in an external logging system or an external logging service. Such logging services are becoming more and more widespread and the term Logging-as-a -Service (LaaS) has been established. Furthermore, research has been carried out to enable secure LaaS, even in untrusted environments [18]. So, from a regulatory point of view it would be sufficient to log into an external logging service and to make this service provider responsible to fulfill the criteria through service level agreements.

There might be regulatory constraints (e.g., data privacy) that prohibit to make use of external logging services. In these cases, we have to consolidate our logs by ourselves. The canonical way to do this in modern cloud engineering is to make

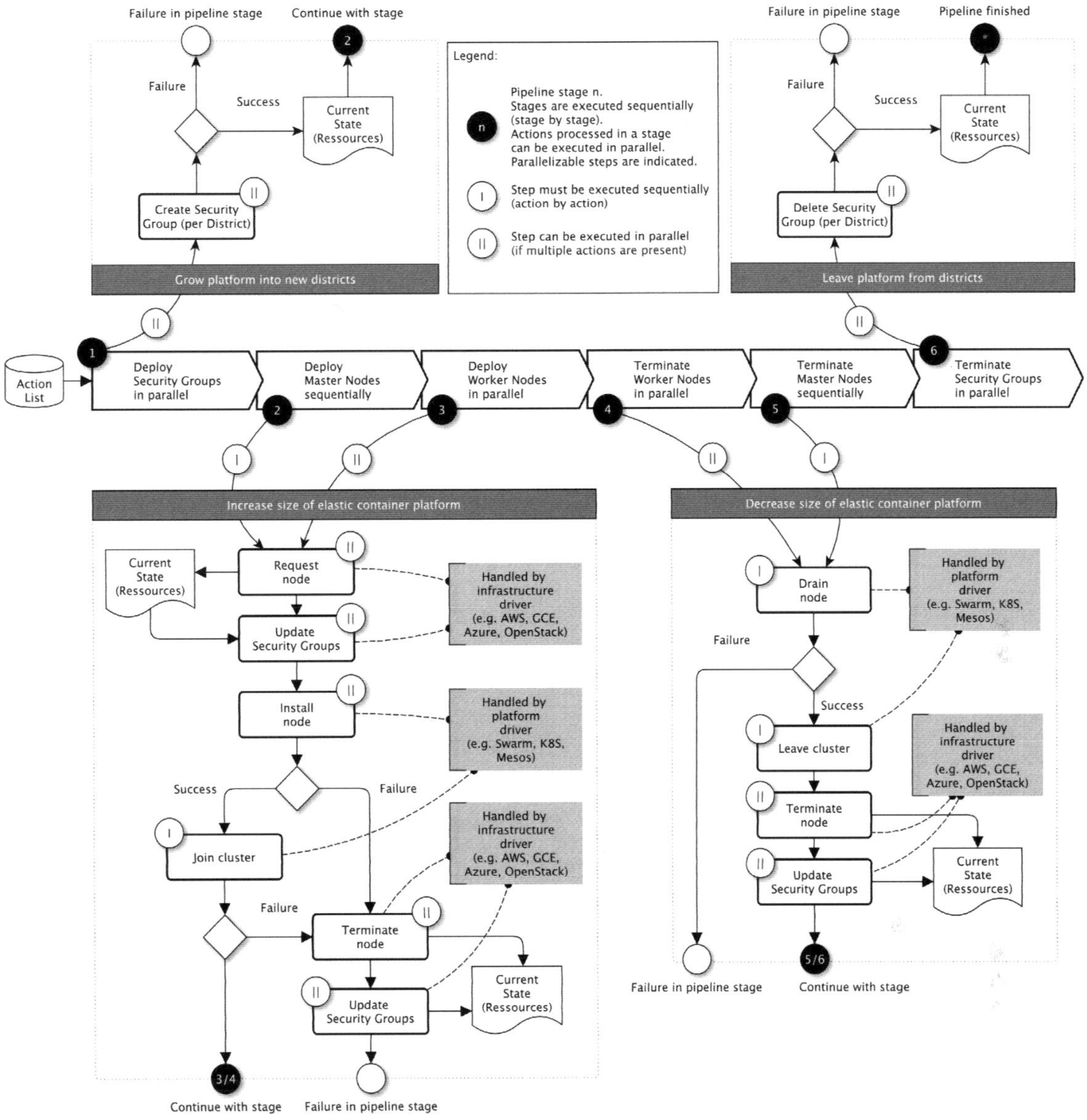

Figure 3. Execution pipeline (explained in details here: [15])

use of logging stacks like the ELK stack (https//elastic.io) or Heapster (https://github.com/kubernetes/heapster) or to use distributed streaming platforms like Kafka [6]. These stacks are composed of three basic tiers. Nodes are instrumented with *metric* and *log shippers* on tier 1 (the nodes of the payload system according to Figure 4). These shippers send their data to distributed and horizontal scalable *timeseries databases* or *streaming platforms* (that can be operated on elastic platforms according to Figure 4). And a visualization and analytical component on tier 3 is responsible to visualize timeseries or streams and perform analytics on log data. These analytical and visualizing components can be run on the same hardware like the timeseries database/streaming platform or somewhere else.

This paper proposes to do the same. However, is has to be considered that the logging system might be compromised as well. And that is why this paper proposes to log and analyze the logging system by a second logging system and vice versa. In fact there are three systems. The *payload system*, a *logging system A* which logs the *payload system* and a second *logging system B* which logs the *logging system A*. The *logging system A* logs and supervises *logging system B* as well, to avoid an unsupervised system. All three systems are operated on regenerating elastic container platforms as shown in Section III that make it hard for an intruder to maintain a foothold in any of these three systems. *Logging systems A* and *B* have not just the responsibility to log but also to detect anomalies in the supervised systems. If they detect anomalies they trigger a node regeneration. Such anomalies

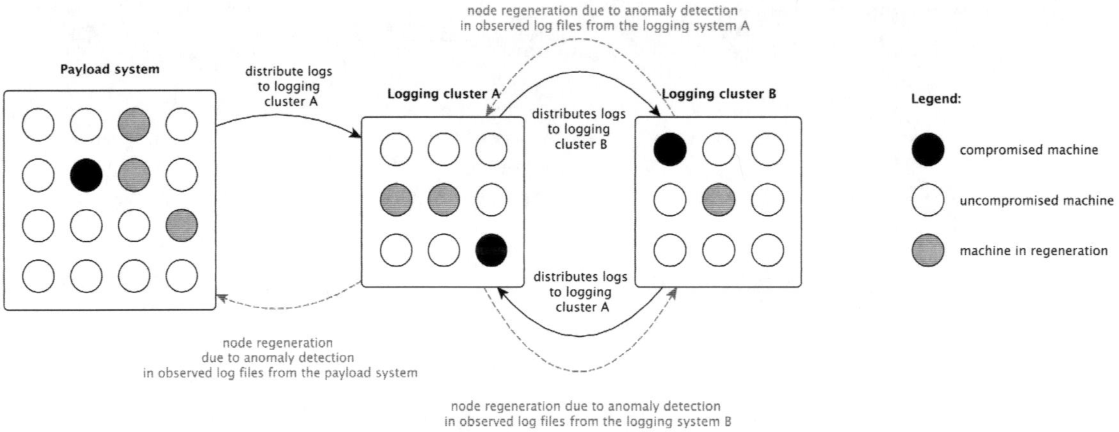

Figure 4. An Immune System Architecture based on a Double Logging System

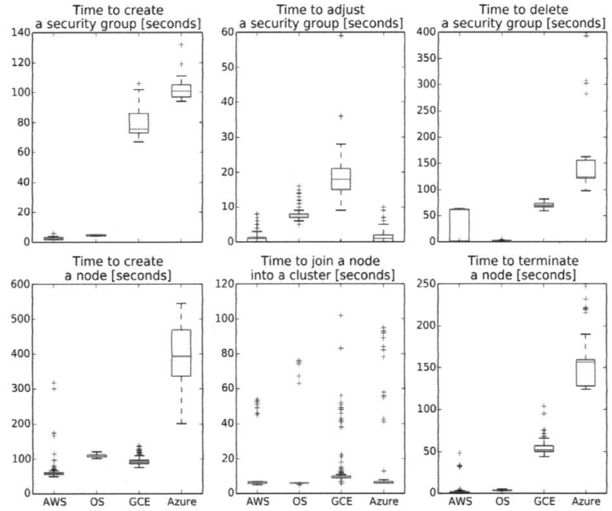

Figure 5. Differences in infrastructure specific regeneration durations [15]

could be detected automatically by approaches described by [19]. And it might be interesting for the reader that there are even approaches making use of bioinformatics tools to detect outliers in log data [20] which is aligned to some degree with our biology analogy throughout this paper. This anomaly detection must not be perfect, it would be sufficient to rate a node just vaguely as suspect (and not as precisely hostile). A false positive would result only in an unnecessary regeneration of one node. However, if there are too many suspects identified, then too many nodes would be attacked unnecessarily by the immune system to be regenerated, thus the system would become "hot" due to a lot of regenerations. The reader might know this health state as "fever" from their own experiences. A medical scientist might even want to talk about an autoimmune disease.

V. Evaluation Results

The execution pipeline presented in Figure 3 was evaluated by operating and transferring two elastic platforms (*Swarm Mode of Docker 17.06* and *Kubernetes 1.7*) across four public and private cloud infrastructures. All experiments were repeated 10 times. The platforms operated a reference "sock-shop" application being one of the most complete reference applications for microservices architecture research [21]. Table IV lists the machine types that show a high similarity across different providers. These machine types have been selected according to [22]. The OpenStack *m1.large* and *m1.medium* are research institute specific machine types that have been intentionally defined to show maximum similarities with the other mentioned machine types.

Although the evaluation of [2] [15] was not done to investigate the current use case, it is possible to use some of the data to estimate reasonable regeneration cycles of elastic container platforms. First of all, the evaluation demonstrated that most time is spent on the IaaS level (creation and termination of nodes and security groups) and not on the elastic platform level (joining, draining nodes). The measured differences on infrastructures provided by different providers is shown in Figure 5. For the current use case the reader can ignore the times to create and delete for a security group (because that is a one time action). However, there will be many node creations and node terminations. According to our execution pipeline shown in Figure 3 a node creation ($\sigma = N \mapsto \sigma' = N + 1$)

TABLE IV. USED MACHINE TYPES AND REGIONS

Provider	Region	Master type	Worker type
AWS	eu-west-1	m4.xlarge	m4.large
GCE	europe-west1	n1-standard-4	n1-standard-2
Azure	europewest	Standard_A3	Standard_A2
OpenStack	*own datacenter*	m1.large	m1.medium

TABLE V. DURATIONS TO REGENERATE A NODE (median values)

Provider	Creation	Adj. Secgroup	Joining	Term.	Total
AWS	70 s	1 s	7 s	2 s	**81 s**
GCE	100 s	8 s	9 s	50 s	**175 s**
Azure	380 s	17 s	7 s	180 s	**600 s**
OpenStack	110 s	2 s	7 s	5 s	**126 s**

involves the durations to **create a node** (request of the virtual machine including all installation and configuration steps for the elastic container platform), to **adjust of security group** the cluster is operated in and to **join the new node** into the cluster. The shutdown of a node ($\sigma = N \mapsto \sigma' = N - 1$) involves the **termination of the node** (this includes the platform draining and deregistering of the node and the request to terminate the virtual machine) and the necessary **adjustment of the security group**. So, for a complete regeneration of a node ($\sigma = N \mapsto \sigma' = N + 1 \mapsto \sigma'' = N$) we have to add the times to create, to join, to terminate the node and to add two times the adjustment of the security group the cluster is operated in. Table V lists these values per infrastructure.

So, even on the "slowest" infrastructure Azure, a node can be regenerated in about 10 minutes. That means one can regenerate six nodes every hour or up to 144 nodes a day or a cluster of 432 nodes every 72h (which is the reporting time requested by the EU GDPR). If the reader compares a 72h regeneration time of a more than 400 node cluster (most systems are not so large) with the median value of 99 days that attackers were present on a victim system in 2016 (see Table II) the benefit of the proposed approach should become obvious.

Obviously there are some open questions and drawbacks regarding this proposal that should be tackled by ongoing research. For example, what would be the penalty of additional load on the cloud infrastructure? What would be the degradation in application performance caused by frequent VMs re-generation? An educated guess would be to expect $1/n$ behavior. At one point in time only one node of a n node cluster is affected. So, the performance degradation would be much more severe for small clusters and hardly observable for larger clusters. However, this has been not investigated so far.

VI. RELATED WORK

To the best of the author's knowledge, there are currently no approach making intentional use of virtual machine regeneration for security purposes [23]. A literature search using Google Scholar and the Semantic Web did not turn up any noteworthy papers in this field. However, the proposed approach stands on the shoulders of giants and is derived from multi-cloud scenarios and their increased requirements on security. And there are several promising approaches dealing with multi-cloud scenarios. So, all of them should show comparable opportunities but come along with a lot of inner complexity. A container based approach seems to handle this kind of complexity better. There are some good survey papers on this [24] [25] [26] [27].

To make the execution pipeline work seamlessly, an efficient and pragmatic deployment description format is needed. The current format is based on JSON and shows similarities with other kind of deployment description languages like **TOSCA** or **CloudML** [28]. Nonetheless, the proposed approach is focused on a more container-centric approach and separates the platform and application level which enables a high-frequency regeneration of hosting virtual machines. This is hardly realizable with TOSCA and comparable approaches without accepting downtimes in regeneration cycles.

Duncan and Whittington emphasize the requirement to beef up the need to use the humble audit trail on all cloud systems to improve the ability to retain some level of forensic trail. They propose to use an immutable database for this purpose, which they suggested to be kept in a remote location from the main cloud system [29] [30]. Further research deals with append-only data structures on untrusted servers [31]. Other approaches propose building a secure and reliable file synchronization service using multiple cloud synchronization services as untrusted storage providers [32]. Further approaches focus on the integrity of logs and ensure their integrity by hash-chain schemes and proofs of past logs published periodically by the cloud providers [18]. The question remains, whether these approaches are scalable enough to provide robust logging means for the forensic trail of up to thousands of nodes. Messaging solutions like Kafka [6] or logging stacks like the ELK-Stack are bullet-proofed technologies for consolidating logs but assume to be operated in a trusted environment which ends in a kind of double logging architecture. So, the above mentioned research approaches show the potential to simplify the double logging architecture and should be considered in ongoing research. The same is true for anomaly detection approaches in log data [19] [20].

Taken all together, the proposed approach leverages more up-to-date container technologies with the intent to be more "pragmatic". On the downside, it might be only applicable for container-based applications being on the level 2 or 3 of the maturity model shown in Table III. But this architecture style gets more and more common in cloud application engineering [3].

VII. CONCLUSION

Once attackers successfully breach a cloud system there is little to prevent them from modifying the forensic trail. This involves a serious challenge - from a security but also from an economic point of view. The forthcoming EU General Data Protection Regulation (GDPR) has a regime of penalties which can rise up to 4% of global turnover in those cases where failure by the company to protect systems in a sufficiently robust manner will be seen as complicit in the loss of customer data.

Although the presented approach evolved mainly from transferability research questions for cloud-native applications, it can be adopted as a foundation for an approach one could call 'immune system" inspired. This paper proposed to regenerate virtual machines (the cells of an IT-system) with a much higher frequency than usual to purge even undetected intruders. Our evaluations on infrastructures provided by AWS, GCE, Azure and OpenStack showed that a virtual machine can be regenerated in somewhere between two minutes (AWS) and 10 minutes (Azure). The reader should compare these times with recent cyber security reports. E.g., the M-Trends report from 2016 reported that an attacker was undetected on a victim system for about 100 days. For an attacker this means that their undetected time on a victim systems drops from months down to minutes, thus minimising the potential for damage.

Nevertheless, even in a very short amount of time an attacker could delete (parts) of the cloud forensic trail. To use external and trusted append-only logging systems seems somehow obvious. However, existing solutions rely on trusted environments. But if that environment can not be assured, the need for complex and "ugly" double logging architectures arises, as Section IV, has shown. Our further research will investigate how "regenerating" platforms and append-only logging systems could be integrated more straightforward.

ACKNOWLEDGMENT

This research is partly funded by the Cloud TRANSIT project (13FH021PX4, German Federal Ministry of Education and Research). I would like to thank Bob Duncan for his efforts making this paper much more readable.

REFERENCES

[1] B. Duncan and M. Whittington, "Compliance with standards, assurance and audit: does this equal security?" in Proc. 7th Int. Conf. Secur. Inf. Networks - SIN '14. Glasgow: ACM, 2014. [Online]. Available: http://dl.acm.org/citation.cfm?doid=2659651.2659711

[2] N. Kratzke, "Smuggling Multi-Cloud Support into Cloud-native Applications using Elastic Container Platforms," in Proc. of the 7th Int. Conf. on Cloud Computing and Services Science (CLOSER 2017), 2017.

[3] N. Kratzke and P.-C. Quint, "Understanding Cloud-native Applications after 10 Years of Cloud Computing - A Systematic Mapping Study," Journal of Systems and Software, vol. 126, no. April, 2017.

[4] N. Kratzke and R. Peinl, "ClouNS - a Cloud-Native Application Reference Model for Enterprise Architects," in 2016 IEEE 20th Int. Enterprise Distributed Object Computing Workshop (EDOCW), Sep. 2016.

[5] L. Bilge and T. Dumitras, "Before we knew it: an empirical study of zero-day attacks in the real world," in ACM Conference on Computer and Communications Security, 2012.

[6] Wang et al., "Building a Replicated Logging System with Apache Kafka," in Proc. of the VLDB Endowment, vol. 8, no. 12, 2015.

[7] FireEye Inc., "Security Predications 2018," 2017, retrieved: 12, 2017. [Online]. Available: https://www.fireeye.com/current-threats/annual-threat-report.html

[8] K. Krombholz, H. Hobel, M. Huber, and E. Weippl, "Advanced social engineering attacks," Journal of Information Security and Applications, vol. 22, 2015.

[9] S. Gupta, A. Singhal, and A. Kapoor, "A literature survey on social engineering attacks: Phishing attack," 2016 International Conference on Computing, Communication and Automation (ICCCA), 2016.

[10] M. Stine, Migrating to Cloud-Native Application Architectures. O'Reilly, 2015.

[11] Fehling et al., Cloud Computing Patterns: Fundamentals to Design, Build, and Manage Cloud Applications. Springer Publishing Company, Incorporated, 2014.

[12] Ashtikar et al., "OPEN DATA CENTER ALLIANCE Best Practices: Architecting Cloud-Aware Applications Rev. 1.0," 2014, retrieved: 12, 2017. [Online]. Available: https://www.opendatacenteralliance.org/docs/architecting_cloud_aware_applications.pdf

[13] A. Balalaie, A. Heydarnoori, and P. Jamshidi, "Migrating to Cloud-Native Architectures Using Microservices: An Experience Report," in 1st Int. Workshop on Cloud Adoption and Migration (CloudWay), Taormina, Italy, 2015.

[14] S. Newman, Building Microservices. O'Reilly Media, Incorporated, 2015.

[15] N. Kratzke, "About the complexity to transfer cloud applications at runtime and how container platforms can contribute?" in Cloud Computing and Service Sciences: 7th International Conference, CLOSER 2017, Revised Selected Papers, Communications in Computer and Information Science (CCIS). Springer International Publishing, 2018, to be published.

[16] B. Hindman, A. Konwinski, M. Zaharia, A. Ghodsi, A. D. Joseph, R. H. Katz, S. Shenker, and I. Stoica, "Mesos: A Platform for Fine-Grained Resource Sharing in the Data Center." in 8th USENIX Conf. on Networked systems design and implementation (NSDI'11), vol. 11, 2011.

[17] R. Peinl and F. Holzschuher, "Docker cluster management state of the art and own solution," Journal of Grid Computing, vol. 14, 2016.

[18] S. Zawoad, A. K. Dutta, and R. Hasan, "Towards building forensics enabled cloud through secure logging-as-a-service," IEEE Transactions on Dependable and Secure Computing, vol. 13, no. 2, 2016.

[19] Q. Fu, J.-G. Lou, Y. Wang, and J. Li, "Execution Anomaly Detection in Distributed Systems through Unstructured Log Analysis," in 2009 Ninth IEEE Int. Conf. on Data Mining, 2009.

[20] M. Wurzenberger, F. Skopik, R. Fiedler, and W. Kastner, "Applying High-Performance Bioinformatics Tools for Outlier Detection in Log Data," in CYBCONF, 2017.

[21] C. M. Aderaldo, N. C. Mendonça, C. Pahl, and P. Jamshidi, "Benchmark requirements for microservices architecture research," in Proc. of the 1st Int. Workshop on Establishing the Community-Wide Infrastructure for Architecture-Based Software Engineering, ser. ECASE '17. Piscataway, NJ, USA: IEEE Press, 2017.

[22] N. Kratzke and P.-C. Quint, "About Automatic Benchmarking of IaaS Cloud Service Providers for a World of Container Clusters," Journal of Cloud Computing Research, vol. 1, no. 1, 2015.

[23] D. A. B. Fernandes, L. F. B. Soares, J. V. P. Gomes, M. M. Freire, and P. R. M. Inácio, "Security issues in cloud environments: a survey," Int. Journal of Information Security, 2014.

[24] A. Barker, B. Varghese, and L. Thai, "Cloud Services Brokerage: A Survey and Research Roadmap," in 2015 IEEE 8th International Conference on Cloud Computing. IEEE, jun 2015.

[25] D. Petcu and A. V. Vasilakos, "Portability in clouds: approaches and research opportunities," Scalable Computing: Practice and Experience, vol. 15, no. 3, oct 2014.

[26] A. N. Toosi, R. N. Calheiros, and R. Buyya, "Interconnected Cloud Computing Environments," ACM Computing Surveys, vol. 47, no. 1, may 2014.

[27] N. Grozev and R. Buyya, "Inter-Cloud architectures and application brokering: taxonomy and survey," Software: Practice and Experience, vol. 44, no. 3, mar 2014.

[28] M. Lushpenko, N. Ferry, H. Song, F. Chauvel, and A. Solberg, "Using Adaptation Plans to Control the Behavior of Models@Runtime," in MRT 2015: 10th Int. Workshop on Models@run.time, co-located with MODELS 2015: 18th ACM/IEEE Int. Conf. on Model Driven Engineering Languages and Systems, ser. CEUR Workshop Proceedings, N. Bencomo, S. Götz, and H. Song, Eds., vol. 1474. CEUR, 2015.

[29] B. Duncan and M. Whittington, "Creating an Immutable Database for Secure Cloud Audit Trail and System Logging," in Cloud Comput. 2017 8th Int. Conf. Cloud Comput. GRIDs, Virtualization. Athens, Greece: IARIA, ISBN: 978-1-61208-529-6, 2016.

[30] ——, "Cloud cyber-security: Empowering the audit trail," Int. J. Adv. Secur., vol. 9, no. 3 & 4, 2016.

[31] T. Pulls and R. Peeters, Balloon: A Forward-Secure Append-Only Persistent Authenticated Data Structure. Cham: Springer International Publishing, 2015. [Online]. Available: https://doi.org/10.1007/978-3-319-24177-7_31

[32] Han et al., "MetaSync: File Synchronization Across Multiple Untrusted Storage Services," in USENIX Annual Technical Conference, 2015.

Could Block Chain Technology Help Resolve the Cloud Forensic Problem?

Yuan Zhao*,Bob Duncan†
Business School
University of Aberdeen, UK
Emails: *y.zhao@abdn.ac.uk,†robert.duncan@abdn.ac.uk

***Abstract*—Many cloud users are blindly heading into a potentially devastating regulatory disaster zone. Given the shortcomings of the cloud due to the cloud forensic problem, this is likely to mean many cloud users will be unable to be compliant with the forthcoming EU General Data Protection Regulation when it comes into effect on 25th May, 2018. We consider the possible use of a crypto-currency based mechanism to address the as yet unsolved cloud forensic problem. Crypto-currencies are becoming a global phenomenon, and gaining more attention from media, venture capitalists, financial and government institutions. We focus on the operational risk and the market risk related to crypto-currencies, especially the dominating Bitcoin. The operational risk encompasses the actions that undermine the technological infrastructure and security assumptions of crypto-currencies. We discuss how the implementation of block chain technology could improve the efficiency of financial infrastructure, as well as the inevitable vulnerabilities of operational risk of software, open-source governance, and code maintenance. The market risk associated with crypto-currencies denotes the fluctuation in the exchange rate between crypto-currency and other currencies or financial asset classes. We summarise the literature findings on the co-movement of crypto-currencies with different currencies, indices, and commodities, to show the role of crypto-currency as a commodity, currency, or a speculative investment under portfolio diversification theory. In the light of the robustness of this approach, we consider whether the underlying block chain technology could, in turn, be practically applied to addressing the cloud forensic problem. This paper looks at the pros and cons of the blockchain/bitcoin approach, the potential benefits offered versus the additional resource costs involved, the increased latency necessarily introduced and considers whether there is any mileage in using such an approach to secure cloud forensic trails.**

Keywords–Cloud forensic problem; GDPR; Blockchain/bitcoin technology.

I. INTRODUCTION

All computing systems are constantly under attack, and for traditional networked computer systems, this presents a serious challenge to ensure a high level of security and privacy can be maintained. For cloud systems, these challenges increase exponentially, due to the increase in complexity in software, and the multiplicity of layers and actors involved in modern cloud ecosystems.

There remains one serious, but as yet, unresolved challenge, namely the cloud forensic problem. This problem arises where an attacker breaches a cloud system and becomes an intruder, whereby there is nothing then to prevent that intruder from escalating privileges and removing all trace of their incursion by deleting or modifying the forensic trail identifying all their actions and routes into the system. Needless to say, they are perfectly happy to remain hidden in the system, where they can carry on stealing information, while continuing to hide their presence.

This is about to become particularly problematic for companies who both use cloud, and are liable to fall under the jurisdiction of, and therefore require to be compliant with, the forthcoming EU General Data Protection Regulation (GDPR) [1]. Those who use cloud will by default be unable to meet compliance requirements. Given the punitive level of possible fines for non-compliance (up to the greater of €20million or 4% of last year's global turnover), this is likely to have a considerable impact on companies who are unable to be compliant.

Given the widespread convenience of cloud use for a great many companies, it is likely that this fact will place them at a competitive disadvantage once the GDPR goes live on 25th May. Given the long lead time required, the enormous costs involved, and the level of expertise needed to securely set up such systems, moving back to distributed network systems is unlikely to present a feasible option for many companies, who will effectively be "sitting ducks" once the legislation takes effect on 25th May 2018.

Therefore, it is imperative that a viable solution be found in the meantime, and as quickly as possible. For this paper, we take a look at the latest global phenomenon of crypto-currencies, and the technologies they use to ensure security. Security for all financial systems takes an necessary ultra high level priority in all financial companies. They are subject to an incredible range of risks, and we believe it may be worthwhile looking at the operational risk which encompasses the actions that undermine the technological infrastructure and security assumptions of crypto-currencies, as well as the market risk related to crypto-currencies.

We start by examining the cloud forensic problem to understand why it is such a challenge for cloud users to become compliant with the GDPR in Section II. Next, we turn to crypto-currencies and consider operational risk in such systems in Section III. In Section IV, we conside the implications of market risk, while in Section V, we look at the co-movement of crypto-currencies with different currencies, indices, and commodities, to show the role of crypto-currency as a commodity, currency, or a speculative investment under portfolio diversification theory. In Section VI, we consider the robustness of this approach for dealing with security issues. In Section VII, we discuss our findings and consider future work, and in Section VIII, presents our conclusions.

II. The Cloud Forensic Problem and GDPR Compliance

All computer systems are continuously subject to attack, and cloud systems are no exception. It is certainly the case that no system is immune to attack, and that is particularly true for cloud systems. During the past decade, a great many research papers have allowed a far greater level of security and privacy to be achieved in cloud systems. However, despite all that effort, no solutions have yet been found to address the cloud forensic problem.

This problem arises once an attacker compromises a cloud system, thus gaining even a small foothold. Once embedded in a system, the attacker becomes an intruder and seeks to escalate privileges until they can access and delete, or modify, the forensic logs in order to hide all trace of their incursion into the system. This allows them to retain a long term foothold within the system, thus allowing them to help themselves to whatever data they wish.

Many companies do not retain records of which database records have been accessed, and by whom, meaning that once a breach occurs, the ability of the company to be able to report which records have been accessed, copied, modified, deleted or ex-filtrated from the system becomes an impossible task. This results in non-compliance with the GDPR, meaning exposure to potentially punitive levels of fines.

To achieve compliance with the GDPR, all companies must first be able to report a breach within 72 hours of discovery. The global average time for all companies between breach and discovery in 2012 was an average of 6 months [2] [3]. This had improved to some 4 weeks by 2016 [4] — still far short of what is needed to understand what has been going on with the intruders while they were undiscovered.

In the light of cloud use, and in particular the Internet of Things (IoT), this raises the question of just how feasible complying with such a time threshold might be. Where a company uses cloud, the company is breached and it has made no special arrangements to ensure the safety of forensic and audit trail data, the 72 hour deadline is moot, since in the first place, it will have no means of knowing that it has been breached, so will have nothing to report, since the requirement is to report within 72 hours of discovery. However, once discovery does occur, there will be no realistic prospect of that company ever finding out just which records have been compromised. When the forensic and audit trail is gone — it is gone!

The IoT, of course, brings a whole new suite of problems to bear, not least of which is the general insecure level of devices, their small resource level, yet high throughput level of data. some of which may be lost in transit. The issue might not be so much with the data lost from IoT devices, rather than with the ability of attackers to easily compromise the devices, thus allowing them access via corporate networks to other more valuable devices in the system. We do not address the IoT within the scope of this paper, but do recognise that any company using IoT devices will require to take special measures to ensure GDPR compliance can be achieved.

Where a company does not take these special measures to safeguard their forensic and audit trail data, they will be less likely to be able to discover the occurance of the breach. Shoud they by chance manage to discover the breach, they would certainly be in a position to report it with 72 hours of discovery, they will simply struggle to be able to report what has been compromised, meaning they will be liable for some level of fine.

Obviously, the longer an intruder has available to spend inside a company system, the more information they will be able to acquire, and the more potential damage they can cause. While the GDPR was changed from "... within 72 hours of a breach occurring..." to a much less stringent "... within 72 hours of discovery ...", this rather misses the point that if a company cannot discover a breach within 72 hours of the breach occurring, how will they possibly be able to discover that is has arisen at all, let alone what data has been compromised once the intruder has deleted all forensic and audit trails?

So, not being able to discover that a breach has arisen, while not putting the company technically in breach of the GDPR, it will certainly make it extremely difficult to enable them to report which records have been compromised once discovery actually occurs. This means the non-compliance will necessarily become far more serious, thus enlarging the exposure to risk of steeper fines.

While there is no specific requirement to encrypt data, there is certainly a strong recommendation that this should take place, and within a reasonable time. Encryption and decryption keys should not be stored on the cloud instance. Failure to address these issues will certainly lead to steeper fines in the event of a breach.

As all firms involved in financial services are generally subject to greater attack than many other market sectors, it is worth taking a look at how they address security requirements. We believe there may be some merit in considering crypto-currencies, since as a new entrant to the market, there is more likelihood that their security approach, being designed from the beginning, might offer better prospects.

III. Operational Risk of Crypto-Currencies

Operational risk referrers to the action that undermines the technical infrastructure and security assumptions relating to crypto-currencies. The vulnerabilities related to crypto-currencies can be found in operator errors and security flaws. And most importantly, the Bitcoin platform also faces potential vulnerabilities from protocol designs. Operational insecurity has been addressed by Moore and Christin [5], who suggests that fraudulence is an issue among cryptocurencies. Exchanges acts as de facto banks, but almost half of them ceased operation due to the resultant impact of security breaches. However, these exchanges failed to reimburse their customers after shutting down. As an alternative approach, other users have instead deposited their Bitcoins in a digital wallet which has also become a target for cyber-criminals.

A small number of theoretical papers written by computer scientists address the mining pool protocols and anonymity. Miners opted out for the pool in long rounds, in which a potential block will be shared with large groups. Based on a peer-to-peer network layer, Babaioff et al. [6] argue that the current Bitcoin protocols do not provide an incentive for nodes to broadcast transactions. This is problematic, since the system is based on the assumption that there is such an incentive. Instead, by focusing on block mining protocol, Eyal and Sirer [7] show that mining is not incentive-compatible and that so-called "selfish mining" can lead to higher revenue for miners who collude against others. Houey [8] observed that larger blocks are less likely to win a block race when including new transactions into blocks. Karame, Androulaki and Capkun [9] analysed the security of using Bitcoin for past payments, and found that double-spending attacks on fast payments succeed with overwhelming probability and can be mounted at lower cost unless appropriate detection techniques are integrated in the current Bitcoin implementation. Regarding the double-spending and selfish mining attacks, Kogias et al. [10] proposed the usage of ByzCoin as a novel protocol to optimise transaction commitment and verification under normal operation while guaranteeing safety and liveness under Byzantine (It leveraged scalable collective signing to commit Bitcoin transactions irreversibly within seconds) faults.

The protection of online privacy and anonymity arises and are both addressed in the literature. Christin [11] examined the anonymous online marketplace in crypto-currencies. Böhme et al. [12] examined what can be learned from Bitcoin regarding Internet protocol adoption. Many studies analysed the public bitcoin transaction history and found a set of heuristics that help to link a Bitcoin account with real word identities. Androulaki et al. [13] quantified the anonymity in a simulated environment and found that almost half of the users can be identified by their transaction patterns. Using two examples, Bitcoin and Linden Dollars, the report focuses on the impact of digital currencies on the use of fiat money. Gans and Halaburda [14] analysed the economics of private digital currencies, but they explicitly focus on currencies issued by platforms like Facebook or Amazon (that retain full control), and not decentralized currencies like Bitcoin. Dwyer [15] provided institutional details about digital currency developments. The security, privacy and anonymity issue related to Bitcoin has been addressed by Krombholz et al. [16], in which they surveyed 990 Bitcoin users to determine Bitcoin management strategies and identifies how users deploy security measures to protect their keys and Bitcoins. They found that about 46% of participants use web-hosted solutions to manage Bitcoins, and over 50% use such solutions exclusively.

Among all the potential causes for operational risk, the denial-of-service attack is the prominent form by Böhme et al. [12], which entails swamping a target firm with messages and requests in such volume that either mining pools or exchanges become very slow and unusable. This type of attack is especially effective on the Bitcoin ecosystem because of its relative simplicity of monetising the attacks.

IV. Market Risk of Crypto-Currencies

Market risk via price fluctuation in the exchange rate is inevitable for users holding Bitcoin and other cryptocurrencies. Figure 1 shows the average US dollar-Bitcoin exchange rate, along with its trading volume. It is clear that the market volatility is tremendous for Bitcoin, leading to a high potential market risk.

There are also some attentions from the literature focusing on the price dynamics and speculative bubbles in the crypto-currency markets. Cheah and Fry [18] claimed that the crypto-currencies are prone to substaintial speculative bubbles, and they found that the fundamental value of Bitcoin is zero, by examining the daily clothing prices of Bitcoin from 2010 to 2014. A more recent study is conducted by Blau [19], which emphasised that high volatility of Bitcoin is not related to the speculative activities in this period. The volatility of Bitcoin has been analysed by Katsiampa [20]), Cheah and Fry [18], and many others.

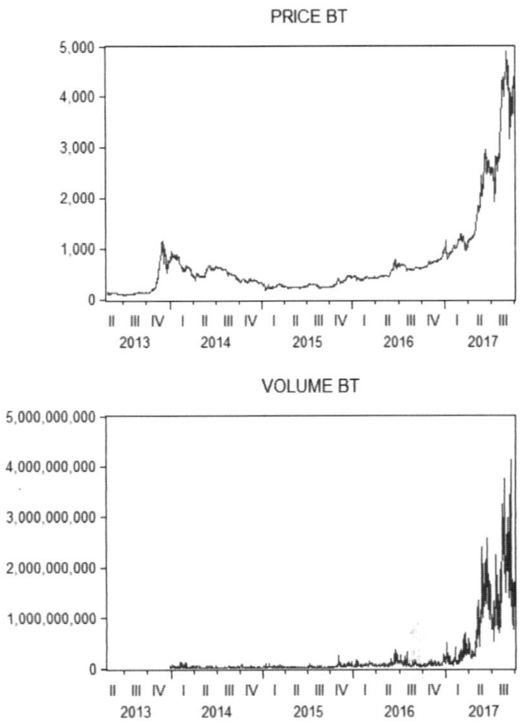

Figure 1. A Comparison Between Price and Volume [17].

There is no conclusive finding on whether the Bitcoin is a speculative investment asset or a currency. Glaser et al. [21] suggest users treat Bitcoin as speculative assets rather than a type of currency. The diversification benefits offered by Bitcoin is also studied by Briére, Oosterlinck and Szafarz [22]. They found Bitcoin can offer diversification benefits after looking into the correlation between Bitcoin and other asset classes. Gandal and Halaburda [23] examined the exchange rates of different virtual currencies to observe the co-movement and identify the opportunities or triangular arbitrage. But they found little opportunity based on daily closing prices. Yermack [24] analysed changes in Bitcoin price against fiat currencies and concludes that its volatility undermines its usefulness as currency. To be qualified as a currency, Bitcoin needs to serve as an intermediary of exchange, as a unit of account and store value. Also, they have been proved not to be able to function as those by Bariviera et al. [25].

V. Co-Movement of Crypto-Currencies and Portfolio Theory

Despite extensive studies on the economics aspects of cryptocurrencies, there are relatively fewer studies conducted on analysing the inter-linkage of cryptocurrencies with other financial assets. A number of papers have analysed the ability of cryptocurrencies, usually Bitcoin, to act as safe havens or hedges mentioned by a series of papers such as [26]–[28]. Dyhrberg [26] analysed the hedge properties of Bitcoin using a selection of explanatory variables such as gold (cash and future), the dollar-euro and dollar-pound exchange rates and the the Financial Times Stock Exchange 100 (FTSE 100) Index. The results of the GARCH model [29] showed that Bitcoin can be used in hedging against the dollar and the UK stock market, showing similar hedging capabilities to gold. In Figure 2, we see how a basket of crypro-currencies compare with each other based on price.

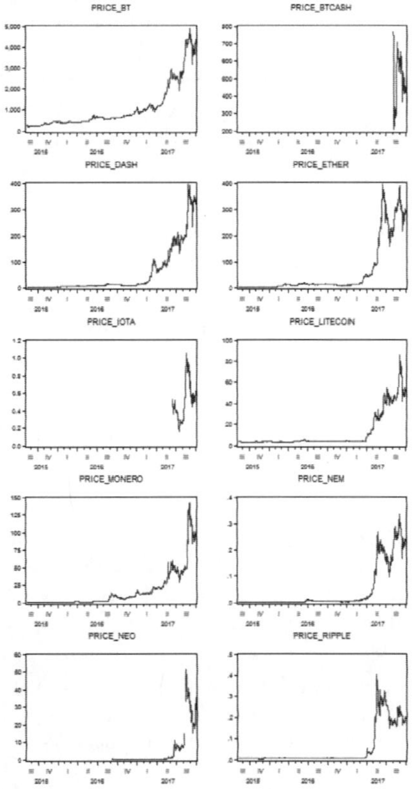

Figure 2. A Co-Movement View of Crypto-Currencies Based on Price [17].

Bouri, Azzi and Dyhrberg [28] used a quantile regression approach to analyse the relationships between the Bitcoin and global uncertainty. The findings demonstrate that at the longer frequencies VIX have strong negative impact on Bitcoin returns, while at the shorter frequencies uncertainty does have positive and significant impacts only on high quantiles. This implies that Bitcoin can hedge against global uncertainty at short investment horizons and in the bull regime only. Another study by them in 2017 investigated interrelationships between Bitcoin and the world equity indices, bonds, oil, gold, the general commodity index and the US dollar index using the bivariate DCC model by Engle [30]. The results show limited evidence of hedging and safe haven properties of the Bitcoin; however, Bitcoin still can be an effective diversifier. In Figure 3, we see how a basket of crypro-currencies compare with each other based on volume.

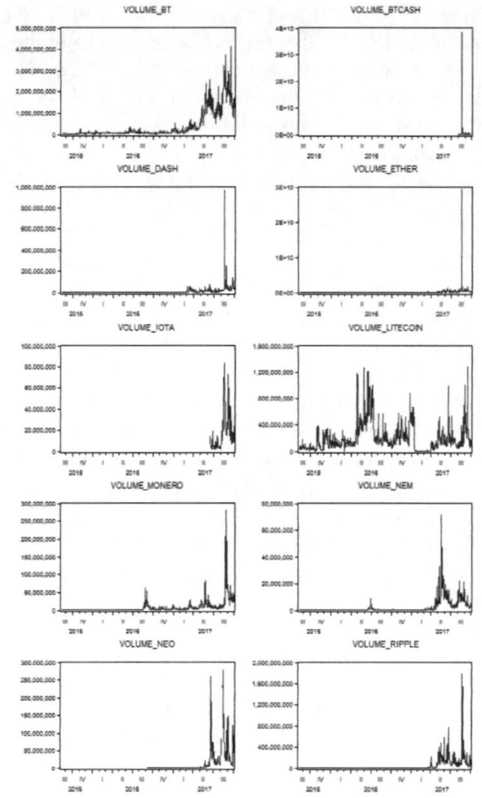

Figure 3. A Co-Movement View of Crypto-Currencies Based on Volume [17].

VI. The Robustness of this Approach for Security Issues

The design of Bitcoin presents distinctive risks that differ from other payment methods and thus pose security issues related to operational risk, market risk, and contagion risks with other cryptocurrencies.

The operational risk occurs when certain actions undermines the technical infrastructure and security assumption of crypotocurrencies, such as fraudulence of exchanges, mining pool inefficiency, double spending attacks, and online anonymity.

The market risk lies in the unpredictable fluctuations in the price of Bitcoin and other cryptocurrencies. As an agent for the storage of value and price goods, the sharp movement of exchange rate of Bitcoin will also cause liquidity issues.

The contagion risk arises when the comovement of price of a bundle of croptocurrencies becomes inevitable. This will cause potential issues for portfolio diversification, despite their innovations and efficiencies. For instance, the Litecoin confirms transactions four time faster than Bitcoin, which is more useful for the retail use and other time-sensitive transactions. NXT [31] reduces the electronic and computational burden of Bitcoin mining by replacing the proof-of-work mining with proof-of-stake, assigning block chain duties in proportion to coin holdings. Zerocash [32], which is not yet operational, will seek to improve privacy protections by concealing identifiers in the public transaction history. Peercoin [33] allows a perpetual 1% annual increase in the money supply.

We can see from what we have looked at, that from a security perspective, in principal, Blockchain technology provides a potentially robust approach to solving this problem. However, in looking at a number of real world instances, we can see that there are potential issues that must be considered. Attacks, such as Denial of Service (DOS) attacks, can prove lethal to both functionality and performance, although Tripathi et al. [34] have suggested a workaround to mitigate this particular issue.

The majority of successful attacks are perpetrated against the storage and containment technology in use, often utilising social engineering or in a recent case, holding of BitCoin owners to ransom until their BitCoins are transferred to the criminal perpetrators.

There are clear core strengths contained in Blockchain technology, but there are practical concerns to be considered. The lack of a clear economic methodology to pay for the use of the technology presents a major concern, as does the volatility of the crypto-currencies inextricably linked to it.

However, if we strip away the currency component, and focus only on the Blockchain technology, putting the financing of processing distributed ledger transactions onto a solid financial basis, with sufficient distributed resources to ensure a robust enough environment can be built to sustain the whole process, there might be a way to move forward.

There needs to be a sufficient incentive for distributed ledger providers to provide a highly secure, robust and low latency mechanism to deliver the means to record irrefutable transactional data rapidly enough to provide a high performing system. It is certainly the case that the use of some Blockchain based mechanism to protect cloud instances could prove a very useful means of doing so. However, it is also obvious that if the Blockchain ledgers are run within the same cloud instance as the system they are trying to protect, then we would be asking for trouble.

The obvious solution to this issue would be to truly distribute the Blockchain instances to a sufficiently diverse number of locations, such as to make it difficult for an attacker to compromise all, or a sufficiently large number of the ledgers to be able to force a permanent illicit change to their own advantage.

On the other hand, while the increased number of distributed ledgers can significantly increase the security, it will also increase the cost and the latency of processing transactions.

VII. DISCUSSION

Thanks to the major weakness posed by the cloud forensic problem, the potential to lose both the audit trail and the forensic trail means that recording the data we require to remain compliant with the GDPR becomes a vitally important task for us. The use of a distributed ledger holds great promise for us. The thinking behind the Blockchain approach affords us with huge redundancy, meaning that an attacker will have to compromise a great many of the distributed ledgers before they can have any impact on the ledger contents. Some would see this as too much redundancy. We would view this as just enough to provide the required assurance. This can therefore provide us with a very strong assurance that the consensus across the ledgers will deliver a high level of comfort as to the veracity of the contents. So, while this represents a big drawback for some, for us, it represents a major advantage!

Some point to the huge volumes of processing generated by the Blockchain process as used in Bitcoin, suggesting that it would be too computationally expensive for our purposes. We take a different view. Because it is a crypto-currency and highly volatile, Bitcoin is subject to transactional volumes measuring in multi-trillions per year. By stripping out the crypto-currency aspect from the equation, we also remove the need for such extreme volumes of transactional data, rendering the approach very manageable for any size of company.

Some express concerns at the impact of selfish miners. We take the view that by removing the need for mining from the equation, and instead having the processing carried out by credible parties for economic cost, this will remove any incentive to try to mess with the system in this way. All processors would be paid at the same rate for the job they perform, so there would be no means available to them, nor any incentive, to try to improve on that.

Yet others point to the dangers of Distributed Denial of Service (DDoS) attacks. Given that there will be no direct financial advantage to be gained by attacking these Blockchain ledgers, the volume of attacks will likely be lower. For a large attack to be financially viable, there has to be a huge financial incentive before it becoms worthwhile to spend the kind of money it takes to perpetrate such an attack.

VIII. CONCLUSION AND FUTURE WORK

It is clear that for any company using cloud, it will prove virtually impossible to achieve compliance with the GDPR in the event of a security breach due to the, as yet unresolved, Cloud Forensic Problem. Discovering this fact after a cyber breach will not be grounds for mitigation from the regulator after the fact. It will be far too late by then. Therefore, cloud users who require to be compliant with the GDPR will have to take steps now to be thoroughly prepared ahead of time.

We have looked at the Operational Risk and the Market Risk of crypto-currencies as well as considering the co-movement of crypto-currencies in the light of portfolio theory. Many of these risks arise through the perceived mass value attributable to these crypto-currencies and the mass transactional processing volumes implicit in their operation. Clearly, by removing the currency aspect from the equation, we can eliminat a huge portion of the risk. We accept that all risk will not be removed, but there will be a significant reduction in risk levels involved.

Our proposal will be to use the underlying concept of a distributed ledger to ensure we are in a position to retain some element of both audit trail and forensic trail data to allow us to meet the compliance requirements of the GDPR, which would othrwise be impossible in the event of a breach. There will be a need to carry out some serious testing in order to find a satisfactory equilibrium between security, privacy, performance, reliability, accessability and the accountability we require for GDPR compliance.

To that end, we plan to conduct a pilot case study on how the technical aspects might be implemented in order to meet all the required goals to ensure compliance can be achieved.

This will run around a miniature cloud system, offering both cloud-based and non-cloud based ledgers to assess what the optimum configuration might be.

REFERENCES

[1] EU, "EU General Data Protection Regulation (GDPR)," 2017. [Online]. Available: http://www.eugdpr.org/ [Retrieved: December 2017]

[2] PWC, "UK Information Security Breaches Survey - Technical Report 2012," London, Tech. Rep. April, 2012. [Online]. Available: www.pwc.com www.bis.gov.uk [Retrieved: December 2017]

[3] Trustwave, "2012 Global Security Report," Tech. Rep., 2012.

[4] Verizon, "2016 Verizon Data Breach Report," Tech. Rep., 2016.

[5] T. Moore and N. Christin, "Beware the middleman: Empirical analysis of Bitcoin-exchange risk," in International Conference on Financial Cryptography and Data Security. Springer, 2013, pp. 25–33.

[6] M. Babaioff, S. Dobzinski, S. Oren, and A. Zohar, "On bitcoin and red balloons," in Proceedings of the 13th ACM conference on electronic commerce. ACM, 2012, pp. 56–73.

[7] I. Eyal and E. G. Sirer, "Majority is not enough: Bitcoin mining is vulnerable," in International Conference on Financial Cryptography and Data Security. Springer, 2014, pp. 436–454.

[8] N. Houy, "The Economics of Bitcoin Transaction Fees." GATE WP 1407 Université de Lyon, Groupe d'Analyse et de Théorie Economique (GATE), February. [Online] Available: http://ssrn.com/abstract=2400519 [Retrieved: December 2017]

[9] G. O. Karame, E. Androulaki, and S. Capkun, "Double-spending fast payments in bitcoin," in Proceedings of the 2012 ACM conference on Computer and communications security. ACM, 2012, pp. 906–917.

[10] E. K. Kogias et al., "Enhancing bitcoin security and performance with strong consistency via collective signing," in 25th USENIX Security Symposium (USENIX Security 16). USENIX Association, 2016, pp. 279–296.

[11] N. Christin, "Traveling the silk road: A measurement analysis of a large anonymous online marketplace," in Proceedings of the 22nd international conference on World Wide Web. ACM, 2013, pp. 213–224.

[12] R. Böhme, N. Christin, B. Edelman, and T. Moore, "Bitcoin: Economics, technology, and governance," The Journal of Economic Perspectives, vol. 29, no. 2, 2015, pp. 213–238.

[13] E. Androulaki, G. O. Karame, M. Roeschlin, T. Scherer, and S. Capkun, "Evaluating user privacy in bitcoin," in International Conference on Financial Cryptography and Data Security. Springer, 2013, pp. 34–51.

[14] J. S. Gans and H. Halaburda, "Some economics of private digital currency," in Economic Analysis of the Digital Economy. University of Chicago Press, 2015, pp. 257–276.

[15] G. P. Dwyer, "The economics of Bitcoin and similar private digital currencies," Journal of Financial Stability, vol. 17, 2015, pp. 81–91.

[16] K. Krombholz, A. Judmayer, M. Gusenbauer, and E. Weippl, "The other side of the coin: User experiences with bitcoin security and privacy," in International Conference on Financial Cryptography and Data Security. Springer, 2016, pp. 555–580.

[17] Coindesk, "Coindesk," 2017. [Online]. Available: https://www.coindesk.com/ [Retrieved: December 2017]

[18] E.-T. Cheah and J. Fry, "Speculative bubbles in bitcoin markets? an empirical investigation into the fundamental value of bitcoin," Economics Letters, vol. 130, 2015, pp. 32–36.

[19] B. M. Blau, "Price dynamics and speculative trading in bitcoin," Research in International Business and Finance, vol. 41, 2017, pp. 493–499.

[20] P. Katsiampa, "Volatility estimation for bitcoin: A comparison of garch models," Economics Letters, vol. 158, 2017, pp. 3–6.

[21] F. Glaser, K. Zimmermann, M. Haferkorn, M. C. Weber, and M. Siering. "Bitcoin—Asset or Currency? Revealing Users' Hidden Intentions." Proceedings of the 22nd European Conference on Information Systems, Tel Aviv, June 2014.

[22] M. Brière, K. Oosterlinck, and A. Szafarz, "Virtual currency, tangible return: Portfolio diversification with bitcoin," Journal of Asset Management, vol. 16, no. 6, 2015, pp. 365–373.

[23] N. Gandal and H. Halaburda, "Can we predict the winner in a market with network effects? competition in cryptocurrency market," Games, vol. 7, no. 3, 2016, p. 16.

[24] D. Yermack, "Is Bitcoin a real currency? An economic appraisal," National Bureau of Economic Research, Tech. Rep., 2013.

[25] A. F. Bariviera, M. J. Basgall, W. Hasperué, and M. Naiouf, "Some stylized facts of the Bitcoin market," Physica A: Statistical Mechanics and its Applications, vol. 484, 2017, pp. 82–90.

[26] A. H. Dyhrberg, "Bitcoin, gold and the dollar–a garch volatility analysis," Finance Research Letters, vol. 16, 2016, pp. 85–92.

[27] A. H. Dyhrberg, "Hedging capabilities of bitcoin. is it the virtual gold?" Finance Research Letters, vol. 16, 2016, pp. 139–144.

[28] E. Bouri, G. Azzi, and A. H. Dyhrberg, "On the return-volatility relationship in the bitcoin market around the price crash of 2013". Economics: The Open-Access, Open-Assessment E-Journal, 11:1–16.

[29] T. Bollerslev, "Generalized autoregressive conditional heteroskedasticity," Journal of econometrics, vol. 31, no. 3, 1986, pp. 307–327.

[30] R. Engle, "Dynamic conditional correlation: A simple class of multivariate generalized autoregressive conditional heteroskedasticity models," Journal of Business & Economic Statistics, vol. 20, no. 3, 2002, pp. 339–350.

[31] NXT, "NXT Platform," 2017. [Online]. Available: https://nxtplatform.org/ [Retrieved: December 2017]

[32] Zerocash, "Zerocash," 2017. [Online]. Available: http://zerocash-project.org/ [Retrieved: December 2017]

[33] Peercoin, "Peercoin," 2017. [Online]. Available: https://peercoin.net/ [Retrieved: December 2017]

[34] S. Tripathi, B. Gupta, A. Almomani, A. Mishra, and S. Veluru, "Hadoop based defense solution to handle distributed denial of service (ddos) attacks," Journal of Information Security, vol. 4, no. 03, 2013, p. 150.

Managing Forensic Recovery in the Cloud

George R. S. Weir
Department of Computer and Information Sciences
University of Strathclyde
Glasgow, UK
e-mail: george.weir@strath.ac.uk

Andreas Aßmuth and Nicholas Jäger
University of Applied Sciences
OTH Amberg-Weiden
Germany
e-mail: {a.assmuth,n.jaeger}@oth-aw.de

Abstract— **As organisations move away from locally hosted computer services toward Cloud platforms, there is a corresponding need to ensure the forensic integrity of such instances. The primary reasons for concern are (i) the locus of responsibility, and (ii) the associated risk of legal sanction and financial penalty. Building upon previously proposed techniques for intrusion monitoring, we highlight the multi-level interpretation problem, propose enhanced monitoring of Cloud-based systems at diverse operational and data storage level as a basis for review of historical change across the hosted system and afford scope to identify any data impact from hostile action or 'friendly fire'.**

Keywords-Cloud security; forensic readiness; multi-level interpretation; secure data retention.

I. INTRODUCTION

For many individuals, the primary use of Cloud computing is remote data storage. Presently, most major online Cloud service providers offer such storage. Apple users may engage iCloud as a supplement to local storage capacity and as an emergency backup for system configuration. Among similar service offerings we find Google Drive, Microsoft OneDrive and Amazon Drive.

Dropbox and its freemium business model, where users may register for a free account with a limited storage size and an option for more storage capacity and additional features for paid subscriptions, is also very popular. The broad appeal and immediate benefits from services of this type are apparent from the proliferation of such offerings, as underlined by the fact that many home broadband contracts include a measure of Cloud storage as standard. Thus, "BT Cloud is a free service for BT Broadband customers that allows you to securely back up, access and share your precious files and folders" [1]. Home broadband users will often rely on their remote storage and backup facility with little recognition that Cloud services are in operation.

Despite the apparent speed with which consumers have adopted Cloud-based services, there is recognition that security issues can arise in the Cloud setting just as in the context of locally hosted systems [2]-[5]. When occasional security issues are reported in the media, the greatest concern may be the availability and privacy of their data [6].

In the following, we outline the characteristics of risks that need to be accommodated in terms of forensic readiness. Firstly, we consider security risks arising from the network context, before focussing specifically on security issues in the Cloud setting. In section IV, we describe the concept of digital forensic readiness and, in Section V, explore the implications of applying this important aspect to the context of Cloud services. We conclude by recommending greater attention to the requirements of Cloud forensic readiness, particularly with regard to the issue of multi-level interpretation. To this end, we propose enhanced monitoring of Cloud-based systems at diverse operational and data storage levels, as well as deployment of several previously advocated techniques for enhancing the security and resilience of recorded forensic readiness data.

II. NETWORK SECURITY RISKS

Addressing security risks is a familiar issue in the context of networked computing. In non-Cloud systems, the principal ingredients in management responses to security take three general forms:

- System hardening
- Software defences
- Data backup

Firstly, system hardening is an attempt to render known threats ineffective. This includes 'conventional' measures that reduce vulnerability, such as authentication, identity management and access control [7], as well as acting to disable unnecessary services, applying regular software updates (patches) and gauging of the relevance and associated risks from newly published exploits [8]. Modern Operating Systems have also been adapted to meet known cyber threats. Counter measures, like address space randomisation, mandatory access control or maybe sandboxing, are state of the art. In addition, advanced users might even build their own operating system and use selected kernel parameters to further harden their system. The second variety of response to address

Application
Middleware
Operating System
Hardware

Figure 1. Layer-based model of a computing system

security issues is the application of software defences. This ranges from antivirus provision to firewalls and may also include some variety of intrusion detection, usually rule-based [9] or anomaly-based [10].

Any computing system may be described by a simple layer-based model as depicted in Figure 1. Obviously, security on any higher layer strongly depends on access control mechanisms of lower layers. Even if users or service providers only aim for access control on a higher level to secure their application, these access control mechanisms in practice are more complex than those on lower layers. In addition, vulnerabilities or inadequate configuration on lower levels may lead to bypassing security measures on higher layers. Therefore, appropriate countermeasures are necessary on all layers.

A third security measure is the provision of regular data backup, as a means of ensuring that any system failure or intrusion does not result in irretrievable data loss.

III. CLOUD SECURITY RISKS

Perhaps unsurprisingly, Cloud configurations are subject to levels of security risk that go beyond those affecting conventional networked computer systems. In consequence, the security measures outlined above may not be sufficient in the Cloud setting. In elaborating this claim, the Cloud issues are best illustrated with reference to the differing Cloud service offerings [11]:

- Infrastructure as a Service (IaaS);
- Platform as a Service (PaaS);
- Software as a Service (SaaS).

These models for Cloud service provision are helpfully elucidated by Gibson et. al. [12], as follows:

- "IaaS provides users with a web-based service that can be used to create, destroy, and manage virtual machines and storage. It can be used to meter the use of resources over a period of time, which in turn, can be billed back to users at a negotiated rate. It alleviates the users of the responsibility of managing the physical and virtualized infrastructure, while still retaining control over the operating system, configuration, and software running on the virtual machines" [op. cit., p. 199].
- "Platform-as-a-Service providers offer access to APIs, programming languages and development middleware which allows subscribers to develop custom applications without installing or configuring the development environment" [op. cit., p. 200].
- "Software-as-a-Service gives subscribed or pay-per-use users access to software or services that reside in the cloud and not on the user's device" [op. cit., p. 202].

Clearly, our earlier noted approaches to system security are also applicable to Cloud-based systems. With an eye specifically on Cloud security, we can consider how each of these service offerings may be at risk and what precautions may be anticipated in response to these risks.

1. Infrastructure as a Service

This kind of service seems most prone to the types of exploit that one would expect with conventional networked computers, principally, because, in most cases, such virtual machines will be presented to the Internet as networked hosts. Here, the customer is deploying a virtual machine with associated Operating System and on-board software applications. This raises the prospect of vulnerabilities at network level, as well as application level issues, e.g., with Web systems and Database servers, Cross-Site Scripting (XSS) or SQL injections. Denial of service attacks are also a legitimate concern, especially since this kind of attack can achieve enormous bandwidths by using IoT devices for their purpose [13]. For these reasons, *system hardening* (especially, defending against known vulnerabilities) and *software defences* are appropriate for IaaS, including precautions such as anti-malware, firewalls, and Intrusion Detection Systems. Provision of these features may be the responsibility of the Cloud Service Provider (CSP), who determines what OS and defensive capabilities are made available. In some settings, the customer may be in a position to bolster the native defences on the virtual system provided by the CSP.

In similar vein, *data backup* is likely to be required by the IaaS customer. Indeed, the protection of customer data may jointly be the concern of the customer and the CSP. The former may enable off-Cloud backup, to avoid a single source of failure. While the CSP may also offer data backup to a separate Cloud data storage facility.

Despite reasonable expectation of such measures, there are indications that Cloud software infrastructure components are not always adequately secured from known vulnerabilities at the virtual machine level [14].

2. Platform as a Service

Computing facilities afforded to the customer of PaaS, are limited to the development of specific middleware or functional components. These services employ technologies such as Docker [15], Containers [16], DevOps [17] and AWS Lambda [18], in order to host customer-defined remote functionality. From a Cloud customer perspective, *system hardening* seems to be irrelevant in this context in relation to the host Operating System. On the other hand, any code developed for use on the Cloud platform must be protected from illicit operations, e.g., process hijacking, output redirection or the elevation of privileges.

Software defences of the variety outlined above seem less relevant to the PaaS context since the operations supported by the middleware are limited to specific data processing and do not afford full operating system access or modification. The primary concern should be the operational effectiveness and resilience of the customer-defined operations. Clearly, such services may also be impaired through illicit access, e.g., stealing authentication details in order to alter code on the host system. Managing this area of concern lies primarily in the hands of the Cloud customer, with the assumption that the

CSP will prevent unauthorised access to customer account details.

3. Software as a Service

SaaS provides the Cloud customer with remote access to third-party data processing facilities via micro-services [19], or RESTful services [20]. Aside from network level attacks, such services should be protected from most other security concerns by having the host system hardened and equipped with suitable software defences. From the customer perspective, so long as their remote Cloud services operate effectively, without interruption or data loss, there would seem to be little cause for concern. Of course, the risk of aberrant customer-side behaviour may arise through social engineering exploits or disgruntled employee actions.

This summary of security concerns affecting the three varieties of service has treated each Cloud model as an isolated networked computing facility. In reality, since the essence of Cloud provision is the virtualisation of services, our overview lacks one further important consideration, i.e., the possibility of service impairment as a result of activity at adjacent, upper or lower levels of the Cloud implementation.

Clearly, any security aspects that affect the operational resilience of the underlying Cloud infrastructure is of direct concern to the CSP and can have a knock-on effect upon customer services. The underlying Cloud technology, i.e., the hardware and software configurations that provision our three Cloud models, may be subject to attack or deliberate manipulation in a fashion that impinges detrimentally upon the Cloud services supported by that particular hardware and software ensemble. This may be construed as a service attack 'from below'. The scope for such attacks are precisely the characteristic exploits that may affect any networked host (listed earlier).

Attacks 'from the side' are a growing concern in Cloud security. 'Side channel attacks', originate with co-hosted customers who manipulate the behaviour of their virtual system to influence the behaviour of the host system and thereby affect co-hosted customers. Several studies suggest that such 'co-tenancy', an essential feature of IaaS and PaaS, carries dangers. Thus, "Physical co-residency with other tenants poses a particular risk" [21], such as "cache-based side-channel attacks" [22], and *"resource-freeing attacks* (RFAs)" in which "the goal is to modify the work- load of a victim VM in a way that frees up resources for the attacker's VM" [23]. Most worrying are contexts where one customer's 'malicious' virtual machine seeks to extract information from another customer's virtual machine on the same Cloud platform [24]. Such risks to Cloud facilities are fundamental to their service provision.

A final attack vector that threatens some Cloud systems is 'from above'. In this case, poorly implemented virtual systems may afford scope for customers to 'break free' of their virtual system and access or directly affect the underlying Operating System or middleware/hypervisor. Clearly, it must be ensured that there is no information leakage from virtual machines and that attackers or malicious customers are not capable of breaking out of the virtual machine and gaining access to the host OS or the virtual machines of other customers [25].

The characteristics of these Cloud service offerings with associated security measures and the likely risk conditions are captured in Figure 2. The prospect of action from one Cloud user affecting another is described as intra-platform interference.

IV. DIGITAL FORENSIC READINESS

The numbers of cases of network intrusion and data breach are on the rise: "there is a massive increase in the records being compromised by external hacking – from roughly 49 million records in 2013 to 121 million and counting in 2015" [26].

Service model	**Main features**	**Security Measures**	**Risks**
Infrastructure (IaaS)	Virtual machines, Operating systems, Storage, Software applications	System hardening, Software defences, Data backup	Social engineering, Intrusion, Malware, Denial of service, Elevation of privileges, *Intra-platform interference*
Platform (PaaS)	APIs, Programming languages, Development middleware, (Containers, Dockers, AWS Lambda, DevOps)	System hardening, Software defences	Social engineering, Elevation of privileges, *Intra-platform interference, Information leakage*
Software (SaaS)	Remote applications, Micro-services, RESTful services	System hardening, Software defences	Social engineering, *Intra-platform interference*

Figure 2. Summary of features, security measures and risks

One positive effect of this growth in unauthorized data access is the raised awareness of digital forensics (DF) and a marked change in its perception from a solely post-event reactive investigative tool to a pro-active policy to establish intelligence capabilities in advance of any incidents. This change in role reflects the concept of digital forensic readiness. Thus, "Pro-active DF management must ensure that all business processes are structured in such a way that essential data and evidence will be retained to ensure successful DF investigations, should an incident occur" [27, p.18].

One might define digital forensic readiness as 'having facilities in place to ensure the comprehensive capture and retention of all system event and user activity data that would be required post-incident in order to determine the precise nature of any data-loss, system modification or system impairment that results from intrusion, system misuse, or system failure".

Naturally, this concept of digital forensic readiness is equally applicable to Cloud systems and novel techniques have been proposed to facilitate the data collection that this entails [28]. Yet, the Cloud context introduces particular problems with respect to forensic readiness.

V. CLOUD FORENSIC RECOVERY

Forensic readiness in the Cloud is complicated by the variety of contexts in which Cloud services are deployed and the diversity of software settings in which security risks may arise. Forensic readiness must accommodate these complexities and, in turn, this suggests that a single infrastructure-based digital forensic readiness solution may be infeasible.

The primary reason for concern is the need to capture relevant data on system operation at the various operational levels of the Cloud system and any potential interaction across these levels. This means capturing program logs, system logs and user activity logs. In any end-customer Cloud facility, the data protected may not extend beyond any currently live information and data held in associated database systems. The ready recycle capability of Cloud services also has implications for the persistence of digital forensic evidence. An intrusion that steals data from a virtual machine and then seeks to reset that machine may well succeed in destroying evidence of the intrusion, thereby removing any forensic traceability on the nature and quantity of stolen data.

Neither is it sufficient to provide each distinct operational layer of Cloud systems with its own comprehensive forensic readiness. At best, this condition will allow for forensic data recovery for that operational layer. But there is no one-size-fits-all solution that can capture all state, interaction and performance data such as would ensure full Cloud forensic recovery. In fact, this insight reveals a fundamental problem that may impact upon Cloud forensic readiness.

There are parallels here with issues in distributed systems and software architecture. Thus, "distributed software systems are harder to debug than centralized systems due to the increased complexity and truly concurrent activity that is possible in these systems" [29, p. 255]. Regardless of whether the Cloud setting is truly distributed in its realisation, its interconnected software functional layers represent a unique challenge when attempting to interpret the relationship between events or changes actioned at one functional level and the operational impact of such changes on other functional aspects of the services afforded by that Cloud.

When considering Cloud systems, from the perspective of software architecture there may be an assumption of 'a component- and message-based architectural style' in which there is 'a principle of limited visibility or *substrate independence*: a component within the hierarchy can only be aware of components "above" it and is completely unaware of components which reside "beneath" it' [30, p.825].

This multi-level interpretation problem is complicated by the fact that events considered anomalous at one level of service offering may arise through actions considered legitimate at a 'lower' level of software implementation. From the digital forensic readiness perspective, this underlines the requirement to go beyond capture of significant events across the Cloud service software and functional levels, since significance is an aspect that may cross the boundaries between such layers in the system as a whole. A hypothetical example may clarify this issue.

A CSP customer may contract access to specific functional components (e.g., a Web service). The operational characteristics of the service are under the control of the CSP and not the customer. An authorised employee of the CSP may modify the algorithmic process and thereby affect the outcome of any service use by the customer. While a change in operational behaviour of the service (i.e., an anomaly) may eventually be detected by the customer, there may be no anomalous activity evident at the level of CSP employee activity. The focus of subsequent forensic investigation may light initially on the nature of customer activity, since this is where the anomaly is apparent, but proper understanding of the issue requires that events across different functional levels of the Cloud system be apprehended.

An informative view on this issue may be borrowed from Granular Computing [31], which aims to develop computational models of complex systems, such as human intelligence. A key characteristic of this work is that it 'stresses multiple views and multiple levels of understanding in each view' [op. cit., p.85]. Here, the emphasis is upon 'holistic, unified views, in contrast to isolated, fragmented views. To achieve this, we need to consider multiple hierarchies and multiple levels in each hierarchy' [op. cit., p.88].

Our proposal for adequate Cloud forensic readiness has two components. Firstly, there is a requirement for data capture. This is the obvious need to record any data at each layer of Cloud facility that may have a role to play in subsequent digital forensic analysis. Secondly, the captured data must be stored off the system being monitored in a manner that both ensures the integrity of the logging and minimises the likelihood that the stored data can be compromised, either as a result of hostile action or 'friendly fire'.

To achieve adequate data capture, we require 'state information' and data management across differing levels of any Cloud service, from the lowest software level up to the most abstracted 'user facing' software component. On their own, such records will not be sufficient to fully capture the potential interplay of differing software levels. For this purpose, subsequent digital forensic analytics will be required in order to establish a multi-dimensional representation of event chronology. This means that timestamps from events and data captured at different software levels of abstraction will be correlated to determine how events across the Cloud system are related.

Our requirement for secure and resilient log storage can build upon default system logging that will be present within the Cloud implementation but this must be supplemented to achieve log reliability.

Instead of using centralised log servers, which of course are attractive targets and easy to spot for attackers, we propose a different approach. In order to prevent adversaries from manipulating log files to hide their tracks, we use chained Message Authentication Codes (MACs) for each entry to the log file on each node. If state-of-the-art MACs are used, this makes it impossible to delete or manipulate text in the log files. Next, each node uses secret sharing techniques as proposed by Adi Shamir [32] to divide the log file into parts. These parts are then sent to random other nodes which store these log data. Even if an adversary succeeds in taking over some of the nodes, he will need a certain number of these fragments to reconstruct the log data. But since for each log entry different nodes are chosen randomly as stated before, the attacker effectively needs to control the whole Cloud ecosystem to stay hidden. Further information on this solution can be found in our previous paper [33].

VI. CONCLUSIONS

As organisations move increasingly away from locally hosted computer services toward Cloud-platforms, there is a corresponding need to ensure the forensic integrity of such instances. The primary reasons for concern are (i) the locus of responsibility, and (ii) the associated risk of legal sanction and financial penalty. In the first place, while Cloud service providers (CSPs) are responsible for the availability and robustness of their commercial offerings, they will not be responsible for the management of such services by their customers, nor for the data security associated with customer-level use of the Cloud services. Responsibility for these aspects resides with the CSP's customers, whose data processing and data management are built upon the purchased Cloud services. In the second place, legislative demands on data protection, such as the forthcoming EU General Data Protection Regulation, will require companies to notify all breaches within 72 hours of discovery, or face significant financial penalty.

These concerns can be addressed and the business risk mitigated through development of forensic readiness in customer-level Cloud systems. We have argued that this requires a range of logging and data capture facilities across the Cloud system software infrastructure that maintain the possibility of tracking activity at different levels of software abstraction (the multi-level interpretation problem). Our second proposition is that such digital forensic readiness must be combined with techniques to ensure that logged data is incorruptible and robust. We have previously proposed techniques for intrusion monitoring that ensure log data credibility and provide robust decentralised log storage and recovery for post-hack scenarios [33].

REFERENCES

[1] British Telecom Customer Support, Available: http://bt.custhelp.com/app/answers/detail/a_id/41948/~/what-is-bt-cloud%3F. [Accessed: Dec. 29, 2017].

[2] M. Nanavati, P. Colp, B. Aiello, and A. Warfield, "Cloud security: A gathering storm", *Communications of the ACM*, *57*(5), pp. 70-79, 2014.

[3] S. S. Tirumala, H. Sathu, and V. Naidu, "Analysis and prevention of account hijacking based incidents in cloud environment", In Proc. *International Conference on Information Technology (ICIT)*, pp. 124-129, 2015.

[4] M. Zhou, R. Zhang, W. Xie, W. Qian, and A. Zhou, "Security and privacy in cloud computing: A survey", In Proc. *Sixth International Conference on Semantics Knowledge and Grid (SKG)*, pp. 105-112, 2010.

[5] Y. Chen, V. Paxson, and R. H. Katz, "What's new about cloud computing security", *University of California, Berkeley Report No. UCB/EECS-2010-5 January, 20*, 2010.

[6] BBC News, Available: http://www.bbc.co.uk/news/technology-29076899. [Accessed: Dec. 29, 2017].

[7] H. Takabi, J. B. Joshi, and G. J. Ahn, "Security and privacy challenges in cloud computing environments", *IEEE Security & Privacy*, 8(6), pp. 24-31, 2010.

[8] M. Carroll, A. Van Der Merwe, and P. Kotze, "Secure cloud computing: Benefits, risks and controls", In Proc. *Information Security South Africa (ISSA), 2011*, pp. 1-9, 2011.

[9] K. Ilgun, R. A. Kemmerer, and P. A. Porras, "State transition analysis: A rule-based intrusion detection approach", *IEEE transactions on software engineering*, vol. 21, no. 3, pp. 181-199. 1995.

[10] P. Garcia-Teodoro, J. Diaz-Verdejo, G. Maciá-Fernández, and E. Vázquez, "Anomaly-based network intrusion detection: Techniques, systems and challenges", *Computers and Security*, vol. 28, no. 1, pp. 18-28, 2009.

[11] P. Mell and T. Grance, "The NIST definition of cloud computing", NIST, 2011. Available: http://faculty.winthrop.edu/domanm/csci411/Handouts/NIST.pdf. [Accessed: Dec. 29, 2017].

[12] J. Gibson, R. Rondeau, D. Eveleigh, and Q. Tan, "Benefits and challenges of three cloud computing service models", In Proc. *Fourth International Conference on Computational Aspects of Social Networks (CASoN)*, pp. 198-205, 2012.

[13] H. Sweetland Edwards, "How Web Cams Helped Bring Down the Internet, Briefly", *Time Magazine*, 25th October 2016. Available: http://time.com/4542600/internet-outage-web-cams-hackers. [Accessed: Dec. 29, 2017].

[14] S. Zhang, X. Zhang, and X. Ou, "After we knew it: empirical study and modeling of cost-effectiveness of exploiting prevalent known vulnerabilities across IAAS cloud", In Proc. *9th ACM symposium on Information, computer and communications security*, pp. 317-328, 2014.

[15] S. Dhakate and A. Godbole, "Distributed cloud monitoring using Docker as next generation container virtualization technology", In Proc. *Annual IEEE India Conference (INDICON)*, pp. 1-5, 2015.

[16] C. Pahl and B. Lee, "Containers and clusters for edge cloud architectures--a technology review. In Proc. *3rd International Conference on Future Internet of Things and Cloud (FiCloud)*, pp. 379-386, 2015.

[17] A. Balalaie, A. Heydarnoori, and P. Jamshidi, "Microservices architecture enables DevOps: migration to a cloud-native architecture", *IEEE Software*, *33*(3), pp. 42-52, 2016.

[18] M. Villamizar et al., "Infrastructure cost comparison of running web applications in the cloud using AWS lambda and monolithic and microservice architectures. In Proc. *16th IEEE/ACM International Symposium on Cluster, Cloud and Grid Computing (CCGrid)*, pp. 179-182, 2016.

[19] D. Namiot and M. Sneps-Sneppe, "On micro-services architecture", *International Journal of Open Information Technologies*, *2*(9), pp. 24-27, 2014.

[20] H. Han et al., "A RESTful approach to the management of cloud infrastructure", In Proc. *IEEE International Conference on Cloud Computing,. CLOUD'09.*, pp. 139-142, 2009.

[21] Y. Zhang, A. Juels, A. Oprea, and M. K. Reiter, "Homealone: Co-residency detection in the cloud via side-channel analysis", In Proc. *IEEE Symposium on Security and Privacy (SP)*, pp. 313-328, 2011.

[22] Y. Zhang, A. Juels, M. K. Reiter, and T. Ristenpart, "Cross-tenant side-channel attacks in PaaS clouds". In Proc. *ACM SIGSAC Conference on Computer and Communications Security,* pp. 990-1003, 2014.

[23] V. Varadarajan, T. Kooburat, T., Farley, T. Ristenpart, and M. M. Swift, "Resource-freeing attacks: improve your cloud performance (at your neighbor's expense)", In Proc. *ACM conference on Computer and communications security*, pp. 281-292, 2012.

[24] Y. Zhang, A. Juels, M. K. Reiter, and T. Ristenpart, "Cross-VM side channels and their use to extract private keys", In Proc. *ACM conference on Computer and communications security,* pp. 305-316, 2012.

[25] T. Vateva-Gurova, N. Suri, and A. Mendelson, "The Impact of Hypervisor Scheduling on Compromising Virtualized Environments", In Proc. *IEEE International Conference on Computer and Information Technology; Ubiquitous Computing and Communications; Dependable, Autonomic and Secure Computing; Pervasive Intelligence and Computing (CIT/IUCC/DASC/PICOM)*, pp. 1910-1917, 2015.

[26] Security Week, "Data Breaches by the Numbers", Available: http://www.securityweek.com/data-breaches-numbers. [Accessed: Dec. 29, 2017].

[27] C. P. Grobler and C. P. Louwrens, "Digital forensic readiness as a component of information security best practice", In Proc. *IFIP International Information Security Conference*, pp. 13-24, Springer, Boston, MA, 2007.

[28] V. R. Kebande and H. S. Venter, "A Cloud Forensic Readiness Model Using a Botnet as a Service", In Proc. *the International Conference on Digital Security and Forensics (DigitalSec2014)*, pp. 23-32, The Society of Digital Information and Wireless Communication, 2014.

[29] P. C. Bates and J. C. Wileden, "High-level debugging of distributed systems: The behavioral abstraction approach", *Journal of Systems and Software*, *3*(4), pp. 255-264, 1983.

[30] N. Medvidovic, R. N. Taylor, and E. J. Whitehead Jr, "Formal modeling of software architectures at multiple levels of abstraction", *ejw*, *714*, pp. 824-837, 1996.

[31] Y. Yao, "Perspectives of granular computing. In Proc. *IEEE International Conference on Granular Computing,* Vol. 1, pp. 85-90, 2005.

[32] A. Shamir, "How to share a secret", *Communications of the ACM*, vol. 22, no. 11, pp. 612-613, 1979.

[33] G. R. S. Weir and A. Aßmuth, "Strategies for Intrusion Monitoring in Cloud Services", In Proc. *Cloud Computing 2017, The Eighth International Conference on Cloud Computing, GRIDs, and Virtualization*, IARIA, Athens, Greece, 2017.

Dark Clouds on the Horizon

The Challenge of Cloud Forensics

Ian Ferguson & Karen Renaud
Division of Cybersecurity
Abertay University
Dundee, Scotland, DD1 IHG
Email: {i.ferguson,k.renaud}@abertay.ac.uk

Alastair Irons
Faculty of Computer Science
University of Sunderland
Sunderland, United Kingdom, SR1 3SD
Email: alastair.irons@sunderland.ac.uk

***Abstract*—We introduce the challenges to digital forensics introduced by the advent and adoption of technologies, such as encryption, secure networking, secure processors and anonymous routing. All potentially render current approaches to digital forensic investigation unusable. We explain how the Cloud, due to its global distribution and multi-jurisdictional nature, exacerbates these challenges. The latest developments in the computing milieu threaten a complete "evidence blackout" with severe implications for the detection, investigation and prosecution of cybercrime. In this paper, we review the current landscape of cloud-based forensics investigations. We posit a number of potential solutions. Cloud forensic difficulties can only be addressed if we acknowledge its socio-technological nature, and design solutions that address both human and technological dimensions. No firm conclusion is drawn; rather the objective is to present a position paper, which will stimulate debate in the area and move the discipline of digital cloud forensics forward. Thus, the paper concludes with an invitation to further informed debate on this issue.**

Keywords–Cloud Forensics; Challenges

I. INTRODUCTION

The seeds of Cloud Computing were sown back in 1963 when Licklider talked about an "*intergalactic computer network*" [1]. He had a vision of a global network allowing people to execute code anywhere and access data anywhere. The world had to wait for the capacity of the Internet before this dream would come to fruition. In 1999, Salesforce delivered services to Enterprise via a website [2]. Soon large companies, such as Amazon and Microsoft, started to offer enterprise and personal computing services. Many organisations now use Microsoft's Office 365 platform to manage their email and store their documents. Licklider's dream has been realised.

Cloud computing offers obvious benefits to companies and individuals [3]. The costs are reasonable, as compared to investing in, and maintaining, their own infrastructure.

Yet there is a flip side too, related to those who use computing power for nefarious purposes. When law enforcement officials investigate crimes it is common practice for them to seize devices for analysis by forensics experts.

Digital forensics, as a science, emerged as cyber crime started to increase, and did so to meet the needs of law enforcement and also to help organisations to reveal the activities of cyber attackers. Rigorous forensics procedures emerged and were adopted by forensics investigators [4]. The advent of the cloud challenges these established procedures, adding a whole new dimension of complexity to forensics investigations. Challenges come from technical, stakeholder, organisational and political levels.

In this paper, we discuss the challenges experienced by the humans involved in usual and cloud forensics investigations [5].

Options for a digital forensic response to the emergent challenges are discussed in the hope of provoking discussion on a response that is grounded not solely in technology but rather one that is multi-disciplinary incorporating elements from various stakeholders in the criminal justice process (law makers, law enforcement) and society at large.

We commence by discussing the progress of technology and introducing forensics in Section II. We then introduce the concept of cloud computing in Section III. We continue our discussion by advancing the argument that progress, in the shape of security technology, may lead to a situation in which information only exists "in the clear" (i.e., unencrypted) as it is input and output (Sections IV and V). All storage and computation will be performed upon a provably securely encrypted representation, resulting in an encryption boundary encircling all data.

We contemplate the concept of a "robust" system and discuss how such a system might arise from the encryption boundary. The consequences for the digital forensics community of the existence of such a system are examined. We also address the concept of the cloud and its impact on digital forensics.

We then discuss existing responses to individual threats in Section VI. Consideration is given to the combined threat and to the technical, legal and ethical aspects of the problem including community roles and attitudes to the problem, taking into account the need to maintain evidential integrity and continuity. Some possible digital forensic responses are discussed, including their technical feasibility, ethical desirability and current admissibility in Section VII. Section VIII concludes by inviting debate on the technical, ethical and legal consequences of the various response options.

II. TECHNOLOGY, PROGRESS & FORENSICS

An ethical paradox lies at the heart of all security research: one that presents a problem to the digital forensics community. The more secure we make things, the less we can get into them when we need to. It is possible that the ordinary security researcher does not worry too much about this on a day-to-day basis. Happy with the assumption that they are on the side of the "good guys", and that their job is to keep the "bad guys" out, they continue to develop ever stronger encryption, more user-friendly security systems and generally, with a defenders mindset, build ever higher digital castle walls.

One specific kind of researcher, namely the digital forensic scientist, is likely to regard these fortifications with trepidation. The obvious question is: *"What happens if the 'bad guys' have seen how we secure our "valuables" and use the same measures?"*

Since Kerckhoff's principle [6] mandates that the "protection plans" should be in the public domain, we must assume that the bad guys will have access to, and employ, the same technology as the good guys.

Current digital forensic techniques can, to some extent, be said to work by accident. It is only because the normal functioning of hardware, operating systems and applications leave artefacts lying around that the reconstruction of user activity is possible. Less sophisticated cyber criminals might still leave sufficient cybertrails at the scene of the cybercrime. Garfinkel [7] has argued that we have been living in a "golden age" of digital forensics. To date, these artefacts and the inevitable human fallibility in implementing "secure" systems have meant that the digital forensic investigator has been able to sneak into the digital storage mechanism and look around.

However, cyber security, and its uptake by criminal elements, will inevitably challenge forensics investigators. The consequences of this may include an "evidence blackout." How we could respond to this is the subject of this paper.

It could be argued that we do not need to worry about this yet. It might be the case that human fallibility will always defeat attempts to make systems secure. However, improving security seems to be the *raison d'être* of the larger security research community and their techniques will inevitably be embraced by criminal elements.

The literature on digital security often identifies the human as the weakest point in any digital security system. What happens if this is reversed and the human, in this case the cyber criminal, becomes the strongest link? How will greater awareness of the strengths and weaknesses of digital investigations help cyber criminals to obfuscate their cybertrails? Recent cases have suggested that this era might well have dawned. Two examples demonstrate this. The first is the San Bernadino case [8] where the US government attempted to force Apple to help them to access data on iPhones. The second is that in the days following the Texas church shooting the FBI complained about not being able to access the shooter's phone [9]. These are evidence of a significant phase change: a new challenge for law enforcement.

There are also signs from Western governments that the use of encryption by subversives is making counter-terrorism efforts challenging [10], [11], [12], [13].

III. CLOUD COMPUTING

The term "Cloud Computing" has various overloaded meanings conventionally categorised as "software as service", "platform as service", "infrastructure as service" etc., and is a growing area of interest in the digital investigation community [14].

Cloud forensics can be defined as *"a hybrid forensics approach (e.g., remote, virtual network, live, large-scale, thin-client, thick client) towards the generation of digital evidence"* [15].

One particular feature of some cloud computing systems likely to prove troublesome to forensic investigators is the idea of the distributed, fragmented file system. Originally conceived partly for reasons of data security and mapping easily onto the cloud paradigm, it has its origins in the work of Shamir [16] and Rabin [17], with implementations such as OceanStore [18], PASIS [19] and more recently the work of Mei *et al.* [20]. Such systems achieve security by storing a file not on one remote networked file server but by splitting a file into fragments and storing each fragment on (potentially geographically separate) servers.

The underlying idea is that if one server is attacked and compromised, then the attackers still do not have access to a file — that requires the more difficult proposition of compromising all the servers across which the file is stored. Couple this with full disk encryption, with each fragment protected by a different key, and we have a perfect storm. Anyone wishing to reconstruct a file is thus potentially faced with the theoretical problem of decrypting multiple encryption regimes and also the practical problems associated with data fragments existing in multiple jurisdictions, and possibly even the knowledge of the file fragments' locations being likewise encrypted and distributed.

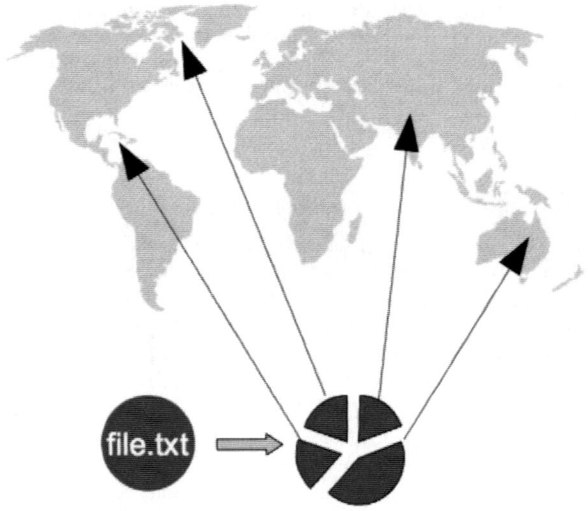

Figure 1. Fragmented file storage in the cloud computing paradigm

In an Internet-wide cloud context, different parts of the same file will be in different computers, different countries and different jurisdictions (See Figure 1). The practical difficulties of obtaining the file are thus indeed daunting. Uptake of the cloud computing paradigm is widespread [21].

IV. INDIVIDUAL TECHNICAL THREATS

In this section, a number of security technologies that may threaten an "evidence blackout" are individually examined before we discuss the consequences of deploying them together. The techniques/technologies considered are: full disk encryption, secure network communication, secure processors, homomorphic encryption and anonymous routing.

A. *Encryption*

It is worth briefly examining the state of the art of encryption technology and its adoption.

Current encryption techniques are based on the idea of computational security. Given encryption keys of sufficient length, cryptanalysis requires infeasible amounts of computing power and/or lengths of time. The existence of techniques and/or computing power able to tackle current cyphers in a meaningful time-scale is not acknowledged by those likely to possess them. Encryption has thus reached the point of being "practically unbreakable".

B. *Full Disk Encryption (FDE)*

Current digital forensic techniques depend largely on artefacts left behind on disk, both explicitly, and as a by-product by the operating system. The first "dark cloud" on the horizon is that these techniques do not perform well when faced with serious attempts at concealment by encrypting full disks [22].

Full disk encryption allows the entire contents of a disk to be protected by a password/key scheme, i.e., no-one without the key (digital investigators included) can read the contents of the disk. To achieve this, a layer is introduced into the Operating System between the file system and storage media device driver. Any data being written to the disk is encrypted on-the-fly as it passes through this layer. Conversely, any data being read is decrypted, provided that the correct decryption key has been provided at the beginning of a session.

The advantage of such a scheme is that it is largely transparent to the user — no special actions are required to conceal particular items of data as *everything* is automatically encrypted/decrypted. Popular implementations of this technology include VeraCrypt [23] and Bitlocker [24].

C. *Secure network communication*

The transmission of strongly encrypted messages, once the province of governments, military and intelligence services is within the grasp of both the ordinary citizen, and the criminal. HTTP Secure (HTTPS), Virtual Private Network (VPN), Internet Protocol Security (IPSec) and all have achieved widespread adoption.

D. *Secure Processors*

Secure processor technology promises to do for memory image forensics what full disk encryption did for disk examination — i.e., render it impossible. In a system with a secure processor, all data outside the boundary of the processor itself i.e., anything in random access memory (RAM), is encrypted. Both program instructions and data are decrypted on-the-fly with block ciphers as data is shifted to and from the various system buses (See Figure 2).

Having their origins in systems such as Aegis [25] and Bastion [26], secure processors were originally intended to provide a secure environment for embedded control systems but continue to develop towards high-end systems. Although they are not yet widely adopted in desktop level systems (mainly due to speed issues in dealing with the large cryptographic overhead) working systems are emerging.

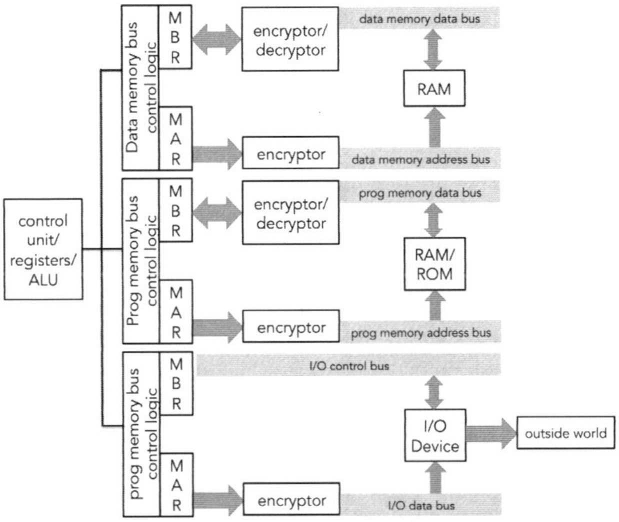

Figure 2. Secure Processor Architecture (MBR=Master Boot Record; MAR=Memory Address Register; ALU=Arithmetic Logic Unit)

E. *Homomorphic Encryption*

Homomorphic encryption (HE) is the idea that computation can be performed directly on the encrypted representation of data without the need first to decrypt it. First proposed by Rivest *et al.* [27] it would enable data not only to be stored securely in the cloud, but also to be processed there without fear of compromise by a corrupt cloud service provider.

The work of Gentry [28], based on ideal lattice cryptography, has shown that such a scheme is viable, but currently the computational overhead involved means that it is not yet practical. Efforts to discover a more computationally tractable scheme continue [29].

F. *Anonymous Routing*

Due to the nature of the protocols underlying the operation of the Internet, it is possible to identify the source and destination of network traffic. Even if encryption is in place, it is thus possible to establish that two parties are in communication.

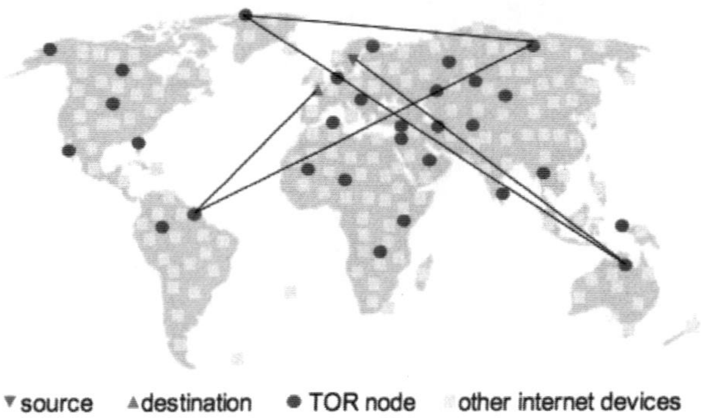

Figure 3. Onion Routing

The advent of anonymous routing (e.g., onion routing as embodied in the The Onion Router (TOR) protocol [30]) removes this source of evidence. The TOR works by separating the concerns of identity and routing. It forwards messages randomly though a network of TOR servers (nodes), with each one applying a layer of encryption (hence the onion metaphor) before forwarding the packet to the next node or ultimately its intended destination. This prevents both the source and destination of the message from being known by every node and prevents traffic analysis (See Figure 3).

Whilst current onion routing implementations have their weaknesses (various attacks against the anonymity have been demonstrated), systems such as the TOR network have demonstrated their viability. Such techniques are available to those with sufficient knowledge and reason to hide the origin and destination of their incoming and outgoing data.

V. The Combination of Threats

Although the threat of encryption has been identified previously in work such as that of Garfinkel [7] and Seigfried *et al.* [31], digital forensics has thus far managed to keep evidence flowing by reducing reliance on the initial acquisition strategy of imaging cold systems and resorting to live imaging/live forensics. How well this approach would scale should the need for it become widespread remains to be seen.

Due to the threats outlined in the previous section it is possible to envisage a computing system in which the only place that data exists "in the clear" (i.e., in unencrypted form) is internally in the processor, during input (mouse, keyboard events, etc.) and when formatted for human consumption i.e., display/rendering (and hence the video RAM, audio and printer buffer etc.). Anything stored in either primary or backing store, or in transit over a communication channel is likely to be strongly encrypted. Thanks to the cloud, homomorphic encryption and anonymous routing threats, not only will any evidence be encrypted, it will also be difficult to find which machine it is on or even where it is physically located. This would lead to an "evidence blackout" as current approaches to investigation (largely based on disk and RAM images) will fail.

Figure 4. A Robust System

In the remainder of this paper, such a system is referred to as a "robust" system (see Figure 4). We define a robust system as one which, when implemented and operated without error, maintains data in an unencrypted form to the least extent commensurate with the fundamental operations of computing.

The cloud is essentially an instantiation of Figure 4 but also spans jurisdictions and continents.

VI. Responses to Threats

This section begins by examining existing responses to the individual threats and then argues that such responses may be ineffective against the combined threat of the "robust" system.

A. Response to the encryption threat

An obvious approach to the encryption-based threats would seem to be to attack the encryption that protects "robust systems". Over time, resources and a concentrated research effort the technologies that make up the "robust system" might well be broken and a way found to reveal the data needed for forensic reconstruction. This would, however, be a something of an "own-goal" for the computer security community that has been making computers progressively harder to break into. The same technologies that protect the terrorist's plot also guard individual privacy, the world's e-commerce systems and bank accounts. We, as a society, ought to have no interest in breaking this encryption other than to identify weaknesses in protecting our own data.

B. Response to Full Disk Encryption (FDE)

Rather than use a technical approach to get around the protection offered by FDE, the UK response (as embodied in Regulation of Investigatory Powers Act (RIPA) Part III, Section 49 [32]) has been one based on legislation. Failure to disclose a password/decryption key following the service of an appropriate court order is now an offence carrying a maximum penalty of a two year custodial sentence (or 5 years in the case of a threat to national security). In the year 2014/2015, 37 "Section 49" notices were issued. 22 refused to comply and three were convicted [33].

It is interesting to note that the initial response to FDE, when it emerged as a threat, was not to try to produce a faster decryption technique, but rather a move towards live-forensics in which a logical image of a machine is taken via a login session during which the necessary decryption keys have already been provided. This move may not merely be because of the undoubted practical difficulty in producing such a technique, but rather that the research cryptographers and cryptanalysts are on the same side. This observation leads to the notion that the threats outlined above should not be considered purely as a computer science problem, but rather as one to which operational solutions might also be applied.

C. Response to Anonymous Routing

When, during World War 2, the cryptanalysts of Bletchley Park were faced with a "blackout" of decrypted signals traffic due to a change in enemy ciphers, some level of useful intelligence was derived from the practice of "traffic analysis". Crudely stated, this allowed the origin and destination of a message to be identified even if the content of the message could not be deciphered. By correlating the volume of traffic between known signal stations, areas of significant enemy activity could be identified. Unfortunately, faced with a similar blackout on intercepting internet traffic due to securely encrypted communications, modern digital forensic investigators may be denied even this limited option.

1) TOR Weaknesses: The current implementation of TOR is vulnerable to certain attacks, which could offer a means of traffic analysis as evidence [34], [35]. However, work is ongoing to remove those vulnerabilities [36]

D. Response to Robust Security.

Currently, responses to the combined threat would be difficult, primarily because of the way that the cloud makes the problem trans-jurisdictional. This presents the twin problems of practical international cooperation and the differing legal attitudes to encryption.

E. Response to Cloud

The most appropriate responses to the threats posed by cloud computing lie outwith the purely technical domain and are more concerned with obtaining the cooperation of the cloud providers and jurisdictions where the servers are located.

VII. Solutions

This section outlines some possible options for maintaining access to evidence in the face of individual threats combining to offer "robust" security. This paper does not seek to suggest that such solutions are either desirable or practical, merely that they are technical possibilities.

A. Acquire evidence that is in the clear

The concept of an "attack surface" is familiar in the computer security world. It seems reasonable in the role-reversed world of the digital investigator trying legitimately to gain access to a suspect system. Whilst the "attack surface" of the "robust system" is minimal it is not non-existent. In the short-term, one technical response to the encryption-based threats is increased reliance on live forensics. Depending as it does on gaining access to a suspect system whilst it is turned on, and while the user logged in with decryption keys having been supplied, it is an option with its practical difficulties. The challenge here is to provide law enforcement with the legislative framework and operational capability routinely to use such techniques on a large scale.

Other technical means of exploiting the reduced attack surface include covert surveillance of screen and printer output by video or the Van Eck technique [37], for example. Difficulties here are obtaining permission to mount the surveillance and the logistics of putting suitable equipment in place, undetected.

The "robust system" concept includes the idea of perfect implementation and, of course, practical systems rarely are. The greatest source of potential weakness of any cryptosystem can be human error, and it is thus reasonable to conjecture that exploiting security implementation or human errors may continue to provide an evidence source long into the future.

B. Black-bag techniques

The hacker community has (and continues to have) great success in gaining illegal access to insufficiently-secured systems, both by technical means and by social engineering. The adoption of some of their techniques (e.g., "black-bag" cryptanalysis [38]) to provide evidence would be challenging from the current rigid legal point of view on admissibility of evidence and the issue of "forensic soundness" [39]. It may be that this stance needs to be modified in order to allow evidence recovered using non-standard means.

Two examples of techniques that have emerged from this community that might be useful are:

- The use of **key-loggers** (both software and hardware) is a well-known hacking technique. However, employing it for evidence gathering counts as the interception of communication and thus requires appropriate authorisation.
- The **Firewire direct memory access (DMA) hack** [40] allows direct access to a system's memory via a firewire port. It offered a means of rapidly imaging a target system's RAM (and potentially the disk) without the need to install and execute software on the target (or indeed alter the state of the RAM).

C. Forensic Readiness/Analysable by design

One possible mitigation might be to universally adopt the discipline of "forensic readiness" [41], in which all systems record their activities and make such a (cryptographically protected) record accessible to law enforcement in a retrospective manner, as required. Three questions emerge: **(a)** is it technically possible? **(b)** is it practical? and **(c)** is it desirable?

1) Technical Feasibility: The question of possibility can be broken down into recording and access aspects.

- **Recording** Part of the discipline of forensic readiness deals with the configuring of operating systems and applications to record their operation in sufficient detail to enable meaningful reconstruction of their usage [42]. Such techniques are commonly deployed on organisational systems rather than those of the private home user. Various suggestions as to how to make operating systems leave analysable artefacts as part of their natural operation have also been put forward, including [43]. These arguments coupled with the ever-increasing capacity of storage device (and consequent decrease in storage costs) make it reasonable to suggest that such forensic logging is feasible.
- **Access** For reasons of security, such a log should be encrypted. Providing a way into it, thus becomes a matter of accessing the appropriate key.

  Current practice in dealing with encryption keys falls under two headings: *key escrow* and *key surrender*. The difficulties associated with key escrow (primarily assuring the security of held keys and designing access mechanisms) have prevented its widespread adoption. Although there are civil liberties problems associated with both forms of key access, the UK has adopted a "key surrender" policy. With a lack of outcry (and possible due scrutiny) that surprised commentators, a policy of Government Access to Keys (GAK) was embodied in the Regulation of Investigatory Powers Act (RIPA) 2000. Failure to disclose an encryption key when presented with a court order demanding its release to an appropriately authorised government agency carries a maximum custodial sentence of 2 years (five years for terrorism and child pornography offences). An as yet unimplemented provision of RIPA allows for a sentence associated with the crime under investigation to be imposed should keys be withheld (i.e., if a suspect is being investigated for murder, and refuses to divulge a key, then the full sentence for murder could be applied). Whilst the length of sentence can be debated, this mechanism at least provides a means of dealing with an unwillingness to divulge keys.

It seems reasonable to assume that any keys protecting a forensic log could be dealt with in a similar manner.

2) Practicality: The techniques of forensic readiness are in the domain of the workplace. IT departments could activate forensic readiness, but there is little incentive for private users to do so and obviously there is a considerable disincentive for anyone planning to commit a cybercrime.

For an evidence database to exist universally, it would have to be built into the system (presumably by system manufacturers at system-build time) and turned on (possibly without the option to turn it off) by default.

For the (non-technical) majority of users, this might suffice to provide a means of acquiring evidence should the need arise. Achieving the necessary universality is more problematic as suitably knowledgeable users could simply construct their own non-forensic-ready system using existing technology. Thus forensic-ready devices will only be adopted by the law-abiding, in whom we have no interest.

A similar legislative technique to that used with encryption technology could be employed, i.e., make it an offence to operate a computer that is not forensically ready. This strategy would suffer from the same "presumption of guilt" objection that accompanies a sentence under RIPA, as well as the difficulties of coping with legacy systems. It is also unclear how well such a strategy might scale as computing becomes ever closer to realising Weiser's vision of the ubiquitous computer [44].

A technical alternative to legislation might be to put in place a requirement for forensic-readiness before a device can access the Internet. Aside from the technical difficulties with enforcing this, and problems with universal adoption in different jurisdictions, how long would it be before an alternative "Dark Internet" arose?

A further practical difficulty is associated with resourcing such a scheme. Encryption is not yet widespread and many police forces report a considerable backlog of digital forensics cases. It is by no means clear that current administration systems could cope with the added burden of obtaining court orders for evidence-log disclosure.

3) Desirability: As a society, we have accepted the desirability of law-enforcement being able to access private, encrypted data, in appropriate circumstances, via RIPA 2000 and legislation of similar purpose in other jurisdictions. It might thus seem that enforcing the deliberate availability of something from which forensic reconstruction of user activity might take place would be equally acceptable. After all, no eyebrows are raised at the current ability to reconstruct the same information as part of an investigation from the traces 'accidentally' left behind by the Operating System. However, evidence-gathering techniques that require the active capture of information are seen as an interception of communications and require higher permission. A distinction is thus made between the *a-priori* capture and the post-hoc reconstruction of (potentially) identical information. The techniques of forensic readiness fall across this divide by capturing data but not allowing its authorised examination until after an event.

The distinction between *a-priori* and *post-hoc* evidence is based on the need to preserve privacy: If a crime has been committed then it is proportionate to acquire and reconstruct evidence, however if a crime is only anticipated, then higher permission for state intrusion upon the privacy of an individual is required.

How should the use of forensic-readiness based evidence thus be regulated? The proposal here is that it becomes a routine technique and, for reasons of cost, speed and efficiency there should be a low barrier to its use.

Stallman [45] has argued against the idea of the "treacherous computer", which the current forensic readiness proposal might be thought to embody. However, a scheme in which the keys that protect the forensic readiness backdoor belong to the owner of the equipment, and are only used in the case of an investigation, may offer sufficient protection from this charge.

The proposed forensic readiness scheme is predicated on the (negative) incentive of a custodial sentence to gain access to the necessary keys. Such a practice can give rise to concerns over its abuse.

Another potential problem is the security of the back-door itself. If it were universally deployed, then one break in would compromise everyone's security. The counter argument here is that such a scheme is only necessary to counter "robust security" in the first place.

4) Cloud Forensics Readiness: If cloud systems could be made forensically ready, then obtaining evidence is at least technically possible. Ensuring that the necessary legislation is in-place and enforceable globally is another matter. The primary objection to this is the *trans-jurisdictional* nature of the Internet. Whilst the creation of a separate jurisdiction for the Internet has been proposed [46], such solutions are a long way from realisation. Obtaining appropriate international cooperation is, however, a human problem rather than an insoluble cryptographic one. Human problems, while seeming intractable, can often be solved in ingenious ways, so this offers some hope.

5) Forensics Readiness Conclusion: The forensic readiness scheme outlined above is, at best, a compromise. Enforcing its universal deployment seems problematic and it maybe that in a "robust security" scenario we might simply have to accept that it offers no hope against the determined, cybercriminal with the knowledge to set up their own system. However by building it into new devices, forensic readiness may offer some utility against the average user who does not fiddle with the security settings.

D. Fundamental Changes

Two extremely fundamental changes would also serve to make things easier in terms of digital forensics. The first is that the Internet no longer permits or supports anonymity. If every Internet user has to prove their identify in an irrefutable way to be permitted to use the Internet, it would make attribution much easier to prove. This does, of course, compromise individual privacy, and might not be an acceptable solution.

Another suggestion is that the Internet be treated as a separate jurisdiction, much as is the case for independent countries. We would then be able to have laws that apply across the Internet. This removes the need for forensics investigators to negotiate multiple jurisdictions in order to carry out an investigation. This would have to be accepted by nearly 200 independent countries across the planet, so is probably infeasible.

VIII. Conclusions

Advances in computer security may be about to nullify many of the current digital forensic techniques. Even if the blackout is not total, now is the time to start thinking about what happens, and what our options could be. One possible option is the widespread use of a cryptographically protected forensic readiness approaches with the disclosure of the keys subject to laws similar to the UK's RIPA.

Despite civil liberties concerns, we have, as a society, already taken the step of demanding access to encryption keys when necessary. Should we take the additional step of demanding some form of universal forensic readiness?

Ultimately, this is not a technological debate about how to facilitate a digital forensic investigation; rather it is an ethical question about whether an individual has the right to keep secrets from the state. In the encryption debate, we have already decided that the answer is "no." Currently a compromise exists whereby those with appropriate technical skills and knowledge can achieve a much greater degree of privacy than the average citizen. The proposed approach might remove such inequality.

Before developing such a technology, exceptionally careful consideration should be given to the ethical implications of the use of the technology — assuming the moral neutrality of the technology and the acknowledgement that the investigators may not always be the "good guys". Of course, there is a debate in the computer ethics literature as to whether technology is value neutral or not, for example, see Johnson [47]

The evidence blackout is not yet with us, but appropriate forensic readiness measures and legislation would take time to develop. In the short term, it is possible that a greater emphasis on surveillance and live seizure will be necessary, along with an appropriate legal and operational framework.

The real challenge to the security/digital forensics community is that we, as the ones who understand the technical issues and their consequences, must be the ones who lead the debate.

References

[1] J. C. R. Licklider, "Memorandum for members and affiliates of the intergalactic computer network," 1963, originally distributed as a memorandum April 23, 1963. Published on KurzweilAI.net.

[2] N. N. Rojas, "CRM Review," undated, http://erpsoftware360.com/salesforce.htm Accessed 6 December 2017.

[3] D. Catteddu, "Cloud Computing: benefits, risks and recommendations for information security," in Web application security. Springer, 2010, pp. 17–17.

[4] R. McKemmish, What is forensic computing? Australian Institute of Criminology Canberra, 1999.

[5] B. Martini and K.-K. R. Choo, "An integrated conceptual digital forensic framework for cloud computing," Digital Investigation, vol. 9, no. 2, 2012, pp. 71–80.

[6] A. Kerckhoffs, "Military cryptography," Journal des sciences militaires, 1883, p. 5–83.

[7] S. L. Garfinkel, "Digital forensics research: The next 10 years," Digital Investigation, vol. 7, 2010, pp. S64–S73.

[8] J. Rubin, J. Queally, and P. Dave, "FBI unlocks San Bernardino shooter's iPhone and ends legal battle with Apple, for now," 2016, march 28 http://www.latimes.com/local/lanow/la-me-ln-fbi-drops-fight-to-force-apple-to-unlock-san-bernardino-terrorist-iphone-20160328-story.html Accessed 6 December 2017.

[9] J. J. Roberts, "The FBI Can't Open the Phone of the Texas Church Shooter Devin Kelley, note=http://fortune.com/2017/11/08/texas-church-shooting-fbi-phone/, accessed november 8 2017,," 2017.

[10] G. Burton, "Amber Rudd: The little people don't need encryption," 1 August 2017, the Enquirer https://www.theinquirer.net/inquirer/news/3014855/amber-rudd-the-little-people-dont-need-encryption Accessed 6 December 2017.

[11] Masnick, "Theresa May Tries To Push Forward With Plans To Kill Encryption, While Her Party Plots Via Encrypted WhatsApp," 12 June 2017, https://www.techdirt.com/articles/20170611/11545237565/theresa-may-tries-to-push-forward-with-plans-to-kill-encryption-while-her-party-plots-via-encrypted-whatsapp.shtml Accessed 6 December 2017.

[12] N. Statt, "Donald Trump thinks he can call Bill Gates to 'close up' the internet," 7 December 2015, https://www.theverge.com/2015/12/7/9869308/donald-trump-close-up-the-internet-bill-gates Accessed 6 December 2017.

[13] R. Roberts, "Prime Minister claims laws of mathematics 'do not apply' in Australia," 15 July 2017, http://www.independent.co.uk/news/malcolm-turnbull-prime-minister-laws-of-mathematics-do-not-apply-australia-encryption-l-a7842946.html Accessed 6 December 2017.

[14] D. Hilley, "Cloud computing: A taxonomy of platform and infrastructure-level offerings," Georgia Institute of Technology, Tech. Rep., 2009.

[15] K. Ruan, J. Carthy, T. Kechadi, and M. Crosbie, "Cloud forensics," in IFIP International Conference on Digital Forensics. Springer, 2011, pp. 35–46.

[16] A. Shamir, "How to share a secret," Communications of the ACM, vol. 22, no. 11, 1979, pp. 612–613.

[17] M. O. Rabin, "Efficient dispersal of information for security, load balancing, and fault tolerance," Journal of the ACM (JACM), vol. 36, no. 2, 1989, pp. 335–348.

[18] J. Kubiatowicz, D. Bindel, Y. Chen, S. Czerwinski, and P. *et al.*. Eaton, "Oceanstore: An architecture for global-scale persistent storage," ACM Sigplan Notices, vol. 35, no. 11, 2000, pp. 190–201.

[19] J. J. Wylie, M. W. Bigrigg, J. D. Strunk, G. R. Ganger, and H. *et al.*. Kiliccote, "Survivable information storage systems," Computer, vol. 33, no. 8, 2000, pp. 61–68.

[20] A. Mei, L. V. Mancini, and S. Jajodia, "Secure dynamic fragment and replica allocation in large-scale distributed file systems," IEEE Transactions on Parallel and Distributed systems, vol. 14, no. 9, 2003, pp. 885–896.

[21] R. Buyya, C. S. Yeo, and S. Venugopal, "Market-oriented cloud computing: Vision, hype, and reality for delivering it services as computing utilities," in High Performance Computing and Communications, 2008. HPCC'08. 10th IEEE International Conference on, 2008, pp. 5–13.

[22] E. Casey and G. J. Stellatos, "The impact of full disk encryption on digital forensics," ACM SIGOPS Operating Systems Review, vol. 42, no. 3, 2008, pp. 93–98.

[23] "VeraCrypt," https://veracrypt.codeplex.com/ Accessed 6 December 2017.

[24] "BitLocker," https://docs.microsoft.com/en-us/windows/device-security/bitlocker/bitlocker-overviewAccessed 6 December 2017.

[25] G. E. Suh, C. W. O'Donnell, and S. Devadas, "Aegis: A single-chip secure processor," IEEE Design & Test of Computers, vol. 24, no. 6, 2007, pp. 63–73.

[26] R. B. Lee, P. Kwan, J. P. McGregor, J. Dwoskin, and Z. Wang, "Architecture for protecting critical secrets in microprocessors," in ACM SIGARCH Computer Architecture News, vol. 33, no. 2. IEEE Computer Society, 2005, pp. 2–13.

[27] R. L. Rivest, L. Adleman, and M. L. Dertouzos, "On data banks and privacy homomorphisms," Foundations of secure computation, vol. 4, no. 11, 1978, pp. 169–180.

[28] C. Gentry, "Fully homomorphic encryption using ideal lattices." in STOC, vol. 9, no. 2009, 2009, pp. 169–178.

[29] J.-S. Coron, D. Naccache, and M. Tibouchi, "Public key compression and modulus switching for fully homomorphic encryption over the integers." in EUROCRYPT, vol. 7237. Springer, 2012, pp. 446–464.

[30] M. G. Reed, P. F. Syverson, and D. M. Goldschlag, "Anonymous connections and onion routing," IEEE Journal on Selected areas in Communications, vol. 16, no. 4, 1998, pp. 482–494.

[31] J. Siegfried, C. Siedsma, B.-J. Countryman, and C. D. Hosmer, "Examining the encryption threat," International Journal of Digital Evidence, vol. 2, no. 3, 2004, [PDF].

[32] UK Government, "Regulation of Investigatory Powers Act 2000," http://www.legislation.gov.uk/ukpga/2000/23 (downloaded 2013).

[33] Open Rights Group, "Regulation of Investigatory Powers Act 2000/Part III," https://wiki.openrightsgroup.org/wiki/Regulation_of_Investigatory_Powers_Act_2000/Part_III#Cases Accessed 6 December 2017.

[34] M. Kumar, "Tor anonymizing network compromised by french researchers," 2011, http://thehackernews.com/2011/10/tor-anonymizing-network-compromised-by.html October 24 (downloaded April 2013).

[35] R. Lemos, "Tor hack proposed to catch criminals," http://www.securityfocus.com/news/11447 SecurityFocus 2007-03-08 (downloaded April 2013).

[36] "TOR," Online,https://www.torproject.org/ (downloaded April 2013).

[37] W. Van Eck, "Electromagnetic radiation from video display units: An eavesdropping risk?" Computers & Security, vol. 4, no. 4, 1985, pp. 269–286.

[38] R. Divya and S. Muthukumarasamy, "An impervious qr-based visual authentication protocols to prevent black-bag cryptanalysis," in Intelligent Systems and Control (ISCO), 2015 IEEE 9th International Conference on. IEEE, 2015, pp. 1–6.

[39] E. Kenneally, "Confluence of digital evidence and the law: On the forensic soundness of live-remote digital evidence collection." 2005, sSRN Papers https://papers.ssrn.com/sol3/papers.cfm?abstract_id=2145647 Accessed 6 December 2017.

[40] "Technical notes, my online memory," undated, http://ilostmynotes.blogspot.co.uk/2012/01/firewire-and-dma-attacks-on-os-x.html Accessed 7 December 2017.

[41] R. Rowlingson, "A ten step process for forensic readiness," International Journal of Digital Evidence, vol. 2, no. 3, 2004, pp. 1–28.

[42] A. Poulter, I. Ferguson, D. McMenemy, and R. Glassey, "Question: Where would you go to escape detection if you wanted to do something illegal on the Internet? Hint: Shush!" Global Security, Safety, and Sustainability, 2009, pp. 1–8.

[43] F. Buchholz and E. Spafford, "On the role of file system metadata in digital forensics," Digital Investigation, vol. 1, no. 4, 2004, pp. 298–309.

[44] M. Weiser, "The computer for the 21st century." Mobile Computing and Communications Review, vol. 3, no. 3, 1999, pp. 3–11.

[45] R. Stallman, Free software, free society: Selected essays of Richard M. Stallman. Lulu.com, 2002.

[46] J. M. Oberding and T. Norderhaug, "A separate jurisdiction for cyberspace," Journal of Computer-Mediated Communication, vol. 2, no. 1, 1996, pp. 0–0.

[47] D. G. Johnson, "Is the global information infrastructure a democratic technology?" ACM SIGCAS Computers and Society, vol. 27, no. 3, 1997, pp. 20–26.

Intruder Detection through Pattern Matching and Provenance Driven Data Recovery

Anthony Chapman
Computing Science
University of Aberdeen
Aberdeen, UK
Email: r01ac14@abdn.ac.uk

***Abstract*—Intruder detection and recovering tampered data is challenging enough without the added complexity of the cloud or the forthcoming EU General Data Protection Regulation (GDPR), which will put greater pressure on companies to strengthen their cyber security or potentially face large fines. Intruder breach reporting and forensic analysis needs to drastically improve in order to avoid these potentially catastrophic fines. We conducted a conceptual exploration of intruder detection and data recovery methods. This paper aims to encourage further research for effective cloud security assurance with a focus on increased protection from tough legislation, such as complying with the forthcoming GDPR. We propose a framework which uses pattern matching to identify tampered data, provenance models for data assurance and audit trails to recover original data.**

***Keywords*—Cloud Security; Audit; Provenance; Tamper Detection; Data Recovery; GDPR**

I. INTRODUCTION

CLOUD computing research has experienced a surge of interest in recent years. Unfortunately, cloud security has advanced at a slower pace than other aspects of cloud systems and given the changes soon to affect the cloud security community, namely the EU GDPR [1], more of our attention must be directed to improve cloud security.

Recent reports have noticed a significant reduction in the global average time between a security breach and reporting a detection to just under 3 weeks in 2016 [2] compared to 1 month in 2015 [3] or 6 months in 2012 [4]. Although this is a significant improvement, in order to comply with the forthcoming GDPR, reporting of a breach must take place within 72 hours of discovery [1]. From this, it is clear that many enterprises will be unable to comply with the requirement to report any and all breaches within 72 hours of detection. It also suggests that system monitoring is not being done properly [5].

The new GDPR, applying in the UK from 25 May 2018 [1], aims to encourage firms to protect their client's personal data by penalising those with inefficient security measures. One of the stronger encouragement measures is fining companies that do not report breaches within 72 hours of discovery. The report should include what the intruder was looking at, what was tampered with, what was deleted and what was stolen. Many companies will struggle to meet this requirement because of the loss of vital forensic records. The longer an intruder remains inside a system undetected, the more damage they can do. The short reporting time (compared to the current average of 3 weeks) could hopefully reduce the amount of damage an intruder is able to do; the sooner a breach is detected and reported.

Detecting and reporting breaches as soon as they happen needs to be at the forefront of security for compliance with the new regulations. There is also a clear, outstanding need for a specified policy to control and track data as it flows throughout cloud infrastructure. This is to ensure that data custodians are meeting their obligations [6].

Corporate governance rules are also constantly changing. The emphasis of these changes are to place more on responsibility and accountability [7], social conscience [8], sustainability [9], [10], resilience [11] and ethics [12] on companies and data custodians. These changes alongside new legislations will force traditional principles of corporate governance towards towards stricter and more robust cyber security measures. Ever evolving technologies (with increasing complexity) heighten exposure to risk, particularly if the technologies (and their potential problems) are not fully understood [13]. Thus, there is a need for a more effective approach to address these security issues.

This paper focuses on tamper detection and data recovery and is structured as follows: Section II describes the motivations, implications and background related to this research. Section III describes the proposed framework and Section IV gives a breakdown of the benefits the framework could have on a system. The remaining sections consist of a discussion, which includes limitations, in Section V, and finally, a conclusion and future work in Section VI.

II. MOTIVATION & BACKGROUND

The new GDPR will displace some pressure from the customers to the data custodians. Although this is positive for customers, the companies who own the data need to radically improve breach detection and reporting as they will be held accountable for any and all unreported security breaches.

A. *Implications*

Intruders within a system have the potential to illegally access, modify, delete and/or extract data. Any of which could financially harm a company as well as damage their reputation [14]. Regulations, such as GDPR, encourage firms to protect personal data by penalising those not seen to be doing so properly.

Post-attack business continuity measures are paramount in minimizing intruder damage [15]. Unfortunately, pre-attack measures (intruder deterrents) have received a lot more academic attention than post-attack measures (data recovery, forensic trails, etc.). Simple post-attack methods such as data recovery through regular back-ups could cause more damage if not done with care. For example, if a safe back-up is updated with unsafe (tampered) data. This can occur for a number of reasons, for instance if tampering is not detected prior to a back-up being taken, it may then be impossible to recover the original data.

The vast majority of financial institutions in the UK are woefully under-prepared to comply with the forthcoming GDPR. Current estimates suggest that UK banks could potentially suffer fines in the first year alone of over €5 Billion [16]. Campbell et al. [17] and Farrow et al. [18] have investigated the impact cyber breaches will have on the stock market value of firms with varying results. They found that the significance and the effect breaches will have is likely to be evolving over time.

Chow et al [19] also consider some implications and discuss difficulties with cloud auditing. They found that cloud doubts largely stem from the perceived loss of control of sensitive data and that current control measures do not address cloud's third party data storage and processing requirements adequately. They also express the likelihood of problems arising from over relying on cloud computing.

Having back-up data could help recover tampered data, unfortunately, it might not be efficient for companies with large amounts of data to store them. Even in cases where back-up data is kept, the intruder may still be able to access it also. Assuming the intruder tampers with a small part of the data, how can we: 1. locate the tampered data and 2. recover the original data?

Duncan and Whittington [20] explore checklists within various fields (medicine and accounting) and examine problems that are inherent with checklists in order to identify strategies that might be adopted by cloud computing to improve efficiency. One benefit found is that checklists enable systems to conform with standards, but note that this does not guarantee improved security. One drawback from checklists is that it may "deny an experienced practitioner the opportunity to develop a rounded understanding of the situation by being forced to focus on the individual trees rather than the wood as a whole".

B. Audit Trail

Audit trails are a fundamental part of accounting and finance, they provide assurance that company managers have presented a "true and fair" view of a companys financial performance and position, underpinning the trust and obligation of stewardship between company management and the owners of the company [21]. Accounting audit can be extended to IT audit, and further to cloud audit, where rather than treat the IT systems as black box components of the company systems, the IT systems themselves are audited to provide assurance that they are capable of delivering what is needed by the company [22].

An area of weakness arises when taking audit professionals from the accounting world out of their comfort zone, and placing them in a more technical field. Whilst the use of people with a computing background can overcome some of these issues, their lack of audit background presents another weakness [23]. Clearly further research is needed in this area [24].

Cloud adoption has not been straight forward either. This may be due to difficulties within cloud audit [25] as well as the possible belief that trust and privacy issues [26]–[29] also need further work before cloud auditing is achieved. A common theme is the recognition that cloud audit is far harder to perform than audit of non-cloud systems.

Forensic audit is used when fraud is discovered, to find and collect suitable evidence for presentation in a court case, whether criminal or civil. This can be extended to IT audit forensic trails which could be used to trace the acts of an intruder or backtrack the steps a system has taken when an error has occurred. This way, we may be able to identify errors and/or see what an intruder may have been interested in [30].

Greater accountability, and particularly a broadening of the scope of Service Level Agreements (SLAs) have been considered as a way to enhance cloud security and privacy. Achieving cloud accountability is a complex challenge; as we now have to consider large-scale virtual and physical distributed server environments to achieve (1) real-time tracing of source and duplicate file locations, (2) logging of a files life cycle, and (3) logging of content modification and access history [31].

C. Data Provenance

Data provenance (also referred as data lineage or pedigree) was introduced to better understand the origins of data within databases [32], [33]. Whole system provenance goes further, it gives the complete picture of a system, from initialisation to shutdown, by tracking metadata and transient system objects [34]. Provenance alone is not enough to detect an intruder in a system, so further components will need to be in play in order to identify a breach [35].

Like auditing, provenance is not well researched within the computing community. One of the reasons why it may not receive so much attention could be that provenance information cannot be trusted unless its integrity is assured. Moreover, provenance must be protected differently than regular data [36]. The fact that provenance models are fairly novel added to the large initial effort required to implement such a system to work within a current firm may be deterring companies from using such models.

Another issue which plagues both auditing and provenance is that the benefits do not become apparent during profitable and calm periods of business. They only appear when something (a security breach, an accounting error, etc.) disrupted normal working procedures or an unwanted result has been reported. Of course, by the time a company realises it might need provenance or auditing it will be too late.

Provenance is currently being used to create models which may be able to distinguish between legitimate and illegitimate behaviour in applications on a large cluster of machines [37]. The model could be extended for data recovery by restoring the data to a pre-breach safe state, the system could then carry out any operations it carried out during the breach to update the system to the desired state. One drawback from this method could be that the data recovery might not justify the potentially large computational expense; if only a small amount of data is tampered with, the whole system will have to be restored, not just the tampered data.

D. Tampered Data Detection

Current tampered data detection focuses on either time stamping [38] or system calls and activity logging [39]. Although both could be used to detect breaches, hackers may be able to access the time stamp files or activity files and remove or alter the activities during a breach. Through forensic analysis, it may be possible to determine when the tampering occurred, what data was tampered with, and perhaps who did the tampering [40].

A complementary soft security solution relying on detecting behavioural anomalies by evidence theory is proposed [41] and although this approach could identify anomalous behaviour as it is happening, it may not identify tampered data. Another possible limitation in such a system could be a lack of backtracking. If a behavioural anomaly is not detected, the damage caused may go unnoticed and may cause future problems without the ability to revert them.

By maintaining an audit log in the background of a system and using cryptographic techniques to ensure that any alterations to entries in the log are stored, we may be able detect unwanted tampering [42]. Unfortunately, such a system could easily become computationally expensive and may not be necessarily viable for large systems, especially if the larger system requires quick processing as this might be affected by the constant monitoring of the audit logs.

A method was proposed for secure logging which relied on secure keys between the logging machines [43]. Two major flaws were detected: (1) truncation attack (a special kind of deletion attack whereby the attacker deletes a contiguous subset of tail-end log entries) and (2) delayed detection attack (Where the system uses an old log file to verify current actions, an intruder could delete a file the system doesn't know exists yet) [44]. Both of which could seriously damage a system unless other mechanisms are in place to reinforce the system's weaknesses.

E. Data Recovery

Forensic trails are at the forefront of data recovery [45], from an efficient auditing system we may be able to find what was looked at, what was modified, what was deleted and possibly how it all happened. With auditing, it is possible to demonstrate compliance with data management policy and/or provide forensic data to determine the cause of any unintended data disclosure [6]. An intruder's objective, once they are embedded within a cloud system, will be to edit or delete forensic data in order to conceal their behaviour and avoid being detected.

Immutable data logging [5] is one part of an audit system which could greatly benefit a system. The advantage of being able to store every movement within a system has to be balanced against the large amount of memory required to store such movements. Another issue arises if an intruder finds a way to tamper with the logging files. If the system relies on the logging files and they are tampered with, then an intruder might be able to conceal their actions long enough to carry out whatever actions they want on the system without being detected.

System calls, storing keystroke and deletion requests are other aspects of an audit system that could be used to recover tampered data. Again, similar to immutable data logs, they can be computationally expensive and may cause greater harm if not used with care. These methods should be used within auditing systems but should be used with other methods in order to provide a complete system. Over relying on parts of auditing could cause more harm than good as aforementioned.

III. Proposed Framework

The proposed framework can be split into two stages. The first stage is tamper detection, this stage will determine where an intruder has breached the system and what data has been tampered with. The first stage will help firms comply with the GDPR breach reporting policy and help avoid potentially large fines which could cripple a company.

The second stage may undo the intruder's damage by recovering the original data through provenance and audit trails. This stage works alongside the first stage by identifying which data has been tampered with and focusing on that data, thus not having to waste computing power recovering non-tampered data.

```
ranges ← initialise pattern model ;
for every day do
    compare model range with data;
    if data within range then
        no breach ;
        update pattern model ;
    else if data outside range then
        investigate ;
        if tamper detected then
            report breach ;
            recover tampered data ;
        else if data untampered then
            update pattern model ;
end
```

Algorithm 1: Pseudo code for tamper detection. This pseudo code is designed to run on a single piece of data, for multiple datasets we can run the system on them individually creating custom ranges. The time between runs can vary according to different needs, we have used "every day" as an example.

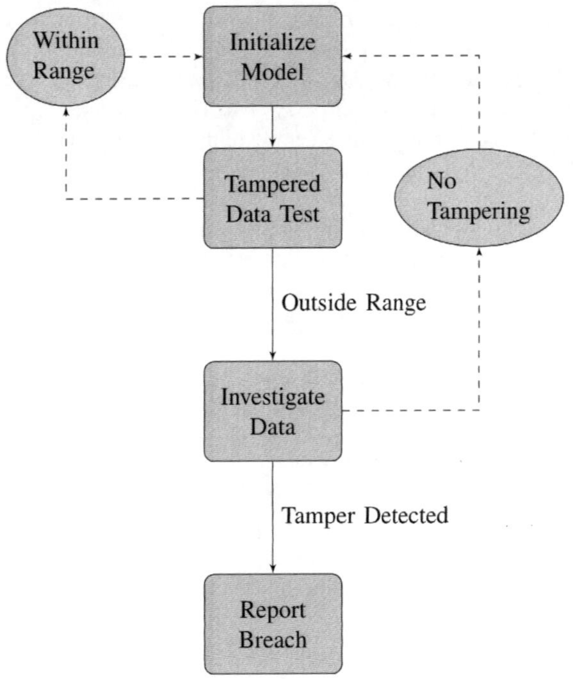

Fig. 1. Tamper detection flowchart.

A. *Tamper Detection*

Missing data prediction (imputation) uses statistical models to predict missing data based on the observed data [46]. These models create a range of possible values for every missing entry. Using this range they impute the missing values and account for uncertainty by running multiple times with a specified probability distribution [47].

We can adapt these methods to create the relationship models and ranges as it would normally do and then use these ranges to compare against the data. We could then identify whether any data falls outside their respective range and investigate whether it has been tampered with or not.

Firstly, we will create an initial model and ranges from the data by creating regression models for every data type, this will create the initial ranges and they will change as the system progresses over time. The initial ranges will be created using data already in the system. Using the initial model and ranges we can then compare, after a chosen time period (i.e. every 12 hours), the ranges from the initial data to the data currently in the system, as shown in Figure 1.

Notice that within the chosen time period, the data will have changed, if the data is within the range, then no tampering has been detected and we can recalculate the model (to include the the new data) and create new ranges. If any data falls outside the range, we should investigate the data and decide whether it has been tampered with or not. If it has, go to stage two (the data recovery stage) and then recalculate a new model and ranges after any tampered data has been recovered.

B. *Data Recovery*

Once tampered data has been detected we must recover the original data. Data provenance models and audit trails could work together to recover tampered data. The provenance models could provide assured data by stating a safe stage that can be trusted by the system. Once the assured data is ready, we can use auditing trails to recreate the original data by applying procedures that occurred between the assured data stage and the tampered data detection.

There are different ways to tackle this problem; one way would use the tamper detection model (the first stage of the framework) to identify which data has been tampered. Doing so will mean we can recover only the tampered data and not have to use unnecessary computing power on the rest of the dataset. Alternatively, we could use all of the assured data and all of the audit trails to recreate the complete data from the time of assured data to present, tamper detection, time. This method would make sure all tampered data during that period is recovered and it is less likely that any tampered data will be missed.

Pasquier et al. [48] proposed an approach based on Information Flow Control (IFC) that allows: (1) the continuous, end-to-end enforcement of data flow policy, and (2) the generation of provenance-like audit logs to demonstrate policy adherence and contractual/regulatory compliance. We can also extend this work to provide data-centric audit logs akin to provenance metadata in a format in which analyses can easily be automated.

IV. Framework Benefits

The proposed framework may be able to not only detect whether data has been tampered with but also locate the tampered data. By locating the tampered data, the system will be able to minimize computing powered required to recover tampered data. This may enable us to only work on the tampered data and not have to use more computing power than necessary dealing with the whole dataset.

Reporting time may be greatly reduced by discovering that your system has been breached. The time between breach and discovery may be reduced by running the tamper checking software on a regular basis. This may enable companies to comply with GDPR's 72 hour breach discovery reporting. Reducing the time from breach to discovery may also reduce the risk of companies having to pay large fines for non-compliance with increasingly strict regulations and also better protect personal and confidential data.

Once tampered data has been detected, the original data can be recreated through provenance and auditing. Being able to re-create data may remove or minimize the need for large data backups, thus reducing memory and hardware required.

Potentially, depending on the size of the data and computing power available, this system could be run daily or even a few times a day. Doing so will enable intruder detection at a daily or even hourly rate, hugely reducing the time it takes to detect an intruder after the system has been breached.

The audit models within the system maybe provide essential forensic data which may improve a company's security and potentially our understanding of the intruder's intentions. Through audit trails, we may be able to see how the intruder infiltrated the system and whether any data was stolen. This, of course, will help firms comply with the new GDPR.

V. Discussion & Limitations

Our proposed framework focuses on detecting (as opposed to preventing) breaches and recovering tampered data. Research regarding breach prevention is crucial to cloud security and having methods to cope with breaches, when preventions mechanisms fail, will only strengthen systems. Tamper prevention mechanisms include user monitoring and anomalous behavior detection [21]. System calls can also be used to ensure the credibility of logged data [49], they could also be used to detect intruders within a system as they may be analysed in order to identify the intruder's malicious intent.

Using pattern matching to detect tampered data may not detect intruders if they do not modify data. In such cases, system calls could be used to capture the intruder's path. Intruders will want to modify these calls, again this may be recognized by the models and alert the company of a security breach. By working together, pattern matching models and system calls may strengthen a system's security.

The new GDPR poses a moral dilemma for firms. The regulations state that a firm has to report a breach within 72 hours of discovery. Notice, it states within 72 hours of discovery, not 72 hours after the system is breached. It could be possible for firms to not apply intruder detection software until it affects the running of the company, thus not having to use time and money complying with GDPR unless the breach affects them. This could potentially expose or compromise personal and confidential data.

When considering the proposed framework a number of limitations were identified, the first one is the computational expense vs benefits from the framework. Businesses will have to consider whether implementing such a system will benefit them enough to justify running it. This will be especially challenging for smaller firms, which are usually (although wrongly so) less likely to be concerned about cyber attacks than larger firms. Additionally, implementing such systems may have bigger initial financial impact on smaller businesses, implying they will be less likely to want to use such systems.

A more technical limitation lies at the heart of modeling theory. Although regressions have great modeling power they also come with a pinch of uncertainty. If not done with care, the data "ranges" proposed in this paper might either overestimate or underestimate data tampering. Overestimating may produce threat warning for data when no breach has occurred, this may waste computational power, labour and ultimately, money. Underestimating may cause the converse problem and may not detect tampered data, this may lead to breaches going unnoticed and possible large fines from governing bodies such as GDPR, not to mention damage to customers whose data has been stolen.

VI. Conclusion & Future Work

This paper has identified some potential weakness which if not corrected before the new GDPR is enforced (25th May 2018 for the UK) could lead to firms being financially penalised. One problem identified is the current average time for breach detection is circa 3 weeks. This time needs to be reduced to minimize the amount of damage caused by breaches. Another problem identified is the lack of post attack coping mechanisms, specifically for rectifying tampered data. Finally we noticed a gap in research for locating tampered data and separating it from the rest of the dataset.

We proposed a framework which may be used to identify tampered data at intervals during the day to minimise the time an intruder spends within a system after they have breached it. The framework proposed includes a method for recovering tampered data in an efficient way by working only on the tampered data by minimising the computing power required to recover data. The method could also solve issues with back-up data recovery by not relying on large digital storage or potentially compromised back-ups.

The framework can be applied at different intervals according to company needs. The companies will have to decide the optimal interval for the framework which both minimizes the time between breach and discovery as well as optimising the computational power allocated for the system. Checking for tampered data too often may take up too much computing power but a large interval may delay detection. The proposed framework will enable firms to not only comply with the new GDPR but also further protect personal and/or confidential data. This is especially important since we live in a world where regulations and corporate governance rules are constantly evolving.

Finally, future investigations could be carried out to address the already discussed limitations. To minimise over and underestimation, testing scenarios should be created which will create empirical data that could be used to better understand the effects of over and underestimation. By better understanding the effects of over and under estimation, we may be able to optimise the system to efficiently detect breaches. When it comes to justifying the software to businesses of all sizes, it might be beneficial to simulate cyber attack behaviour and have user studies demonstrating how the software might work. Only by educating the users (not just financial institutions are at risk) of cyber security risks and potential financial damage posed by ever changing regulations, will they be able to make a fully informed decision on whether this type of framework is suitable for them

References

[1] ICO. (2017) Overview of the general data protection regulation (gdpr). [Online]. Available: https://ico.org.uk/for-organisations/data-protection-reform/overview-of-the-gdpr/ [Last Accessed: 22 Dec 2017]

[2] Verizon, "2016 data breach investigations report," 2016.

[3] Verizon, "2015 data breach investigations report," 2015.

[4] Verizon, "2012 data breach investigations report," 2012.

[5] R. A. K. Duncan and M. Whittington, "Creating an immutable database for secure cloud audit trail and system logging," in *Eighth International Conference on Cloud Computing, GRIDs, and Virtualization, 19 February 2017-23 February 2017, Athens, Greece*, 2017, pp. 54–59.

[6] T. F.-M. Pasquier, J. Singh, J. Bacon, and D. Eyers, "Information flow audit for paas clouds," in *Cloud Engineering (IC2E), 2016 IEEE International Conference on*. IEEE, 2016, pp. 42–51.

[7] M. Huse, "Accountability and creating accountability: a framework for exploring behavioural perspectives of corporate governance," *Brit J. Mgt*, 2005, pp. 65–79.

[8] A. Gil, "Corporate governance as social responsibility : A research agenda," *Berkeley J. Intl L.*, 2008, pp. 452–478.

[9] C. Ioannidis, "Sustainability in information stewardship: Time preferences, externalities and social co-ordination," *WEIS 2013*, 2013.

[10] A. Kolk, "Sustainability, accountability and corporate governance: Exploring multinationals reporting practices," *Business Strategy and the Environment*, 2008, pp. 1–15.

[11] F. S. Chapin, "Principles of ecosystem stewardship: Resilience-based natural resource management in a changing world," *Springer*, 2009.

[12] S. Arjoon, "Corporate governance: An ethical perspective," *J. Bus Ethics*, 2005, pp. 343–352.

[13] E. Zio, "Reliability engineering: Old problems and new challenges," *Reliability Engineering & System Safety*, 2009, pp. 125–141.

[14] L. A. Gordon, M. P. Loeb, W. Lucyshyn, and L. Zhou, "Increasing cybersecurity investments in private sector firms," *Journal of Cybersecurity*, vol. 1, no. 1, pp. 3–17, 2015.

[15] J. Singh, T. Pasquier, J. Bacon, H. Ko, and D. Eyers, "Twenty security considerations for cloud-supported internet of things," *IEEE Internet of Things Journal*, vol. 3, no. 3, pp. 269–284, 2016.

[16] P. Tobin, M. McKeever, J. Blackledge, M. Whittington, and B. Duncan, "UK Financial Institutions Stand to Lose Billions in GDPR Fines: How can They Mitigate This?" in *Br. Account. Financ. Assoc. Scottish Area Gr. Annu. Conf.*, BAFA, Ed., 2017, p. 6.

[17] K. Campbell, L. A. Gordon, M. P. Loeb, and L. Zhou, "The economic cost of publicly announced information security breaches: empirical evidence from the stock market," *Journal of Computer Security*, vol. 11, no. 3, pp. 431–448, 2003.

[18] S. Farrow and J. Szanton, "Cybersecurity investment guidance: Extensions of the gordon and leob model."*Journal of Information Security*,vol. 7, no. 2, pp. 15, 2016.

[19] R. Chow et al., "Controlling data in the cloud: outsourcing computation without outsourcing control," in *Proceedings of the 2009 ACM workshop on Cloud computing security*. ACM, 2009, pp. 85–90.

[20] B. Duncan and M. Whittington, "Reflecting on whether checklists can tick the box for cloud security," in *Cloud Computing Technology and Science (CloudCom), 2014 IEEE 6th International Conference on*. IEEE, 2014, pp. 805–810.

[21] M. Neovius and B. Duncan, "Anomaly Detection for Soft Security in Cloud based Auditing of Accounting Systems," in *Closer 2017 - 7th Int. Conf. Cloud Comput. Serv. Sci.*, 2017, pp. 1–8.

[22] B. Duncan and M. Whittington, "Compliance with standards, assurance and audit: Does this equal security?" in *Proceedings of the 7th International Conference on Security of Information and Networks*. ACM, 2014, p. 77.

[23] B. Duncan and M. Whittington, "Enhancing cloud security and privacy: broadening the service level agreement," in *Trustcom/BigDataSE/ISPA, 2015 IEEE*, vol. 1. IEEE, 2015, pp. 1088–1093.

[24] R. A. K. Duncan and M. Whittington, "Enhancing cloud security and privacy: the power and the weakness of the audit trail," *Cloud Computing 2016*, 2016.

[25] H. S. Herath and T. C. Herath, "It security auditing: A performance evaluation decision model," *Decision Support Systems*, vol. 57, pp. 54–63, 2014.

[26] R. K. Ko, P. Jagadpramana, and B. S. Lee, "Flogger: A file-centric logger for monitoring file access and transfers within cloud computing environments," in *Trust, Security and Privacy in Computing and Communications (TrustCom), 2011 IEEE 10th International Conference on*. IEEE, 2011, pp. 765–771.

[27] R. K. Ko, B. S. Lee, and S. Pearson, "Towards achieving accountability, auditability and trust in cloud computing," *Advances in Computing and Communications*, pp. 432–444, 2011.

[28] S. Pearson, "Taking account of privacy when designing cloud computing services," in *Proceedings of the 2009 ICSE Workshop on Software Engineering Challenges of Cloud Computing*. IEEE Computer Society, 2009, pp. 44–52.

[29] S. Pearson and A. Benameur, "Privacy, security and trust issues arising from cloud computing," in *Cloud Computing Technology and Science (CloudCom), 2010 IEEE Second International Conference on*. IEEE, 2010, pp. 693–702.

[30] B. Duncan, "Enhancing cloud security and privacy: The cloud audit problem," *The Seventh International Conference on Cloud Computing, GRIDs, and Virtualization*, 2016.

[31] R. K. L. Ko, B. S. Lee, and S. Pearson, "Towards achieving accountability, auditability and trust in cloud computing," *Commun. Comput. Inf. Sci.*, vol. 193 CCIS, pp. 432–444, 2011.

[32] P. Buneman, S. Khanna, and W. C. Tan, "Why and where: A characterization of data provenance." Springer.

[33] A. Woodruff and M. Stonebraker, "Supporting fine-grained data lineage in a database visualization environment," in *Data Engineering, 1997. Proceedings. 13th International Conference on*. IEEE, 1997, pp. 91–102.

[34] T. Pasquier et al., "Practical whole-system provenance capture," in *Proceedings of the 2017 Symposium on Cloud Computing*. 2017, pp. 405–418.

[35] T. Pasquier et al., "Data provenance to audit compliance with privacy policy in the internet of things," *Personal and Ubiquitous Computing*, pp. 1–12, 2017.

[36] A. Bates, B. Mood, M. Valafar, and K. Butler, "Towards secure provenance-based access control in cloud environments," in *Proceedings of the third ACM conference on Data and application security and privacy*. ACM, 2013, pp. 277–284.

[37] X. Han et al., "Frappuccino: Fault-detection through runtime analysis of provenance,". 2017.

[38] A. Imran, N. Nahar, and K. Sakib, "Watchword-oriented and time-stamped algorithms for tamper-proof cloud provenance cognition," in *Informatics, Electronics & Vision (ICIEV), 2014 International Conference on*. IEEE, 2014, pp. 1–6.

[39] H. Nguyen et al., "Cloud-based secure logger for medical devices," in *Connected Health: Applications, Systems and Engineering Technologies (CHASE), 2016 IEEE First International Conference on*. IEEE, 2016, pp. 89–94.

[40] K. E. Pavlou and R. T. Snodgrass, "Forensic Analysis of Database Tampering," *ACM Trans. Database Syst.*, vol. 33, no. 4, pp. 30:1–30:47, nov 2008.

[41] M. Neovius and B. Duncan, "Anomaly detection for soft security in cloud based auditing of accounting systems," in *Proceedings of the 7th International Conference on Cloud Computing and Services Science*. SciTePress, 2017.

[42] R. T. Snodgrass, S. S. Yao, and C. Collberg, "Tamper detection in audit logs," in *Proceedings of the Thirtieth international conference on Very large data bases-Volume 30*. VLDB Endowment, 2004, pp. 504–515.

[43] B. Schneier and J. Kelsey, "Secure audit logs to support computer forensics," *ACM Transactions on Information and System Security (TISSEC)*, vol. 2, no. 2, pp. 159–176, 1999.

[44] D. Ma and G. Tsudik, "A new approach to secure logging," *ACM Transactions on Storage (TOS)*, vol. 5, no. 1, p. 2, 2009.

[45] S. Thorpe et al., "Towards a forensic-based service oriented architecture framework for auditing of cloud logs," in *Services (SERVICES), 203 IEEE Ninth World Congress on*. IEEE, 2013, pp. 75–83.

[46] D. McNeish, "Missing data methods for arbitrary missingness with small samples," *Journal of Applied Statistics*, vol. 44, no. 1, pp. 24–39, 2017.

[47] S. van Buuren and K. Groothuis-Oudshoorn, "mice: Multivariate imputation by chained equations in r," *Journal of Statistical Software*, vol. 45, no. 3, pp. 1–67, 2011

[48] T. F.-M. Pasquier, J. Singh, and J. Bacon, "Clouds of things need information flow control with hardware roots of trust," in *Cloud Computing Technology and Science (CloudCom), 2015 IEEE 7th International Conference on*. IEEE, 2015, pp. 467–470.

[49] G. R. Weir and A. Aßmuth, "Strategies for intrusion monitoring in cloud services," in *The Eighth International Conference on Cloud Computing, GRIDs, and Virtualization*, 2017, pp. 1–5.

Establishing Situational Awareness for Securing Healthcare Patient Records

Aaron Boddy, William Hurst, Michael Mackay, Abdennour El Rhalibi
Department of Computer Science
Liverpool John Moores University
James Parsons Building, Byrom Street
Liverpool, UK, L3 3AF
Email: A.Boddy@2011.ljmu.ac.uk; {W.Hurst, M.I.Mackay, A.Elrhalibi}@ljmu.ac.uk

Abstract— **The healthcare sector is an appealing target to attackers due to the high value of patient data on the black market. Patient data can be profitable to illegal actors either through direct sale or extortion by ransom. Additionally, employees present a persistent threat as they are able to access the data of almost any patient without reprimand. Without proactive monitoring of audit records, data breaches go undetected and employee behaviour is not deterred. In 2016, 450 data breaches occurred affecting more than 27 million patient records. 26.8% of these breaches were due to hacking and ransomware. In May 2017, a global ransomware campaign adversely affected approximately 48 UK hospitals. Response to this attack, named WannaCry, resulted in hospital networks being taken offline, and non-emergency patients being refused care. Hospitals must maintain patient trust and ensure that the information security principles of Integrity, Availability and Confidentiality are applied to Electronic Patient Record EPR data. With over 83% of hospitals adopting EPRs, access to healthcare data needs to be monitored proactively for malicious activity. Therefore, this paper presents research towards a system that uses advanced data analytics techniques to profile user's behaviour in order to identify patterns and anomalies. Visualisation techniques are then applied to highlight these anomalies to aid the situational awareness of patient privacy officers within healthcare infrastructures.**

Keywords-*Electronic Patient Records; Patient Privacy; Patient Confidentiality; Information Security; Data Analysis; Visualisation; Healthcare Infrastructures.***

I. INTRODUCTION

Healthcare infrastructures are complacent towards the risks of patient privacy violations [1]. Reduced information visibility due to data complexity, fragmentation, interoperability and lack of specialisation undermine the security of these organisations [1]. Visualisation techniques can provide both awareness and modelling capabilities for critical infrastructures [2]. Applying these techniques to aids the understanding of how patient data is accessed within healthcare infrastructures. The goal of security engineers is to develop tools capable of detecting malicious, multi-stage intrusion attacks. These tools should weight the individual attacks, and compare them against the enormous and disparate database of attacks within the network [3]. An intruder's objectives should be determined based on the analysis of the entire dataset of attacks as a whole, rather than just an individual attack [3].

Electronic Patient Record (EPR) systems are vulnerable to both insider and outsider threats [4]. A potential insider threat refers to a legitimate user looking at data when it is not appropriate to do so; such as looking at the record of a celebrity. An external threat is comprised of the theft of a legitimate user's credentials, allowing the attacker uninhibited access to EPR data. This is known as an Active Persistent Threat (APT). It is, therefore, a challenge to mitigate both types of threats.

Current Rules-Based solutions to these issues are effective at detecting predictable insider threats. They can process the large quantities of audit data, and can process rules against that data. For example, a rule can be set to inform Information Security if anyone other than a set list of clinicians accesses the patient record of a celebrity or famous individual. Any violation of this will then be reported automatically to the Information Security team. However, this cannot detect the threat of an attacker who has acquired the logon credentials of a clinician; which is achieved through either phishing or social engineering techniques and enables EPR data exfiltration. Additionally, rules are also be set to detect if a user is looking at the record of a patient with the same surname as them to identify potential patient confidentiality violations. Similarly, if an attacker has unauthorised login credentials (and is surveying a patient's record) the rules set would not make provisions for the detection.

Therefore, this paper proposes an advanced data analytics and visualisation-based approach to patient privacy violation detection within EPR systems. Advanced data analytics algorithms have the capability to learn patterns of data and profile users' behaviour, which can then be represented visually. Advanced data analytics detect when a user's behaviour has changed, by comparing behaviours, such as the type of actions being taken and the patients they are viewing.

It is unfeasible to detect fully all illegitimate access within EPR systems, but it is feasible to eliminate legitimate access. In doing so, it becomes possible to focus the attention of information security analysts to where it is needed, within the comprehensive EPR audit datasets.

The remainder of this paper is as follows. Section II presents a literature review of the background research on patient privacy within EPR systems. Section III outlines the systematic approach and presents our results and a sample of test data. Section IV discusses conclusions and the future work to be done.

II. Background

Authorised users can access EPR data from virtually anywhere; allowing increased productivity compared with paper-only records and allowing clinicians to make informed decisions towards improving healthcare quality for patients [5]. The management of patient data in electronic form decreases healthcare administration costs, strengthens care provider productivity and increases patient safety [6].

The proliferation of technology within healthcare has brought the advantages of improved efficiency of record keeping, easier detection and prevention of fraud, waste and abuse, and an improvement on the overall quality of care [7]. However, with the added benefits of technology in healthcare, the potential for unauthorised and illegal access to patient information has increased [8]. Users may abuse their privileges for personal reasons, such as viewing records of relatives, friends, neighbours, co-workers or celebrities [5]. Therefore, patients are becoming increasingly concerned regarding the privacy and security of their health data [9]. The cost to a healthcare organisation caused by a security breach is one of the highest of any industry and leads to the loss of trust of patients [10].

A. *EPR Audit Logs*

When there is reason to suspect that unauthorised accesses have occurred, a review of the audit logs is undertaken by a security expert. This is inefficient, as it requires the information to be collated and reviewed by a security expert. It is a process that is purely retrospective [5]. Therefore, there is a motivation to automate and alleviate the burdens associated with this process [7]. The fundamental limitations in privacy officers manually reviewing audit logs for potentially suspicious accesses are threefold [5]. Firstly, the volume of audit records means that audit logs are only practically useful as adjuncts to investigate suspected breaches, rather than a tool that can be utilised to proactively find inappropriate accesses. Secondly, audit records can only provide data regarding the access itself, and contains no situational or relationship information or knowledge regarding the access. Thirdly, the process is labour-intensive, without guidance of where to look for potential breaches, inappropriate accesses are buried amongst the audits of appropriate accesses.

B. *Access Control*

Healthcare systems typically employ access control solutions [11], where once an individual has been authenticated, they are allowed unhindered access inside the perimeter [5]. It is a challenge to impose an access control policy on employees in a healthcare setting due to the dynamic and unpredictable care patterns of hospital care [7].

The Access Matrix Model (AMM) is a conceptual framework that specifies each user's permissions for each object in the system [12]. Although it allows for a thorough mapping of access rights, it does not scale well, and lacks the ability to support dynamic changes of access rights, which makes it difficult to apply to EPRs [13].

Role-Based Access Control (RBAC) maps users to roles and maps permissions to the roles [14]. Job positions within the enterprise and tasks the employees need to perform are identified, and privileges are assigned to these positions to enable the employees to accomplish their tasks [15]. Whilst more computationally tractable, RBAC roles tend to be static and inflexible, and therefore not responsive to the shifting nature of roles [16].

Attribute-Based Access Control (ABAC) provides flexible, context-aware access control through evaluating the attributes of entities, it's subject and object, the operation, and the contextual environment of the request [17]. Boolean logic can then be applied to the operational request to determine access rights. ABAC therefore allows for a higher number of discrete inputs and provides a larger, more definitive set of rules to express policies than RBAC.

Experience Based Access Management (EBAM) emphasises the accountability and use of audit data to detect illegitimate access [15]. EBAM enterprises often manually review the audit logs of VIPs to determine inappropriate accesses [18]. Break The Glass (BTG) is a policy, which allows users to override access controls in necessary instances [19]. EBAM enterprises would manually review the audit logs every time a user broke the glass [15].

Task-based Access Control (TBAC) extends the user-object relationship though the inclusion of task-based and contextual information [20]. However TBAC is limited to contexts that relate to tasks, or workflow progress and EPRs cannot always be easily portioned into tasks [13].

Team-based Access Control (TeBAC) groups users in an organisation and associates a collaboration context with the activity to be performed [21]. However, these models have not been fully developed or implemented and it remains unclear how to implement them within a dynamic framework [13].

C. *Detection Approaches*

The following section examines several related common detection approaches to anomaly detection in large datasets:

- Signature detection is a rules-based algorithm that constructs a set of rules based on historic breaches and can detect correctly known patterns whilst being interpretable [22]. However, it cannot detect unseen patterns and cannot assign risk scores [23].
- Anomaly detection compares incoming instances to previously built profiles and can detect novel patterns, although it requires a large quantity of historic data [24]. Additionally, the output is known to be problematic to interpret and the technique produces false positives [25].
- Clustering is invoked to integrate similar data instances into groups [26]. Clustering evaluates each instance with respect to the cluster it belongs to, while nearest neighbour analyses each instance with respect to its own local neighbourhood [13].
- Spectral Projection estimates the principal components from the covariance of the training data of normal events [27]. The testing phase compares each point with the components and assigns an anomaly score based on the points distance from the principal components [13].

- Classifier detection determines a classification function based on a labelled training set [28] and can be fast, accurate and assign risk scores to all events [29]. However, acquiring class labelled data is expensive and scoring unlabelled events is important in large scale data mining, as human validation is limited and costly [30].

D. Related Work

Machine learning models are trained on historical access data to classify future data access patterns [7]. Supervised machine learning models, such as Support Vector Machines (SVMs), linear regression and logistic regression have been applied successfully to the challenge of detecting inappropriate access within Electronic Patient Record systems [5][7][10].

For example, Community-based Anomaly Detection System (CADS) is an unsupervised learning framework to detect insider threats based on information recorded in audit logs of collaborative environments [13]. It is based on the observation that typical users tend to form community structures, so users with a low connection, to such communities, are indicative of anomalous behaviour. The model consists of two primary components. Firstly, relational pattern extraction, which infers community structures from access logs and subsequently derives communities, which serve as the CADS core. Secondly, potentially illicit behaviour, where CADS uses a formal statistical model to measure the deviation of users from the inferred communities to predict which users are anomalies [13]. CADS does not implement supervised learning techniques to further classify the data with feedback from patient privacy officers.

AI^2 is another example of a cyber-security machine learning system, which improves its accuracy over time through feedback from security analysts [31]. AI^2 is composed of the following four components. Firstly, a Big Data Processing System, which quantifies the behaviours and features of raw data. Secondly, an Outlier Detection System, which learns a descriptive model of data features extracted via unsupervised learning, using either density, matrix decomposition, or replicator neural networks. Thirdly, a Feedback Mechanism and Continuous Learning, which incorporates analyst input through a user interface. The system highlights the top *k* outlier events or entities and tasks the analyst with identifying whether they are malicious; the feedback is then input back into the supervised learning module. Fourthly, a Supervised Learning Model, which predicts whether a new incoming event is normal or malicious, and uses analysts feedback to refines the model. Raw data is input into AI^2 that computes features describing the entities of the data set. Using these features, an unsupervised machine learning module identifies extreme and rare events in the data. These events are then ranked based upon a predefined metric and presented to the analyst, who ranks the behaviours as normal or malicious (and as pertaining to a particular attack type). Finally, these labels are input to the supervised learning module. The novelty of the system proposed in this paper, to that of AI^2, is the addition of visualisation techniques to aid the analyst to understand and explore the data. There is also a specific focus on EPR data, which differ from other enterprise infrastructures due to their reliance on insecure medical devices, legacy systems, and bespoke software.

The use of statistical and machine learning techniques have previously been used to detect fraud in financial reporting [32], to detect fraud in credit card transaction data [33], to construct a spam email detector [34], and to solve a fraud detection problem at a car insurance company [35].

III. Approach

As the background demonstrates, there is a clear need to address the issue of lack of situational awareness on the part of information security professionals within healthcare infrastructures. In this section, an approach is put forward for analysing data within healthcare infrastructures, processing it to eliminate low-risk data points and visualising it in such a way that data anomalies become apparent. Our research to date has focused on the development of a system for modelling data flow within healthcare infrastructures [36][37]. The system assists information security officers, within healthcare organisations, to improve the situational awareness of patient data confidentiality risks.

A. Approach

The novel contribution presented in [36][37] involves the use of advanced data analytics techniques, in addition to an analyst-in-the-loop and the use of visualised attack events. Low-risk data is analysed, processed and pre-filtered using advanced data analytics techniques before the visualisation of the data. This is then visualised and presented to an analyst. The analyst then classifies events within the presented visualisation, which provides feedback to the system. Through the use of the analyst-in-the-loop both models are used to continuously defend the healthcare infrastructure against current attack vectors. The aim is to collect, process, and filter big data sets to provide users of an overall understanding of system behaviour in order to detect security breaches and general anomalies.

The system provides contextual awareness to detect anomalous behaviour within EPR audit activity. The main challenge of the work involves big data analytics to process datasets generated by healthcare infrastructures.

The system put forward in this paper combines several related data sets and presents them, in such a way, as to identify relationships between them. EPR audit data and behavioural patterns are understood, in order to assist end users in finding the potential vulnerabilities within the health care infrastructure. The data analysis techniques involve interpreting dataset patterns and identify potential on-going patient privacy violations.

The visualisations cluster together salient points and use size to indicate potential threat levels. This gives the analyst a broad overview of the current EPR security at a glance. From here, the visualisation can be interacted with, explored by the analyst to investigate the data points and find in-depth technical information about each data point. Additionally, the analyst can provide feedback to the system and rank the highlighted data points as either safe, or as pertaining to a patient privacy violation.

B. Case Study

In this section, a case study of the EPR audit data is presented. This rich dataset contains 1,007,727 rows of audit logs of every user and their EPR activity in a UK hospital over a period of 18 months (28-02-16 – 21-08-17). Each User UID, Patient UID and Device name is tokenised through isolating the unique entries and assigning each value an incrementing number. There are 1,515 unique User UIDs, 72,878 unique Patient UIDs and 2,270 unique Devices within the dataset.

The dataset consist of the following fields:

- *Date* - The date the patient record was accessed
- *Time* - The time the patient record was accessed
- *Device (Tokenised)* - The name of the device the patient record was accessed
- *User UID (Tokenised)* - A tokenised representation of the User who accessed the patient record
- *Routine* - The routine performed whilst accessing the patient record (was the record updated, was a letter printed etc.)
- *Patient UID (Tokenised)* - A tokenised representation of the patient record that was accessed
- *Duration* - The number of seconds the patient record was accessed (this number counts for as long as the record is on the screen, so may not always be an accurate reflection of how long the User was actively interacting with the data)
- *Latest Adm Date* - The date the patient was last admitted to the hospital
- *Latest Dis Date* - The date the patient was last discharged from the hospital

A snapshot of the first 10 rows in the dataset is presented in Table 1.

TABLE I. EPR AUDIT SAMPLE DATA

Date	Time	Device	User U	Routine	Patient	Durat	LocationLa	Latest Di:
28-02-16	00:00	362	865	PHA.ORD	58991	54	28-02-16	29-02-16
28-02-16	00:02	103	677	ASF	4786	13	22-07-08	22-07-08
28-02-16	00:02	103	677	ASF	4786	54	22-07-08	22-07-08
28-02-16	00:02	923	199	REC REC:	17278	77	15-02-16	15-02-16
28-02-16	00:04	103	677	ASF VH	14067	39	28-09-04	28-09-04
28-02-16	00:04	845	1489	PHA.ORD	49304	22	23-01-02	23-01-02
28-02-16	00:04	923	199	REC UK.C	62121	147	08-02-16	08-02-16
28-02-16	00:06	923	199	REC REC:	60948	165	08-01-16	08-01-16
28-02-16	00:08	775	568	NOTE	32826	75	25-01-12	25-01-12
28-02-16	00:10	393	1361	PHA.ORD	28106	49	16-08-06	16-08-06

In Figure 1, a heatmap is presented of the dataset comparing User UID to the duration of the patient record access. The graph shows that there is consistent point density of up to 47,341 in the first row of the matrix, indicating that most patient records are only accessed for fewer than 300 seconds (5 minutes). This would represent *normal* behaviour within the hospital. Representing the data as a heatmap highlights clear anomalies in the data.

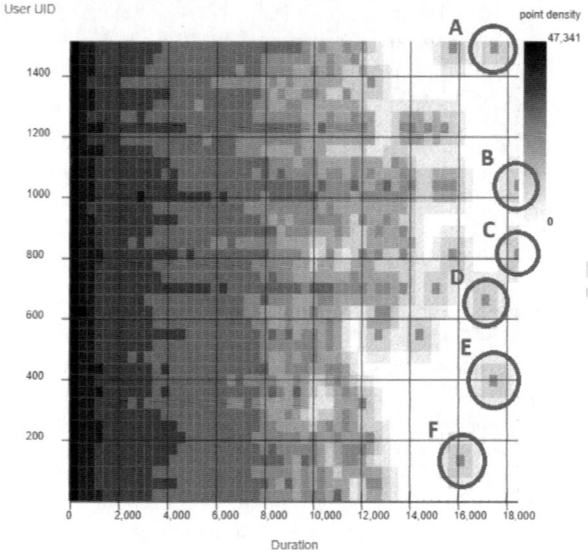

Figure 1 - Heatmap - User UID and Duration

Notably, as displayed in Figure 1, users B and C are identified spending over 18,000 seconds (over 5 hours) accessing patient records. Additionally users, A, D, E and F all spent over 16,000 seconds (almost 4.5 hours) accessing records. These anomalies can be investigated by an analyst indicating potentially illegitimate access to EPR data.

C. Discussion

These initial results display only preliminary explorations of the dataset and demonstrate the potential insights the dataset holds. Once feature selection and pre-processing work has been completed on the data, machine learning models will be used to explore the data further, with a particular emphasis on unsupervised learning such as clustering. This will allow initial patterns within the data to be identified to understand the data and identify illegitimate access to patient records within this real world EPR dataset. Extracting features from this data (such as mean, median, mode and range of duration), will be used to train classifiers to autonomously learn normal and abnormal patterns through supervised learning techniques. This process will occur once the data has been clustered through the use of unsupervised learning algorithms. In combing both unsupervised and supervised machine learning techniques, the system will aid privacy officers in their situational awareness of access to patient records and identify outliers for investigation.

IV. CONCLUSION AND FUTURE WORK

Electronic Patient Record (EPR) data is both sensitive and valuable. Patients need to be assured of three crucial security principles regarding their healthcare data. Firstly, patients need to be assured that the data stored is trustworthy and accurate. Secondly, patients need to be assured that the data can be reliably accessed by healthcare professionals when needed. And thirdly, patients need to be assured that only authorised healthcare professionals have access to the data, and only access it when it is appropriate to do so. It is therefore of utmost importance that the Information Security principles of Integrity, Availability and Confidentiality are applied to EPR data. Therefore, this paper presents research towards a system, which can detect unusual data behaviour through the use of advanced data analytics and visualisation techniques. Machine learning algorithms have the capability to learn patterns of data and profile users' behaviour, which can be represented visually. The proposed system is tailored to healthcare infrastructures by learning typical data behaviours and profiling users. The system adds to the defence-in-depth of the healthcare infrastructure by understanding the unique configuration of the EPR and autonomously analysing user's access.

Future work will build on the visualisation work undertaken in the research case studies presented in this paper. The visualisations will allow the user to explore the data and understand the patterns and trends within the comprehensive EPR audit data sets. Unsupervised machine learning techniques will be implemented to classify this data in future work as there is limited abnormal data and a lack of labelled training data. Feedback from the analysts will inform the machine learning algorithms and refine the results to reduce alert fatigue. Machine Learning algorithms will allow the system to pick up on patterns and trends in the date without being explicitly taught them, as in Rules-Based Analytics. For example, if a user typically only logs into their account on weekdays, then if the account is logged in on a weekend, it may be an indication that the users' username and password has been compromised by an attacker. The attacker could either be illegally accessing hospital records, or searching for further vulnerabilities within the EPR in order to perform a privilege escalation attack.

Additionally, the machine learning algorithms will be automated and tested on "live" real-world data once it has been refined. This will allow the process outlined in this paper to alert information security analysts of illegitimate shortly after they occur. Over time, the analyst will be able to provide feedback to the system through the use of supervised machine learning algorithms, and the algorithms will be refined and tailored to the unique threat landscape and infrastructure of the hospital.

REFERENCES

[1] J. Stoll and R. Z. Bengez, "Visual structures for seeing cyber policy strategies", in *2015 7th International Conference on Cyber Conflict: Architectures in Cyberspace*, pp. 135–152, 2015.

[2] M. Merabti, M. Kennedy, and W. Hurst, "Critical infrastructure protection: A 21st century challenge", in *2011 International Conference on Communications and Information Technology (ICCIT)*, pp. 1–6, 2011.

[3] J. J. Walker, T. Jones, and R. Blount, "Visualization, modeling and predictive analysis of cyber security attacks against cyber infrastructure-oriented systems", in *2011 IEEE International Conference on Technologies for Homeland Security (HST)*, pp. 81–85, 2011.

[4] M. Rahman and C. Kreider, "Information Security Principles for Electronic Medical Record (EMR) Systems", *AMCIS 2012 Proc.*, Jul. 2012.

[5] J. Kim *et al.*, "Anomaly and signature filtering improve classifier performance for detection of suspicious access to EHRs.", *AMIA ... Annu. Symp. proceedings. AMIA Symp.*, vol. 2011, pp. 723–31, 2011.

[6] N. Menachemi and R. G. Brooks, "Reviewing the benefits and costs of electronic health records and associated patient safety technologies.", *J. Med. Syst.*, vol. 30, no. 3, pp. 159–68, Jun. 2006.

[7] A. K. Menon, X. Jiang, J. Kim, J. Vaidya, and L. Ohno-Machado, "Detecting Inappropriate Access to Electronic Health Records Using Collaborative Filtering.", *Mach. Learn.*, vol. 95, no. 1, pp. 87–101, Apr. 2014.

[8] O. of T. A. U.S. Congress, "*Electronic Record Systems and Individual Privacy.*" (Washington, DC: Federal Government Information Technology, 1986.

[9] D. C. Kaelber, A. K. Jha, D. Johnston, B. Middleton, and D. W. Bates, "A Research Agenda for Personal Health Records (PHRs)", *J. Am. Med. Informatics Assoc.*, vol. 15, no. 6, pp. 729–736, Nov. 2008.

[10] A. A. Boxwala, J. Kim, J. M. Grillo, and L. Ohno-Machado, "Using statistical and machine learning to help institutions detect suspicious access to electronic health records", *J. Am. Med. Informatics Assoc.*, vol. 18, no. 4, pp. 498–505, Jul. 2011.

[11] D. F. Ferraiolo, R. Sandhu, S. Gavrila, D. R. Kuhn, and R. Chandramouli, "Proposed NIST standard for role-based access control", *ACM Trans. Inf. Syst. Secur.*, vol. 4, no. 3, pp. 224–274, Aug. 2001.

[12] K. Sikkel, "A Group-based Authorization Model for Cooperative Systems", in *Proceedings of the Fifth European Conference on Computer Supported Cooperative Work*, Dordrecht: Springer Netherlands, pp. 345–360, 1997.

[13] Y. Chen and B. Malin, "Detection of Anomalous Insiders in Collaborative Environments via Relational Analysis of Access Logs.", *CODASPY Proc. ... ACM Conf. data Appl. Secur. privacy. ACM Conf. Data Appl. Secur. Priv.*, vol. 2011, pp. 63–74, 2011.

[14] G.-J. Ahn, D. Shin, and L. Zhang, "Role-Based Privilege Management Using Attribute Certificates and Delegation", Springer, Berlin, Heidelberg, pp. 100–109, 2004.

[15] W. Zhang, C. A. Gunter, D. Liebovitz, J. Tian, and B. Malin, "Role prediction using Electronic Medical Record system audits.", *AMIA ... Annu. Symp. proceedings. AMIA Symp.*, vol. 2011, pp. 858–67, 2011.

[16] R. S. Sandhu, E. J. Coyne, H. L. Feinstein, and C. E. Youman, "Role-based access control models", *Computer (Long. Beach. Calif).*, vol. 29, no. 2, pp. 38–47, 1996.

[17] V. C. Hu, D. R. Kuhn, and D. F. Ferraiolo, "Attribute-Based Access Control", *Computer (Long. Beach. Calif).*, vol. 48, no. 2, pp. 85–88, Feb. 2015.

[18] Z. Zhou and B. J. Liu, "HIPAA compliant auditing system for medical images", *Comput. Med. Imaging Graph.*, vol. 29, no. 2–3, pp. 235–241, Mar. 2005.

[19] A. Ferreira *et al.*, "How to Break Access Control in a Controlled Manner", in *19th IEEE Symposium on Computer-Based Medical Systems (CBMS'06)*, pp. 847–854, 2006.

[20] T. A. Sandhu, T. A. Sandhu, and R. K. Thomas, "Task-based Authorization Controls (TBAC): A Family of Models for Active and Enterprise-oriented Authorization Management", *Proc. IFIP WG11.3 Work. DATABASE Secur. LAKE TAHOE*, pp. 166--181, 1997.

[21] C. K. Georgiadis, I. Mavridis, G. Pangalos, and R. K. Thomas, "Flexible team-based access control using contexts", in *Proceedings of the sixth ACM symposium on Access control models and technologies - SACMAT '01*, pp. 21–27, 2001.

[22] D. Barbara, *Applications of Data Mining in Computer Security*, vol. 6. Springer US, 2002.

[23] Wenke Lee, S. J. Stolfo, and K. W. Mok, "A data mining framework for building intrusion detection models", in *Proceedings of the 1999 IEEE Symposium on Security and Privacy (Cat. No.99CB36344)*, pp. 120–132, 1999.

[24] K. Das, J. Schneider, and D. B. Neill, "Anomaly pattern detection in categorical datasets", in *Proceeding of the 14th ACM SIGKDD international conference on Knowledge discovery and data mining - KDD 08*, p. 169, 2008.

[25] A. Patcha, J. Park, "An overview of anomaly detection techniques: Existing solutions and latest technological trends", *Comput. Networks*, vol. 51, no. 12, pp. 3448–3470, Aug. 2007.

[26] Z. He, X. Xu, and S. Deng, "Discovering cluster-based local outliers", *Pattern Recognit. Lett.*, vol. 24, no. 9–10, pp. 1641–1650, Jun. 2003.

[27] M.-L. Shyu, S.-C. Chen, K. Sarinnapakorn, and L. Chang, "Principal Component-based Anomaly Detection Scheme", in *Foundations and Novel Approaches in Data Mining*, Berlin/Heidelberg: Springer-Verlag, pp. 311–329, 2005.

[28] A. Shen, R. Tong, and Y. Deng, "Application of Classification Models on Credit Card Fraud Detection", in *2007 International Conference on Service Systems and Service Management*, pp. 1–4, 2007.

[29] S. Mukkamala, G. Janoski, and A. Sung, "Intrusion detection using neural networks and support vector machines", in *Proceedings of the 2002 International Joint Conference on Neural Networks. IJCNN'02 (Cat. No.02CH37290)*, pp. 1702–1707, 2002.

[30] J. Zhu, H. Wang, B. K. Tsou, and M. Ma, "Active Learning With Sampling by Uncertainty and Density for Data Annotations", *IEEE Trans. Audio. Speech. Lang. Processing*, vol. 18, no. 6, pp. 1323–1331, Aug. 2010.

[31] K. Veeramachaneni, I. Arnaldo, V. Korrapati, C. Bassias, and K. Li, "AI2: Training a Big Data Machine to Defend", in *Proceedings - 2nd IEEE International Conference on Big Data Security on Cloud, IEEE BigDataSecurity 2016, 2nd IEEE International Conference on High Performance and Smart Computing, IEEE HPSC 2016 and IEEE International Conference on Intelligent Data and S*, pp. 49–54, 2016

[32] T. B. Bell and J. V. Carcello, "A Decision Aid for Assessing the Likelihood of Fraudulent Financial Reporting", *Audit. A J. Pract. Theory*, vol. 19, no. 1, pp. 169–184, Mar. 2000.

[33] Tao Guo and Gui-Yang Li, "Neural data mining for credit card fraud detection", in *2008 International Conference on Machine Learning and Cybernetics*, pp. 3630–3634, 2008.

[34] K. Yoshida *et al.*, "Density-based spam detector", in *Proceedings of the 2004 ACM SIGKDD international conference on Knowledge discovery and data mining - KDD '04*, p. 486, 2004.

[35] J. M. Pérez, J. Muguerza, O. Arbelaitz, I. Gurrutxaga, and J. I. Martín, "Consolidated Tree Classifier Learning in a Car Insurance Fraud Detection Domain with Class Imbalance", Springer, Berlin, Heidelberg, pp. 381–389, 2005.

[36] A. Boddy, W. Hurst, M. MacKay, and A. El Rhalibi, "A Study into Detecting Anomalous Behaviours within HealthCare Infrastructures", *9th Int. Conf. Dev. eSystems Eng.*, pp111-117, 2016.

[37] A. Boddy, W. Hurst, M. Mackay, and A. El Rhalibi, "A Study into Data Analysis and Visualisation to increase the Cyber-Resilience of Healthcare Infrastructures", *Internet Things Mach. Learn.*, 2017.

Using Unikernels to Address the Cloud Forensic Problem and help Achieve EU GDPR Compliance

Bob Duncan
Computing Science
University of Aberdeen, UK
Aberdeen, UK
Email: bobduncan@abdn.ac.uk

Andreas Happe
Dept. Digital Safety & Security
Austrian Inst. of Tech. GmbH
Vienna, Austria
Email: andreas.happe@ait.ac.at

Alfred Bratterud
Dept. of Computer Science
Oslo and Akershus University
Oslo, Norway
Email: alfred.bratterud@hioa.no

***Abstract*—IT security and privacy is a challenging problem to address, and when cloud is used, there is an exponential increase in the challenge. A particular challenge is the cloud forensic problem, which arises when an attacker succeeds in breaching a cloud system, because one of the first aims is to delete the forensic trail, and there is little to prevent this from happening in cloud. Quite apart from the obvious difficulties this will present to finding out who has breached the system and how they got in, there will now be a far more pressing problem to be dealt with, namely, the forthcoming European Union General Data Protection Regulation. Once a breach has been identified, it is also necessary for the company to report the impact of the breach, to include which records were accessed, modified, deleted, or ex-filtrated, on pain of punitive levels of fine. Where the forensic trail has been compromised, this might prove to be a huge challenge to comply with. We propose addressing this problem through the use of Unikernel based monitoring systems which can ensure both full forensic and audit trails can be maintained.**

Keywords–Cloud Forensic Problem; unikernels; EU GDPR, compliance.

I. Introduction

Every business is the subject of cyber attacks, no matter whether it is a public corporation, a private firm, a financial institution, a government agency, a non-government agency or a charity. No matter what type of organisation is involved, all will be subject to the rules of the forthcoming European Union (EU) General Data Protection Regulation (GDPR) [1], which comes into effect on 25th May 2018. It will apply to every single organisation that deals with any individual who is resident anywhere within the EU; and in a post-Brexit world, the UK Government has indicated that the GDPR will still apply in the UK. Indeed, the UK Government have indicated that the UK GDPR will be enforced with greater rigour, and will accord greater rights to private individuals.

The rules of the GDPR will mean considerable extra work, and expense, for all these organisations who fall under the scope of the GDPR, which will basically include any organisation, anywhere on earth, who process the personal data of any EU resident, anywhere within the EU. Each organisation will require to appoint a data controller, who either must have the requisite technical skills, or must be assisted by a person with such technical skills. This will no doubt be an unwelcome additional expense. They must also have a data processor and a data protection officer, meaning more costs. In addition, they will have to take all necessary technical steps to ensure the security and privacy of all Personally Identifiable Information (PII) belonging to data subjects of the organisation, at yet more expense.

A great many companies are totally unprepared for this. Many believe that because the reporting requirement has been changed from "within 72 hours of a breach occurring" to "within 72 hours of discovering a breach", they will have no problem being compliant [2]. They will be wrong! They must also be able to report which records were accessed, modified, deleted or ex-filtrated from the system.

Once an attacker breaches a system and becomes resident as an intruder, one of their first tasks is to delete the forensic trail of their incursion into the enterprise systems, so that their presence becomes more covert, thus allowing them to remain hidden inside the system. This allows them to harvest whatever information or secrets they desire for as long as they can stay hidden in the system.

Once the forensic trail has been deleted as part of the attacker seeking to retain an ever more capable foothold inside the system, there may be a reduced ability to actually comply with this particular GDPR requirement. In some cases, compliance may even be completely impossible. This will particularly be the case with cloud systems, since there is nothing to prevent such an intruder from deleting not only the forensic trail, but anything else they desire, including the very running cloud instance that they are hiding within.

Since failure to comply can result in fines which can rise to the greater of €20 million or 4% of global turnover, then this will certainly have a substantial impact, although there are many who still fail to grasp this important point.

We start by considering the cloud forensic problem in Section II, and discuss why this is such a challenge for GDPR compliance in cloud systems. We are concerned with achieving both good security and good privacy. While it is possible to have security without privacy, it is not possible to have privacy without security. Thus our approach will be to first ensure a good level of security can be achieved, and to that end, we start by listing the specific security issues we seek to address and discuss how we propose to tackle them in Section III. The remainder of the paper is organized as follows: in Section IV, we consider how we might go about finding a cloud based solution, in Section V, we discuss the outline technical details of our proposed approach; In Section VI, we consider possible attack vectors. In Section VII, we consider just how robust a unikernel approach might be. In Section VIII, we discuss our conclusions.

II. The Cloud Forensic Problem and the GDPR

Cloud computing has been around now for over 10 years, and a great deal of good quality research has been carried out, particularly regarding matters of security and privacy. Cloud systems have become highly popular with companies due to the flexibility of cloud offerings. The speed of starting a cloud instance, the removal of long lead times to access compute and storage resources, the ability to scale up, as well as down, to match demand presents a particularly good incentive to use cloud computing. The fact that companies can write costs off entirely against revenue provides a further attractive incentive for their use. Kratzke [3] has long warned of the dangers of thinking that conventional software is just the same as cloud-native software. Kratzke et al [4] do suggest the possibility of using existing Container technologies to improve cloud-native programming.

There have been many good papers produced on both security [5]–[9] and privacy [10]–[14], and we laud the efforts of countless researchers who have tried to provide this area with better security and privacy, which speaking generally, has been successfully achieved over the years. But there remains one fundamental weakness that has not been resolved, namely the "cloud forensic problem". All computer systems are the subject of attack, and cloud systems are no exception. Unfortunately, no system is immune to attack, and that is certainly true for cloud systems.

The primary goal of an attacker is to breach a system. This can involve quite a considerable amount of work on the part of a serious attacker. They will perform surveillance and compile many analyses of how the company systems are organised. Many will carry out huge amounts of work to understand the people of the organisation, since they are usually the weakest link. This intelligence gathering will be very extensive, usually covering every possible aspect of all the systems of the company in order to discover everything they can about the business architecture before they start their attacks.

Other attackers, are much less organised. They will simply try to hack in to company systems, without a thought of the overview of the company concerned. They will merely look for known vulnerabilities and try to attack them. Yet other attackers will attack the people of the company through social engineering, email attacks through malicious links and malware payloads, web based drive by attacks, phishing, vishing and many other approaches.

No matter which type of attacker they are, they all share one fundamental goal — to penetrate the system in order to become an intruder. The aim here is not just to get in, and out, as quickly as possible, but to develop a long term foothold inside company systems which will allow them to return, time and again, to help themselves to whatever they wish, as they escalate privileges more and more, the longer they remain inside the system.

It is rather unfortunate that they are often greatly aided in this quest by the companies themselves. Usually, this occurs through a degree of laziness whereby the companies are clearly failing to monitor server logs properly. Looking at previous cyber breach reports [15], at which time there was a global average of 6 months between breach and discovery, it is clear that had these companies been more rigorous about reading and analysing their server logs, they would have been in a better position to discover intruders rather more quickly. Even last year, where the time between breach and discovery has dropped to a number of weeks rather than months [16], this is still not good enough. Some companies contribute further by refusing or failing to update security patches to both operating systems and software systems, usually under the guise of "last time I did a security update, all the systems crashed".

This all leads towards the, as yet unresolved, cloud forensic problem — namely, that once an intruder is in the system, and has escalated sufficient privileges, there is absolutely nothing to prevent them from deleting the forensic trail, which allows them to hide all evidence of their successful penetration. Worse, by this stage they will also have control of all the system logs and audit trails, and there is nothing to prevent them from deleting every last trace of their intrusion and ongoing ex-filtration of private data.

Surely that has nothing to do with the GDPR you might ask? Sadly, that is not the case. In the event of a breach, you are required to report the breach within 72 hours of discovering the breach. You must be able to report how many relevant records have been compromised, whether by having been read, amended, deleted or ex-filtrated from the system. Given that many system logs are not even turned on by default, this means identifying which records have been compromised, whether by having been read, amended, deleted or ex-filtrated from the system, will present a serious enough challenge in the first place. However, given that the intruder will likely have done a complete job on all forensic trails in the system, the likelihood of being able to realise that a breach has occurred in the first place will be very slim, let alone having the ability to properly identify which records have been compromised.

From a holistic perspective, it would have been helpful if these matters might have been addressed by the Cloud implementation itself. However, no such attempt has taken place during the past decade, no doubt due to the massive challenge involved. Consequently, all organizations subject to the provisions of the GDPR are required to safeguard their own systems and therefore take such steps as are necessary to ensure adequate privacy is achieved.

This will mean non-compliance with the GDPR, which can then trigger fines which can rise to the greater of €20,000,000 or 4% of global turnover. This will certainly catch the attention of top management within organisations. Considering that these fines can be levied for every single breach, and that the upper limit is based on turnover rather than profit, that should be sufficiently concerning to get some serious attention. Of course, all sensible Cloud users should have been thinking about this long before now, and we are aware of many who on hearing that notification 'within 72 hours of discovery of a breach', rathr than 'within 72 hours of occurrence of a breach', heaved a collective sigh of relief and stopped worrying about implementing a solution. This is what motivates our work.

III. How do we tackle the problem?

At this time, no system is fully secure. Operating systems, transport protocols, software applications — all of this software has evolved during previous decades. Any relevant standards were defined decades ago. The primary goal at that time was functionality. Security and privacy were very much an afterthought, which has remained the case for decades.

Security and privacy has very much been a case of "Let us bolt something on to tackle that". Default settings are geared for ease of setting up, not for security and privacy. This means proper security and privacy presents a massive challenge, which increases exponentially for cloud, Internet of Things and Big Data.

We could opt to use Containers, such as Docker, LXD or Rocket. However, Bratterud et al [17] warn of some security issues with this approach, and Ktatzke [18] also warns of the unexpected, and unwelcome overhead these solutions can bring.

In previous work, [19], we considered how well unikernels might be used to improve on dealing with our target list of security goals, and found the potential for an improved approach. In [20], we developed a suitable framework, providing detailed definitions of how this might be tackled. In [21], we demonstrated how a unikernel based solution could reduce complexity, while improving security and privacy. We also considered in [22], whether unikernels could help address some of the key weaknesses introduced by use of the Internet of Things (IoT). In each case, we build on the work of the previous papers, in order to ensure we do not miss anything important as we develop the system.

Unikernels run natively on cloud, they have an exceptionally small footprint, they run without many of the conventional "toys" associated with normal web based cloud instances. This means a seriously minimal attack surface. They are lightweight, can be activated "on demand", and are extremely difficult to attack. Virtually every single conventional attack fails due to there being a heavily restricted means of accessing the running unikernels. A typical cloud instance will be over 150MB in size. Even Docker containers will be a minimum of 24MB in size, whereas a unikernel instance can be as little as 2MB in size.

Given the limitation we face in terms of most software being insecure, how can we approach developing a potential solution for this problem? In [23] [24] Duncan and Whittington proposed that all cloud based systems which would be subject to compliance under the GDPR, should have ALL audit trails and forensic logs captured and stored off-site in a highly secure immutable database running on a dedicated and highly secure server.

These proposals suggest the immutable database be set up off-site from the cloud instance. While we accept that advice might be highly appropriate given the pervasive extent of the cloud forensic problem, could there be any other way that we might be able to find a cloud based solution? As we shall see in the next section, there may be a way to achieve just that objective.

IV. Finding a Cloud Based Solution

We certainly do accept the sensible logic proposed by Duncan and Whittington [23] [24] to keep the immutable database separated from all running cloud instances. While that makes perfect sense, there is no reason, other than the cloud forensic problem, why the immutable database should not run on a cloud system. However, we do agree that it should not run on the same system as the company system it is trying to protect.

So the question we must first address is how we might go about solving this problem. This is where the unikernel based system might be able to help.

Let us first consider the advantages from a security point of view of unikernels:

- The larger a piece of software, the more vulnerabilities are usually present. As we already stated, a unikernel instance can be as little as 2MB;
- The smaller an instance is, the faster a new instance loads;
- The smaller instances are, the cheaper they are to run;
- There is no terminal to log into. The terminal presents one of the easiest attack routes into any system and is usually not well protected from attack. If the attacker cannot log in, achieving a successful attack will be rather difficult to perpetrate;
- The running instance of any unikernel runs with immutable code, meaning no user may inject code into the running unikernel instance.

And now, let us look at any potential disadvantages of unikernels:

- No terminal to log into — a disadvantage for most sys admins. We view this as a huge advantage. If the sys admin cannot login, the attacker has no chance of doing so;
- The running instance is immutable, so it cannot handle changes. We view this as a positive. We are particularly keen to be able to log all changes, system, forensic and audit trail data in a persistent and immutable storage medium off-site. If we cannot change anything, neither can the intruder.

In our view, every item in the above list of advantages and disadvantages are all positive attributes. From a performance, cost, reduced latency and minimised attack surface perspective, all the attributes are highly beneficial for our purposes. In the next section, we will look at how we might deploy these instances to help solve our security challenge.

V. Outline Technical Solution Proposed

We have seen that our unikernel instances can be extremely lightweight, are immutable in operation, have a very small attack surface, perform well, are cheap to run with reduced latency. Because of these advantages, we can use a number of these instances to build a much more robust system.

If we use the analogy of a bee hive, we can apply this approach as part of our solution. In a bee hive, there are a number of specialised bees — there is a single queen bee, hundreds of male drones (whose responsibility is to mate with a queen, after which they die), anything up to 80,000 female worker bees, who look after developing eggs, larvae and pupae, as well as the whole hive, gathering food from flowers outside the hive and defence duties, which they perform to the death, if needed. Each bee performs a specialised function depending on its age. And in the event a queen leaves, gets lost, or dies accidentally, the colony is capable of generating new queens, either full queens, or temporary queens. The ultimate in sustainability.

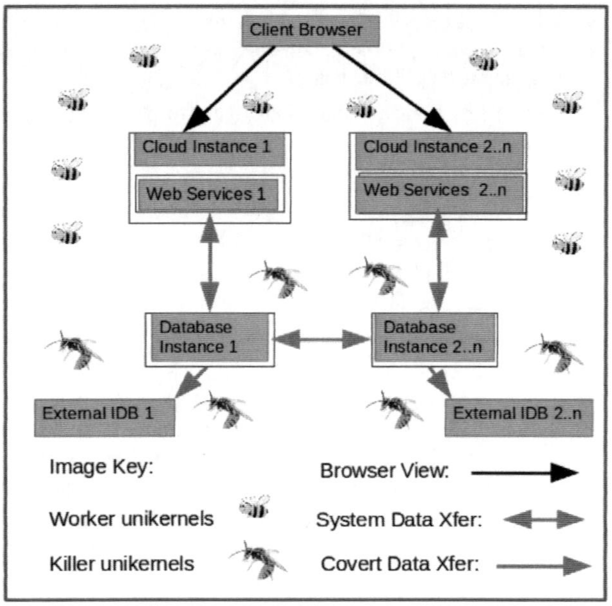

Figure 1. A Unikernel Based Solution to the Cloud Forensic Problem.

Our main company system will have a presence on a cloud platform, using one or more cloud instances as needed, which will be running on a conventional cloud setup. The cloud instance will have the capability to replicate at scale as demand increases and also to shut down instances when demand falls. The main cloud instance system will not be able to be shut down from within. We shall call this the front end Cloud Instance 1.

A conventional database management system will be included in all cloud instances in the normal way except they will instead be removed from within these instances and will run inside a single instance with every non-required function removed from that running instance in order to reduce the attack surface. Should database replication be later required, this can be accommodated through setting up similar database instances. We shall call this original Database Instance 1.

Thus Database Instance 1 will only accept input from the known running front end Cloud Instance 1. There will be no direct access allowed from outside the cloud environment. In the event that replication is required, Cloud Instance 1 will setup as many replicated instances as needed, including Database Instance 2..n, which will all be replicated, expanding to deliver the required resources.

Worker unikernels will be assigned to each Cloud Instance as they are spooled up, and shut down as no longer needed. They will have specific tasks to perform, such as policing, audit, or whatever. Killer unikernels will be assigned to the task of protecting database systems. Their primary goal will be to ensure the safety of both the forensic trail and the audit trail for all database components, which will be safely stored in the immutable database. These records cannot be deleted. If required, these killer unikernels can turn on attackers trying to breach the systems. All unikernel instances will be tracked, with forensic data collected also for them.

As we can see, each different type of instance is specialised, sticking to its own designated tasks. So what is special about this, apart from splitting up the functions? When a cloud instance runs with a variety of different types of software running on it, this can present a big challenge to configure the overall package in a secure way. By specialising each instance, it becomes much easier to configure securely, because every single unused port can be shut down. Security controls can focus on only what they have to, thus cutting down the potential attack surface.

Any new front end instance, if not registered with the control instance, will not be allowed access to any database instance. Likewise where any new database instance is not registered with the control instance, the front end instances will refuse to connect with it.

The secure immutable database for storing system logs, forensic and audit trail data. These should not be directly visible to the client browser. Each running instance will send a copy of all system logs, forensic and audit trail data to the immutable database instance as it is generated. The source and timing of all events will be logged by the immutable database.

With the unikernel instances, because they are so lightweight, we can deploy as many of them as we need to carry out very specific tasks. We can have some to police various events, some to carry out audit tasks, some to keep a track of what is live within the system. Each of the components of the main system can be looked after by a number of dedicated unikernel instances, whose sole function will be dedicated to looking after the one conventional cloud instance. Since these unikernels are self sufficient, there is unlikely to be any real adverse impact on the running main instances.

Figure 1 shows a cross-section of the proposed solution. The Client browser will see the front end which provides conventional running cloud instances, with controllers hidden behind the scenes. These controllers can be protected by 'killer bee' unikernels. The external Immutable Database instances will be hosted elsewhere, and can also be protected by 'killer bee' unikernels. The 'worker bee' unikernels clustering around the conventional cloud instances will carry out normal policing and other required tasks. Additional 'bee workers' of whatever kind needed can be spooled up as required. They are fast to provision, take little space and will carry out their programmed task.

As to the question of how many of each type of unikernel we should aim to use, we believe that it would be pointless to speculate at this stage until we can test what will be optimal after we carry out some live experimentation to establish what works well in various loading scenarios. With the use of proper control systems, we can ensure that each new instance is properly registered, constantly and properly monitored, with the control system having the capability to spool up new instances as needed qhickly and efficiently, as well as shutting down those which are no longer required. We expect that such flexibility will allow a highly scalable system to be developed, which can offer minimal running cost, in conjunction with a low latency approach to dealing with attacks. This testing will form part of our future work.

VI. Possible Attack Vectors to Consider

Since we are mostly working with web services, we will look at the Open Web Application Security Project (OWASP) 2017 Top 10 Web Vulnerabilities [25].

A1:2017-Injection Vulnerability: Injection flaws, such as Structured Query Language (SQL), Not Only SQL (NoSQL), Operating System (OS) injection and Lightweight Directory Access Protocol (LDAP) injection, occur when untrusted data is sent to an interpreter as part of a command or query. The attacker's hostile data can trick the interpreter into executing unintended commands or accessing data without proper authorization. **Solution:** Use a strong Application Programming Interface (API), separate content from commands in the database, and sanitise **ALL** user input.

A2:2017-Broken Authentication Vulnerability: Application functions related to authentication and session management are often implemented incorrectly, allowing attackers to compromise passwords, keys, or session tokens, or to exploit other implementation flaws to assume other users' identities temporarily or permanently. **Solution** Implement multi-factor authentication; no default passwords, especially from admins; reject all top 10,000 worst passwords.

A3:2017-Sensitive Data Exposure Vulnerability: Many web applications and APIs do not properly protect sensitive data, such as financial, healthcare, and PII. Attackers may steal or modify such weakly protected data to conduct credit card fraud, identity theft, or other crimes. Sensitive data may be compromised without extra protection, such as encryption at rest or in transit, and requires special precautions when exchanged with the browser. **Solution:** Encrypt all PII.

A4:2017-XML External Entities (XXE) Vulnerability: Many older or poorly configured eXtensible Markup Language (XML) processors evaluate external entity references within XML documents. External entities can be used to disclose internal files using the file Uniform Resource Identifier (URI) handler, internal file shares, internal port scanning, remote code execution, and denial of service attacks. **Solution:** Whenever possible, use less complex data formats such as JavaScript Object Notation (JSON), and avoiding serialization of sensitive data.

A5:2017-Broken Access Control Vulnerability: Restrictions on what authenticated users are allowed to do are often not properly enforced. Attackers can exploit these flaws to access unauthorized functionality and/or data, such as access other users' accounts, view sensitive files, modify other users' data, change access rights, etc. **Solution:** With the exception of public resources, deny by default; no unrestricted access to users; log all failures.

A6:2017-Security Misconfiguration Vulnerability: Security misconfiguration is the most commonly seen issue. This is commonly a result of insecure default configurations, incomplete or ad hoc configurations, open cloud storage, misconfigured Hypertext Transfer Protocol (HTTP) headers, and verbose error messages containing sensitive information. Not only must all operating systems, frameworks, libraries, and applications be securely configured, but they must be patched/upgraded in a timely fashion. **Solution:** Secure installation processes should be implemented. Keep it simple and log all errors.

A7:2017-Cross-Site Scripting (XSS) Vulnerability: XSS flaws occur whenever an application includes untrusted data in a new web page without proper validation or escaping, or updates an existing web page with user-supplied data using a browser API that can create Hyper Text Markup Language (HTML) or JavaScript. XSS allows attackers to execute scripts in the victim's browser which can hijack user sessions, deface web sites, or redirect the user to malicious sites. **Solution:** Preventing XSS requires separation of untrusted data from active browser content.

A8:2017-Insecure Deserialization Vulnerability: Insecure deserialization often leads to remote code execution. Even if deserialization flaws do not result in remote code execution, they can be used to perform attacks, including replay attacks, injection attacks, and privilege escalation attacks. **Solution:** The only safe architectural pattern is not to accept serialized objects from untrusted sources or to use serialization mediums that only permit primitive data types.

A9:2017-Using Components with Known Vulnerabilities Vulnerability: Components, such as libraries, frameworks, and other software modules, run with the same privileges as the application. If a vulnerable component is exploited, such an attack can facilitate serious data loss or server takeover. Applications and APIs using components with known vulnerabilities may undermine application defenses and enable various attacks and impacts. **Solution:** There should be a patch management process in place to ensure known vulnerabilities are never used.

A10:2017-Insufficient Logging&Monitoring Vulnerability: Insufficient logging and monitoring, coupled with missing or ineffective integration with incident response, allows attackers to further attack systems, maintain persistence, pivot to more systems, and tamper, extract, or destroy data. Most breach studies show time to detect a breach is over 200 days, typically detected by external parties rather than internal processes or monitoring. **Solution:** This paper is all about solving this problem!

And for no 11 of 10, go check out your site and make sure your system is not vulnerable.

There are, of course, many more vulnerabilities you can check out, and you should. The more you eliminate, the stronger and more robust your system becomes. You can be sure the attacker already knows all the potential vulnerabilities, so you need to make sure you do too, and plug them.

VII. DISCUSSION

We strongly believe that a unikernel based system would have a positive and robust impact because of the extra muscle offered to check and log everything that is happening within the system. Given that unikernel instances have a very low attack surface, no conventional attacker 'toys', are immutable in operation, and highly compact, as well as everything being logged to the immutable database - we are cutting out a huge range of vulnerabilities from existing cloud systems. By ensuring the cloud instance running can also withstand the OWASP top ten web vulnerability test, we are in a very strong position to resist a great many attacks.

Some experimentation will be required to identify what the optimal setup of the 'unkernal hive' instances will be in order to obtain the most effective approach. We need to ensure the cotroller instances are efficiently organised to allow scalability of the overall cloud installation, while at the same time ensuring maximum security and privacy can be achieved. At this time, the Cloud Forensic Problem means that conventional cloud systems cannot guarantee GDPR compliance for cloud users. Container based solutions are likely to be sugject to the same issues as conventional cloud instaces. While they may very well offer some improvement, it is likely that improvement will come at an overhead cost.

Using the unikernel approach, it is likely that it will certainly be possible to be compliant with the GDPR, that the overhead of running the unikernel instances will be minimal, and that the system can be highly responsive to the need for scalability. Not only that, but the ability to provide a means for compliance for cloud systems has to be big improvement on the status quo.

While we have carried out a number of minor tests on various aspects of our proposal, we have still to carry out any serious testing, which will form the main thrust of our next stage of the work. We are very keen to develop something that can provide a proper solution.

VIII. Conclusion and Future Work

As we have already stated, the Cloud Forensic Problem presents a very serious challenge for all cloud users, especially in light of the forthcoming GDPR. We have proposed a possible solution for this problem, which is a little different from conventional approaches. However, it offers a highly robust solution to a major challenge for all organisations who will be subject to compliance with the GDPR.

We believe this solution offers such merit that we plan to run a pilot test to establish just how well it will be able to cope with a system under serious attack. Initially, it will run on a private network, under attack from professional penetration testers. Once we are sure of how well the solution is likely to perform, we will set up a real live cloud instance to see just how well it might perform.

When the GDPR comes on stream, there will not be time for organisations to mess about. If they cannot comply with the regulation, and they are breached, resulting in a loss of PII, then they can expect huge fines, the like of which they have never seen before. It is time to wake up and smell the coffee.

References

[1] EU, "EU General Data Protection Regulation (GDPR)," 2017. [Online]. Available: http://www.eugdpr.org/ [Retrieved: December 2017]

[2] EU, "Reform of EU data protection rules," 2016. [Online]. Available: http://ec.europa.eu/justice/data-protection/reform/index_en.htm [Retrieved: December 2017]

[3] N. Kratzke and P.-C. Quint, "Understanding cloud-native applications after 10 years of cloud computing-a systematic mapping study," Journal of Systems and Software, vol. 126, 2017, pp. 1–16.

[4] N. Kratzke, P.-C. Quint, D. Palme, and D. Reimers, "Project cloud transit-or to simplify cloud-native application provisioning for smes by integrating already available container technologies," European Project Space on Smart Systems, Big Data, Future Internet-Towards Serving the Grand Societal Challenges. SCITEPRESS. In print, 2017.

[5] R. K. L. Ko, P. Jagadpramana, M. Mowbray, S. Pearson, M. Kirchberg, Q. Liang, and B. S. Lee, "TrustCloud: A framework for accountability and trust in cloud computing," Proceedings - 2011 IEEE World Congress on Services, SERVICES 2011, 2011, pp. 584–588.

[6] R. K. L. Ko, B. S. Lee, and S. Pearson, "Towards achieving accountability, auditability and trust in cloud computing," Communications in Computer and Information Science, vol. 193 CCIS, no. PART 4, 2011, pp. 432–444.

[7] N. Papanikolaou, S. Pearson, and M. C. Mont, "Towards Natural-Language Understanding and Automated Enforcement of Privacy Rules and Regulations in the Cloud: Survey and Bibliography," Analysis, 2011, pp. 1–9.

[8] S. Pearson, "Taking account of privacy when designing cloud computing services," Proceedings of the 2009 ICSE Workshop on Software Engineering Challenges of Cloud Computing, CLOUD 2009, 2009, pp. 44–52.

[9] S. Pearson, "Towards Accountability in the Cloud," IEEE Internet Computing, vol. 15, no. 4, jul 2011, pp. 64–69.

[10] W. Jansen and T. Grance, "Guidelines on Security and Privacy in Public Cloud Computing," NIST, Tech. Rep. 7, 2011. [Online]. Available: http://csrc.nist.gov/publications/nistpubs/800-144/SP800-144.pdf [Retrieved: December 2017]

[11] NIST, "Security and Privacy Controls for Federal Information Systems and Organizations Security and Privacy Controls for Federal Information Systems and Organizations," Natioinal Institute of Standards and Technology, Gaithersburg, MD, Tech. Rep. February, 2014. [Online]. Available: http://nvlpubs.nist.gov/nistpubs/SpecialPublications/NIST.SP.800-53r4.pdf [Retrieved: December 2017]

[12] S. Pearson, "Privacy and Security for Cloud Computing," in Privacy and Security for Cloud Computing. e: Springer, 2013, pp. 3–42.

[13] S. S. Shapiro, "Privacy by Design," Communications of the ACM, vol. 53, no. 6, jun 2010, p. 27.

[14] J. Singh, T. F. J. M. Pasquier, and J. Bacon, "Securing tags to control information flows within the Internet of Things," 2015 International Conference on Recent Advances in Internet of Things, RIoT 2015, 2015.

[15] Verizon, "2012 Data Breach Investigations Report," Verizon, Tech. Rep., 2012.

[16] Verizon, "2016 Verizon Data Breach Report," Tech. Rep., 2016.

[17] A. Bratterud, A.-A. Walla, H. Haugerud, P. E. Engelstad, and K. Begnum, "IncludeOS: A Minimal, Resource Efficient Unikernel for Cloud Services," 2015 IEEE 7th International Conference on Cloud Computing Technology and Science (CloudCom), 2015, pp. 250–257.

[18] N. Kratzke, "About microservices, containers and their underestimated impact on network performance," arXiv preprint arXiv:1710.04049, 2017.

[19] B. Duncan, A. Bratterud, and A. Happe, "Enhancing Cloud Security and Privacy: Time for a New Approach?" in Intech 2016, Dublin, 2016, pp. 1–6.

[20] A. Bratterud, A. Happe, and B. Duncan, "Enhancing Cloud Security and Privacy: The Unikernel Solution," in Cloud Computing 2017: The Eighth International Conference on Cloud Computing, GRIDs, and Virtualization, 2017, pp. 1–8.

[21] A. Happe, B. Duncan, and Alfred Sewitsky Bratterud, "Unikernels for Cloud Architectures: How Single Responsibility can Reduce Complexity, Thus Improving Enterprise Cloud Security," in COMPLEXIS 2017 - Proceedings of the 2nd International Conference on Complexity, Future Information Systems and Risk, Porto, Portugal, 2017, pp. 1–12.

[22] B. Duncan, A. Happe, and A. Bratterud, "Enterprise IoT Security and Scalability: How Unikernels can Improve the Status Quo," in 9th IEEE/ACM International Conference on Utility and Cloud Computing (UCC 2016), Shanghai, China, 2016, pp. 1–6.

[23] B. Duncan and M. Whittington, "Creating an Immutable Database for Secure Cloud Audit Trail and System Logging," in Cloud Computing 2017: The Eighth International Conference on Cloud Computing, GRIDs, and Virtualization. Athens, Greece: IARIA, ISBN: 978-1-61208-529-6, 2017, pp. 54–59.

[24] B. Duncan and M. Whittington, "Creating and Configuring an Immutable Database for Secure Cloud Audit Trail and System Logging," International Journal On Advances in Security, vol. 10, no. 3&4, 2017, pp. 155–166.

[25] OWASP, "OWASP home page," 2017. [Online]. Available: https://www.owasp.org/index.php/Main_Page [Retrieved: December 2017]

Securing 3rd Party App Integration in Docker-based Cloud Software Ecosystems

Christian Binkowski
Ostbayerische Technische Hochschule
Amberg-Weiden
Amberg, Germany
Email: c.binkowski@oth-aw.de

Stefan Appel
Siemens AG
Erlangen, Germany
Email: stefan.appel@siemens.com

Andreas Aßmuth
Ostbayerische Technische Hochschule
Amberg-Weiden
Amberg, Germany
Email: a.assmuth@oth-aw.de

Abstract—**Open software ecosystems are beneficial for customers; they benefit from 3rd party services and applications, e.g., analysis of data using apps, developed and deployed by other companies or open-source communities. One significant advantage of this approach is that other customers may benefit from these newly developed applications as well. Especially software ecosystems utilizing container technologies are prone to certain risks. Docker, in particular, is more vulnerable to attacks than hypervisor based virtualisation as it directly operates on the host system. Docker is a popular representative of containerisation technology, which offers a lightweight architecture in order to facilitate the set-up and creation of such software ecosystems. Popular Infrastructure as a Service cloud service providers, like Amazon Web Services or Microsoft Azure, jump on the containerisation bandwagon and provide interfaces for provisioning and managing containers. Companies can benefit from that change of technology and create software ecosystems more efficiently. In this paper, we present a new concept for significant security improvements for cloud-based software ecosystems using Docker for 3rd party app integration. Based on the security features of Docker, we describe a secure integration of applications in the cloud environment. Our approach considers the whole software lifecycle and includes sandbox testing of potentially dangerous 3rd party apps before these became available to customers.**

Keywords–Docker; Cloud; security.

I. INTRODUCTION

Cloud computing developed within the last 10 years as the Internet is well spread all over the globe with an acceptable bandwith. With the development of Web 2.0, in the beginning of the 21st century, cloud computing started spreading. Big companies like Amazon, Google or Microsoft started hosting services for companies and their applications. Cloud computing was a breakthrough technology for smaller companies as it reduced the costs of datacenter maintenance. Another important benefit is the elasticity, which makes it easy for users to upscale the resources and increase the performance. Nowadays, companies are able to push their software ecosystems easily to foreign servers instead of deploying it on their own. Another fundamental technology that was beneficial for cloud computing is the use of virtualisation. Creating multiple host systems based on shared enhanced hardware is the basis of modern cloud computing. Today, it is common to run services in virtual machines on servers but in the last few years containerisation is in the focus as a new virtualisation technology. A server runs a base Linux and the services run in lightweight containers with a small OS, which reduces storage costs immensely. Every container has a small host OS, the base image, which may be shared with other containers. If one user installs an Apache Server on top of the base image, Docker will add one layer to the image. Another user can install a Python environment and run scripts. This will also add another layer to the base image. This makes it easier to distribute updates to containers, as only the layer needs to be shipped to the other containers.

But containerisation does not only have benefits. A major problem of Docker or other containerisation services is security. The user has to adjust settings and install optional packages to create a safe environment for the use of containers.

One of the main advantages of Docker is Docker Hub with an immese amount of preconfigured images. However, in 2015 a study from BanyanOps showed that a lot of images uploaded to the platform are vulnerable and contain security breaches [1]. They tested official releases like Debian images and general images from private distributors. One third of the official images included critical vulnerabilities like the Heartbleed bug in OpenSSL, not being patched for some time. The rest of the tested images contained high and medium rated vulnerabilities. They also tested about 1700 general images supplied by 3rd parties and the number of vulnerabilities found was even higher. The results may be interpreted as follows: even official images have weak spots and the user has to be careful when bringing these images into his environment.

As the trend of cloud computing showed, many companies are creating their own cloud platforms offering different services. Some of them allow 3rd parties to integrate applications into their ecosystems. In the context of Docker, it means that a customer can push his container into the environment and interact with the provided platform services. Therefore, a security and test concept for the integration is indispensable as customers upload and process their data to the platforms. A data breach may not only result in financial consequences due to the new General Data Protection Regulation (GDPR) coming on 25th of May 2018, which forces companies to be more transparent about attacks. Any security breach then needs to be reported within 72 hours after discovery, otherwise the company has to pay up to 2% of the worldwide turnover as a fine for a first offense [2]. Beside the financial consequences the loss of trust of customers can cause an image damage of the company, too.

In Section II, we first present common attacks in the Docker environment, and in Section III we discuss the Docker security features and how to increase Docker security. Section IV describes a security concept how new containers should be able to interact with other containers. Section V discusses a test concept for containers, and in Section VI, we discuss our conclusions and future work.

II. ATTACKS

Researchers are finding exploits day by day and often Docker or other container environments are affected. Many different and sometimes also unconventional ways involving, e.g., social engineering, lead to damage on a Docker system. In this paper, we present mechanisms to prevent attacks using three categories of attack vectors:

- Overloading the network: Denial of Service (DoS) attacks
- Elevation of privileges: container breakout & exploits
- Compromising the network: ARP spoofing

A. Denial of Service Attacks

DoS attacks cause different effects. One purpose is bringing the host down or stop the system from operating. DoS attacks are against any kind of services, interfaces or devices like the memory or cpu of the host system. Docker, not configured in the right way, is prone to DoS attacks.

As Docker refers to user namespaces every container image based on a Linux system has user IDs (UID). For example, a UID 0 in a Docker container can relate to a UID 500 on a host system. Docker implements a constant span between the virtual UID in the container and the real UID on the host system. If a system launches 20 containers, which all contain a UID 0 then every container UID will refer to the real UID 500 on the host system. This being implemented may cause DoS attacks by hitting specific user limits. Different examples exist for this phenomenon described in the following paragraph [3].

Every user in a Linux host system is provided a specific number of signals in order to let processes communicate with each other. A signal can stop, kill a process or transport a simple message like a number. To perform a DoS attack one container tries to queue the user maximum amount for signals. As other containers share the same UID and so also refer to the same user limits they are not able to send signals anymore due to the boundaries. This may not cause a complete host takedown but some containers may freeze and will not be able to operate properly anymore. To prevent this from happening it is useful to create different users in the containers whenever possible [3].

Another way to burst user limits is by increasing the number of user processes. This can bring down the Docker environment. It can be realised by creating a fork bomb. The father process forks itself many times and creates a lot of processes in a short time. This leads to an exceedance of the process user limit. In tests, this behaviour leads to bringing down the whole Docker environment but not the host.

In conclusion, different ways to burst user specific limits exist. Further ways, like allocating disk space or increasing cpu usage, can cause the same effects - the host is taken down or damaged afterwards. Not only the Docker environment also the host can be attacked in this way. Attacks based on increasing disk space or cpu usage can be prevented easily by configuring the Docker environment correctly. Docker gives the user the possibility to limit the cpu usage or memory that can be used by a single container.

B. container breakout & exploits

Linux Kernel exploits enable attackers to break out of the container and infect the system by installing a stable backdoor and channeling malicious code. After breaking in the attacker is then able to take over control of the host system or the hosted container in the environment.

A famous Linux kernel exploit is called "Dirty COW", which stands for "Dirty Copy On Write". In this exploit, the standard user tries to write to a file that only a user with root permissions can write to [4]. According to Current Vulnerabilities and Exploits (CVE) [5], almost half of the Linux exploits found are DoS exploits in order to bring the host system down followed by privilege elevation and information leakage. As Linux is the host system it is important to have a look at the published kernel vulnerabilities. It is also important to watch out for Docker vulnerabilites or even vulnerabilities inside the containers. This raises the potential of possible weak spots immensely. The deduction of this attack scenario is to keep the kernel, Docker, as it is a fast living environment, and software inside of containers updated and patching the system by creating new container images with updated software.

C. Address Resolution Protocol (ARP) spoofing in the container network

ARP spoofing is popular when it comes to network sniffing and so called Man in the Middle attacks. Although Docker containers communicate over a private network they are prone to these attacks. One container could contain malicious code to spoof the private network. The following section and Figure 1 will explain ARP spoofing shortly [6].

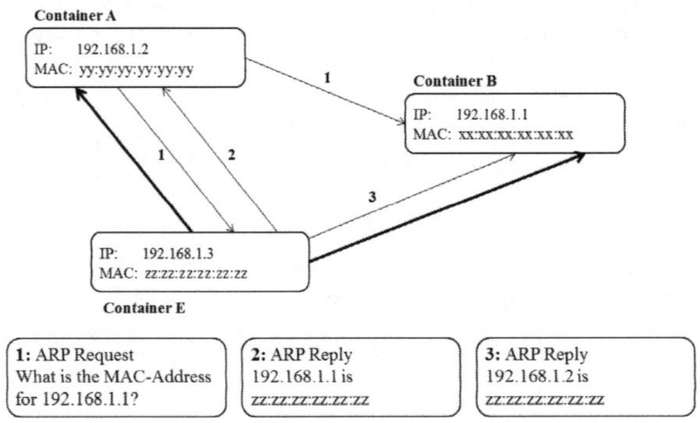

Figure 1. ARP Spoofing

Container A wants to communicate with container B and sends an ARP message, which asks for the MAC address related to the IP address container A wants to communicate with. The attacking container E sends a manipulated ARP message pretending to be container B and transmits his own MAC address. Instead of establishing a connection with container B, A is now connected with container E. All packages container A tries to send to container B now arrive at container E, which can read the packages, forward them to the container B or just drop them. After spying, e.g., passwords or other credentials, container E can drop packages, which leads to a loss of a connection. To perform a complete Man in the Middle attack, the malicious container has to pretend to be A when

B tries to connect to container A. As both received the same MAC address they will send the packages to container E. Now he can eavesdrop on the entire communication between both containers and what attacker E just has to do is forwarding the packages between A and B. Known from public networks, e.g., cafes, spoofing and sniffing in the end can cause serious problems.

Using TLS as communication standard makes it more difficult for attackers to intercept and read communications. Containers identify themselves with certificates issued by a root certificate authority. In order to prevent Man in the Middle attacks with fake or self-signed certificates, certificate pinning should be used [7][8].

III. Docker Security Features

Compared to hypervisor based virtualisation a container based virtualisation tends to be more vulnerable to attacks. As a hypervisor based virtualisation has an own host OS installed, an additional layer of security is brought between the virtualised hardware and the host OS. To understand security in the Docker framework it is necessary to explain how the resources are virtualised in the Docker environment. Docker comes with some Linux specific security features that ensure the security of each container. The following two mechanisms are essential in the Docker virtualisation:

- Cgroups: provides the possibility to limit the resources every container is able to access [9]
- Namespaces: namespaces lead to a separation of spaces. In conclusion, every container thinks of itself as the only container running on the system (Figure 2) [10]

Docker uses a process isolation to prevent a container from accessing the process management of other containers. The isolation is guaranteed by providing each container a unique namespace for every container, limiting the permissions and the visibility of underlying processes in other containers or the host systems. The process ID namespace isolates the process number space from the host. The process hierarchy is also a benefit for the containers as it only sees the processes in its own container or child processes.

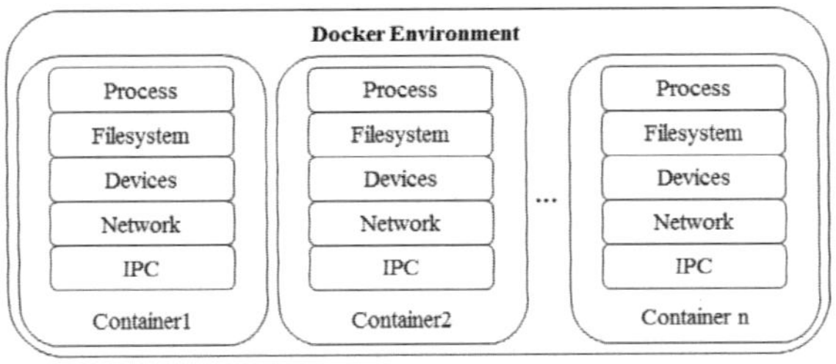

Figure 2. Namespacing in Docker

The host OS and the containers must be protected from unauthorized access and modification of the file system. Thus, every container has its own filesystem and therefore can operate in its own home directory. However, some of the kernel files are not virtualised. This means that every container shares these files with the other containers. As a Docker container is able to see the files, the system is prone to attacks like the already discussed Dirty COW attack. At least, a container is generally not able to write kernel files.

Another key feature of container based virtualisation is device isolation. Access to important device nodes like the physical memory or storage can cause serious damage to the host system. To prevent this from happening Docker uses the device whitelist controller, which limits the access to devices for Docker. Processes are also prevented from creating new device nodes in containers.

Shared memories, pipes or semaphores are ways to interact with other processes. Here, Docker creates an own namespace to guarantee that every container only uses its own resources and does not communicate with processes or overwrites data in foreign shared memories. Thus, containers can't interact with processes from other containers.

Containers can communicate with each other only over a network connection. Every container has its own network interface including IP address, routing table, network device and stack. Docker establishes a Virtual Ethernet Bridge to communicate between container and the host system. This link can be found on the host system and is named Docker0. All hosted containers are connected to the bridge and to the eth0 interface of the container.

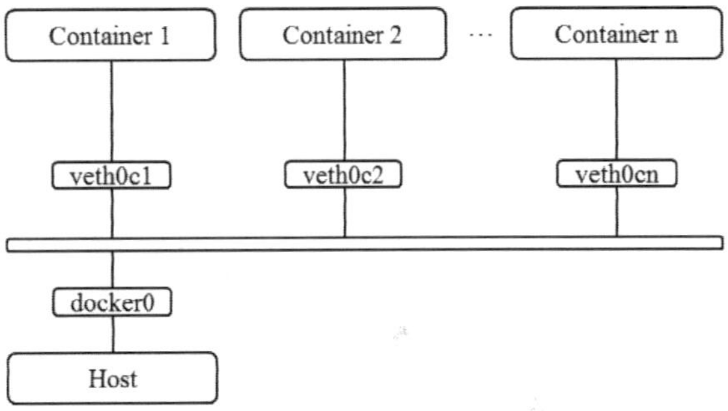

Figure 3. Docker Virtual Network

As Figure 3 depicts, there is a stable connection between the containers and the host. With the default settings of this network setup the Docker environment is vulnerable to ARP spoofing and Man in the Middle attacks as described before.

To prevent DoS attacks Docker uses the cgroups functionality that allows users to configure how many resources, like cpu usage or memory, each container can access; a container is not able to consume the entire host system anymore. With the start of a container the operator can tell Docker that the container is only allowed to access a certain fraction of the available memory. Once Docker recognises a memory limit violation it will enforce the set rule.

Besides namespacing and cgroups Docker also offers other security features. It allows users to run processes in two modes:

- privileged mode: using superuser permissions and no permission checks
- unprivileged mode: full permission checks

The following measures are introduced in order to harden the host system. All newer Linux kernels provide the possibility to assign capabilities to superusers [11]. Capabilities are rights for super users, e.g., CAP_NET_ADMIN, if assigned, can be used to administrate the IP firewall or to modify the routing table. By default, many of these capabilities are disabled even if the container is running in privileged mode. In conclusion, disabling capabilities makes containers safer and the host system less vulnerable.

Third party applications can enhance Linux security. SELinux was created by the NSA in corporation with the Linux distributor Red Hat [12]. The user or process has access to the files based on a Mandatory Access Control (MAC) system, which implements rules for the user to access files. These rules can be related to categorisation or labels. Standard Linux applies a Discretionary Access Control (DAC) where decisions depend on the identity of the user.

SELinux offers the user a type enforcement mode that lets the user define the type of a file. The user can grant a process access to a specific type of file and doesn't have to specify the user rights for every file. Another key security feature is called Multi-category security (MCS) [12]. This prohibits access to data of a foreign container. When a container is launched, the Docker daemon randomly picks a label and attaches it to every file and process that is launched or created in the container. Only containers with the consistent label can access processes or data inside the container.

AppArmor is a different approach to harden containers and preventing them to cause damage on the host system [13]. The concept of the Linux extension refers to loading profiles in each application. Administrators can configure two modes. In enforcement mode, the policies in the profile are enforced strictly. In learning mode, violations are permitted but also logged on the system. The generated log file can be analysed to develop new profiles. Docker has a possibility to load profiles into containers in enforcement mode. If the user has not created any profile, it loads the default profile with less capabilities and no access to important filesystems.

IV. Security Concept

In the following section, the paper will propose a security concept, which ensures a secure integration of 3rd party applications in an existing Docker container environment. This section will introduce a security concept for 3rd party app integration, methods regarding to communication, authentication and how network analysis can improve security.

We want to present a concept for intra container communication, as this is crucial for 3rd party application integration. Open software platforms are an important foundation for innovative business models. However, this openness comes with risks for platform operators and customers. Especially security is an extremely important aspect; it becomes ever more challenging, when apps are not only delivered to customers, e.g., Apple/Android. Platforms allowing the execution of web-based 3rd party apps need to be secured against potentially malicious components. On the other side, it is very important to open the platform for other developers as it will only grow with external input.

Cloud was an enabler for ecosystems in recent years. Developers easily pushed their deployments on servers in cloud farms and could scale the applications without maintaining a big datacenter on their own. That is not only a benefit for the developer, also the customer profits by a growing variety of Software as a Service (SaaS) offers.

A number of researchers already have demonstrated that Docker has some serious security concerns. They focused their research on container hardening to minimize the number of weak spots of a Docker container. Others refer to hardening the host and its services in order to reduce the attack surface for Docker containers [14].

We offer a solution for the 3rd party app integration in the docker environment and are adding another layer of security in addition to hardening the host and containers. Our solution focuses on the services architecture [15]. The ecosystem is based on small services that interact with a Representational State Transfer (REST) Application Programming Interface (API) concept. An API Gateway routes the requests to the demanded services. As the services are not bound to programmining languages it is easy for 3rd parties to develop a service in a Docker container and integrate it into the ecosystem. If one container is down, the platform still can be up and running because the services are not centralised on a single host.

A. Request Forwarding

As described in Section II all containers share the same network interface, which allows every container to communicate within the network. Once a new container is integrated into the platform, it could interact with the other containers without restrictions. To prevent this, a proxy container is introduced into the network.

This prohibits two containers from exchanging messages directly. The functionality of a network proxy is described briefly:

- The client requests a service.
- The proxy receives the request and forwards the message to the original server.
- The response of the server will be processed by the proxy, which will forward the response to the client in the end.

A proxy depicts a Man in the Middle, which can control the network traffic. 3rd party application in the environment should only be allowed to access a selected services that are available in the environment. In this concept, we would like to introduce two proxies for different use cases.

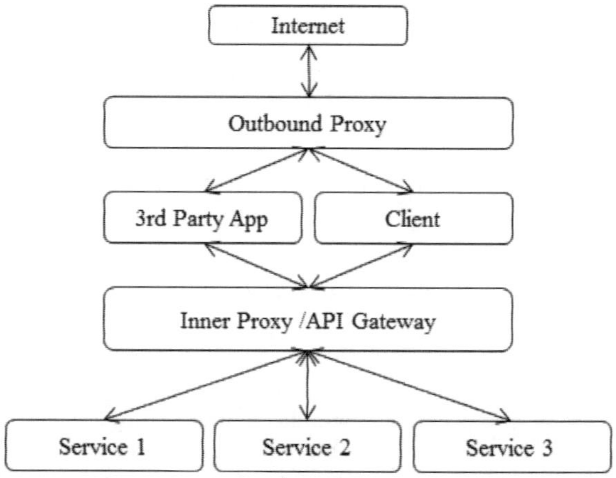

Figure 4. Proxy Setup

There is one proxy, also called API Gateway that will handle the requests regarding to the backend services of the platform. The second proxy is used for the outbound traffic towards the Internet. Both proxies can implement rules to refuse or drop connections, which a container wants to establish. Although this makes the communication more complex, it adds a security layer between the backend services and the 3rd party and also a additional layer between the Internet and the foreign application. The communication and benefits of this setup is described in the sub paragraphs Logging and Whitelisting. Another benefit of a proxy is that the operator can ask for authentication and authorisation before granting access to the services. Only containers with the correct credentials or registration are able to use the proxy and thus the services in other containers. This is a first step to isolate services from direct requests in order to make them more secure.

B. Encrypted Communication

As described in Section III, ARP spoofing or Man in the Middle attacks are a risk. As mitigation we propose to implement secure connections by using Transport Layer Security (TLS) [16]. TLS is a protocol to establish an encrypted and authenticated connection. During the handshake, client and server perform a key exchange. We recommend to use strong ciphersuites to mitigate the risk of an attacker being able to crack the keys. Both, client and server, identify themselves via X.509 certificates issued by a root certificate authority (CA). By signing the key exchange messages with the X.509 certificate, server and client prove that they are the sender of these messages. As the platform can't be reached directly from the Internet (Figure 4) an internal Public Key Infrastructure can be deployed. After the handshake the communication between server and client is encrypted, and message authentication codes additionally provide authenticity.

ARP spoofing attacks are based on rerouting packages to a wrong MAC address. If an attacker performs ARP spoofing in a network which deploys TLS, the attacker will receive encrypted messages, which he can't decrypt without the correct key. A successful spoofing attack now requires using fake certificates to pretend being a different container. Those fake certificates can only be issued, if the root CA was attacked. In conclusion, by using TLS and certificates the gain of security is immense. A container can't easily spy on credentials or authentication keys, which might elevate his rights in the system to gather confidential information, e.g., customer data. Another extension to prevent Man in the Middle attacks is certificate pinning. When certificate pinning is deployed, the container requests a server connection and the server will pin the transmitted certificate to the container that sent the request. The server then only accepts connections when the submitted certificate matches the pinned certificate. An attacker could add a self signed or other certificates via a proxy and so bypass the TLS security mechanisms. Certificate pinning can prevent this scenario as the server does not trust all connections that would be verified by a root certificate. This extension was added to the handshake protocol as CA's lost trust due to attacks and fake certificates.

C. Logging

The API Gateway protects the services from direct requests from a 3rd party app. The Gatway reroutes the requests to the required platform service. But the proxy besides rerouting can extend the functionality and log incoming requests. Analysis of requests and the HTTP/HTTPS status codes can help to identify malicious behaviour. We want to present three different ways for a container to act in a malicious way.

A correct request leads to HTTP status code 200. If a container sends a request with a wrong syntax, the server will respond with status code 400. When the inquiring container uses a wrong access token or is not registered to the service, the service will respond with a status code 401. A container can also send too many requests in order to bring it down (DoS attack), the API Gateway can measure that as well. Thus, the operator can create statistics on container behavior and identify suspicious activities. For example, a user tries to access the weather API and the database API with no permission. After a certain time the API gateway detects that the container sends too many requests without the correct permission. The gateway can automatically evaluate the received status codes and ban the container from the network if the numbers of unauthorized requests is too high. Besides unauthorized and wrong requests, the number of requests enable the gateway to identify DoS attacks. If a single container sends too many request in a short time period, e.g., calling the weather API for 1000 times in five seconds in order to bring the service down, the API gateway can identify the malicious container and reduce its bandwith or block requests and isolate it from the platform services [8].

As logging data is highly valuable for digital forensics and analysis it is important to store the collected data in a secure way. Right now, we are also working on a concept to mitigate the risk of data loss or manipulation. In general, a system based on the approach of Weir and Aßmuth, which includes Message Authentication Code (MAC) chains and secret sharing, may be a first step towards securing monitoring data [17].

D. Whitelisting/Blacklisting

Also the outgoing traffic to the Internet (Figure 4) from containers can indicate attacks. Some commands inside the container require additional downloads from the Internet. Downloaded content from the Internet can include malicious software or exploit code that tries to cause damage in the platform. For instance, a container might download new kernel exploits to elevate permissions and damage the host system. To prevent unbridled downloads, the platform operator has to create mechanisms to keep the risk of malicious downloads small. For this reason we propose the outbound proxy in Figure 4. One possible measure is to define guidelines for developers of 3rd party containers on allowed traffic. In case of a detected rule violation, the container can be banned from the network immediatly. In addition, the administrator can create a whitelist of IP adresses in the proxy, which every container is allowed to reach out to. Every IP address or host name not included in the whitelist is blocked. The platform operator can ensure that containers only download software from trusted sources like IP addresses from specific countries or sources. So locating the IP address of a request going to the Internet can help to improve security in the network.

E. Application Authorisation

Once a request has passed the API gateway it will be directed to the service. The container has to prove that it has the permission to use the service which brings in authentication. A common standard for securing API's is OAuth2 [18]. Instead of submitting username and password to the server to gain access to services, OAuth2 follows a token-based approach for this. Once a container wants to access a service he needs to request authorisation of the resource owner. This step is required to identify the container can be seen as a replacement for identifying through username and password in every request. The service operator allows access to the service and therefore will send an authorisation string to the client. Every time the container wants to access the service he has to reach out to the authorisation server with the authorisation string. The server will compute an access token and send it back to the container. In further service API requests, the client has to submit the token to the server in order to receive the required information. Access tokens have a certain time span. If the access token expires, the client has to request another token. As described before, the user doesn't need to submit username and password to the server as he only sends a randomly chosen access string. This leads to anonymity as an attacker can't refer to the specific user if the connection is eavesdropped. Combined with TLS in connection establishing the system is secured. Now it is hard for attackers to spy on credentials. If the attacker is able to manage an attack against TLS, the distributor can issue a new identification string and can make the cracked authorisation string invalid.

In summary, the platform services are now secured from direct access through the API gateway. In addition, the logging functionality enables the operator to identify malicious activities. As the Docker network is prone to ARP spoofing and Man in the Middle attacks the implemented TLS hardens the network communication and hard for a container to spy on data, e.g credentials. With OAuth2 we anonymise the user requests and secure the API's from unauthorized access. The outbound proxy filters requests towards the Internet and therefore protects the platform from downloaded exploits. These security features help an operator to mitigate the risk of an attack.

V. Test Concept

To mitigate the risk of damage in the container ecosystem, it is indispensable to test the components before integrating them into the system. In the software lifecycle, test is an important step before the final product release. It is common to test software to find bugs and to improve software quality but ensuring the security of products has also become more important in recent years. In this section, we will propose three different methods to improve security by testing the software:

- Static Code Analysis
- Dependency Checks
- Sandbox Testing

A. Static Code Analysis

Static code analysis can take place before the functionality of the software is tested [19]. The purpose of the test is improving software quality by finding bad coding styles or duplicate code. But not only from the quality perspective it is important to perform a static code analysis. This process also helps to improve the security of the written software. Test tools are able to find vulnerabilities like race conditions, buffer overflows or memory leaks before an attacker can exploit them.

But static code analysis has to be performed in the providing company, as no company will voluntarily share their source code and know-how with the hoster of the platform. A vendor of a platform has to create guidelines, which tell the developers what security standards must be implemented and what kind of tests need to be performed before application submission. One important part of testing will be described in the next section.

B. Dependency Checks

Most software make use of libraries. The libraries themself can also use other libraries, which creates a tree of library dependencies. The scenario, shown in Figure 5, helps to illustrate the possible weak spot in the source code.

```
source code
├─library1 v2.0
├─library2 v1.3
│ └─library1 v1.0
├─library3 v12.0
│ ├─library1 v1.0
│ └─library4 v3.0
│   └─library2 v1.0
│     └─library5 v3.7
└─library4 v4.0
```

Figure 5. Example Dependency Tree

For instance, the developer always uses the updated versions while the other layers may include outdated versions of the libraries. Those old versions may be prone to vulnerabilities, which an attacker can exploit. When the application then runs in a container, the container could be inherited by a 3rd party like an attacker, but also the vendor of the application can use these unstable or vulnerable libraries to create backdoors on purpose in order to perform malicious activities. Hence, it is important to check the dependencies of the source code before the integration of the container. As stated previously it might be difficult to get the original source code, so the developer could hand over some kind of "header file" that reports, which libraries are used in the application. Then the container hoster can continously check the header files against a vulnerability database and send out reports if the used libraries are exploitable. The developer could be forced to update his application within a certain timespan or it might be excluded from the platform. In order to keep the platform stable and secure, the vulnerability database needs to be updated regularly.

C. Sandbox Testing

The final step before the integration of the container into the platform is to perform a sandbox test. Sandbox testing is a good way to evaluate how the application interacts with the provided services. The hoster creates a development space next to the "Live Space", which can be used to test the applications and how they react in different scenarios.

Sandbox testing can also be helpful for the developer to see how the application works in a live system. The developer cannot cause any damage to a live system as he tests the software in a different space. This test is meant to reduce possible downtime of a host system.

Once an application doesn't show any malicious activities and worked fine in the sandbox environment, it can be integrated into the live system. However, a sandbox has to be developed, equipped with analysis tools in order to monitor behavior correctly, maintained and hosted. To reduce effort, a smaller demo environment, which represents only the critical interfaces of the platform may be helpful to monitor the behavior of a container.

The sandbox can not only be used to identify possible malicious containers, it also helps to improve the security of the system as it reveals possible vulnerabilities. Some of the containers are maybe not meant to be malicious on purpose and therefore show the behavior due to bugs in the software. So the operator has to distinguish between an attacker that wants to harm the system and a developer who did not write the software properly. All in all, a sandbox environment can strengthen the security of a platform especially when it allows 3rd parties to develop and deploy apps into the ecosystem.

VI. Conclusion & Future Work

Our approach considers the whole software lifecycle and also includes sandbox testing of potentially dangerous 3rd party apps before these became available to the customers. We presented different techniques in order to secure the system from the described attacks. The described architecture and security features help the operator to decouple and secure services from the 3rd party app. Hence, the foreign app is not able to access the services without permission and control. Testing can be tough as the app developer will not supply the operator with the source code. Developer guidelines can help to streamline the process and ensure high quality

We are currently working on a proof of concept system to get these concepts into practice. We intend to build backend services and protect them with an API Gateway as depicted in Figure 4. Afterwards we will attack this demo system in various ways - our results will then be published.

References

[1] J. Gummaraju, T. Desikan and Y. Turner, "Over 30% of Official Images in Docker Hub Contain High Priority Security Vulnerabilities," 2015, URL: https://banyanops.com/blog/analyzing-docker-hub/ [accessed: 2018-1-8].

[2] "GDPR Regulations," 2017, URL: http://www.eugdpr.org/the-regulation.html [accessed: 2018-1-8].

[3] J. Hertz, "Abusing privileged and unprivileged linux containers," nccgroup, Tech. Rep., 2016.

[4] "Dirty COW ," 2016, URL: https://dirtycow.ninja/ [accessed: 2018-1-8].

[5] "Linux Vulnerability Statistics," 2017, URL: http://www.cvedetails.com/product/47/Linux-Linux-Kernel.html?vendor_id=33 [accessed: 2018-1-8].

[6] S. Fouant, "Man in the Middle (MITM) Attacks Explained: ARP Poisoining," 2010, URL: http://www.shortestpathfirst.net/2010/11/18/man-in-the-middle-mitm-attacks-explained-arp-poisoining/ [accessed: 2018-1-8].

[7] F. Callegati, W. Cerroni and M. Ramilli, "Man-in-the-Middle Attack to the HTTPS Protocol," IEEE Security & Privacy, vol. 7, no. 1, 2009, pp. 78–81.

[8] C. Evans, C. Palmer and R. Sleevi, "Public Key Pinning Extension for HTTP," RFC Editor, techreport 7469, Apr. 2015, URL: https://tools.ietf.org/html/rfc7469 [accessed: 2018-1-8].

[9] Docker, "Docker security," 2017, URL: https://docs.docker.com/engine/security/security/#control-groups [accessed: 2018-1-8].

[10] M. Ridwan, "Separation Anxiety: A Tutorial for Isolating Your System with Linux Namespaces," 2014, URL: https://www.toptal.com/linux/separation-anxiety-isolating-your-system-with-linux-namespaces [accessed: 2018-1-8].

[11] "Capabilities - Overview of Linux Capabilities," 2017, URL: http://man7.org/linux/man-pages/man7/capabilities.7.html [accessed: 2018-1-8].

[12] D. J. Walsh, "Your visual how-to guide for SELinux policy enforcement," 2013, URL: https://opensource.com/business/13/11/selinux-policy-guide [accessed: 2018-1-8].

[13] Ubuntu, "Apparmor," 2017, URL: http://manpages.ubuntu.com/manpages/trusty/man7/apparmor.7.html [accessed: 2018-1-8].

[14] Center for Internet Security, "CIS Docker Community Edition Benchmark," Center for Internet Security, techreport, 2017.

[15] C. Richardson, "Pattern: Microservice Architecture," 2016, URL: http://microservices.io/patterns/microservices.html accessed: 2018-1-8].

[16] T. Dierks and E. Rescorla, "The Transport Layer Security (TLS) Protocol Version 1.2," RFC Editor, techreport, Aug. 2008, URL: https://www.ietf.org/rfc/rfc5246.txt [accessed: 2018-1-8].

[17] G. R. S. Weir and A. Aßmuth, "Strategies for intrusion monitoring in cloud services," The 8th International Conference on Cloud Computing, GRIDs, and Virtualization, Proceedings, 2017, pp. 49–53.

[18] D. Hardt, "The OAuth 2.0 Authorization Framework," RFC Editor, techreport, Oct. 2012, URL: https://tools.ietf.org/html/rfc6749 [accessed: 2017-1-8].

[19] OWASP, "Static code analysis," 2017, URL: https://www.owasp.org/index.php/Static_Code_Analysis [accessed: 2018-1-8].

Can Forensic Audit Help Address the Cloud Forensic Problem in Light of the Requirements of the Forthcoming European Union General Data Protection Regulation?

Bob Duncan*, Mark Whittington†
Business School
University of Aberdeen
Aberdeen, UK
Emails: *robert.duncan@abdn.ac.uk, †mark.whittington@abdn.ac.uk

***Abstract*—There is no doubt that the forthcoming European Union (EU) General Data Protection Regulation (GDPR), which comes into effect on 25th May 2018, will certainly concentrate many corporate minds. As for those who rely on cloud computing, there is likely to be even more consternation in the ranks, due to the issues surrounding dealing with the Cloud Forensic Problem. While it is the case that all computing systems are constantly under serious attack, this particular problem arises due to the fact that once an attacker gains a foothold in a cloud system and becomes an intruder, there is very little to prevent the intruder from gaining sufficient privileges to then completely delete all trace of their incursion, possibly deleting far more records than they need to in the process. Additionally, there is nothing to prevent them from then helping themselves to any amount of data covered by the GDPR, either by viewing it, modifying it, deleting it or ex-filtrating it from the victim system. This, then, will present a compliance nightmare to a great many cloud users, many of whom are poorly prepared to cope with this serious practical and financial challenge. In this paper, we consider how the use of robust forensic audit techniques from the accounting world might be applied to mitigate this serious challenge for such companies.**

Keywords*–*Forensic audit; GDPR compliance; cloud forensic problem.

I. Introduction

Achieving information security with conventional distributed network computer systems presents a significant challenge, but this challenge increases exponentially when we introduce cloud computing to the mix, due to the multiplicity and complexity of hardware and software layers and the number of actors with differing agendas, involved in any cloud ecosystem. The principal reason for the difficulty of this challenge is the so called "Cloud Forensic Problem".

This arises once an attacker gains a foothold in a cloud system and becomes an intruder. Once this happens, there is little to prevent the intruder from helping themselves to any amount of data, either by viewing, modifying, deleting or ex-filtrating it from the victim system. Worse still, there is nothing to prevent the intruder from gaining sufficient privileges to completely delete all trace of their attack.

The forthcoming EU General Data Protection Regulation (GDPR) [1] comes into effect on 25th May 2018, and a principal requirement is the protection of personally identifiable information held by any organisation, anywhere in the world, on pain of severe financial penalties. Given that the cloud forensic problem presents a potentially insurmountable compliance problem, a great many organisations are likely to be exposed to incalculable potential penalties for the inevitable string of cyber breaches that are likely to ensue.

We start in Section II, by considering the cloud forensic problem and the challenges it poses. We turn to the accounting world to see which techniques we could implement to help address these serious challenges in Section III, where we look at accounting, audit and forensic accounting to see how it works for the accounting world, and in Section IV, we consider how we might develop some of these well established techniques to help us address this significant cloud security problem. In Section VI, we look at how we might use the immutable database as the core of this approach. In Section VIII, we discuss our conclusion and future work.

II. The Cloud Forensic Problem

Cloud systems are extremely popular with companies due to the flexibility offered by cloud. Speed of start-up, ease of scalability to match the demand curve and the revenue nature of the costs involved all provide a strong incentive for companies to use cloud services. Cloud computing has been with us now for over 10 years, and while much of the early research concentrated on usability [2] [3] and performance [4]–[6], it was not long before thoughts of security [7]–[9] and privacy [10] [11] started to surface.

While the US National Institute for Standards and Technology (NIST) were one of the first organisations to propose standard definitions [12] [13], interest in security [14]–[17] and privacy [18]–[20] started to grow.

Thoughts also started turning to accountability [8] [21]–[23], given the evolving complexities of cloud ecosystems.

While there have been some really positive advances in both security and privacy during this time, there remains one fundamental weakness that has not been resolved, namely the "cloud forensic problem". All computer systems are subject to continuous and serious attack, and cloud systems are no exception. It would be realistic to state that no system is immune to attack, and this is particularly true for cloud systems.

The main focus of an attacker is to breach a system, which can involve a considerable amount of work on their part. The more diligent will first perform surveillance, compile many analyses of how the various company systems are structured and how they interact with each other. Often, they will also carry out huge amounts of work to understand the people of the organization, since they are usually the weak link in the chain [24]. This extensive intelligence gathering will usually cover every conceivable aspect of all company systems to ensure they discover everything they need to know about the company. This why it is so important to analyse system logs, in order to gain a better understanding of who is actually attacking their systems.

Other attackers, will be much less organised, simply trying to hack in to company systems, without a thought of the overview of the company concerned. They will merely look for known vulnerabilities and try to attack them. There are other attackers who will specifically attack the people of the company through social engineering and other similar approaches. The first objective of all attackers is the same — to penetrate the system in order to become an intruder.

The aim is not just to get in, and out, as quickly as possible, but to develop a long term foothold, secrete themselves into corporate servers and other systems which will allow them to return to help themselves whenever they want. The longer they remain in the system, the more they are likely to try to escalate privileges to give them access to more and more possible information. All too often, they are helped along the way by the companies themselves, often through an element of laziness on the part of system administrators [25].

If we look back five years ago, at previous cyber breach reports [26], there was a global average time of 6 months between breach and discovery. With more rigorous attention paid to reading and analysing their server logs, it is obvious they could have discovered intruders much more quickly. By 2016, the time between breach and discovery had dropped to a matter of weeks rather than months [27], however, this is still not good enough to keep on top of what is going on in corporate systems.

Companies often contribute to their own downfall by failing to update security patches to both operating systems and software systems, complexities from legacy applications applications and risks of outages being reasons or excuses for slow implementation [28]. All of these issues conspire to lead inexorably to the, as yet unresolved, cloud forensic problem — namely, that once an intruder is in the system, and has escalated sufficient privileges, there is nothing to prevent them from deleting the forensic trail, all system logs and audit trails, thus hiding all evidence of their successful penetration and of the size and nature of their crime.

Under the forthcoming GDPR [1], any breached organisation must report the breach within 72 hours of discovery of the breach. They must also report how many relevant records have been compromised, whether by having been read, amended, deleted or ex-filtrated from the system. Given that many system logs are also not turned on by default [41], this means identifying which records have been compromised, whether by having been read, amended, deleted or ex-filtrated, will present a serious enough challenge in the first place, but since the intruder will likely have deleted all forensic trails in the system, the likelihood of an organisation being able to properly identify which records have been compromised may be impossible to determine.

This means not only non-compliance with the GDPR, triggering fines, but failure to tackle some elementary steps will then cause these fines to escalate following repeated events to the greater of €20million or 4% of global turnover. The size of the potential fines, along with the bad publicity will surely get the attention of organizations.

III. USEFUL TECHNIQUES FROM THE ACCOUNTING WORLD

The process of accounting has been around for millennia, with the underlying standard approach of double entry bookkeeping in use for over 500 years, with the generally accepted story placing its creation in Italy. Accounting is primarily seen as a technique for collecting, measuring, processing and communicating financial information about the economic performance of entities, in order to provide decision useful information for interested parties, such as management, investors, creditors and regulators [30]. The International Accounting Standards Board (IASB) issued a similar, but more user-constrained definition in 2015, namely "The objective of general purpose financial reporting is to provide financial information about the reporting entity that is useful to existing and potential investors, lenders and other creditors in making decisions about providing resources to the entity. Those decisions involve buying, selling or holding equity and debt instruments, and providing or settling loans and other forms of credit." [31]

Auditing, too, has been around for millennia, as there has always been a need to provide assurance that accounts and financial statements present a "true and fair view" of the business under review. Naturally, many accounting and auditing techniques can also be applied to anything else that is measurable, and in this case, of particular interest to us is data. Hence, seeking to apply the more evolved and time tested techniques from accounting and auditing techniques to the management and governance of data in the cloud would seem logical.

A further extension of the processes of accounting and audit is forensic (OED [32] "pertaining to, connected with, or used in courts of law; suitable or analogous to pleadings in court") accounting, which as the definition suggests is the process of preparing evidence suitable for use in a court of law.

We can use these techniques, which have long been developed in the accounting world to good effect in helping us secure our cloud data. We can then liken the database system to an accounting system, whereby we collect, measure, process and communicate non-accounting information concerning a business to the people for whom it is intended or relevant.

In principal, we can then use cloud audit to provide assurance of the data provenance of all the data held in the database system, and in the event of a security breach, we can easily apply cloud forensic techniques, learning from the accounting world, in order to help us bring about a successful prosecution in the courts and be aware of the steps needed to improve security for the future. In practice, this will, of course, be far harder to achieve.

Of course, it is worth pointing out that for centuries, accountants have enjoyed the benefits of working with hard copy books, written with quill pen and ink. This medium presents the benefit of providing a hard ink trail to follow, something which we shall later see is no longer available with modern cloud systems.

IV. FORENSIC CLOUD AUDIT

An interesting distinction in definition between "forensic accounting" and "cloud computing forensic science" is the presence of that last word science. Hopwood et al., [33] give the following definition for forensic accounting:

Forensic accounting is the application of investigative and analytic skills for the purpose of resolving financial issues in a manner that meets standards required by courts of law. Notice that forensic accounting is not limited to the use of financial investigations that result in legal prosecution; however, if this is the purpose, the investigation and analysis must meet the standards required in the court of law that has jurisdiction. (page 3)

Whilst NIST [34] provides the following discussion and definition:

Many experts consider forensic science to be the application of a broad spectrum of sciences and technologies to the investigation and establishment of facts of interest in relation to criminal, civil law, or regulatory issues. However, the resulting techniques may also be used for purposes outside the scope of law to reconstruct an event that has occurred. Cloud computing forensic science is the application of scientific principles, technological practices and derived and proven methods to reconstruct past cloud computing events through identification, collection, preservation, examination, interpretation and reporting of digital evidence.

Note that the forensic accounting definition does not include the word science, despite the area (see for example two textbooks Taylor [35] and Hopwood et al., [33]) including scientific methods. Taylor [35], as a more introductory text, focuses initially and at some length on the need to understand background and environmental issues, using this as a backdrop before moving on to, again, a largely discursive review of the wide range of relevant criminal activities that might require the attention of the forensic accountant. He also addresses risk management issues in relation to IT systems, briefly including the cloud, and the process of investigation. Hopwood et al., [33] have a similar structure but give a little greater weight to forensic science and computer forensics.

From the computer science camp, Choo and Dehghantanha [36], a more scholarly work, reflects a greater weight placed on technical issues, the tools and techniques needed, for forensic cloud investigations. Almulla et al., [37] review the cloud forensic literature and find some discursive, though many technical papers.

Issues requiring computer forensic audit are likely to involve the stealing of money, the stealing of monetizable data or the misrepresentation of data to personal or group advantage. These are areas which accountants have strived to address over decades in less technical and complex settings. It would seem logical that their group learning over time would have some relevance and currency to the new cloud situation.

Like most professions, accountants have well organised professional exams. The Association of Chartered Certified Accountants (ACCA), an international professional body with over 200,000 members [38], has an exam at its professional stage, Advanced Auditing and Assurance [39], that includes a section on forensic audit though it should be noted that it is only a small part. It would seem that qualified accountants are ill-prepared for the complexities of the cloud environment, both in terms of understanding the environmental issues, though there is accessible material for them to pick up some of this (see Taylor [35] and Hopwood et al., [33]), as well as comprehending the technical ones, which would be a far more complex and difficult step. Whilst there are a few small organisations focusing on forensic accounting and audit, these appear peripheral (for example..), it does not seem that many qualified accountants have moved into this more rarefied space by adding years of further learning to their accounting badge.

From the other direction, computer specialists clearly have an understanding of the technology and some understanding of the softer environmental, legal and behavioural issues (see Choo and Dehghantanha [36]) though little if any accounting awareness.

So, it would seem, that apart from a few exceptional, motivated, highly skilled individuals there is not yet a significant body that balances the three areas in the venn diagram below. The diagram is, of course, highly simplistic intending to just give a broad view of the difficulties in bringing the wide range of knowledge and experience required for forensic cloud investigation.

Whilst there are many audit tools, the computing literature already uses the "audit trail" [37] when discussing evidence integrity, however in previous work [40]–[43], we have questioned the level of development of these audit trails and whether all the lessons from the rich accounting history in this area have been taken on board. One stark difference between the accounting approach and the computing one is that of redundancy. To the accountant, there is an expectation of keeping more rather than less, with computer scientists having a focus on efficiency and minimising costs. Another is some level of agreement on what should be in an audit trail. For example, Bernstein [44] sees the trail including: events, logs, and the analysis of these, whilst Chaula [45] gives a longer, more detailed list: raw data, analysis notes, preliminary development and analysis information, processes notes, and so on. Pearson et al. [9], as far back as 2010, accept that attaining consistent, meaningful cloud audit trails is a goal rather than reality. More worryingly, Ko et al. [21] point out that it is possible to delete the audit trail along with a cloud instance, meaning there is no record then remaining. Ko [46] details the requirements for accountability.

V. THE SPECIAL SKILLS MIX NEEDED FOR CLOUD FORENSIC AUDIT

As we mentioned earlier, with modern cloud systems, we no longer are able to enjoy the benefits of the permanent ink trail. While reasonable alternatives can be available with conventional distributed network systems, this is not the case for cloud systems. We discussed the Cloud Forensic Problem earlier, and it is this security weakness inherent in cloud systems that makes this job significantly harder to accomplish effectively.

When considering cloud forensic issues, it is now clear that we can no longer afford to rely on conventional discipline boundaries when trying to address these issues, as it is now likely that all the disciplines affected are likely to suffer from a potentially significant knowledge gap. Clearly, the cloud environment is considerably different from conventional distributed network models under the sole control of a company. There are also a great many actors involved in such an environment, each potentially with its own agenda. Legal and regulatory issues are a lot less clearly defined for cloud environments, with the increased likelihood of multiple companies and jurisdictions.

We also have to contend with a number of uninvited actors — namely, the attackers and the intruders, with the latter presenting the greater challenge.

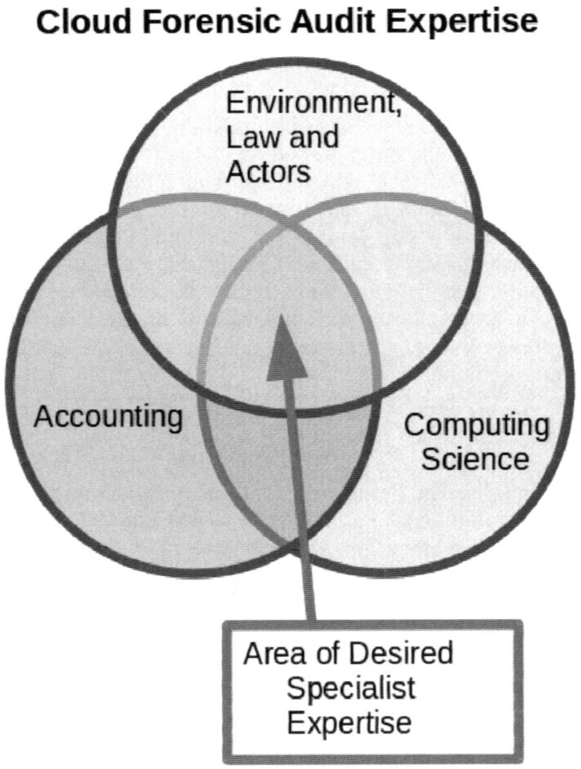

Figure 1. The Area of Desired Expertise

This means we can no longer consider addressing cloud forensic audit from an insular perspective, since accountants, computer scientists and legal, regulatory and other actors within the cloud environment will all suffer from incomplete knowledge, which rather suggests there are likely to be weaknesses in their various individual approaches. Equally, in the absence of the solid 'ink trail', this increases the complexity of the task exponentially. In Figure fig:venn, we show the overlapping Area of Desired Expertise that is needed for all three disciplines to fully understand where this knowledge gap needs to be addressed.

Currently, when it comes to Cloud, intruders have it all their own way. Once they are in the system, it is merely a matter of time until they have sufficient privileges to delete the forensic trail, thus allowing them to bed down for the long run. Since they are likely to be deleting all audit and forensic trails as they go, this also means an increase in difficulty, verging on the impossible, for data controllers to safely keep the organisation fully compliant with all regulatory and legislative requirements they must adhere to in order to achieve compliance, security and privacy.

There are, therefore, two major goals that must be dealt with. First, we need to restore the permanent 'ink trail' so that we have something to follow, and this is where the immutable audit trail process comes in. Second, we have to fill the various knowledge gaps to ensure that all parties involved in Cloud Forensic Audit are fully up to speed. This will come down to a combination of collaboration and proper training. This latter is outside the scope of this paper, but the first is very much a part of it, and we discuss this further in the next section.

VI. THE IMMUTABLE DATABASE

We can see that compliance with the GDPR is not a readily achievable goal that can be easily met by any organisation using Cloud services, due to the difficulties associated with the Cloud Forensic Problem. Thus, we must ensure we create and maintain both a secure forensic and audit trail in order to have any chance of making this happen.

We need to consider very carefully exactly what we need to log to ensure we can achieve compliance with the GDPR. This means we need to monitor our Cloud instances, we need to monitor who is accessing our systems and we need to monitor what is happening with our database systems.

We start by considering our Cloud instances. As Duncan and Whittington have shown in [41] [47] [42], a working solution can be found using an immutable database at its core to record all the relevant information we would require. This means we must first consider carefully exactly what that information should be.

We would want to log all significant events as they transpire during the life cycle of each Cloud instance, with the first significant event being the creation of the Cloud instance, and the last being the shutting down of that instance. Under normal circumstances, these, and all other lifetime events, would be logged on the instance itself. This, as we know from Ko et al. [21], is a dangerous thing to do; thus our first step will be to ensure this data is logged additionally onto an external secure immutable database to ensure it achieves full persistence.

This external database must run on a dedicated secure server, protected by an Intrusion Detection System (IDS), and the database must be immutable, i.e., append only. This secure server will also use dedicated software agents to police the activities being logged, so that the occurrence of any significant event (such as the shutting down of a Cloud instance) will be instantly identified and reported for approval/further investigation.

Turning to the question of who is using our systems, we want to understand who is logging in to our systems, where they come from and what they do once they have successfully logged in. Thus we must capture the relevant detail from the access logs. The detail of how this may be carried out will depend on the systems architecture deployed, the type of access control credentials used and means of controlling access to the various systems available to specific users. A multi-factor authentication approach is always better than access by password. Proper logging of each step in the process is also always preferable.

Once a user gains access to any system, we still want to know where the user came from, and we certainly want to know what the user is doing with the system after they gain access. Thus we should be logging all the steps that the user takes, regardless of whether access is via physical presence or via remote login. In other words, we need to log every single query made or instruction given to the system. We might wish to consider whether we want to record what the result of that query would be, since this might generate inordinate amounts of data in the case of a database query. Whatever we decide is required, we must ensure a separate copy of the queries recorded are stored into our dedicated secure immutable database. It is clear that redundancy can be a good thing.

VII. Discussion

Having devloped a workable solution to this problem, we may well have some questions, such as:

- How easy is it to implement?
- How quickly and how well will interested parties adhere to such a solution?
- In the event of a breach, who will be responsible and what might the consequences be?

The answer to the first question is that we take the view that this approach needs to be simple to implement and simple to maintain. It is as simple as switching on the necessary forensic and audit trail logging, then writing a chron job to forward the resulting logs to the immutable database. Wherever possible, such programmes should be set to immutable to make it difficult for attackers and intruders to delete them. A regular check on the configuration files would also be a useful thing to do.

For the second question, it is likely that the easier something is to implement, the more likelihood that it will be implemented. It is not challenging to implement, nor to maintain, and the cnsequences of failing to do so could have a huge adverse impact, so there is a considerable incentive to both implement and maintain this approach.

As to the third question, it is not a question of 'in the event of a breach', but rather a case of accepting there will be breaches, and these are likely to be a continuous feature. As soon as a breach occurs, a forensic trail will be generated and stored both within the Cloud instance , as well as in the off-site immutable database. Under normal circumstances, the attacker will now attempt to dig deep, escalate privileges and delete the forensic trail. The longer the intruder remains inside the system, the more likelihood that a successful deletion of the audit trail will take place. However, with a covert copy of the forensic and audit trail data available, this will allow some potentially fruitful investigative work to take place.

In the event that an attack against the Cloud instance is successful, where will liability sit? The GDPR regulation is quite clear. In the event of a breach, the Data Controller has a legal obligation to notify the Supervisory Authority within 72 hours of becoming aware of a breach. Individuals must also be notified in the event that encryption is not used. Clearly the use of encryption would be a prudent approach to minimise the impact of the breach, as well as the amount of any possible fine.

VIII. Conclusion and Future Work

We have seen that compliance with the EU GDPR for all Cloud users is likely to present a significant challenge. Without special measures being taken, it is likely that compliance will prove impossible to achieve. This is likely to expose such Cloud users to the full force of the penalties of this regulation, which are significant.

It is clear that a minimal requirement will be to generate both a secure forensic trail and an audit trail, in order to have the basic requirements to be able to consider fulfilling the regulatory requirements in the event of a breach. Without this in place, it is likely to be impossible to comply with the legislation, thus rendering the organisation liable to some serious penalties.

In this paper, we have identified the particular issues that companies who are Cloud users and are liable to be GDPR compliant must be able to deal with. There is no point in relying on Cloud service providers to take care of this matter. The company data controller is accountable to the regulator for ensuring the company is compliant, and without both a forensic trail and a full audit trail for the PII held on behalf of EU residents, then compliance will not be possible. This will lead to potentially massive fines being applied — a situation that is potentially avoidable.

We are in the process of building a miniature real life Cloud system on which to test our ideas. The server will run a full Cloud management system, which will be used to run a number of independent Cloud instances, all of which will run web servers with database back ends to replicate the approach of many Cloud users. This will be subject to rigorous attack, with the view to discover whether the immutable database approach can allow Cloud users to be GDPR compliant.

We have a range of permutations to test, and we seek to find the optimum solution providing the right balance between usability, performance, cost and ease of dealing with breaches. We shall be reporting our results later this year, and we will be working towards delivering a workable solution to keep Cloud users compliant.

References

[1] EU, "EU General Data Protection Regulation (GDPR)," 2017. [Online]. Available: http://www.eugdpr.org/ [Retrieved: December 2017]

[2] T. Takahashi, Y. Kadobayashi, and H. Fujiwara, "Ontological Approach toward Cybersecurity in Cloud Computing Categories and Subject Descriptors," in Science And Technology, 2010, pp. 100–109.

[3] L. M. Vaquero, L. Rodero-Merino, J. Caceres, and M. Lindner, "A Break in the Clouds: Towards a Cloud Definition," ACM SIGCOMM Computer Communication Review, vol. 39, no. 1, 2008, p. 50.

[4] M. Alhamad, T. Dillon, C. Wu, and E. Chang, "Response Time for Cloud Computing Providers," Response, 2010, pp. 8–10.

[5] D. Durkee, "Why Cloud Computing Will Never Be Free," Communications of the ACM, vol. 53, no. 5, may 2010, p. 62.

[6] S. Fraser et al., "Cloud Computing Beyond Objects: Seeding the Cloud," Communications, 2009, pp. 847–850.

[7] A. Haeberlen, "A Case for the Accountable Cloud," ACM SIGOPS Operating Systems Review, vol. 44, no. 2, 2010, p. 52.

[8] S. Pearson, "Towards Accountability in the Cloud," IEEE Internet Computing, vol. 15, no. 4, jul 2011, pp. 64–69.

[9] S. Pearson and A. Benameur, "Privacy, Security and Trust Issues Arising from Cloud Computing," in 2010 IEEE Second International Conference on Cloud Computing Technology and Science, no. December. Ieee, nov 2010, pp. 693–702.

[10] R. Buyya, C. S. Yeo, S. Venugopal, J. Broberg, and I. Brandic, "Cloud computing and emerging IT platforms: Vision, hype, and reality for delivering computing as the 5th utility," Future Generation Computer Systems, vol. 25, no. 6, 2009, p. 17.

[11] L. M. Kaufman, "Data security in the world of cloud computing," IEEE Security and Privacy, vol. 7, no. 4, jul 2009, pp. 61–64.

[12] P. Mell and T. Grance, "Effectively and Securely Using the Cloud Computing Paradigm," NIST, Information Technology Laboratory, vol 2, no 8, pp 304-311.

[13] P. Mell and T. Grance, " The NIST definition of cloud computing.,"Tech. Rep., 2011. [Online]. https://doi.org/10.6028/NIST.SP.800-145 [Retrieved: December 2017]

[14] S. Bradshaw, C. Millard, and I. Walden, "Contracts for Clouds: Comparison and Analysis of the Terms and Conditions of Cloud Computing Services," International Journal of Law and Information Technology, vol. 19, no. 3, 2011, pp. 187–223.

[15] K. Hon, C. Millard, and I. Walden, "The Problem of 'Personal Data' in Cloud Computing - What Information is Regulated ?" 2011. [Online]. Available: http://ssrn.com/abstract=1562461 [Retrieved: December 2017]

[16] M. Iansiti and G. L. Richards, "Economic Impact of Cloud Computing," Economics of Innovation and New Technology, vol. 7, no. 2000, 2010, pp. 1–42.

[17] N. Papanikolaou, S. Pearson, M. C. Mont, and R. K. L. Ko, "Towards Greater Accountability in Cloud Computing through Natural-Language Analysis and Automated Policy Enforcement," Engineering, 2011, pp. 1–4.

[18] Data Protection Working Party, "Opinion 05/2012 on Cloud Computing," 2012. [Online]. Available: http://ec.europa.eu/justice/data-protection/article-29/documentation/opinion-recommendation/files/2012/wp196_en.pdf [Retrieved: December 2017]

[19] W. Jansen and T. Grance, "Guidelines on Security and Privacy in Public Cloud Computing," NIST, Tech. Rep. 7, 2011. [Online]. Available: http://csrc.nist.gov/publications/nistpubs/800-144/SP800-144.pdf [Retrieved: December 2017]

[20] N. Papanikolaou, S. Pearson, and M. C. Mont, "Towards Natural-Language Understanding and Automated Enforcement of Privacy Rules and Regulations in the Cloud: Survey and Bibliography," Analysis, 2011, pp. 1–9.

[21] R. K. L. Ko et al, "TrustCloud: A framework for accountability and trust in cloud computing," Proceedings - 2011 IEEE World Congress on Services, SERVICES 2011, 2011, pp. 584–588.

[22] R. K. L. Ko, B. S. Lee, and S. Pearson, "Towards achieving accountability, auditability and trust in cloud computing," Communications in Computer and Information Science, vol. 193 CCIS, no. PART 4, 2011, pp. 432–444.

[23] S. Pearson and A. Charlesworth, "Accountability as a way forward for privacy protection in the cloud," Lecture Notes in Computer Science (including subseries Lecture Notes in Artificial Intelligence and Lecture Notes in Bioinformatics), vol. 5931 LNCS, no. December, 2009, pp. 131–144.

[24] M. Hammock, "A Review of the Economics of Information Security Literature," pp. 1–38, 2010. [Online]. Available: http://ssrn.com/abstract=1625853 [Retrieved: December 2017]

[25] A. M. Froomkin, "Government Data Breaches," Berkeley Technology Law Journal, 2009, pp. 1–42.

[26] Verizon, "2012 Data Breach Investigations Report," Verizon, Tech. Rep., 2012.

[27] Verizon, "2016 Verizon Data Breach Report," Tech. Rep., 2016.

[28] D. Kossmann, T. Kraska, and S. Loesing, "An evaluation of alternative architectures for transaction processing in the cloud," in Proceedings of the 2010 International Conference on Management of Data. Indianapolis, Indiana: ACM Press, 2010, pp. 579–590.

[29] B. Duncan and M. Whittington, "Enhancing Cloud Security and Privacy: The Cloud Audit Problem," in Submitted to Cloud Computing 2016, Rome, 2016, pp. 1–6.

[30] A. A. A. C. to Prepare a Statement of Basic Accounting Theory, A statement of basic accounting theory. American Accounting Association, 1966.

[31] IASB, "IASB ED/2015/3 - Exposure Draft Conceptual Framework for Financial Reporting Comments," IASB, Tech. Rep., 2015.

[32] "forensic, adj. and n." OED Online. Oxford University Press, December 2017. [Retrieved: December 2017.]

[33] W. S. Hopwood, J. J. Leiner, and D. G. R. Young, Forensic accounting and fraud examination. McGraw-Hill, 2012.

[34] NIST, "NIST Cloud Computing Forensic Science Challenges," 2014, p. 51.

[35] J. Taylor, Forensic accounting. Financial Times Prentice Hall, 2011.

[36] K.-K. Choo and A. Dehghantanha, "Contemporary Digital Forensics Investigations of Cloud and Mobile Applications," in Contemporary Digital Forensic Investigations of Cloud and Mobile Applications. Elsevier, 2017, pp. 1–6.

[37] S. A. Almulla, Y. Iraqi, and A. Jones, "A State-of-the-Art Review of Cloud Forensics," Journal of Digital Forensics, Security and Law, vol. 9, no. 4, 2014, pp. 7–28.

[38] ACCA, "ACCA celebrates hitting 200,000 members worldwide with a global tour to honour each and every one," London, 2018.

[39] ACCA, "Advanced Audit and Assurance: Syllabus and Study Guide September 2018 to September 2019," 2017.

[40] B. Duncan and M. Whittington, "Compliance with standards, assurance and audit: does this equal security?" in Proceedings of the 7th International Conference on Security of Information and Networks - SIN '14. Glasgow: ACM, 2014, pp. 77–84.

[41] B. Duncan and M. Whittington, "Enhancing Cloud Security and Privacy: The Power and the Weakness of the Audit Trail," in Cloud Computing 2016: The Seventh International Conference on Cloud Computing, GRIDs, and Virtualization, no. April. Rome: IEEE, 2016, pp. 125–130.

[42] B. Duncan and M. Whittington, "Creating an Immutable Database for Secure Cloud Audit Trail and System Logging," in Cloud Computing 2017: The Eighth International Conference on Cloud Computing, GRIDs, and Virtualization. Athens, Greece: IARIA, ISBN: 978-1-61208-529-6, 2017, pp. 54–59.

[43] B. Duncan and M. Whittington, "Creating and Configuring an Immutable Database for Secure Cloud Audit Trail and System Logging," International Journal On Advances in Security, vol. 10, no. 3 & 4, 2017, pp. 155–166. [Online]. Available: ISSN: 1942-2636, http://www.iariajournals.org/security/index.html [Retrieved: December 2017]

[44] D. Bernstein, E. Ludvigson, K. Sankar, S. Diamond, and M. Morrow, "Blueprint for the intercloud - Protocols and formats for cloud computing interoperability," in Proceedings of the 2009 4th International Conference on Internet and Web Applications and Services, ICIW 2009, 2009, pp. 328–336.

[45] J. A. Chaula, "A Socio-Technical Analysis of Information Systems Security Assurance: A Case Study for Effective Assurance," Ph.D. dissertation, 2006. [Online]. Available: http://scholar.google.com/scholar?hl=en&btnG=Search&q=intitle:A+Socio-Technical+Analysis+of+Information+Systems+Security+Assurance+A+Case+Study+for+Effective+Assurance#1 [Retrieved: December 2017]

[46] R. K. L. Ko, "Data Accountability in Cloud Systems," in Security, Privacy and Trust in Cloud Systems. Springer, 2014, pp. 211–238.

[47] B. Duncan and M. Whittington, "Cloud cyber-security: Empowering the audit trail," International Journal on Advances in Security, vol. 9, no. 3 & 4, 2016, pp. 169–183. [Online]. Available: https://www.iariajournals.org/security/tocv9n34.html [Retrieved: December 2017]

Management of Virtual Desktops in Energy Efficient Office Environments Using Thin Clients

Christina Sigl, Alexander Faschingbauer and Andreas Berl
Deggendorf Institute of Technology, Germany
Email: [christina.sigl, alexander.faschingbauer, andreas.berl]@th-deg.de

Abstract—**There are different approaches to make office computer environments more energy efficient: terminal server environments and virtual desktop infrastructures. While in both environments money saving thin clients are used to connect a server, this paper presents an alternative approach, that uses several distributed workstations instead of a server. Therefore, this topology allows some savings concerning power consumption, as well as procurement cost, because no centralized server is required. Theoretical consideration for a typical use case showed a potential for energy savings using this approach. Moreover, the model is especially interesting for small office environments. Existing workstation computers can be used and replaced step by step through thin clients without purchasing an expensive virtualization server.**

Keywords–VDI; virtualization; distributed hypervisors; thin client; virtual desktops; energy efficiency

I. Introduction

In times of climate change, the energy demand of enterprises becomes a point of interest. Often the term Green IT is used with the goal to reduce CO_2 emissions. For modern office environments, this means reducing energy consumption and hence energy costs. Therefore, the approaches of terminal servers and virtualization are used to implement energy efficient infrastructures. Whereby, these environments are mainly using energy efficient and cost effective thin clients. Using terminal servers, end users are connected to a central server, where all the calculations are done. The other cost effective tool in computer technology is virtualization. Using this technique, user environments with operating system and all required applications are virtualized using virtual machines running on a centralized server with one hypervisor. Thus, the utilization rate of a server can be enhanced [1]. Nowadays, it is especially used in medium to large scale enterprises, in form of a Virtual Desktop Infrastructure (VDI) [2].

This paper presents an extended and distributed approach of the traditional VDI architecture. Here, virtual desktops are provided by several office workstation computers instead of a central server. Additionally, a set of workstation computers is also replaced by thin clients. Remaining workstations are used as user workspaces and virtualization platform (distributed hypervisors). The paper is focused on the concept of the Workstation based Virtual Desktop Infrastructure (WVDI) model. It covers the question, weather this approach may be used to achieve energy savings. Furthermore, a theoretical evaluation of this approach, using a typical use case in a small office environment, is presented. Thereby it is shown, that WVDI has a theoretical potential to reduce energy consumption within an office infrastructure.

This paper is organized as follows. In section II, the technical background and related work are given. Section III presents the concept of WVDI. Possible limitations of this approach are pointed out in section IV. A theoretical evaluation of the presented model is done in section V. Finally, in section VI we conclude the paper and indicate some further work.

II. Related Work

A. *Terminal Servers*

Applications installed on very powerful servers and providing user sessions for connected terminals are referred to as terminal servers. Usually, terminals are thin clients, which merely create remote connections to terminal server sessions. Since only a video stream, as well as mouse and keyboard input are transmitted over network, a higher degree of data security within an enterprise is reached. Attack surface via network is thus reduced significantly. Compared to environments using workstations or personal computers, terminal servers have many beneficial aspects. Due to centralization, PC maintenance costs decrease. All settings and software installations are accessed and applied centrally. Thus, applications are available to a large number of users. In large companies usage of terminal servers may reduce costs. Compared to a normal workplace, power consumption of a terminal server is only a 1/8th the amount. Further savings can be achieved by replacing expensive workstations with low-cost thin clients. Due to their structure, these environments are reliant on powerful servers [3] [4].

The thin clients and the use of remote display connections are important, but central servers are not used and not regarded further in this paper.

B. *Virtualization Technologies*

Another approach for energy efficient computer environments is virtualization. Many virtualization technologies, which differ with respect to the component to be virtualized exist. Below, two virtualization technologies are described.

1) Server Virtualization: On a physical server hardware a hypervisor, that distributes physical resources to Virtual Machines (VMs), is installed. Each virtual desktop can use physical hardware to a share determined by hypervisor, which ensures that VMs are separated logically and can not interfere or manipulate each other. Virtual desktops can be migrated between physical host systems dynamically, depending on hypervisor and any additional products, without being noticed by the user or operating system running in a VM. This virtualization technology offers greater flexibility, load distribution and reliability. It makes Data Centers (DCs) much more efficient and saves energy [5].

2) Desktop Virtualization: In general, desktop virtualization is similar to server virtualization. The difference is that VMs can be streamed across platforms such as personal computers, laptops or thin clients. Using hosted VDI-Desktops, users work with dedicated virtual desktops on a server. Each user has its work environment in an own VM, that can only be accessed via network. The user terminal serves only for input and output operations and needs almost no computing power. Depending on server performance and VM usage, a variable number of virtual desktops can be deployed on a hypervisor simultaneously [6].

In the approach presented in this paper, hypervisor based server virtualization shall be used on workstations. Therefore, it will be further developed in the course of this paper. Since thin clients can not provide the required computing performance, they are used in combination with hosted VDI-Desktops or VDIs, where programs are executed on a server centrally. Thus, usage of thin clients in VDI is possible, which is relevant for this work.

C. Virtual Desktop Infrastructure

In VDI, user desktop environments are virtualized and converted into VMs. Powerful central servers are equipped with a hypervisor to host and run virtual desktops. Workstations or desktops can be used as terminals on user side and are only used to establish a connection to VMs via a remote display protocol over network. To create a connection to a server hosted virtual machine little computing power is necessary. Hence, inexpensive and energy efficient thin clients are used instead of workstations or personal computers [7]. A central Connection Broker (CB) distributes requests for a remote connection from thin clients and forwards them to correct VMs. Users can login to any terminal device and work with their virtual desktop. VDIs are used in medium to large enterprises and are focused on virtualization of desktop PCs. Use of workstations and desktop computers requires an effort regarding installation, configuration, as well as high procurement and operating costs. Therefore, virtualization becomes interesting and its popularity increases. Usually, for a user it does not matter whether he is connected to a VM from a workstation, desktop or thin client. In case of failure or replacement of an end-device, it is easy to set up a replacement device, because no complex installation and configuration is necessary. The user can work almost seamlessly [8] [9] [10].

D. Virtual Desktop Infrastructure without central servers

Based on VDIs there is an approach without central servers [11] [12]. Here, hosting of VMs is done only on workstations and a software is utilized for virtualization. Employees may use a random workstation to connect to their virtual desktop over network. Virtual machines are located arbitrarily on workstations in an office environment. Depending on workload of individual workstations, virtual machines can be migrated dynamically between them. In this way, the highest possible energy efficiency can be achieved, which is the primary goal of this approach. This approach provides no infrastructure with servers in a server room or DC, but an office environment consisting exclusively of workstations. These are equipped with a hypervisor each, so that virtual desktops can be distributed to workstations variably.

Since thin clients are not yet used, an extension of this approach that allows their usage in such an environment, is presented in this paper. Thin clients have no hypervisor function, but use remote display protocols to connect to VMs hosted on workstations. As thin clients have a much lower power consumption than workstations, energy efficiency can be increased significantly. In addition, savings are possible with regard to cost of ownership, because thin clients are far more economically priced than workstations.

III. Workstation based Virtual Desktop Infrastructure

An extension for a VDI environment is the WVDI model, that uses the approach of replacing servers by workstations to take care of virtualization. In addition, to an environment composed of only workstations, a share of them is replaced by thin clients to achieve further energy savings and reduce procurement costs. Servers are not required, because already existing workstations are hosting VMs [11] [12].

A. Architecture

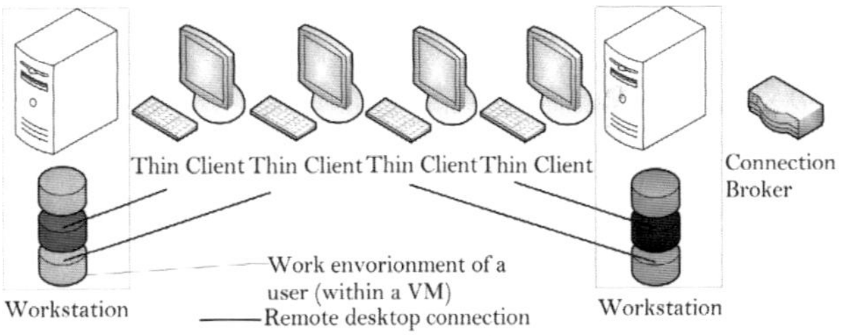

Figure 1. VDI-environment based on workstations

Figure 1 shows an abstract representation of an office environment including two workstations and four thin clients. Workstations provide users the same functionality as thin clients do, namely enable remote access to VMs. Further, there is a virtualization layer on each workstation, that provides virtual desktops (round hard disk icons). On the left and right, both VMs located on top illustrate a virtual desktop accessed via workstation. The other four are accessed via thin clients. Main task of a thin client is to create remote desktop connections to virtual desktops. A CB is illustrated, that takes care of management tasks. It is either implemented on an independent computer or run in a separate virtual machine on a workstation. This approach applies hypervisor based virtualization exactly like VDI, so users can choose their operating system individually. Maximum number of VMs on a workstation is limited by hardware performance. Thus, not as many as on a high performance server can be run. The number of hosted virtual desktops depends on processor performance, memory and hard disk space of a workstation. To run VMs in an office environment, it must consist of at least one workstation with hypervisor.

B. Management concept

A CB is responsible for maintenance of connection requests from the user side. For correct transfer to an appropriate virtual desktop, each user is assigned to a personal VM. The CB knows which hypervisor hosts a proper virtual desktop and manages migrations between workstations centrally, to allow a uniform, but also energy efficient, load distribution.

Goal is to adapt the CB, so that workstations are always utilized to their capacity and also without performance losses, to require less workstations with hypervisor. Remaining workstations can be shut down, but local working users should be considered. Moreover, migration is done in off or on state (Live-Migration). By monitoring utilization of all virtual desktops and workstations, it is decided whether to migrate VMs to another workstation for better performance. This is done completely autonomous and remains unnoticed by users. If a virtual machine has to be run, the respective workstation is woken up via Wake-On-LAN.

C. Assignment of virtual machines

The approach works with static and dynamic assignment of VMs, that can be moved manually, e.g. replace workstations or perform maintenance work. Using static assignment a certain virtual desktop always remains on a specific, previous defined host and is migrated independently of the load level of a workstation. Worst case is if all workstations are switched on and only one virtual desktop is run on each. This is not particularly energy efficient, but implementation is simpler and the CB can be omitted, because organizing and monitoring of dynamic migration is not needed. Alternatively, virtual desktops can be migrated dynamically. Migration can take place at any time, regardless whether a VM is running or not. A CB initiates and monitors all migrations. It is always aware, which workstation is hosting a certain virtual desktop and brokers connection requests accordingly. Migration should be performed in following cases:

1) Start and end of work: At start of work, in most cases, VMs are scattered on switched off workstations. For each additional user who begins to work, the corresponding virtual desktop and hosting workstation are localized and started if necessary. The more users start working, the more workstations have to be run. Depending on the number of VMs run in total and their load, a consolidation on a few or distribution to several workstations, may be useful. If users shut down their virtual desktops or place them in idle state, workstations without running VMs are shut down, unless migrations or backup tasks are pending. Not all users stop working at once. Usually, this extends over a longer period of time. Migration is useful to consolidate still running VMs to as few workstations as possible at an early stage. Thus, energy efficiency increases.

2) Lack of hard disk space: One or more VMs must be migrated to another workstation, if the amount of free disk space of the workstation decreases. Particularly in case of thin-provisioning, where hard disk space for virtual desktops is assured but not physical available at all.

3) High and low utilization: For high workstation utilization in form of processor and memory utilization, it is advisable to migrate VMs to another workstation in order to provide sufficient performance for all users. If necessary, a switched off workstation has to be started. If utilization of workstations is low, it may be advisable to consolidate VMs on less workstations. This increases energy efficiency, because remaining workstations are utilized more efficiently and others are released from their current work and can thus be switched off.

D. Energy savings

In principle, two things establish energy savings using WVDI in office environments. First, many workstations are replaced by energy saving thin clients. Secondly, an intelligent management uses dynamic migration. Resources of workstations are exploited as efficient as possible by running as many VMs per host as feasible. Maximum of hosted VMs are determined by utilization and performance of physical available hardware. In case of high utilization rates of individual workstations, remaining ones, which are not used, can be switched off automatically. Overall, energy savings are achieved through non running workstations. In a scenario where one workstation and three thin clients are used, possible energy saving is theoretical 50% compared to an environment with workstations alone, since mainly thin clients are used for better utilization of workstations. In order to achieve high energy efficiency, just as many workstations as required are switch on. This is possible if running workstations are well utilized, but limitation of performance is reasonable for users.

IV. Possible limitations of WVDI

WVDI enables virtualized office environments to be run energy efficient without a server infrastructure, by using energy saving thin clients and existing workstations with hypervisors to provide VMs. Therefore, energy savings are achieved by replacing some workstations with energy saving thin clients. Analyzing WVDI, possible problems can be identified for practical implementation. Some of these are presented and discussed below.

A. Wake up of Workstations

A CB decides if a workstation is woken up, to serve as hypervisor. This can be done via Wake-On-LAN by sending a magic packet, to give the boot command. A problem cloud be that in an already existing office environment workstations may not be Wake-On-LAN capable or behave incorrectly, e.g. do not follow the usual boot sequence.

B. Properties of virtual desktops

A virtual desktop is located in a VM. Size of a VM can vary arbitrarily, but it must not exceed the local hard disk size, even if thin-provisioning is used, that allows to allocate more hard disk space, than physically available. If allocated memory, that is not physically present, is used entirely, it may lead to a destruction of the VM. Using dynamic migration, maximum hard disk size should be equal to storage capacity of the smallest hard disk integrated in all workstations. Alternatively, VMs, that have not as much physical disk space as allocated, can be prevented from being copied. Depending on virtualization degree, several VMs located on a workstation share space. The size of a virtual machine has a direct impact on migration duration. Further, no special requirements are imposed on the operating system of a virtual desktop, but it has to be supported by hypervisor.

C. Exceeding maximum storage capacity of a workstation

In WVDI, hard disk space can not be added easily. Depletion of storage capacity depends on physical available hard disk space and space already occupied by other VMs. Both values are variable since each workstation can have a different hard disk size and VMs with different virtual disks. Here, an optimization by the CB is necessary, to migrate virtual desktops to other workstations in time and thus an overflow of hard disk is avoided. For static allocation of VMs, it should be sufficient to allocate as much virtual disk space as physical available.

D. Simultaneous start and end of work at all workplaces

If many users start their VMs simultaneously (for example at start of work), virtual desktops must be deployed or upgraded. Because simultaneous switching on/off of multiple VMs requires more hardware performance, this may lead to initial performance limitations. In case of static distribution of virtual machines, this performance limitation is restricted to its boot time. Using (dynamic) migration can cause more limitations. If many migrations take place simultaneously, network load is high correspondingly and depending on network hardware, performance bottlenecks can occur. In the worst case, all VMs are on a single workstation initially and requested concurrently. Then, a majority of VMs is migrated to other workstations, to make the same amount of hardware available for each virtual desktop. To prevent this scenario, the CB has to be parameterized with a maximum number of storable VMs, for each workstation. This number should be chosen individually, depending on the available hardware resources. Virtual desktops have to be distributed to workstations in roughly equal proportions, so that no performance losses occur due to a simultaneous start of all workstations. It is similar if all employees go off duty simultaneously, but do not have to wait for shut down or migration. Instead, this is done in background autonomously, after office hours.

E. Hardware failure of a workstation

If a workstation crashes e.g. due to a disk defect, all stored data and VMs are lost. A backup strategy should be designed, that regular backs up all virtual desktops to a Network Attached Storage (NAS), to prevent data loss. This could be performed every night, when network load is low anyway. Alternatively, VMs could always be migrated to at least two workstations to ensure redundancy. This could be done automated, always after a virtual desktop is shut down. However, this would require additional memory and thus limit the total number of VMs. In addition, network traffic is increased each time a VM is shut down or copied to an additional workstation.

F. Integration of a central management unit for WVDI

A centralized management is necessary to manage VMs and to perform and monitor dynamic migration. This can be implemented on a small computer with low computing power, since high performance is not required for its tasks. Alternatively, a management unit can also be installed on an existing workstation. However, this workstation must be active at all times or at least for the time when a workstation or a thin client is to be used, because it handles incoming connection requests and manages migration processes. Alternatively, an allocation table of VMs could be stored in thin clients and workstations permanently. This may result in a greater administrative management if a device needs to be replaced.

G. Data security and safety

Using WVDI, implementations for physical access protection like in conventional offices are far more difficult, because data is stored in users VMs, that are located on workstations and are thus exposed to third party access. In order to ensure data security, encryption should be used. The best case is to encrypt all VMs entirely if possible and appropriate regarding performance. Further, communication between user workplaces and VMs shall be encrypted.

H. Flexible selection of workplace and telework

The approach allows users to work from home via remote desktop connections. Energy savings are achieved by not running a dedicated workstation for each user separately. A further advantage is, that it is not required to shut down a VM when leaving, but calculations are still pending. Users simply turn off thin clients while virtual desktops are running in background. When working within a virtualized infrastructure, opportunity to change the workspace and continue working is given. Here, the VM continues to run on a respective hypervisor without interruption and only the connection is established from another end device, which may be a thin client, workstation or a computer at home.

I. Operating conditions of a virtual machine

If a VM is paused, the current system state is frozen and written to hard disk. After this, a virtual desktop no longer needs any resources. Power consumption in this state corresponds to a proper turned off VM. A user only has to turn off thin client and peripheral devices, such as a screen or printer. Returning from break, a user starts his thin client and the virtual desktop is woken up, that is again in exact the same state, as left previously so work can be continued seamlessly. This can be problematic if application programs are connected to a central database server directly. It can lead to unwanted results if the database server is disconnected due to timeout, resulting in inconsistencies within database. Another option is to continue to run VMs if a user disconnects and turns off thin client. Time exposure is equal to the other option here. Any further calculations can be continued or database connections maintained. Energy savings are only possible if thin client and its peripherals are turned off. On hypervisor side, no savings can be achieved as the VM is continues running. When returning to work, a user only needs to restart his thin client and the corresponding remote connection.

V. Evaluation of WVDI

To evaluate WVDI, its energy efficiency is compared with conventional workstation or desktop PC solutions. For calculations, power consumption values of respective components were taken into account. The purpose is to determine whether the use of WVDI can save energy or not. The number of necessary workstations and thin clients is determined by the virtualization rate and total number of required workspaces.

Definition: *The **virtualization rate** specifies the maximum number of VMs that can be run on a hypervisor.*

According to this definition, a virtualization rate of three means, on a hypervisor (up to) three VMs can be run. In WVDI a hypervisor runs on a workstation and a user can work with the virtual desktop on it directly. A virtualization rate of three in WVDI means there are a workstation and two thin clients. A virtualization rate of three is noted in this work as VR = 3.

A. General conditions

Certain reference hardware and their parameters (power consumption) are used for a simplified and theoretical evaluation. A workstation serves as a hypervisor and is available to a user as workplace. For remote connection to a VM, a thin client is used as local end device. A desktop computer and workstation (without hypervisor) are used for comparison with conventional desktop PC or workstation based solutions. Performance of all considered components is interpreted for an average user type called "medium user". This user is characterized by using two or three applications at the same time, including e.g. word processing, spreadsheet, database or client/server applications [13]. In order to obtain concrete and realistic performance data, widely used and adapted hardware components for this user type are considered.

1) Workstation: The Fujitsu's CELSIUS W530 Premium Selection workstation with a power consumption of 38 Watts in IdleMode, 100 Watts in Maximum and 44 Watts in OnMode is used as a reference workstation. This workstation is recommended for virtualization tasks by the manufacturer. Values for power consumption (IdleMode and Maximum) were given by the ECO Declaration Sheet [14]. Power consumption of 44 W in OnMode was calculated and rounded using the formula defined in the Product Cases Report of the European Commission [15]:

$$OnMode[W] = 0,9 \cdot IdleMode[W] + 0,1 \cdot Maximum[W]$$

A fixed (38 Watts in IdleMode) and a variable power consumption are included in the total power requirement for each workstation. Variable power consumption is determined by the number of VMs run. A virtual desktop causes an additional power consumption on the host system of up to about five watts [16]. Since they are not always run under full load, an additional power consumption of four watts is assumed for each additional VM. The fact that power consumption is nonlinear according to processor utilization, is neglected, because deviations are minimal to the final result but would increase calculation effort considerably.

2) Thin Client: The Igel UD5-LX thin client with following data is used as a reference device. It has a typical power consumption of 11 Watts. No distinction is made between IdleMode, OnMode and Maximum, since no calculations are performed by thin clients in the actual sense, only a remote session is provided. Hence, utilization is almost always the same.

3) Desktop PC: The Fujitsu's ESPRIMO P720 E90+ desktop PC with following data is used for comparison with WVDI. For each PC a power consumption of 24,2 Watts in OnMode is assumed [17]. It is an all-round PC, dimensioned for conventional office work and has been selected for this reason. For following calculations, a rounded value of 25 watts (OnMode) is used for its power consumption.

In addition, the CB (to manage host assignments of VMs) is not regarded. Since this is only a single small computer or even a single virtual desktop, it is hardly important here. In addition, higher network traffic resulting from a dynamic migration of VMs is not taken into account. Dynamic migration is shown in the best case scenario. With dynamic migration it is possible to cause and approximate the best case. Power consumption of peripheral components are not included here, because these are required in any case, regardless of whether a conventional installation or WVDI is implemented.

B. Energy efficiency in an office environment model

WVDI was designed to enable small enterprises usage of VDI without a dedicated server. Small enterprises typically consist of up to 50 employees. Since in most cases not all users are present at the same time and there are part time employees, this evaluation is based on a more realistic scenario with 30 workplaces. Power consumption is calculated at different virtualization rates. Virtualisation rates of two, four, eight and ten were chosen, since these appear reasonable and realistic. The goal is to determine whether WVDI allows energy savings. For the sake of a clear presentation, an evaluation of the virtualization rates was relinquished. A specific number of workstations and thin clients is required for each virtualization rate. Table I shows how many workstations and thin clients are required for several numbers of virtualization rates.

TABLE I. REQUIRED NUMBER OF WORKSTATIONS AND THIN CLIENTS PER TOTAL NUMBER OF WORKPLACES AND VIRTUALIZATION RATE

	30 Workplaces	
	Workstations	Thin Clients
VR=2	15	15
VR=4	8	22
VR=8	4	26
VR=10	3	27

1) Worst case scenario: Users work on thin clients only and use VMs, which are hosted on different workstations. For each user a thin client and a workstation has to be started. Power consumption is thus higher compared to solutions using only workstations or thin clients. When all workstations have started, only power consumption of thin clients and VMs are added for each additional user. This problem could be solved by organizational measures in the company or by usage of dynamic migration of VMs, but this is not taken into account here. Figure 2 shows that at first, power consumption

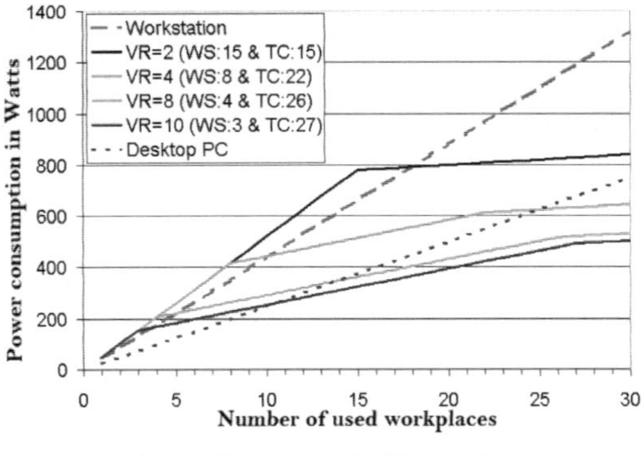

Figure 2. Worst case with 30 workplaces

for all virtualization rates is slightly above the conventional workstation solution. This is due to the fact, that not only a workstation but also a thin client and a VM have to be run per user. Starting from VR=4, it can be seen that even in the worst case, power consumption for ten workplaces is below a workstation solution. Starting from 25 workplaces, power consumption is even below that of a pure desktop computer solution. This is analogous to other virtualization rates. Using a virtualization rate of VR=2, more than 18 workplaces have to be used in order to achieve energy savings compared to a pure workstation solution. Using 30 workplaces power consumption in WVDI is about 400 Watts lesser than the workstation solution. Even if 30 workplaces are used, power consumption of a desktop computer solution is about 100 Watts below the WVDI solution.

2) Best case scenario: The most favorable and thus most energy efficient situation when using WVDI is represented. In this case, it is assumed that users are distributed at their workplaces, so that as few workstations as possible have to be run. This can be done in two ways: Firstly, users are organized in such a way that certain groups of users work with their VMs on the same workstation simultaneously. Thus, only as few workstations as necessary are run. However, this could be difficult to implement, because of a significant reduction in flexibility and higher administrative and organizational effort. Secondly, dynamic migration is implemented. All required VMs are moved dynamically to as few workstations as possible during operation, so that as many workstations as possible can be switched off. This option is much more complex regarding implementation on technical side, but is hardly noticeable to users. Here, the maximum number of VMs per workstation is utilized fully and as few workstations as possible are run. In Figure 3 curves for workstation and desktop computer

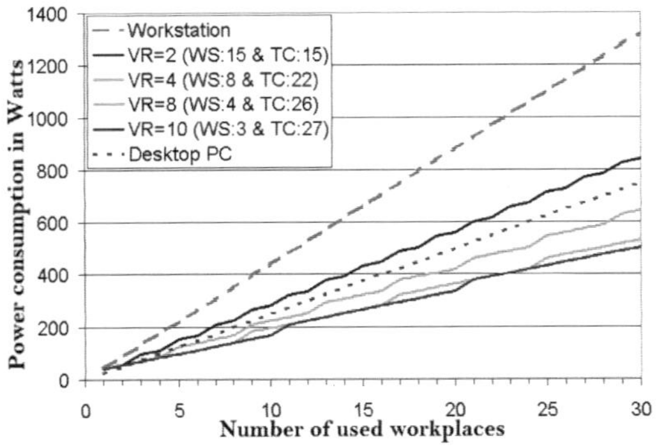

Figure 3. Best case with 30 workplaces

solutions are exactly the same as in the worst case scenario. A further workstation is switched on for each significant increase of a WVDI curve. The Figure shows that using WVDI with the lowest virtualization rate of VR=2, power consumption is below a workstation solution. Using a virtualization rate of VR=3, power consumption is below the desktop PC solution. With a virtualization rate of VR=4, power consumption is half as much compared to a workstation solution. If a best case distribution is ensured by organizational measures or dynamic migration, energy efficiency can be increased significantly, as well as energy savings. It is analogous to other virtualization rates. The best case scenario shows that power consumption of WVDI using a virtualization rate of VR=2 with 30 workplaces is about 400 Watts below a pure workstation solution. Further, the desktop computer solution is about 100 Watts below the WVDI solution. This is the same as in the worst case scenario. Starting with a virtualization rate of VR=4 in the best case, power consumption in WVDI is below a desktop computer solution whereas in the worst case power consumption is lesser than a desktop computer solution if more than 25 workplaces are used.

VI. CONCLUSION

Using WVDI compared to conventional solutions, energy savings, as well as lower procurement costs are possible. Compared to a solution consisting of only workstations, procurement cost savings are already achieved using a virtualization rate of VR=2. Using a virtualization rate of VR=4, procurement costs are already half as much. Even in the worst case scenario, the power consumption of WVDI is below a pure workstation solution, if a minimum virtualization rate of VR=4 with ten workplaces is used. Starting form 25 workplaces, power consumption is also below a desktop computer solution. In the best case, power consumption is already below a pure workstation solution using a virtualization rate of VR=2. This solution is suitable particularly for small office environments, where procurement and maintenance of a large and cost intensive server infrastructure is not worthwhile. Using WVDI, small office infrastructures can still benefit from the advantage of virtualization and increase energy efficiency. Energy savings in WVDI are theoretically determined and illustrated using specific power consumption values for exemplary hardware components (workstations, thin clients and desktop PCs). It is assumed, that execution time is nearly the same in both cases, therefore the decline in power consumption translates to energy savings. Which solution is the one with highest energy efficiency for a respective IT environment, depends on the number of devices, but also on their power consumption.

The result of the research question shows, that WVDI can save energy in theory. Further, the following points have to be considered within the next steps. This paper provides only theoretical calculations, hence, the real number of possible VMs on a host is not considered. Therefore, further steps will be required to evaluate possible limitations of the WVDI model, such as communication and load balancing. Since WVDI is an distributed hypervisor system, network traffic may rise due to an increasing number of required migration processes for consolidation. This may also lead to potential performance cost if those migrations become more frequent. But it must also been taken into account, that a high consolidation rate may decrease performance, because workstations are not as powerful as servers. Another important aspect to be worked on regards data security and privacy assurance in WVDI. Finally, potential drawbacks of WVDI have to be analyzed further, to substantiate energy savings.

ACKNOWLEDGEMENT

This paper is based on the master thesis "Management of Virtual Desktops in Energy Efficient Office Environments Using Thin Clients" of Julian Willerding (Email: julian@willerding.de) written at the University of Passau [18]. The authors would like to thank Julian Willerding for providing his preliminary work for publishment in this paper.

REFERENCES

[1] S. Dutta and A. K. Gupta, "Green computing: A greener approach towards IT," in 2016 3rd International Conference on Computing for Sustainable Global Development (INDIACom), Mar. 2016, pp. 50–53.

[2] M. Plettenberg and R. Spruijt, "State of the VDI and SBC Survey 2017 Edition," Login VSI und VDI Like A Pro, Tech. Rep., Jun. 2017.

[3] C. Kehl and N. Frangos, "The Efficient Installation and Operation of Terminal Server Farms (original title: Die effiziente Installation und der Betrieb von Terminalserverfarmen)," visionapp GmbH, White Paper, April 2007, URL: https://slidedocument.com/die-effiziente-installation-und-der-betrieb-von-terminalserverfarmen [accessed: 2017-12-19].

[4] K. Usvub, A. M. Farooqi, and M. A. Alam, "Edge Up Green Computing In Cloud Data Centers - ProQuest," International Journal of Advanced Research in Computer Science, Tech. Rep., Mar. 2017, URL: https://search.proquest.com/openview/8ad22aad54ab6364be896bb80aaf46d8/1?pq-origsite=gscholar&cbl=1606379 [accessed: 2017-12-12].

[5] VMware, "Virtualization Overview," VMware Inc., White Paper, 2006, URL: http://www.vmware.com/pdf/virtualization.pdf [accessed: 2017-12-20].

[6] D. K. Sachsenmaier, "Energy-efficient Computer Workstations in Office Environments: Technologies and Comparison (original title: Energieeffziente Computerarbeitsplaetze in Bueroumgebungen: Technologien und Vergleich)," Bachelor thesis, University of Passau, September 2013.

[7] L. Casanova, Marcel, and E. Kristianto, "Comparing RDP and PcoIP protocols for desktop virtualization inVMware enviroment," in 2017 5th International Conference on Cyber and IT Service Management (CITSM), Aug. 2017, pp. 1–4.

[8] K. Feldhusen, "Sizing of Virtual Desktop Infrastructures," Whitepaper, Fujitsu Technology Solutions GmbH, White Paper, 2011, URL: http://www.fujitsu.com/downloads/HK/wp-vdi-sizing.pdf [accessed: 2017-12-20].

[9] A. Murphy, "Optimizing VMware View VDI Deployments with F5," F5 Networks Inc., White Paper, 2009, URL: https://www.pei.com/wp-content/uploads/2013/01/Optimizing-VMware-VDI.pdf [accessed:2047-12-19].

[10] E. VMware, Cisco, "Enterprise Virtual Desktop Infrastructure: Design for Performance and Reliability," VMware, Cisco, EMC, White Paper, 2009, URL: http://www.emc.com/collateral/hardware/white-papers/white-paper-vdi.pdf [accessed: 2017-12-20].

[11] A. Berl and H. de Meer, "An Energy Consumption Model for Virtualized Office Environments," Future Generation Computer Systems, vol. 27, no. 8, Oct. 2011, pp. 1047–1055, URL: http://www.net.fim.uni-passau.de/pdf/Berl2011b.pdf http://linkinghub.elsevier.com/retrieve/pii/S0167739X11000616 [accessed: 2017-12-20].

[12] A. Berl, N. Race, J. Ishmael, and H. de Meer, "Network Virtualization in Energy-Efficient Office Environments," Computer Networks, vol. 54, no. 16, Nov. 2010, pp. 2856–2868, URL: http://www.net.fim.uni-passau.de/pdf/Berl2010d.pdf http://linkinghub.elsevier.com/retrieve/pii/S1389128610002513 [accessed: 2017-12-20].

[13] E. Weidner et al., "Ecological Comparison of PC and Thin Client Workplace Devices (original title: Oekologischer Vergleich von PC und Thin Client Arbeitsplatzgeraeten)," Fraunhofer-Institut fuer Umwelt-, Sicherheits-, Energietechnik UMSICHT, Oberhausen, Tech. Rep., Dec. 2006.

[14] D. Feuerer, "Product environmental attributes - THE ECO DECLARATION - Workstation CELSIUS W530," Fujitsu Technology Solutions GmbH, ECO Declaration, Juli 2013.

[15] R. Kemna, M. van Elburg, W. Li, and R. van Holsteijn, "Methodology Study Eco-design of Energy-using Products (MEEUP): product cases report," Delft, Netherlands: VHK-Van Holsteijn en Kemna BV, 2005.

[16] Q. Chen et al., "Profiling Energy Consumption of VMs for Green Cloud Computing."

[17] Fujitsu Technology Solutions GmbH, "Energy Consumption ESPRIMO P720 E90+," White Paper, Fujitsu Technology Solutions GmbH, White Paper, June 2013.

[18] J. Willerding, "Management of Virtual Desktops in Energy Efficient Office Environments Using Thin Clients (original title: Management von virtuellen Desktops in energieeffizienten Broumgebungen unter Verwendung von Thin Clients)," Master thesis, University of Passau, December 2014.

Virtual Machines' Migration for Cloud Computing

Mohamed Riduan Abid
Alakhawayn University
Ifrane, Morocco
R.Abid@aui.ma

Karima Kaddouri
Alakhawayn University
Ifrane, Morocco
Ka.Kaddouri@aui.ma

Moulay Driss El Ouadghiri
Moulay Ismail University
Meknes, Morocco
dmelouad@gmail.com

Driss Benhaddou
University of Houston
TX, USA
dbenhadd@central.uh.edu

Abstract— **Virtualization is strongly emerging back as a fundamental Cloud Computing (CC) technology enabler whereby CC services are mainly provided via the instantiation of Virtual Machines (VMs). These instantiations follow a stochastic pattern, which is mainly dictated by the nature of the CC services requests and Cloud "elasticity". Consequently, a load-balancer emerges as indispensable to intervene in situations where VMs need to be dynamically migrated from a data center site to another in order to sustain optimal CC operation. In this paper, we briefly survey available VM migration techniques, delineate their pros and cons, and shed further light into the novel aspects to consider when approaching, these VM migration techniques, from a CC perspective, e.g., considering Mobile Cloud Computing (MCC) and Network Function Virtualization (NFV). In addition, we propose a novel VM migration scheme (soft-migration) inspired from mobile communication.**

Keywords-Virtual machines; Cloud computing; Live migration; Soft migration

I. INTRODUCTION

Virtualization has its roots in the mainframe era. The late 1960s witnessed the release of a novel memory time-sharing operating system known as the IBM 360 mainframe model 67 (a.k.a CP-67) to share scarce computing resources among multiple users. This was a major innovation: Personal users and organizations were actually able to use computing capabilities at a lower cost without having to own a computer. Some of the key customers to benefit from these time-sharing capabilities were MIT, Princeton University, Bell labs and General Motors [1]. Still, this early project encountered several issues, one of them being thrashing [2].

Optimizing resource utilization, in an era where computing demands are dramatically increasing, is a must. This can only be met through resource sharing and underutilization avoidance. Cloud Computing (CC) leverages optimal use of resources via the promotion of *computing as a utility* instead of a *product*. As a utility, users have on-demand access to computing resources in a similar way to other public utilities, e.g., electricity, water, and natural gas. Besides, users are charged only on what they have used, i.e., pay-per-use. To implement "pay-per-use", CC services need to be dynamically allocated and released, i.e., on-demand, and this is where virtualization. The latter is the main technology enabler behind CC. CC services are, in fact, provided via the instantiation of VMs whose "sizes" can be dynamically decided on, and can be created and released whenever needed. VMs are but image files that can be stored, updated, retrieved for execution, and even migrated from a physical station to another.

CC provides three basic service models: Software as a Service (SaaS), Platform as a Service (PaaS), and Infrastructure as a Service (IaaS) [4]. IaaS is provided via the instantiation of virtual machines (VMs). VMs refer to several virtual instances of an operating system running in isolated partitions within a physical machine [5]. In analogy with "time-sharing", which was developed to optimize resource utilization while giving each user the illusion of having access to a complete set of system resources, VMs take this idea further by providing users with complete system environments, each with its own operating system that manages virtualized hardware resources.

Due to the high and ever-growing demand that strains Cloud resources, the maintenance and management of CC operations against the heavy demand on CC services is a primary concern, especially that the requests on the CC services follow mostly a stochastic pattern which depend mainly on the time when the user requests a CC service and when it releases it. As a consequence, CC providers will witness a dynamic load on their data centres which can only be mitigated via the deployment of optimal load-balancing schemes. Besides, leveraging "elasticity", which is a fundamental aspect in CC, would further worsen the situation.

Elasticity is a major "pillar" in CC [4]. With elasticity, CC users can be allocated VMs with elastic sizes depending on the demand. For instance, an e-Commerce web service would need to be allocated further extra resources (e.g., number of vCPU, memory, etc.) during peak periods (e.g., week-ends and holidays). These extra resources need to be released once the need is over. The acquisition and release of these extra resources should be instantaneous, a fact that puts further pressure on the load dynamicity of CC data centers, and thus renders the deployment of an optimal Load-balancer (LB) indispensable. Besides deciding on whether to admit a VM request or not, the LB would often need to move (i.e., migrate) a VM from one Cloud site to another one as a consequence of an instantaneous increase (elasticity) in the size of the current running VMs.

The process of moving a virtual machine from one physical host to another is labelled migration [6]. This merely consists on the transfer of the VM state, which is dictated by the actual memory image, virtual CPUs states, and the states of attached IO devices. There are basically two main migration techniques: pre-copy [7] and post-copy [8]. Initially, these techniques were not tailored to fit the CC services. Thus, they need to be adapted and fine-tuned to fit in the CC contest. Two key performance metrics are considered to evaluate a migration technique: downtime and migration time. Downtime is the time during which the VM is unreachable to the user because the VM is in the period of transiting from a site to another, and migration time, which is the total amount of time that is needed to transfer the VM from source to destination while keeping it accessible. With the arousal of VM migration, and in order to move a VM between two physical machines, it was obligatory to completely shut down the VM, prepare the destination host resource-wise, move the VM files and then start the VM in the new machine. Nowadays, thanks to several migration techniques, we can move VMs with minimum downtime.

In this paper, we shed further light into the subtleties of VM Migration. We survey available VM migration techniques, present their strengths and weaknesses, and advocate considerations to account for when approaching it from a Cloud Computing point of view, mainly Mobile Cloud Computing (MCC) which is rapidly increasing domain marrying CC and Mobile Computing, and Network Function Virtualization (NFV) which is deemed as the key towards the Cloudification of the Telecommunication world.

Besides, we present a novel VM migration (soft-migration) scheme that is inspired from mobile computing. This promotes the complete elimination of the downtime by managing a time interval whereby VM requests are served simultaneously by the source and target VMs in a similar way to the soft hand-off process in cellular telephony. This will assure the elimination of the downtime.

The rest of the paper is organized as follows: Section II briefly surveys the different VM migration techniques In Section III, we address VM migration from a CC perspective and present relevant live migration use cases, e.g., MCC and NFV. In Section IV, we present our novel soft-migration scheme, and finally, we conclude and set future work in Section V.

II. VM MIGRATION TECHNIQUES

There are two main techniques for moving VM's memory state: pre-copy [7] and post-copy migration [8]. In a memory transfer we have three phases. First, we have the (i) *Push phase* where the original VM keeps its running status whereas some of the memory pages are being pushed through the network to the target host. To make sure the transfer is consistent, updated pages have to be retransmitted thereafter. Second, in the (ii) *Stop-and-copy phase*, the original VM is stopped, all the remaining dirty pages are copied to the destination, and the VM is resumed on the destination host. Finally, in the (iii) *Pull phase*, the copied VM begins its execution. If it comes across a page that has not yet been transferred, this results in a page fault from the VM.

Pre-copy migration combines both the push phase and the stop-and copy phase. The post-copy approach combines the pull phase and the stop-and-copy phase. In *pre-copy memory migration* (figure 1), the hypervisor copies all the memory pages in an iterative fashion from source to destination while the VM is still running at the source. If some memory pages change (i.e., they become dirty) during this process, they will be re-copied. Once enough pages are transmitted (Threshold on the maximum number of iteration is defined by the user at run time.), the VM is suspended at the source and the remaining state is relocated to the destination [7]. In *post-copy migration* (figure 2), the transfer is initiated by suspending the VM at the source. With the VM suspended, a minimal subset of the execution state of the VM (CPU state, registers, non-pageable memory) is transferred to the target. The VM is then resumed at the target. At the destination, if the VM tries to access a page that has not yet been transferred, it generates a page fault. Concurrently, the source dynamically pushes the remaining memory pages of the VM to the target - a technique known as *pre-paging*, which minimizes page faults [8].

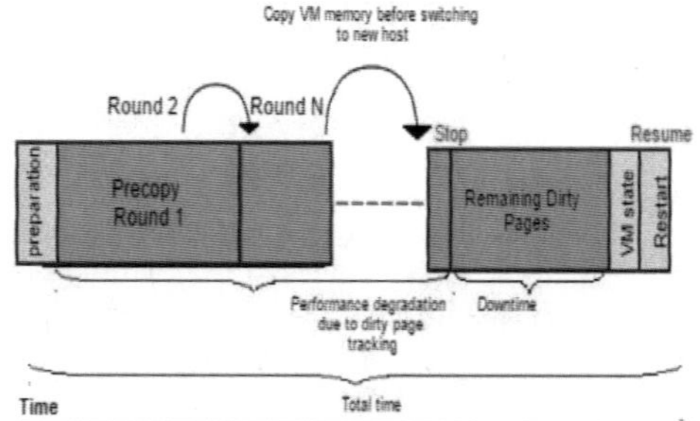

Figure 1. Pre-copy migration

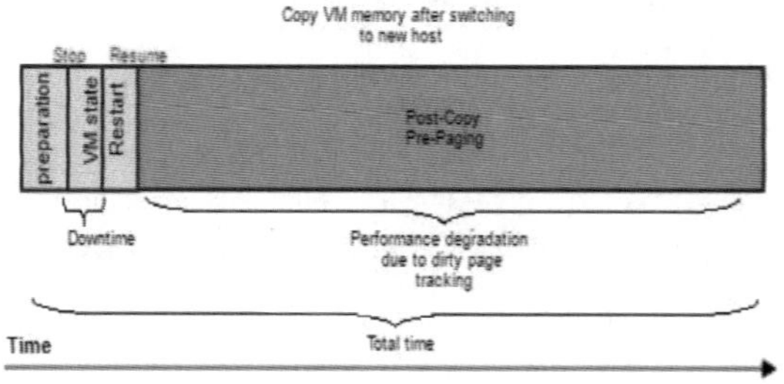

Figure 2. Post-copy migration

The techniques discussed above have been remodelled and readapted by a number of researchers to minimize downtime when live migrating VMs.

E. Zaw et al. [9] propose an updated version of the pre-copy approach. The designed framework is built to include a pre-processing phase in order to decrease the size of transferred data. A working set prediction algorithm is used to implement the pre-processing step. The suggested algorithm predicts the least recently used memory pages that directly affects the total migration time. As a result, the transferred memory page size is diminished. Evaluation of the algorithm showed that the proposed solution –compared with traditional pre-copy- can decrease the total migration time by 11.45%.

With the objective to optimize virtual machine migration based on pre-copy as well, H. Deng et al. suggest a memory compression solution. Similar to the previously mentioned work, the idea of reducing the size of migrated data to improve the performance of VM migration is applied. In the source node, data being transferred is first compressed by a compression algorithm then, upon arrival to the destination node, it is decompressed. The added metric here, compression time, is an extra overhead caused by the compression jobs. In [11], J. Changyeon et al. propose a shared storage based technique for live migrating VMs. Only unique memory pages are sent directly from the source to the destination. Pages that are replicated and found on shared storage are fetched directly by the destination node, so duplicated data is not sent by the source node. The authors demonstrated the efficacy of their suggested technique by running a set of experiments with the XEN hypervisor. There was an improvement in total migration time between 30%-60% with minimal downtime rise, hence improving the migration performance.

T. Wood et al. [12] present CloudNet, a CC platform that attempts to deliver smooth connectivity between enterprise and datacenter sites. It also implements wide area network (WAN) migration of VMs. The objective once more was to minimize the size of transferred data, migration time, and user downtime. This framework uses asynchronous and synchronous disk duplication to reduce downtime. The performance of this platform was evaluated in a setting composed of three geographically separated data centers and a local testbed. The result showed that memory transfer time was decreased by 65%.

III. LIVE MIGRATION IN CC

Live migration refers to the process of moving a virtual machine from one physical host to another while the VM is continuously powered-up. When properly done, this process takes place without any perceptible effect from the point of view of the end user. When a VM is running a live service, it is important that this transfer occurs in a manner that balances the requirements of minimizing both downtime and total migration time. Thus, live VM migration is crucial for dynamic resource management and proper carrying of CC services in Cloud-based systems.

The idea of viewing computing resources given by Cloud providers as a single unified pool is ideal. However, the reality is far from this vision because these resources are distributed across geographically separated and interconnected datacenters. This presents a real challenge for live VM migration in CC. The majority of authors presented previously tackle live migration techniques from the local area network (LAN) perspective, under the assumption of a shared file system that allows migrating only memory data and evading disk state transfers. The situation is further worsened with the arousal of MCC [13] whereby mobile devices will be mostly seeking Cloud services in order to mitigate their inherent limitation on the computer power and energy/battery.

MCC is strongly arising as a promising technology leveraging Mobile Computing and Cloud computing. MCC is driven by the emergence of novel IT ecosystems alike IoT (Internet of Things) [14], Smart Cities [15], and Smart Grids [16] whereby mobile devices, e.g., sensors/actuators, will be all the time connected to the Cloud.

Due to the inherent limitations in energy and compute power, mainly due the restriction in device size, these devices will be mostly sending data for processing in the Cloud. The mobility and ad-hoc topology of these sensors/actuators will generate a dynamic load on the Cloud, thus requiring an optimal load-balancer. The load-balancer needs to account for this dynamicity by migrating VMs (that will process mobile devices requests) into "closer" locations. This is crucial for providing and maintaining requested QoS, especially the delay.

Most of the previously proposed VM migration techniques were not accounting for the novel mobile Cloud services. With the rising demand for mobility of resources, the requirement for MCC also increased, and nowadays users rely on mobile devices. These devices can be effortlessly connected to the Cloud, and accordingly, mobile applications can easily access Cloud resources. Next section delineates the most prominent contributions for VM migration in MCC.

A. *VM Migration for Mobile Cloud Computing*

1) State of the Art

The development of mobile agents plays an important role in remote access, data retrieval, and most importantly mobile Cloud computing. M. Zaa et al. [17] tackle the issue of migrating resources between the Cloud and mobile devices using mobile agents. They can migrate from one host to another host in search of resources. In particular, they can be used to transport resources such as the VM's state from one environment to another, with its data remaining intact and capable of executing in a new environment.

Chun et al. [18] focus on VM migration using VM state cloning. Their system, CloneCloud, duplicates the runtime environment and then executes the application-level VM either on the Cloud or the device. The goal is to achieve better performance with a boosted CPU and memory resources that can be exploited proficiently. However, the application on the Cloud needs to access physical hardware on the mobile devices. Henceforth, reproducing a device and then executing it on the Cloud also adds more complexity.

K. Ma et al. [19] highlight VM state migration using the Stack on Demand (SOD) concept. Instead of using live VM migration which can be too "massive" (i.e., bulky data unfit for mobile devices), they propose a compressed migration scheme intended for stack-based virtual machines. This mechanism migrates the minimal portion of the VM state to the destination host for continued execution. Inspired by the stack concept, it chops the stack into segments and only transfers the top segment at a time. M. Islam et al. [20] propose a Genetic Algorithm based VM migration scheme for a heterogeneous MCC system. Their genetic algorithm leverages both user mobility and the load of the Cloud servers to enhance the efficacy of VM migration. It chooses the fittest Cloud server from the pool for a mobile VM and decreases the total number of VM migrations. Thus, it ensures a smaller task execution time. In [21], a technique called dynamic VM synthesis was presented. This is based on Cloudlets. A Cloudlet is a small-scale Cloud intended for delivering computing resources to high-performing mobile applications. In this scheme, a VM overlay (i.e. file that captures a VM state) is sent by a mobile device to a Cloudlet that has the base VM from which this overlay was created. The Cloudlet merges the overlay with the base to synthesize the ready-for-launch VM, which starts execution at the exact state the mobile communicated.

2) *Discussion*

In [17], the mobile agents used to transport the VM state from one environment to another also need to be migrated, and depending on their availability, there can be some downtime. Although the solution in [18] boosts performance and considerably decreases user response time, there still is minimal downtime when a migration point is reached. The VM thread is suspended and its state sent to a clone. There, the thread state is instantiated into a new thread and execution resumes. In [19] when the top stack segment finishes and pops, the return values are sent to the next site for continued execution. However, there are often freeze times between the multiple hops from one site to another. For [20], when an adequate Cloud is found for the mobile VM, there still is suspend time occurring as the VM state is loaded on the Cloud. While significantly decreasing response time, the solution in [21] still generates a few milliseconds of downtime before the application is executed on the Cloudlet. Furthermore, in the case when the Cloudlet is not available nearby, the mobile device would need to connect to a distant Cloud, which degrades performance.

In all of the previously mentioned contributions, the main object of migration, the VM, is mainly an OS, a server or an application. However, this is not always the case. There are other use cases for live VM Migration not limited to this. Thus there is a need to delve deeper and investigate other use cases that justify the need for live migration. This is particularly relevant for the paradigm shift we are witnessing nowadays in networks, in what is referred to as Network Functions Virtualization (NFV) [31].

B. *NFV and Live VM migration*

Network operators are becoming saturated with an increasingly large quantity of network hardware appliances. Launching a new network service usually necessitates finding the space and power needed. Accommodating these resources is becoming more and more challenging due to the increasing costs of energy and capital investment, but also the scarcity of skills essential to design, integrate, and operate such complex hardware.

Furthermore, dedicated hardware quickly reaches end of life, which implies that the purchase-integrate-deploy cycle to be repeated is with little or no revenue benefit at all. Even worse, with the current technological innovation acceleration, hardware lifecycles are becoming even shorter as dedicated hardware becomes rapidly obsolete. This highly impedes on revenues innovation in a progressively network-focused connected world.

NFV's goal is to leverage one particular technology that enables CC: Virtualization. Hardware Virtualization is needed to link traffic between VMs and physical interfaces. This connection is possible with the use of hypervisors and other virtualized resources such as virtual Ethernet switches (vSwitches). Cloud infrastructures provide mechanisms to enhance resource availability, organization, and administration. It also delivers automatic forking of VM resources, the re-launch of failed VMs, and the migration of VMs. These provide a much needed boost for incorporating NFV in the cloud infrastructure.

NFV is a radical adjustment to the way network operators design networks. It applies virtualization technologies to consolidate network hardware onto virtualized servers, switches and storage. These resources might be located in datacenters, network nodes, or in the end user location. It requires the implementation of network functions at the software level made to run on standard server hardware, also called "commodity of the shelf" (COTS). These network functions can be migrated to, or forked in various places in the network as required by demand, without the need ever for installing and deploying new hardware equipment.

Software-Defined Networking (SDN) [23] is a concept related to NFV. SDN is a model that decouples the data plane from the control plane, in such a way that the control plane is central and the forwarding components remain distributed. NFV is not dependent on SDN. It is completely feasible to implement NFV as a standalone entity using existing networking technologies. However, the two are complementary and there are benefits to using SDN concepts to develop and orchestrate an NFV infrastructure.

Last but not least, the network functions to virtualize (e.g., BBU (BaseBand Unit), switches, routers) might need to be migrated as well, and the trend is not the same as with ordinary VMs which consist on an OS on top of a virtual hardware.

IV. Soft Migration

Our contribution in this survey is our proposition of a soft-handover inspired framework for VM migration, that we named soft-migration. Soft-handover [24] is a scheme where a mobile phone is concurrently connected to two or more radio base stations during a phone call. The cell receiver combines the signals of both base stations for a bit stream of better quality. If any one of the signal fades, there will still be acceptable signal strength from the remaining radio station.

We can use this concept of simultaneous connection with the VM migration scheme (see Figure 3), where the VM is connected to both hosts during migration time. This allows it to run continuously regardless of the transfer state, permitting a seamless VM migration. Thanks to unceasing memory transfer from both servers, there would ideally be very minimal disruptions and downtime.

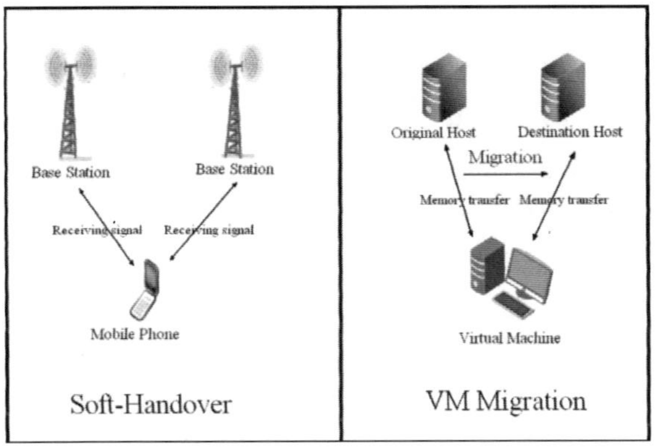

Figure 3. Soft-Migration

Our soft-handover inspired idea aims to minimize downtime as its primary objective. The pre-copy and post-copy approaches have different suspend time gaps.

In post-copy, the suspend phase is at the very beginning, when the VM is stopped and a minimal subset of it gets copied to the target. Then, VM resumes execution at the new host whilst the remaining pages get sent. The problem here would be the high number of page faults that might get generated if the user only accesses the pages that have not yet been copied. This would result in further suspend time when the wanted pages are being pulled from the source. With pre-copy, the memory pages are copied without stopping the execution of the VM. Then occurs the suspend phase where the remaining and dirtied pages get sent, and finally, execution is resumed on the new host. Here, there is no page faults issue. Since the suspend phase does not occur at the beginning, the majority of memory pages are copied before the VM gets paused. Our proposed scheme can be deemed as a "hybrid" approach between the pre-copy and post-copy techniques, and consists of 2 phases, see figure. 4:

Phase 1: Similar to the pre-copy approach, memory pages are copied from the original host to the target host without stopping the execution of the VM.

Phase 2: After the maximum number of iterations is reached (defined by the user), we switch to the new host and resume execution there. There is no suspend phase. Instead, and similar to the post-copy approach, the rest of the pages will be dynamically pushed. If the user tries to access a non-copied page or a dirty page being replaced, this will generate a page fault. The missing page is dynamically pulled from the source.

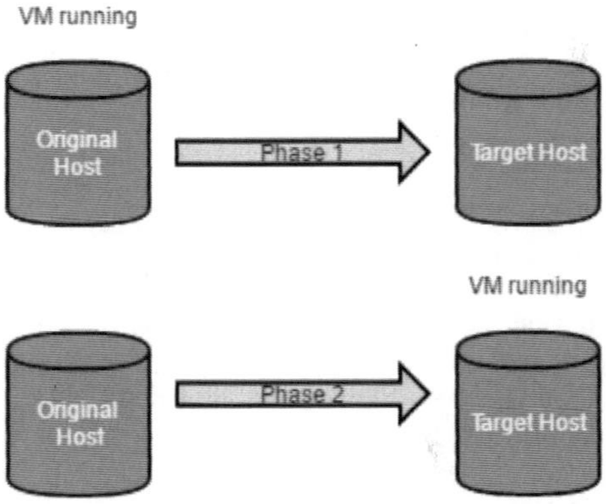

Figure 4. Proposed Migration Process

This approach ensures that the user is continuously connected to either host during the VM transfer (see Figure 5), just as mobile users do in the hand off scenario.

The main advantage of the proposed scheme is that there is *no* suspend time, and thus we have less *down time*: VM execution is continuous even when the original host replaces dirty pages and transfers remaining ones. Still, we have to keep track of which pages are dirty and which are not in order to minimize page faults, and this mandates the implementation of module, within the Load-balancer, that logs relative VM pages migrations.

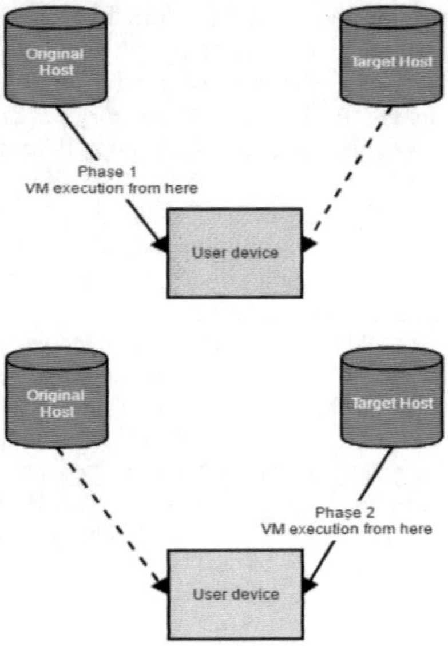

Figure 5: User is never disconnected

V. Conclusion and Future Work

In this paper, we surveyed main VM Migration and addressed its particularity from a Could Computing perspective, mainly when dealing with MCC services, and when migrating network function either using NFV or SDN., We also presented our own soft-migration technique inspired from the soft-handoff mechanism in mobile communication.

Our future work consists of implementing the soft-migration scheme and study its performance. In addition, we will investigate plausible schemes for network function migration in 5G whereby most of the (telecommunications) functions are to be virtualized.

References

[1] D, Morton, "IBM Mainframe Operating Systems: Timeline and Brief Explanation for the IBM System/360 and Beyond", IBM, 2015.

[2] P. J. Denning, "Thrashing: Its causes and prevention". Fall Joint Computer Conference, pp. 915-922, 1968

[3] D. Dale, "Server and Storage Virtualization with IP Storage", Storage Networking Industry Association (SNIA), 2008.

[4] P. Mell and T. Grance, "The NIST Definition of Cloud Computing". National Institute of Standards and Technology, pp. 1-3, 2011.

[5] J. Smith and R. Nair, Virtual Machines: Versatile Platforms for Systems and Processes, Elsevier, 2005.

[6] C. Christopher, et al, "Live migration of virtual machines". In Proceedings of the 2nd conference on Symposium on Networked Systems Design & Implementation pp 273–286, 2005.

[7] D. Botero, "A Brief Tutorial on Live Virtual Machine Migration from a Security Perspective", Princeton University, 2011.

[8] Hines, U. Deshpande, and K. Gopalan, "Post-Copy Live Migration of Virtual Machines", SIGOPS Operating Syst. Review, 43(3):14–26, July 2009.

[9] E. Zaw and N. Thein, "Improved Live VM Migration using LRU and Splay Tree Algorithm", International Journal of Computer Science and Telecommunication, vol. 3, no. 3, 2012.

[10] H. L. Deng, S.W. Shi and X. Pan, "Live Virtual Machine Migration with Adaptive Memory Compression", IEEE, 2009.

[11] J. Changyeon, E. Gustafsson, J. Son and B. Egger. "Efficient Live Migration of Virtual Machines Using Shared Storage", in the 9th ACM SIGPLAN/SIGOPS international conference on Virtual execution environments, pp 41-50, 2013.

[12] T. Wood, P. Shenoy, K.K. Ramakrishnan and J. Van der Merwe CloudNet, "Dynamic Pooling of Cloud Resources by Live WAN Migration of Virtual Machines". In Proceedings of the 2011 ACM SIGPLAN/SIGOPS international conference on Virtual execution environments, pp 51–60, 2011. ACM.

[13] T. Dinh et al, "A Survey of Mobile Cloud Computing: Architecture, Applications, And Approaches", Wireless Communications and Mobile Computing Wirel. Commun. Mob. Comput, pp: 1587–1611, 2013.

[14] F.Xial et al, "Internet of Things", International Journal of Communication System Int. J. Commun. Syst. pp: 1101–1102, 2012.

[15] H. Chourabi, T. Nam and S. Walker, "Understanding Smart Cities: An Integrative Framework", 45th Hawaii International Conference on System Sciences, pp: 2289-2297, 2012.

[16] J. R. Roncero, "Integration Is Key to Smart Grid Management", CIRED Seminar 2008: SmartGrids for Distribution Frankfurt, 2008.

[17] M. Zaa, J.P, Gabhane and A.V Dehankar. "A Survey on Migration of Task between Cloud and Mobile Device". International Journal of Advanced Research in Computer Engineering & Technology (IJARCET), pp. 610-613, vol 2, no. 2, 2013.

[18] B. Chun et al, "CloneCloud: Elastic execution between mobile device and Cloud," In Proc. Of Eurosys, 2011.

[19] K. K. Ma et al, "A Stack-On-Demand Execution Model for Elastic Computing," In Proc. of the 39th Intl. Conf. on Parallel Processing (ICPP2010), pp. 208-217, 2010.

[20] M. Islam, A. Razzaque and J. Islam, "A genetic algorithm for virtual machine migration in heterogeneous mobile Cloud computing," 2016 International Conference on Networking Systems and Security (NSysS), pp. 1-6, 2016.

[21] M. Satyanarayanan et al, "The Case for VM-based Cloudlets in Mobile Computing", IEEE Pervasive Computing, 2009.

[22] B. Han, V. Gopalakrishnan, L. Ji and S. Lee, "Network function virtualization: Challenges and opportunities for innovations", IEEE Commun. Mag., vol. 53, no. 2, pp. 90-97, 2015.

[23] "Software-Defined Networking: The New Norm for Networks", ONF White Paper, April 13, 2012.

[24] Juan et al, "Verification of Mobility-Based Soft Handover Algorithm using WCDMA Measurements Data", IEEE 63 rd Vehicular Technology Conference, 2006.

Cloud Documents Storage Correctness

Aspen Olmsted
Department of Computer Science, College of Charleston
Charleston, SC 29401
e-mail: olmsteda@cofc.edu

Abstract— **In this paper, we investigate the problem of providing correctness guarantees when representing transaction data in semi-structured documents in cloud-based systems. We compare traditional relational database correctness guarantees including normalization and domain constraints with our correctness guarantees for document-oriented databases. In this research, we specifically focus on transactional data that would have traditionally been stored in a relational database system. We ensure that our new guarantees improve the data quality while not reducing the availability of the systems.**

Keywords-web services; distributed database; modeling

I. INTRODUCTION

In this work, we investigate the problem of representing transactional data in a platform as a service (PAAS) cloud-based document storage system. Document-oriented storage systems are excellent in providing availability to client applications. Unfortunately, they sacrifice consistency and durability to achieve this availability. The CAP theory [1] [2] states that distributed database designers can achieve at most two of the properties: consistency (C), availability (A), and partition tolerance (P).

In traditional relational databases, database normalization is used to ensure that redundant data is not stored in the system. Redundant data can lead to update anomalies if the developer is not careful to update every instance of a fact when modifying data. Normalization is also performed to ensure unrelated facts are not stored in the same tuples resulting in deletion anomalies.

Relational databases also provide data correctness guarantees through the use of constraints. Constraints can take the form of domain constraints where the value of an attribute is limited using either the specific attributes data type, check constraints or referential integrity. Out of the box, document-oriented databases allow each document to have its own structure. The designer can write validation code, but that code cannot check other records stored in the system.

There are two major document-oriented database systems in production today. They are named CouchDB [3] and MongoDB [4]. Both systems store schema-less semi-structured data with the goal of providing high availability and redundancy. International Business Machines (IBM) offers a cloud service based on CouchDB named Coudant [5].

Our goals in this research are to allow the developer the high availability provided by these cloud-based document-oriented data storage systems and also have a higher level of correctness guarantees. In this work, we provide normalization algorithms and domain checks for both data types and referential guarantees.

The organization of the paper is as follows. Section II describes the related work and the limitations of current methods. In Section III, we give a motivating example where our normalization and correctness algorithms will be helpful. Section IV describes standards used for semi-structured data validation. Section V explores breaking our model into a directed graph and how to partition that graph for normalization. Section VI contains information on how we can add semantics to the data model to help in our partitioning algorithm. Section VII describes how we generate the validation function to ensure the correctness of documents on creation and modification. We conclude and discuss future work in Section VIII.

II. RELATED WORK

Constraint specification and enforcement have been a part of relational database model research since Codd [6] originally wrote the specification. Recently work on the auto-generation of SQL code to enforce these constraints from the UML model has been done by Heidenreich, et al. [7] and Demuth, et al. [8]. In both these works, the focus is on the generation of the SQL code for relational databases for the invariants. Document-oriented databases require additional work to ensure the constraints can be guaranteed while not decreasing the availability of the service.

Research in the distributed database community has been conducted for decades on finding a balance between availability and consistency. Recent research can be grouped into one of three goals: 1.) to increase the availability with strict replication, 2.) to increase consistency with lazy replication, and 3.) to use a hybrid approach to increase the availability. Document-oriented databases were developed to allow the implementer to have a high availability while sacrificing immediate consistency. We can group the consistency and availability research into four groups.

1) Increasing Availability of Strict Replication: Several methods have been developed to ensure mutual consistency in replicated databases. The aim of these methods is eventually to provide one-copy serializability (1SR). Transactions on traditional replicated databases are based on reading any copy and writing (updating) all copies of data items. Based on the time of the update propagation, two main approaches have been proposed. Approaches that update all replicas before the transaction can commit are called eager update propagation protocols; approaches that allow the propagation of the update after the transaction is committed are called lazy update propagation. While eager update propagation guarantees mutual consistency among the replicas, this approach is not scalable. Lazy update propagation is efficient, but it may result in a violation of mutual consistency. During the last decade, several methods have been proposed to ensure mutual consistency in the presence of lazy update propagation (see *[9]* for an overview.) More recently, Snapshot Isolation (SI) *[10] [11]* has been proposed to provide concurrency control in replicated databases. The aim of this approach is to provide global one-copy serializability using SI at each replica. The advantage is that SI provides scalability and is supported by most database management systems.

2) Increasing Consistency in Lazy Replication: Breitbart and Korth *[12]* and Daudjee, et al. *[13]* propose frameworks for master-slave, lazy-replication updates that provide consistency guarantees. These approaches are based on requiring all writes to be performed on the master replica. Updates are propagated to the other sites after the updating transaction is committed. Their framework provides a distributed serializable schedule where the ordering of updates is not guaranteed.

The approach proposed by Daudjee et al. provides multi-version serializability where different versions of data can be returned for requests that read data during the period that replication has not completed.

3) Hybrid Approach: Jajodia and Mutchler *[14]* and Long, et al. *[15]* both define forms of hybrid replication that reduce the requirement that all replicas participate in eager update propagation. The proposed methods aim to increase availability in the presence of network isolation or hardware failures. Both approaches have limited scalability because they require a majority of replicas to participate in eager update propagation. Most recently, Irun-Briz et al. *[16]* proposed a hybrid replication protocol that can be configured to behave as eager or lazy update propagation protocol. The authors provide empirical data and show that their protocol provides scalability and reduces communication cost over other hybrid update protocols. In addition to academic research, several database management systems have been developed that support some form of replicated data management. For example, Lakshman and Malik *[17]* describe a hybrid system, called Cassandra, which was built by Facebook to handle their inbox search. Cassandra allows a configuration parameter that controls the number of nodes that must be updated synchronously. The Cassandra system can be configured, so nodes chosen for synchronous inclusion cross data center boundaries to increase durability and availability.

4) Buddy System: In our previous work *[18]-[20]*, we provide an architecture and algorithms that address three problems: the risk of losing committed transactional data in case of a site failure, contention caused by a high volume of concurrent transactions consuming limited items, and contention caused by a high volume of read requests. We called this system the Buddy System because it used pairs of clusters to update all transactions synchronously. The pairs of buddies can change for each request allowing increased availability by fully utilizing all server resources available. Consistency is increased over lazy-replication because all transactional elements are updated in the same cluster allowing for transaction time referential integrity and atomicity.

An intelligent dispatcher was placed, in front of all clusters, to support the above components. The dispatcher operated at the OSI Network level 7. The high OSI level allowed the dispatcher to use application specific data for transaction distribution and buddy selection. The dispatcher receives the requests from clients and distributes them to the WS clusters. Each WS cluster contains a load balancer, a single database, and replicated services. The load balancer receives the service requests from the dispatcher and distributes them among the service-replicas. Within a WS cluster, each service shares the same database. Database updates among the clusters are propagated using lazy-replication propagation.

After receiving a transaction, the dispatcher picks the two clusters to form the buddy pair. The dispatcher selects the pair of clusters based on versioning history. If a version is in progress and the request is modifying the data, then the dispatcher chooses set containing the same pair currently executing the other modify transactions. Otherwise, the set contains any pair with the last completed version. The primary buddy receives the transaction along with its buddy's IP address. The primary buddy becomes the coordinator of a simplified commit protocol between the two buddies. Both buddies perform the transaction and commit or abort together.

The dispatcher maintains metadata about the freshness of data items in the different clusters. The dispatcher increments a version counter for each data item after it has been modified. Any two service providers (clusters) with the latest version of the requested data items can be selected as a buddy. Note, that the database maintained by the two clusters must agree on the requested data item versions but may be different for the other data items.

Unfortunately, the buddy system required greenfield engineering to leverage the new algorithms. This current work allows a developer who has deployed a document-oriented database in the hope of high availability to regain some consistency.

III. MOTIVATING EXAMPLE

We demonstrate our work using a Ticketing Reservation System (TRS). The TRS uses web services to provide a variety of functionalities to the patrons who are attending a performance. To understand the impacts on a real organizations' data we used the New York Philharmonic Orchestra's data for the past 10 years. We simplified their relational data model to allow for a better illustration of the challenges in moving from the relational to a semi-structured data model. Figure 1 shows the Entity Relationship (ER) model we used for our experimentation. In the model, each

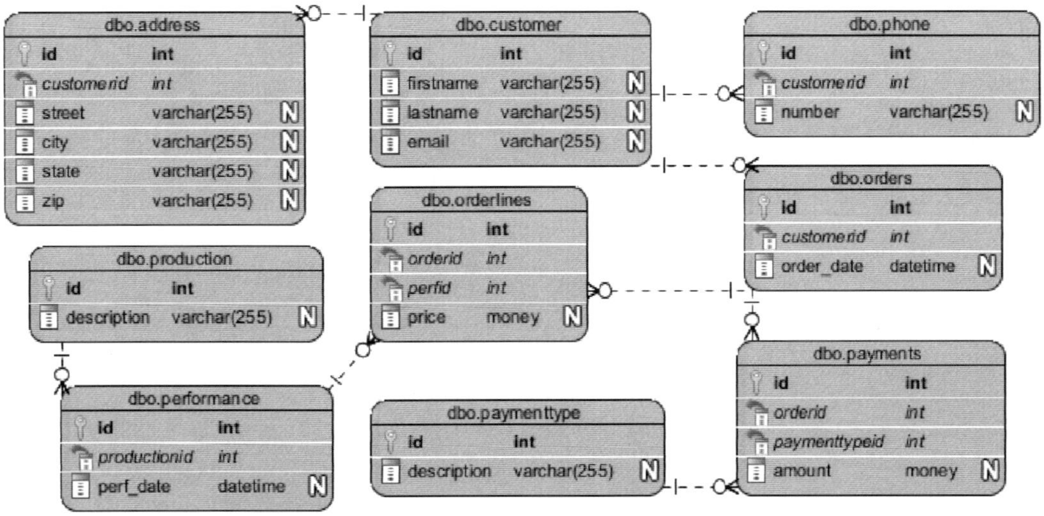

Figure 1. Relational Model

individual customer can have many addresses, many phone numbers and many orders tracked by the system. Each order can have many order lines entities and many payments entities. The order table stores a record of each order for tickets purchased by the individual customer. The order line entity has a many-to-one relationship to a performance record. The performance record represents a specific performance of the orchestra of a production. The production has the description of the pieces performed and the orchestra members. For example, on a weekend one production would have two performances. This relationship is represented by a many-to-one relationship from the performance table to the production table. In our research, we take the relational model in Figure 1 and convert the model into a CouchDB [3] data model.

IV. Semi-Structured Data, Schemas & Validation

There are two main formats used in semi-structured data stores; JavaScript Object Notation (JSON) and Extensible Markup Language (XML). JSON documents are in a format that is easily read by the JavaScript programming language. XML documents are an older format that allows any language to create well-formed documents by creating a language of tags to mark the data. The XML Schema format has matured to the level of being governed by a standards body where the JSON Schema [21] is relatively new and is not governed by a standards body as of yet. XML Schema is governed by the World Wide Web Consortium (W3C) [22].

Both Schema formats allow you to define custom entities, attributes, and the hierarchy of the entities stored in a single document. The two formats diverge in relation to references across documents. XML Schema allows one document to reference the existence of data in another document where JSON schema validation is only within a single document.

The two document-oriented databases we analyzed in this research use the JSON document format but do not support JSON schemas. Both systems support a document validation function that fires before a document is inserted or updated. In the case of MongoDB, there is a declarative structure that can limit the domain of the data type using enumerations and regular expressions. CouchDB and the Cloudant system allow unlimited validation functions that parse the records using JavaScript code. The functions can throw exceptions that stop the data operation from completing.

V. Rooted Trees and Partitioning

The data model shown in Figure 1 can be partitioned in many ways. We could store every object in a single document representing the complete hierarchy. The problem with this approach is normalization. We will have many copies of the same facts if the graph is not a complete directed

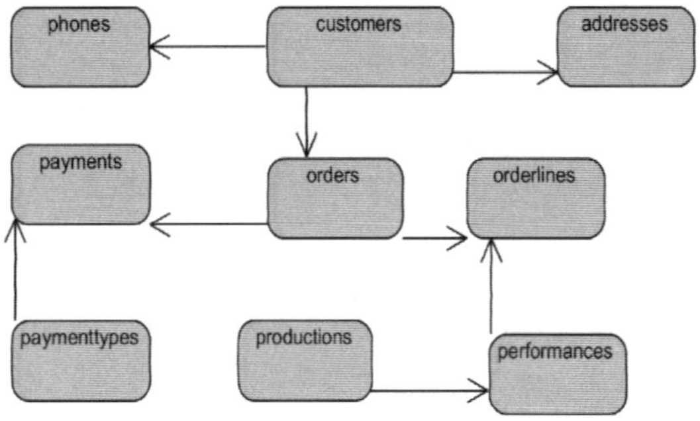

Figure 2. Directed Graph of Data Model

acyclic rooted graph [23]. This type of graph can be referred to as a rooted tree.

We can turn the ER diagram into a graph by using foreign keys as direct edges that travel from the one node to the many nodes. Each table in the ER diagram becomes a node in the graph. Once we have the graph, our algorithm can try each node, and if it can visit every other node and we do not have a cycle then our start node can be the root, and we have a rooted tree. If we have a cycle, then we had foreign keys that pointed in both directions between two entities. Cycles are only possible if we are starting from a relational database that allows constraint validation at transaction time instead of action time. Most relational databases do not allow transaction time constraint enforcement. In the case of cycles, we can merge the entities as they are truly one-to-one relationships. Figure 2 shows a directed graph generated from our data model in Figure 1.

In the case of Figure 1, we do not have a single rooted tree. We have three subtrees each with their own root; starting from customers, payment types, and productions. In this case, we would be required to store duplicate values across several documents depending on the root we choose. If we choose customers for the root node, then we will duplicate payment type, production, and performance information. This can lead to an update anomaly if we modify an attribute in one of those nodes but do not update all nodes that contain the duplicate information.

To eliminate the vulnerability of an update anomaly we need to partition the document into 3 sperate documents. Clearly, the three possible roots belong in their own document. We can continue traversal from these nodes to include other nodes in the separate documents. Unfortunately, we end up with two nodes (payments and order lines) that are placed into two separate documents. To decide which document these nodes should be stored in we will turn to the design documents and pull the required semantics from those documents.

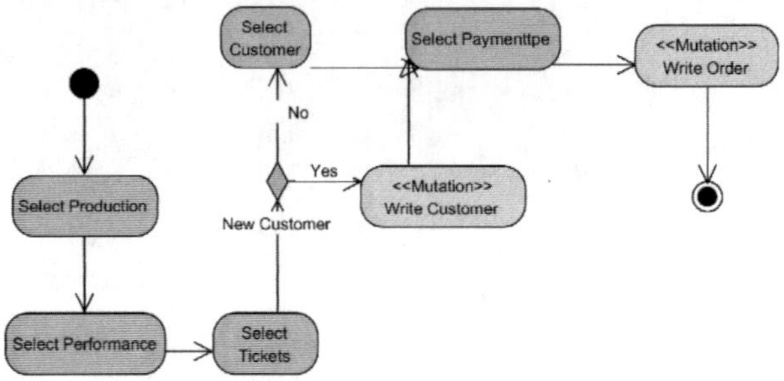

Figure 3. UML Activity Diagram for a Transaction

VI. UML SEMANTICS

Additional semantics for the data model can be acquired from the integration of the matching UML Activity and Class diagrams. UML provides an extensibility mechanism that allows a designer to add new semantics to a model. A stereotype allows a designer to extend the vocabulary of UML in order to represent new model elements [24]. We utilize this mechanism to understand the read and write semantics of activities that consume and generate the data in our data model. Figure 3 is an activity diagram with two stereotypes used to model activities that are read-only and activities that write and update data. The activity model is the main type of transaction that reads and writes the data in our data model. This transaction model is the process of purchasing a ticket for a specific performance. The "Write Order" activity modifies data as part of the transaction. This ability is represented by the stereotype of "Mutation" The

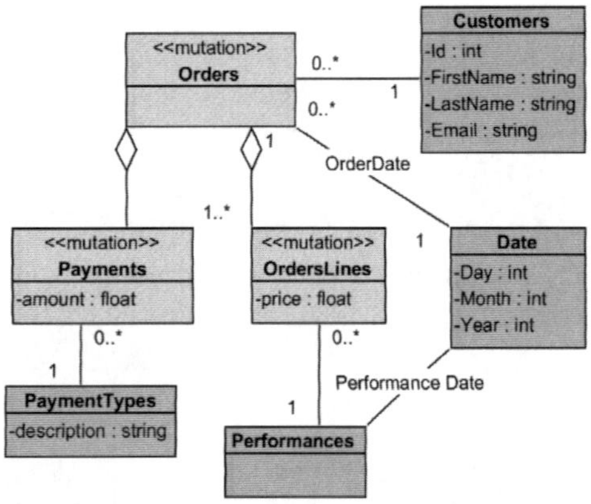

Figure 4. Class Diagram for "Write Order" Activity

Algorithm 1. Partition Algorithm

INPUT: ER Diagram, Activity Diagrams (XMI representation of UML class diagram) and Class Diagrams (XMI representation of UML class diagram)
OUTPUT: document partition

```
docPartions = empty array
foreach activityDiagrm in activityDiagrams
foreach activity in activtiyDiagram
if activity is a mutation
foreach rootedSubtree
documentFound = FALSE
foreach entity in rootedSubtree orderby tree nav
if entity in activity and class is a mutation
  if NOT documentFound
    push new curDocument on docPartitions
    documentFound = TRUE
  else
    add readonlyMidBranches to curDocument
  add entity to curDocument
else
  if documentFound
    add entity to readonlyMidBranches
```

"Write Customer" activity can also mutate data but is not required in every execution path.

```
(['red', 'green', 'blue'].indexOf(doc.field) >= 0)
```

Figure 5. Enumeration Validation

Each activity in the activity diagram has a matching UML class diagram that represents the internal structure of the code that manages the activity. Figure 4 displays the matching class diagram for the "WriteOrder" activity. We utilize the same stereotypes as we used in the activity diagram to model which elements are read-only and which can be modified in the activity. We use Algorithm 1 to choose the proper document partition based on the semantics of the UML model.

Algorithm 1 first creates an empty array to hold the document partitions. The algorithm takes a complete set of activity diagrams and matching class diagrams and navigates through the activity diagrams. The UML diagrams are passed into the algorithm in XMI format. XMI is a standard XML format for representing UML diagrams. Having the model in XML allows us to automate our algorithm, as any programming language can read the XML representation of the model. If the activity diagram is a mutation, then the algorithm will loop over the rooted subtrees from the ER diagram and will add the path from the beginning mutated document to the last mutated document. In our example application, we did not have overlap across the partitions. There is the possibility of overlap, and in that case, the documents will need to be merged to ensure each entity is only in one document. The overlap should be straightforward as it should represent different workflows to generate similar data. For example, in the motivating example for this research, we could have an activity diagram for a self-service web transaction to purchase a ticket and a phone order transaction with a back-office system operator. In both workflows, the partition documents would be almost exact.

In our example four partitions were created:

1. customers, addresses, phones
2. orders, orderlines, payments
3. payment types
4. performances, productions

The new structure eliminates both update and deletion anomalies. Deletion anomalies occur when a fact is lost because all related facts are deleted. With the rooted tree structure, the parent's facts need to exist by definition for the child facts to exists.

VII. DOCUMENT VALIDATION

Now that we have solved the normalization problem through the partitioning of our documents, we want to ensure that updates are validated for domain consistency. There are three types of domain consistency we are concerned with:

1. Simple Data Types – Simple data types including integers, floats, dates, times and strings.
2. Enumerations – Enumerations are limitations of the valid instances of a simple data type. For example, we could have an attribute of enumeration type color that takes in three possible strings: 'Blue,' 'Red,' 'Green.'
3. Referential Integrity – In relational databases, we used foreign keys to link column values to tuples stored in another table.

In CouchDB and the IBM cloud-hosted version Cloudant, design documents are just JSON documents stored in the database. This means we can add design documents via the HTTP interface programmatically. We developed an application that will iterate through our relational model and generate a design document per partitioned document to enforce our three domain consistency types. JSON Schema could be used for the first two domain consistency concerns but not for referential integrity. JSON Schema does not have the notion of referential integrity, and the validation function does not have access to other documents. So instead of trying to implement JSON schema validation in the JavaScript validation function, we took a novel approach that allows us to solve all three of the potential domain consistency issues.

To enforce the simple data types, we were able to use the built-in JavaScript parse methods such as parseInt, parseFloat.and Date.parse. To enforce the enumerations, we read the enumerations from the information schema of the database model and generate a validation test such as is shown in Figure 5. The left-hand side of the code includes a list of the possible enumerated values.

Referential integrity is handled in two ways depending on the partitioning of the document. If the foreign entity is stored in a separate document, then we handle the situation similarly to how we handled the enumerations. For each read all the possible values from the document store and generate validation check to ensure the new value is one of the possible options. If the foreign entity is in the current document tree, we navigate the document to check for its existence.

The challenge with our foreign key solution is in timing. For example, in our motivating example when a new performance is created, no new "orderlines" entities can be written without a new version of the design document being generated that includes the new performance in the valid list. To solve this problem, we implemented a client application that was written in Java. The application executes on a local machine in the end-user organization location. The application utilizes the continuous changes API in CouchDB and Cloudant to receive change notifications on the lookup tables. The continuous changes API allows the application to see the changes as they come in using a single HTTP connection between the application and the database service. When the application sees a change in the lookup data, it will generate a new revision of the design document to include the changed values in the validation function for the foreign key checks. This allows our validation function to have a low latency between the time new facts are inserted into the document store and the time they can be used in related documents.

Our solution works well except in the case of surrogate identifiers in parent entities. Surrogate ids are used when there is not a natural identifier. Entities that use surrogate identifiers tend to have a large number of entities in the collection, and our solution does not work when the foreign key list is large. In our motivating example, the customer's entity has a surrogate identifier for the id attribute. When we partitioned the document so that the orders entity is stored in a different document from the customer entity the validation function for the orders needs to have a list of valid customers. In practice, the number of customers would be too large to handle this way. To solve this problem, we merge the two documents, so we end up with a single document that covers the complete rooted tree consisting of customers, addresses, and payments. This solution does not break the normalization and simplifies the validation so that the validation can happen in a single document.

VIII. CONCLUSION

In this paper, we propose algorithms for semi-structured document normalization and domain value correctness and validation. We develop a test implementation to automate our implementation and validate that your solutions provide the guarantees for the normalization of the semi-structured data and for the consistency of domain values. Our solutions are based on navigating the relationships in both ER and UML diagrams and using additional semantics applied to the models.

In this research, we studied a specific application domain related to the entertainment industry. We believe the algorithms can be applied to other application domains without a significant amount of modification. Future work needs to test our algorithms in other application domains to ensure the work applies across different application domains. We also plan to add additional guarantees of correctness for these semi-structured documents.

REFERENCES

[1] S. Gilbert and N. Lynch, "Brewer's conjecture and the feasibility of consistent, available, partition-tolerant web services," *SIGACT News,* vol. 33, pp. 51-59, 2002.

[2] D. Abadi, "Consistency tradeoffs in modern distributed database system design: Cap is only part of the story," *Computer,* vol. 45, pp. 37-42, 2012.

[3] The Apache Software Foundation, "couchDB relax," 2017. [Online]. Available: http://couchdb.apache.org/. [Accessed 27 August 2017].

[4] MongoDB, Inc., "MongoDB for Giant Ideas," 2017. [Online]. Available: https://www.mongodb.com/. [Accessed 31 August 2017].

[5] International Business Machines, "IBM Cloudant," 2017. [Online]. Available: https://www.ibm.com/analytics/us/en/technology/cloud-data-services/cloudant. [Accessed 31 August 2017].

[6] E. F. Codd, The Relational Model for Database Management, Boston, MA: Addison-Wesley Longman Publishing Co., Inc., 1990.

[7] F. Heidenreich, C. Wende, and B. Demuth, "A Framework for Generating Query Language Code," *Electronic Communications of the EASST,* 2007.

[8] B. Demuth, H. Hußmann and S. Loecher, "OCL as a Specification Language for Business Rules in Database Applications," in *The Unified Modeling Language. Modeling Languages, Concepts, and Tools.*, Springer, 2001, pp. 104-117.

[9] M. T. Ozsu and P. Valduriez, Principles of Distributed Database Systems, 3rd ed., Springer, 2011.

[10] H. Jung, H. Han, A. Fekete and U. Rhm, "Serializable snapshot isolation," *PVLDB,* pp. 783-794, 2011.

[11] Y. Lin, B. Kemme, M. Patino Martiınez and R. Jimenez-Peris, "Middleware based data replication providing snapshot isolation," in *Proceedings of the 2005 ACM SIGMOD international conference on Management of data, ser. SIGMOD '05*, New York, NY, 2005.

[12] Y. Breitbart and H. F. Korth, "Replication and consistency: being lazy helps sometimes," *Proceedings of the sixteenth ACM SIGACT-SIGMOD-SIGART Symposium on Principles of database systems, ser. PODS '97,* pp. 173-184, 1997.

[13] K. Daudjee and K. Salem, "Lazy database replication with ordering," in *Data Engineering, International Conference on*, Boston, MA, 2004.

[14] S. Jajodia and D. Mutchler, "A hybrid replica control algorithm combining static and dynamic voting," *IEEE Transactions on Knowledge and Data Engineering,* vol. 1, pp. 459-469, 1989.

[15] D. Long, J. Carroll and K. Stewart, "Estimating the reliability of regeneration-based replica control protocols," *IEEE Transactions on,* vol. 38, pp. 1691-1702, 1989.

[16] L. Irun-Briz, F. Castro-Company, A. Garcia-Nevia, A. Calero-Monteagudo and F. D. Munoz-Escoi, "Lazy recovery in a hybrid database replication protocol," in *In Proc. of XII Jornadas de Concur-rencia y Sistemas Distribuidos*, 2005.

[17] A. Lakshman and P. Malik, "Cassandra: a decentralized structured," *SIGOPS Oper. Syst. Rev.,* vol. 44, pp. 35-40, 2010.

[18] A. Olmsted and C. Farkas, "High Volume Web Service Resource Consumption," in *Internet Technology and Secured Transactions, 2012. ICITST 2012*, London, UK, 2012.

[19] A. Olmsted and C. Farkas, "The cost of increased transactional correctness and durability in distributed databases," in *13th International Conference on Information Reuse and*, Los Vegas, NV, 2012.

[20] A. Olmsted and C. Farkas, "Coarse-Grained Web Service Availability, Consistency and Durability," in *IEEE International Conference on Web Services*, San Jose, CA, 2013.

[21] Jjson-schema Organisation, "JSON Schema," 2017. [Online]. Available: http://json-schema.org/. [Accessed 27 August 2017].

[22] World Wide Web Consortium, "Schema," 2017. [Online]. Available: https://www.w3.org/standards/xml/schema. [Accessed 27 August 2017].

[23] Wikipedia, "Rooted graph," 2017. [Online]. Available: https://en.wikipedia.org/wiki/Rooted_graph#CITEREFGrossYellenZhang2013. [Accessed 30 August 2017].

[24] O. M. Group, "Unified Modeling Language: Supersturcture," 05 02 2007. [Online]. Available: http://www.omg.org/spec/UML/2.1.1/. [Accessed 08 01 2013].

A Comparison and Critique of Natural Language Understanding Tools

Massimo Canonico

Department of Science and Innovation Technology
University of Piemonte Orientale
Italy
Email: massimo.canonico@uniupo.it

Luigi De Russis

Department of Control and Computer Engineering
Politecnico di Torino
Italy
Email: luigi.derussis@polito.it

***Abstract*—In the last 10 years, various cloud platforms enabled developers to easily create applications able to understand, with some limitations, natural languages. Nowadays, such cloud platforms for natural language understanding (NLU) are widely used, thanks to the rise of multiple chat services and conversational assistants on our mobile devices. This paper compares and analyses the main cloud-based NLU platforms, both from a descriptive and from a performance-based point of view. For the descriptive analysis, a taxonomy is proposed and six cloud platforms are analyzed. The performance evaluation, instead, compares three of these platforms, highlighting strengths and weaknesses of the different NLU tools.**

Keywords–Natural Language Understanding; Cloud Platform; Comparison; NLU Taxonomy.

I. INTRODUCTION

Over the last 20 years, computational linguistics has grown very fast both in scientific research and practical technology that are being incorporated into customer products (for example, in applications such as Apple's Siri [1] or in hardware components such as Google Home [2]). This has been possible thanks to four key factors: (i) a vast increase in computing power, (ii) the huge amount of linguistic data available, (iii) the improvement of Machine Learning, and (iv) a better understanding of the structure of human language.

Natural Language Understanding (NLU) is a subfield of computer science concerned with the usage of computational techniques to learn, understand, and produce human language content [3]. NLU can have multiple purposes: from aiding human-human communication (e.g., Skype Translator [4]) to improve technical support in human-machine communication (nowadays the first questions for technical support are being managed by conversational agents). The importance of NLU is also witnessed by the various cloud-based platforms proposed by the major IT companies such as Facebook (i.e., with wit.ai [5]), Google (i.e., with Dialogflow [6]), IBM (i.e., with Watson Conversation [7]) Microsoft (i.e., with LUIS [8]) and so on. Thanks to Cloud Computing, these NLU platforms can be easily accessible from everywhere, they can exploit huge computational power (as provided by the biggest IT companies like Google), and they are ready-to-go, always updated, without any software to install of hardware requirement to satisfy.

This paper compares the most relevant NLU cloud platforms from two points of view: descriptive and performance-based. To the best of our knowledge, this is the first attempt to fully compare and analyze the most important cloud-based NLU tools. For the descriptive analysis, the paper proposes a taxonomy to represent and explore different NLU solutions. The taxonomy is, then, applied to six NLU platforms, for which we discuss their specific characteristics. Furthermore, for the performance-based analysis, we compare the performance of the best three NLU tools analyzed through an experimental evaluation and we discuss their relative strengths and weaknesses.

The remainder of the paper is organized as follows. In Section II, we review existing work, while in Section III, we describe the most relevant Natural Language Understanding cloud platforms. Then, in Section IV, we discuss the taxonomy used to analyze the NLU tools, and in Section V, we evaluate the weaknesses and strengths of such tools. Finally, in Section VI, we conclude the paper.

II. RELATED WORKS

In 1972, T. Winograd wrote a paper entitled "Understanding natural language" [9], which describes a computer system for understanding English. The paper describes in details the main components of the system (such as a parser, a recognition grammar, a semantic analyzer, and a general problem solving system) and it proposes a sample parsing program. These components are still the key components of the modern NLU system and only in the last 10 years they have been fully implemented with the advent of a new technology called *conversational assistant* (or "ChatBot"): a computer program designed to interact with users via textual or auditory methods using NLU systems, typically hosted in the cloud. Despite the spread of chatbots in many contexts (for example, customer care support, food order, shopping assistant, reservation) and the increase of NLU systems, to the best of our knowledge the scientific literature has not proposed yet a complete comparison concerning the main cloud NLU system available nowadays. As a matter of the fact, in [10] the authors discuss how it is possible to implement a conversational assistant by using three cloud providers (in particular, Microsoft Azure, IBM Watson, and Heroku) but they do not provide any experimental evaluation for the adopted NLU system. In [11], the authors describe ideas to extend the way of verbal lecture visually and verbally. For the visualization of lecture talk, they created a chatbot by using DialogFlow (formerly called api.ai) without a preliminary comparison with other NLU systems. Furthermore, there are specific blogs, bulletin boards, and other web resources focused on chatbots that provide a very superficial comparison with a few of those NLU systems. In particular, in [12] the authors make a comparison with just two of them (i.e., DialogFlow and wit.ai) by considering a specific task: order a pizza. Finally, in [13], the authors compare 4 NLU platforms only from a performance-based point of view without providing a taxonomy to represent and explore the difference between the NLU solutions. In this work, we plan to fill this gap by providing an exhaustive and complete comparison of the main cloud-based NLU systems available nowadays, according to a proposed taxonomy.

III. Natural Language Understanding Platforms

In the last 10 years, several companies opened their cloud-based NLU tools with the aim of allowing developers and engineers (a) to extend the capabilities of their own NLU products or (b) to create new conversational assistants with ease.

In the former case, four actors dominate the NLU panorama: Apple with Siri, Google with Google Assistant, Amazon with Alexa, and Microsoft with Cortana. These companies release APIs and libraries to extend the capabilities of their respective conversational assistants: as an example, Apple provides *SiriKit* for iOS app developers, while Amazon allows developers to create new *skills* for Alexa. In this paper, we are not interested in investigating and comparing these NLU tools since they are pre-trained for end-users and continuously improved by their respective companies.

We would, instead, compare and critique the latter case, i.e., cloud-based NLU platforms personalized and trained by developers. In this way, we aim at evaluating the "bare" algorithms and cloud services. In this category, we identify six main NLU cloud platforms: 1) Google's *DialogFlow* [6], 2) Facebook's *wit.ai* [5], 3) Microsoft *LUIS* [8], 4) IBM *Watson Conversation* [7], 5) *Amazon Lex* [14], and 6) *Recast.ai* [15].

All these platforms are powered by machine learning algorithms that are totally transparent for the developers. They share some common functionality (e.g., they are cloud-based, they support various programming languages and different natural languages, etc.) but differ significantly in other aspects.

They rely on two concepts for performing NLU operations: **intent** and **entity**. An *intent* represents a mapping between what a user says and what action should be taken by the chatbot. It represents a portion of a conversation. An *entity*, instead, is a tool for extracting parameter values from natural language inputs. Any important data you want to get from a user's request, will have a corresponding entity. To better understand, the sentence "What is the weather in Paris?" is the input part of the intent for *asking the weather*, while "Paris" is an individual of a possible entity named *City* that collect the names of any city in the world. Such NLU platforms allow both the definition of new intents and new entities, as well as the reuse of existing intents and entities (called *pre-build intents* and *pre-build entities*, respectively). In the remainder of this Section, we describe the main characteristics of each NLU platform analyzed.

A. DialogFlow

DialogFlow, previously known as *api.ai*, is a NLU cloud platform owned and maintained by Google. It is a free to use conversational platform, i.e., it is possible to refine a dialog without repeating the context of the conversation. It supports various languages, different programming languages, and it has a series of built-in integration with other chatbot-based platforms (e.g., Telegram, Google Assistant, Amazon Alexa).

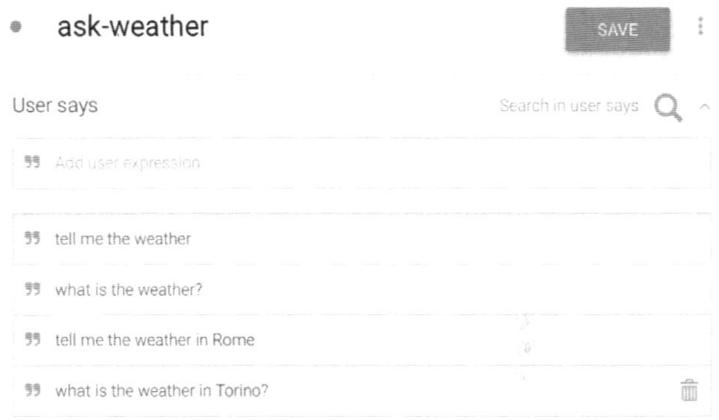

Figure 1. An example of the DialogFlow composition interface: speaking about the weather.

A developer interested in creating a new conversational assistant, or in expanding the conversational capabilities of their existing chatbot, can use one or more forms in a web-based user interface (Figure 1). Each form represents a portion of the conversation, structured as a users' question and some answers. In the DialogFlow form, the developer has to insert some examples of input sentences (i.e., what the portion of the dialog is about) and the "answers" provided by the NLU tool. Answers can be inserted directly into the web interface or can be provided by an ad-hoc server application through the *webhook* mechanism, enabled by the DialogFlow APIs. It is possible to mix, in a single intent, multiple languages.

B. wit.ai

wit.ai is a NLU cloud platform owned and maintained by Facebook. Like DialogFlow, it is a free to use platform, with support of several natural languages but only 3 programming languages.

Differently from all the other NLU tools examined here, wit.ai focuses on extracting meaning from single sentences. In other words, it acts more as a NLU parser than a complete NLU platform: in fact, wit.ai does not provide any integration with other chatbot-based platform, any web interface for handling portions of a conversation, nor any mechanism for maintaining the context through a conversation. All these and other features are in charge of the developers, that should realize in their own code any integration, conversational aspects, etc., in which they are interested.

C. LUIS

Language Understanding Intelligent Service (LUIS) is the NLU platform of Microsoft. Differently from the previous two tools, it is part of the Azure cloud services. Being part of Azure, LUIS shares the pricing schema with it and can access to some additional features. It supports various languages, but only 4 SDKs are available (i.e., C# SDK, Python SDK, Node.js SDK, and Android SDK). All its applications are centered on a domain-specific topic or are content related. Active learning technology is one of LUIS's features. It is possible to use pre-existing, world-class, pre-built models from Bing and Cortana. Models deployment to an HTTP endpoint is a one-click operation; it returns easy-to-use JavaScript Object Notation (JSON) documents. LUIS offers a set of programmatic REST APIs that can be used by developers to automate the application creation process.

D. Watson Conversation

Watson Conversation is the NLU platform of IBM, part of the IBM Bluemix cloud services. It shares Bluemix pricing schema and may access to additional features. It is a conversational platform with the support of various programming and natural languages: it is built on a neural network (one billion Wikipedia words), understands intents, interprets entities and dialogs. It achieves accuracy by attempting to assess as much context as possible. It gets that context both within the passage of the question and from the knowledge base (called a corpus) that is available to it for finding responses. Watson teases apart the question and potential responses in the corpus, and then examines it and the context of the statement in hundreds of ways. Watson then uses the results to gain a degree of confidence in its interpretation of the question and potential answers.

E. Amazon Lex

Amazon Lex is the NLU platform part of the Amazon Web Services (AWS). It shares the pricing schema with AWS and may access to additional features. It is a conversational platform that supports various programming languages but only one natural language (i.e., English). Amazon Lex is a service for building conversational interfaces into any application using voice and text. In particular, it provides the advanced deep learning functionalities of automatic speech recognition (ASR) for converting speech to text, and natural language understanding (NLU) to recognize the intent of the text, to enable developers building applications with highly engaging user experiences and lifelike conversational interactions. Amazon Lex exploits the same deep learning technologies that power Amazon Alexa.

F. Recast.ai

Recast.ai is the only analyzed NLU platform owned and maintained by a startup. It is a NLU cloud platform, free to use, with support for multiple natural and programming languages. Recast.ai allows the creation of complex conversational assistants (e.g., like DialogFlow) but also provides a series of dedicated APIs/web services to perform textual and lexical analysis (e.g., like wit.ai).

Figure 2. An example of the block-based interface available from Recast.ai.

To create a conversational assistant, a developer should define an intent in a two-step process: with a form-based interface, they have to define the input sentences (with their entities) of an intent; then, with a block-based interface (Figure 2), they can define the other elements of the intent (chatbot responses and actions) as well as the connections with other intents. It is possible to mix, in a single intent, multiple languages.

Recast.ai is the only platform that allows a developer to publicly share their intents and entities, to be used by other users of the Recast.ai community.

IV. NLU TAXONOMY

To describe the *core features* of cloud-based NLU tools, we propose a taxonomy that focuses on 13 different facets. The taxonomy aims at providing a descriptive overview of such NLU platforms, thus enabling a comparison of different tools. In particular, we validate the taxonomy by describing and comparing the six NLU platforms briefly presented in the previous Section. The taxonomy with the description of those six NLU tools is reported in Table I.

The taxonomy focuses on 13 facets, ranging from supported languages to pricing, to advanced and automatic NLU features like fallback intents.

1. **Usability** indicates the perceived usability and ease of use of the user interface provided by the NLU platform. It can assume the following values: a) *high*, simple and intuitive for a developer; b) *medium*; c) *low*, difficult to use for a developer and without supporting documentation.
2. **Languages** reports how many natural languages the platform supports. It also indicates whether those languages can be mixed inside a single intent.
3. **Programming Languages** shows how many programming languages the platform officially supports and maintains.
4. **Pre-build Entities** indicates how many pre-build entities the NLU tool offers.
5. **Pre-build Intents** reports how many pre-build groups of intents the NLU platform offers.
6. **Default Fallback Intent** indicates whether the platform has a fallback mechanism for intents. The *fallback mechanism* allows the proper classification of sentences that are not recognized as part of an existing intent; without a dedicated fallback mechanism, every sentence will belong to a defined intent. For example, suppose to have only one intent that is related to the weather and the sentence "My name is Mark"; without a fallback mechanism the sentence will be classified as pertaining to the "weather" topic.
7. **Automatic Context** reports whether the NLU platform can automatically manage the context in a conversation or it is left to the developer's code.

8. **Composition Mode** shows which is the composition modality adopted by the tool (e.g., form-based, block-based).
9. **Online Integration** reports which third-party integrations are available in the cloud platform.
10. **Webhook/SDK Availability** indicates whether and how a developer can integrate his/her conversational assistant with other software, independently from the available online integrations.
11. **All-in Platform** reports whether the NLU tool is a platform able to provide multiple NLU-related services by its own, i.e., it is not too basic or part of a family of different web services.
12. **Linkable Intents** indicates if it is possible to link one intent to another, directly in the platform.
13. **Price** is the pricing for using the NLU platform.

As detailed in Table I, most of the analyzed NLU platforms show a good usability and support various languages as well as programming languages, so that they can be easily used by developers. They mainly differ, instead, in the *automatic* features that pertain to NLU: default fallback intent, automatic context handling, and linkable intents. These three aspects are fundamental for allowing a developer to get started immediately in creating their own conversational assistant. From a descriptive point of view, we can assure that DialogFlow is the most complete NLU platform since it provides the best solutions for the majority of facets considered in the taxonomy.

V. Experimental Evaluation

To conduct a performance evaluation of the NLU platforms, we focused on those tools that exhibit an automatic handling of NLU-related features. In particular, we selected the three NLU platforms with a default fallback intent, so that the handling of unknown sentences is delegated to the platform's algorithm and not to the developer's experience and code.

We evaluated DialogFlow, LUIS, and Watson Conversation concerning two intents: a *weather* intent, created equally in the three platforms, and the *default fallback* intent already provided by each NLU tool. The goal of the evaluation was to understand at which extent each platform detects the intention of the user and the parameters in the sentences. In other words, we were interested in whether the NLU platform placed a sentence in the "right" intent, and whether all the entities present in the trained intent were identified. The language selected for the evaluation was English.

A. Procedure

We created a "weather" intent and enabled the *default fallback* intent in each of the three NLU platforms. Then, for each NLU tool, we trained the intent with the following five sentences (five is the minimum number of training sentences suggested by NLU platforms documentation, such as Watson):

1) Should I take an umbrella outside today?
2) Show me the forecast for next Monday
3) What's it like outside my office?
4) Is it sunny in Rome today?
5) What will be the weather tomorrow in San Francisco?

For each sentence, we highlight to the NLU tool the presence of specific entities and whether they are mandatory or not. In particular, we used two pre-build entities for *date* and *location*, and we instructed the platforms to require the location for every sentence of the "weather" intent. For the *date* entity, we selected the "@sys.date" entity in DialogFlow, "datetimeV2" in LUIS, and "@sys-date" in Watson. For the *location* entity, instead, we selected the "@sys.location" entity in DialogFlow, "geography" in LUIS, and "@sys-location" in Watson (marked as a beta entity). If the *location* entity was absent from a sentence, we trained each NLU platform to ask "Where?" before providing a fixed answer (i.e., "It will be sunny in {location}").

To exemplify the workflow, if a user submit the sentence "*Should I take an umbrella outside today?*", the NLU platform should recognize that the sentence belongs to the "weather" intent and ask "*Where?*", since no location is present in the original sentence. The user, at this point, should indicate a location (e.g., "*In Rome*") and the platform will reply "*It will be sunny in Rome.*"

After this training procedure, we submitted 24 sentences to each NLU platform, by paying attention to reset the context in those platform with an automatic context management. By doing so, we assure that each sentence is evaluated independently from the previous one. The 24 sentences were divided in the following way: (a) 3 sentences were taken from the training set, (b) 13 sentences were about the weather, (c) 8 sentences were not about the weather. For the last set of sentences, we chose various non-weather sentences considering three categories: (i) sentences that are completely not related to the weather (i.e., "Ice cream"), (ii) questions with cities names (i.e., "What is the time in Venice now?") and, finally, (iii) general questions/greetings (i.e., "Which information may you provide?"). The answer provided by the platform in these cases can be decided by the developers (for example, the answer could be "Could you reform your request, please?".).

We stored the results provided by each platform in terms of response, accuracy of the recognition, and classified intent. The full list of sentences, split in the three areas, along with the main results about intent classification are reported in Table II. In the Table, we highlighted in bold the wrong results (intent name and accuracy).

B. Results and Discussion

As mentioned before, we split the full list of sentence in 3 areas: (i) sentences from the training set, (ii) sentences about weather, and (iii) sentences not related to weather. In this section we discuss the results obtained by the NLU platforms for each area.

For the first area, as expected, all NLU platforms were able to detect the right intent (i.e., weather) with maximum confidence level (1.0). Conversely, for the second area, we noted significant differences between the NLU platforms behavior. In particular, DialogFlow detected the default intent for 8 sentences (out of 13) instead of the weather one. The other two NLU platforms performed better since they identified the weather intent with an high confidence level for all the 13 sentences. In particular, LUIS returned an high accuracy (i.e., ≥ 0.99) for all sentences while Watson returned a slightly

TABLE I. THE DESCRIPTIVE TAXONOMY FOR THE SIX NLU PLATFORM EXAMINED

Platform	*Usability*	*Languages*	*Programming Languages*	*Pre-build Entities*	*Pre-build Intents*	*Default Fallback Intent*	*Automatic Context*	*Composition Mode*	*Online Integration*	*Webhook/ SDK Availability*	*All-in Platform*	*Linkable Intents*	*Price*
Dialog-Flow	High	15, from English to Chinese	11, from Java to Ruby	60, from addresses to colors	34, from small talks to currency converters	Yes	Yes	Form-based	14, from Telegram to Alexa	Webhook and SDKs	Yes	Yes	Free
wit.ai	Medium	50, from Albanian to Ukrainian	3: Node.js, Python, and Ruby	22, from location to email	Zero	No	No	Form-based	Zero	SDK	No	No	Free, contact heavy usage
LUIS	Medium	10, from English to Chinese	4: Android, Python, Node.js, and C#	13, from numbers to geography	20, from calendar to fitness	Yes	No	Form-based	Zero	Webhook and SDK	No, other services are in Azure	No, other services are in Azure	Free up to 10k requests per month
Watson Conversation	High	12, from English to Chinese	6, from Node.js to Java	7, from time to person	Zero	Yes	Yes	Form and block-based	Zero	SDK	No, other services are in Bluemix	Yes	Free up to 10k requests per month
Amazon Lex	Low	1: English	9, from Java to Go	93, from Alexa	15, from Alexa	No	Yes	Form-based	3: Twilio SMS, FB Messenger, and Slack	SDK	No, other services are in AWS	Yes	Free for the 1st year (with limits)
Recast.ai	Medium	16 at the standard level	7, from Python to Go	31, from colors to distance	3, several from the community	No	No	Form and block-based	Zero	Webhook and SDK	Yes	Yes	Free

TABLE II. THE MAIN RESULTS OF THE EVALUATION: THE RECOGNIZED INTENTS WITH THEIR ACCURACY

Sentences	*DialogFlow*	*LUIS*	*Watson*
What will be the weather tomorrow in San Francisco?	weather (1.0)	weather (1.0)	weather (1.0)
Show me the forecast for next Monday	weather (1.0)	weather (1.0)	weather (1.0)
What's it like outside my office?	weather (1.0)	weather (1.0)	weather (1.0)
Is it cold outside?	**default**	weather (0.99)	weather (0.85)
What will the weather be like in Paris?	weather (0.71)	weather (0.99)	weather (0.91)
What's the weather like in 3 days?	weather (1.0)	weather (0.99)	weather (0.92)
Is it windy today?	**default**	weather (0.99)	weather (0.88)
I want the weather in New York, in two weeks	weather (0.39)	weather (0.99)	weather (0.26)
Is it raining today?	**default**	weather (0.99)	weather (0.88)
What will the weather be like at my vacation home this weekend?	**default**	weather (0.99)	weather (0.92)
What is the weather like near my next meeting?	**default**	weather (0.99)	weather (0.92)
Is it a beautiful day for a walk?	**default**	weather (0.99)	weather (0.85)
Is the weather good for a walk today?	**default**	weather (0.99)	weather (0.90)
Should I take an umbrella in Oslo, tomorrow?	weather (0.90)	weather (1.0)	weather (0.96)
What is the weather for the next three days in Dublin?	weather (0.54)	weather (0.99)	weather (0.93)
Is it raining in San Diego now?	**default**	weather (0.99)	weather (0.83)
What is the time in Venice now?	default	**weather (0.99)**	**weather (0.37)**
What is the timezone of New York?	default	**weather (0.99)**	**weather (0.37)**
Hello!	default	**weather (0.99)**	default
My name is Mark.	default	**weather (0.99)**	**weather (0.25)**
Ice cream	default	**weather (0.99)**	default
<a word with random chars>	default	default	default
I need help	default	**weather (0.99)**	default
Which information may you provide?	default	**weather (0.99)**	default

lower accuracy (i.e., ≥ 0.85) for the majority of the sentences. It is worth noticing that the sentence with the lowest accuracy is "*I want the weather in New York, in two weeks*" for both DialogFlow (with accuracy = 0.39) and Watson (with accuracy = 0.26). In this second area, LUIS was the NLU platform which performed better than the other two. In the last set of sentences, the performance of the tools varied considerably. In particular, DialogFlow was the only tool which correctly detected the default intent for all sentences. As a matter of fact, both LUIS and Watson detected the weather intent for some sentences. In particular, LUIS performed badly: only the word with random chars was detected as default intent, in all other case, LUIS detected the weather intent with high accuracy (i.e., ≥ 0.99). Watson performed slightly better than LUIS: for three sentences it detected the weather intent, albeit with a low accuracy (i.e., ≤ 0.37). As mentioned before, concerning the entity identification, all NLU platforms were able to recognize them with 1.0 level of accuracy.

In general, we can say that Watson is the best NLU platform in our study since it detects wrong intents only for 3 sentences over 24. Moreover, for these 3 sentences it provides a low accuracy level that can be exploited by a developer to improve the Watson's intent detection algorithm.

VI. CONCLUSION AND FUTURE WORKS

The idea of being able to hold a conversation with a computer has fascinated people for a long time and has featured in many science fiction books and movies. With recent advances in spoken language technology, artificial intelligence, and conversational interface design, coupled with the emergence of smart devices, it is now possible to "ask" these devices to perform many tasks by using natural language [16]. In this paper, we compared and critiqued the main cloud platforms for natural language understanding from a descriptive and performance-based point of view. In particular, we proposed a taxonomy that focuses on 13 different characteristics of a NLU platform and we then conducted a functional evaluation to understand at which extent each platform is able to detect the intention of the user. From the results, we can affirm that Watson is the platform who performs best since it is able to assign the right intent in the majority of the cases studied and, moreover, even when it detects the wrong intent, the accuracy level is low so that a developer can exploit this information to train Watson to improve its intent detection algorithm. As future work, we plan to extend our experimental evaluation by considering many different intents at the same time and we will evaluate how the NLU platforms exploit the context in a more complex conversational dialog.

REFERENCES

[1] M. Galeso, Apple Siri for Mac: An Easy Guide to the Best Features. USA: CreateSpace Independent Publishing Platform, 2017.

[2] A. Nijholt, "Google Home: Experience, support and re-experience of social home activities," Information Sciences, vol. 178, no. 3, 2008, pp. 612–630.

[3] J. Hirschberg and C. D. Manning, "Advances in natural language processing," Science, vol. 349, no. 6245, 2015, pp. 261–266.

[4] W. D. Lewis, "Skype translator: Breaking down language and hearing barriers," Translating and the Computer (TC37), vol. 10, 2015, pp. 125–149.

[5] "The wit.ai project," https://wit.ai, accessed: 2017-11-01.

[6] "The Dialogflow project," https://dialogflow.com, accessed: 2017-11-01.

[7] R. High, "The era of cognitive systems: An inside look at IBM Watson and how it works," IBM Corporation, Redbooks, 2012.

[8] "The LUIS project," https://luis.ai, accessed: 2017-11-01.

[9] T. Winograd, Understanding Natural Language. Orlando, FL, USA: Academic Press, Inc., 1972.

[10] P. Amit, K. Marimuthu, R. A. Nagaraja, and R. Niranchana, "Comparative study of cloud platforms to develop a chatbot," International Journal of Engineering & Technology, vol. 6, no. 3, 2017, pp. 57–61.

[11] S. Matsuura and R. Ishimura, "Chatbot and dialogue demonstration with a humanoid robot in the lecture class." Lecture Notes in Computer Science, vol. 10279, 2017, pp. 233–246.

[12] "Api.ai vs wit.ai (or is it Google vs Facebook?)," https://www.themarketingtechnologist.co/api-ai-vs-wit-ai/, accessed: 2017-11-01.

[13] D. B. et al., "Evaluating natural language understanding services for conversational question answering systems," in Proc. of the 18th Annual SIGdial Meeting on Discourse and Dialogue, 2017, pp. 174–185.

[14] "Amazon Lex," https://aws.amazon.com/lex/, accessed: 2017-11-01.

[15] "Recast.ai," https://recast.ai, accessed: 2017-11-01.

[16] M. McTear, Z. Callejas, and D. Griol, "The conversational interface," New York: Springer, vol. 10, 2016, pp. 978–3.

An Architecture Model for a Distributed Virtualization System

Pablo Pessolani
Facultad Regional Santa Fe
Universidad Tecnológica Nacional
Santa Fe – Argentina
e-mail: ppessolani@frsf.utn.edu.ar

Fernando G. Tinetti
III-LIDI Facultad de Informática- UNLP
Comisión de Inv. Científicas, Prov. Bs. As
La Plata, Argentina
e-mail: fernando@info.unlp.edu.ar

Toni Cortes
Barcelona Supercomputing Center & UPC
Barcelona – España
e-mail: toni.cortes@bsc.es

Silvio Gonnet
INGAR - Facultad Regional Santa Fe
CONICET - Universidad Tecnológica Nacional
Santa Fe - Argentina
e-mail: sgonnet@santafe-conicet.gov.ar

***Abstract* — This article presents an architecture model for a Distributed Virtualization System, which could expand a virtual execution environment from a single physical machine to several nodes of a cluster. With current virtualization technologies, computing power and resource usage of Virtual Machines (or Containers) are limited to the physical machine where they run. To deliver high levels of performance and scalability, cloud applications are usually partitioned in several Virtual Machines (or Containers) located on different nodes of a virtualization cluster. Developers often use that processing model because the same instance of the operating system is not available on each node where their components run. The proposed architecture model is suitable for new trends in software development because it is inherently distributed. It combines and integrates Virtualization and Distributed Operating Systems technologies with the benefits of both worlds, providing the same isolated instance of a Virtual Operating System on each cluster node. Although it requires the introduction of changes in existing operating systems, thousands of legacy applications would not require modifications to obtain their benefits. A Distributed Virtualization System is suitable to deliver high-performance cloud services with provider-class features, such as high-availability, replication, migration, and load balancing. Furthermore, it is able to concurrently run several isolated instances of different guest Virtual Operating Systems, allocating a subset of nodes for each instance and sharing nodes between them. Currently, a prototype is running on a cluster of commodity hardware provided with two kinds of Virtual Operating Systems tailored for internet services (web server) as a proof of concept.**

Keywords: Virtualization, Virtual Machines, Containers, Distributed Operating Systems.

I. INTRODUCTION

Current virtualization technologies are massively adopted to cover those requirements in which Operating Systems (OS) have shown weakness, such as performance, fault, and security isolation. They also add features like resource partitioning, server consolidation, legacy application support, management tools, among others, which are attractive to Cloud service providers.

Nowadays, there are several virtualization technologies used to provide Infrastructure as a Service (IaaS) mounted in a cluster of servers linked by high-speed networks. Storage Area Networks (SAN), security appliances (network and application firewall, Intrusion Detection/Prevention Systems, etc.), and a set of management systems complement the required provider-class infrastructure.

Hardware virtualization, paravirtualization, and OS-level virtualization are the most widely used technologies to carry out these tasks, although each of them presents different levels of server consolidation, performance, scalability, high-availability, and isolation.

The term "*Virtual Machine*" (VM) is used in issues related to hardware virtualization and paravirtualization technologies to describe an isolated execution environment for an OS and its applications. *Containers*, *Jails*, *Zones* are the names used in OS-level virtualization to describe the environments for applications confinement. Regardless of the definition of the virtualization abstraction, its computing power and resource usage are limited to the physical machine where it runs.

Current IaaS providers use SANs in their Data Centers for storage virtualization, supplying disk drives for VMs. In some way, the resources (disks) of a VM expand outside the host and this can be seen as an exception to the above statement. If this processing mode is extended to several types of services and resources, it becomes a new model of distributed processing in virtualization technologies. The proposed architecture model takes this approach, distributing processes, services, and resources to provide virtual environments based on OS factoring and OS containers. The outcome is a Distributed Virtualization System (DVS), which combines and integrates OS-virtualization and Distributed Operating Systems (DOS) technologies, providing the same isolated instance of a Virtual Operating System (VOS) [1] on each node of a virtualization cluster.

Nowadays, to deliver high performance and scalability levels, Cloud applications are usually partitioned in several

VMs/Containers, running on the nodes of a virtualization cluster (as Docker-enabled applications) [2]. Developers often use those kinds of processing models as Platform as a Service (PaaS) because the same instance of the OS is not available on all nodes and, hence, they must use some kind of middleware, which provides the cluster with Application Programming Interfaces (APIs) and services. A DVS is suitable as infrastructure for this new trend in software development, like applications based on microservices architecture (MSA) [3], because it is inherently distributed. Furthermore, thousands of legacy applications would benefit because they would not require modifications to take advantage of DVS features. Migration of legacy applications from on-premises servers to a Cloud execution environment requires changes in their design and coding. If a standard interface, such as POSIX is available in the Cloud, the migration task is simplified by reducing costs and time.

A DVS fits the requirements for delivering high-performance cloud services with provider-class features as high-availability, replication, elasticity, load balancing, resource management, and process migration. Furthermore, a DVS is able to run several instances of different guest VOS concurrently, allocating a subset of nodes for each instance (resource aggregation), and to share nodes between them (resource partitioning). Each VOS runs isolated within a Distributed Container (DC), which could span multiple nodes of the DVS cluster as it is presented in the topology example in Fig.1. The proposed model keeps the appreciated features of current virtualization technologies, such as confinement, consolidation and security, and the benefits of DOS, such as transparency, greater performance, high-availability, elasticity, and scalability.

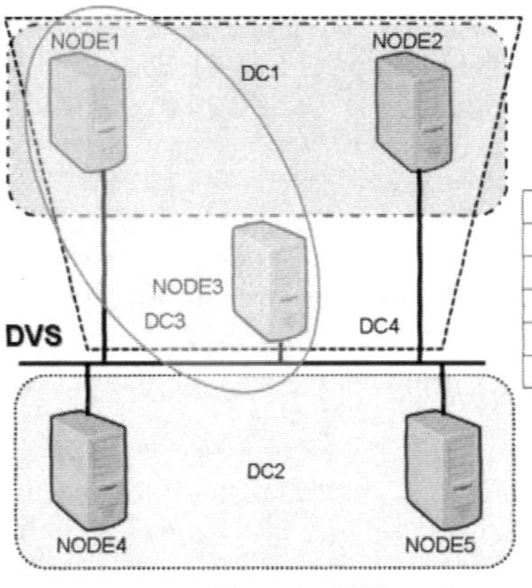

	DC1	DC2	DC3	DC4
NODE1	X		X	X
NODE2	X			X
NODE3			X	X
NODE4		X		
NODE5		X		

Figure 1. DVS topology example.

A DVS allows running multiple Distributed VOSs as guests that can extend beyond the limits of a physical machine. Each DVOS could have more computing power and could provide greater scalability and elasticity in its configuration as a consequence of resource and computing power aggregation. The set of resources (both physical and abstract) and the set of processes that constitute a DVOS can be scattered (and eventually replicated) in the nodes of a cluster.

This work is intended to contribute proposing a new model of virtualization that allows building several isolated execution environments that take advantage of the aggregation of computational, storage, and network resources of the nodes of a cluster.

The use of a DVS is based on the same arguments/grounds for the use of DOSs. Several related processes (in the same DC) could be executed in different nodes using the same abstract resources as those offered by the VOS. This feature simplifies application (or library) programming since standard APIs, such as operations on semaphores, message queues, mutexes, etc. can be used. On the other hand, the process location transparency is helpful for application administrators since it avoids dealing with IP addresses, ports, URLs, etc., simplifying applications deployment and management, and reducing costs and implementation times.

Let us suppose a configuration of a database server (DBMS) running on a host (or VM), and the need to perform an online backup which ensures consistency of a restored database. The backup process should run on a host (or VM), other than the DBMS for performance reasons, but connected to the same network, and both processes connected to the same SAN. As each process runs on its own OS, the DBMS process and the backup process must communicate using an ad-hoc protocol through the network in order to synchronize the access to the database. This requires setting up IP addresses, ports, names, etc. to describe the topology.

In a DVS configuration, both processes (DBMS and backup) could run on the same VOS, but on different nodes. Therefore, they can synchronize the access to the database using semaphores, mutexes, signals or any other facilities offered by the VOS.

The remainder of this paper is organized as follows. Section II explains background and related works. Section III describes the proposed architecture model, its design, and details of a prototype implementation. Section IV presents performance results of several components of the prototype. Finally, the conclusions of this contribution and future work are summarized in Section V.

II. Background and Related Work

The term *virtualization* is usually associated with such technologies, which allow the partition of hardware resources to conform isolated execution environments called *Virtual Machines*. But there is a technology which has the opposite goals: *Reverse Virtualization*. As suggested by its name, it integrates hardware resources from multiple computers (nodes of a cluster) to provide the image of a virtual Symmetric Multiprocessing System or vSMP. Works related to Distributed Virtualization present a cluster as a virtual shared memory multiprocessor. v-NUMA [4], and the University of Tokyo's Virtual Multiprocessor [5] allow multiple physical computers to host a single OS instance. ScaleMP [6] virtualizes an SMP and defines its virtualization paradigm as an *aggregation* of computational resources as opposed to *partitioning*. Somehow, Reverse Virtualization and a DVS share the same goals, but the latter allows not only the aggregation of resources but also their partitioning.

Since there are plenty of articles which can be used as surveys of virtualization [7][8], this section will include details only about those technologies on which the DVS model is based and other related works.

A. Background

Classical definitions about Operating System mention that it is a layer of software located between applications and hardware. In OS-virtualization technology, the guest OS does not manage real hardware, but operates on virtual devices provided by a lower layer of software, such as a host-OS. Therefore, it seems appropriate to refer to the guest-OS as a VOS. There is a noticeable similarity with the paravirtualization [9] approach, the difference lying in the fact that there is a host-OS instead of a hypervisor in the lower layer. Instead of requesting services by means of hypervisor-calls, the guest-OS uses system calls. Hence, OS-virtualization and paravirtualization share the same benefits and drawbacks.

A well-known project that allows running multiple instances of Linux over other native Linux (as host) is User-Mode Linux (UML) [10]. CoLinux [11] is another project that allows running Linux as a guest-OS, but on a Windows host. Minix over Linux (MoL) [12] allows running multiple instances of a multi-server OS, such as Minix [13] over a Linux host.

MoL emulates Minix Interprocess Communications (IPC) mechanisms using TCP sockets, so that processes of the same instance of MoL can be executed in different hosts. This was the germinal version of the architecture model proposed in this article, but the use of Linux provided IPC and a pseudo-microkernel process running in user-mode turns performance its main weaknesses. To improve it, a microkernel with its own IPC mechanisms was developed to be embedded in the Linux kernel named M3-IPC (as a lightweight co-kernel) [14][15]. Later, it was extended to exchange messages and data among processes of the same MoL instance running on several nodes, allowing a multi-server VOS to be turned into a DVOS.

Other technologies that were sources of inspiration for the proposed model are those used by DOSs [16]. They fully developed and investigated in the 1990s as a consequence of the limited performance of a single host and the growing demand for computing power and scalability. Unlike Reverse Virtualization, which is a technology that virtualizes an SMP computer, a DOS performs distributed processing by expanding OS abstract resources to all its nodes. These resources are analogous to those provided by a centralized OS, such as users, processes, files, pipes, sockets, message queues, shared memory, semaphores, and mutexes.

Software factoring is a well-known approach in the field of OSs used by microkernel technologies. Servers and processes communicate with one another by passing messages through an IPC facility furnished by the OS kernel [17]. Unlike monolithic OS, a microkernel-based OS factors the kernel functions and services into multiple layers. Each layer is made up of several isolated processes running in user-mode, and the lowest layer runs the microkernel in supervisor mode [18]. Since upper layer servers and tasks do not have the right privileges to handle the hardware by their own, the microkernel provides services which allow them to operate on the hardware indirectly. A similarity between a microkernel OS and a paravirtualization system becomes evident [19]. In some ways, the microkernel acts as a para-virtualization hypervisor for a single VM, consisting of a set of user-space processes that constitute the guest-OS. Factoring an OS into multiple user-space tasks and servers provides the isolation required by a virtualization system and allows the distribution of processes in multiple nodes of a cluster.

The proposed model takes advantage of another technology: OS-based virtualization. It is a system call level virtualization, partitioning OS resources into isolated instances of execution environments. The host-OS isolates sets of user-space applications in Containers, Jails or Zones. Linux implements Containers [20] with two main kernel features; 1) *cgroups* [21]: It allows to isolate, prioritize, limit, and account for resource usage of a set of processes named *Control Groups*; 2) *namespaces* [22]: Usually, an OS provides a global namespace for OS abstract resources like UIDs, PIDs, file names, sockets, etc. All Containers provide applications with their own execution environment, but they all share the same OS. Therefore, the isolation property seems to be weaker against hardware virtualization and paravirtualization, but the performance gain is significant [23].

Any virtualization system whose aim is to provide IaaS with provider-class quality must consider high-availability as a requirement in its design. As a distributed system, a DVS must support the dynamic behavior of clusters where nodes are permanently added and removed. In a data center, several kinds of failures occur: in computers, in processes, in the network, and in operations; hence, they should be all considered in system design. Generally, component replication is the mechanism adopted to tolerate faults. Although there is extensive research about fault handling in distributed systems and because it is a complex issue [24], it is better to use tested tools, such as Distributed Consensus [25] and Group Communications Systems (GCS) [26] for achieving fault-tolerance through replication. Birman [26] states that: "*The use of a GCS should be considered for standardization, complexity, and performance reasons*". As Birman suggests, the prototype built as a proof of concept of a DVS is based on the use of an underlying GCS, which helped in the development of fault-tolerant components. Moreover, the use of a GCS allows the decoupling of a distributed application from the group communication mechanisms and from its failure detectors.

If a critical application runs on a DVS and its distributed components are strongly coupled, a fault on one member could result in a complete application failure. A GCS could be used by critical services, such as file servers, storage servers, web servers, etc. to solve the replication issue, providing more reliable services.

B. Related Works

Clustered Virtual Machines [27] is a technology used to run applications in a distributed way across a group of containers spread on several nodes of a cluster. On *Clustered Virtualization*, each application component runs within a container using the services of the host-OS in which each container is located.

Mesosphere's Data Center Operating System (DC/OS) [28] allows developers and administrators to consider a data center as a single computer that runs applications in software containers, but it is not really an OS; it is rather a container cluster manager with frameworks that provides PaaS. *JESSICA2* [29] is a distributed Java Virtual Machine implemented as a middleware, which supports parallel execution in a networked cluster environment, but it is limited to Java applications. Another software architecture model used for application development proposes to partitioning the application in autonomous components named Microservices [3]. With a set of microservices running on a cluster of servers the application's computing and resource needs are distributed, thus increasing application performance and scalability.

Unlike *Clustered Virtualization*, running a distributed application on a DVS can share the same instance of a DVOS allowing references to the same resource namespaces and system objects (such as users, pipes, queues, files, PIDs, sockets, etc.) as if they were running on the same host. This key feature can be sometimes used by developers when they need legacy applications to migrate to the Cloud, as well as for applications specifically developed to run in the Cloud.

III. DESIGN AND IMPLEMENTATION

Thinking of a distributed virtualization technology seems to make sense to achieve higher performance and increase service availability. OS-based virtualization and DOS technologies lead the authors to think about their convergence to achieve these goals, extending the boundaries of the virtual execution environment to multiple hosts and thereby multiplexing a cluster among multiple isolated instances of a DVOS.

An OS-based distributed virtualization approach will explore aggregation with partitioning. In such systems, a set of server processes constitutes a DVOS running within an execution environment made up of Distributed Containers (DC). Processes belonging to a DC may be spread on several nodes of a cluster (aggregation); and processes of different DCs could share the same host (partitioning).

Several hardware virtualization products offer high-availability and fault-tolerance by replicating a VM with its inner OS and all its processes. In such systems, load distribution is made using a VM migration facility that moves a complete VM from one server to another as a whole. A DVS could allow replication and migration of either all processes of DVOS or only some of them, such as the critical ones.

DOSs implement their policies and mechanisms, such as load balancing, process migration, leader election, consensus, fault detection, etc., within the system itself. As a result of this monolithic design, software modules are strongly coupled to one another and to the kernel, so that they cannot be reused by other applications. It is also difficult to change one of these components without changing the whole system. The DVS model relaxes the coupling among components, breaking them up as independent services with specific liabilities.

A. DVS Architecture

The main components of the DVS architecture are (see Fig. 2):

1) Distributed Virtualization Kernel (DVK): It is the core software layer that integrates the resources of the cluster, manages and limits the resources assigned to each DC. It provides interfaces for low-level protocols and services, which can be used to build a VOS, such as IPC, GCS, synchronization, replication, locking, leader election, fault detection, mutual exclusion, performance parameter sensing, processes migration mechanism, and key-value services. The DVK provides interfaces to manage all DVS resources, such as nodes, DCs and processes. Process management allows the DVS administrator to assign processes to a DC and to allocate nodes for it. The node in which the process runs can be changed, as in case of a migration, or when the process was replaced by another one, such as a backup process. For communication purposes, location changes made by the replacement or migration of a process are hidden from the other processes within the DC.

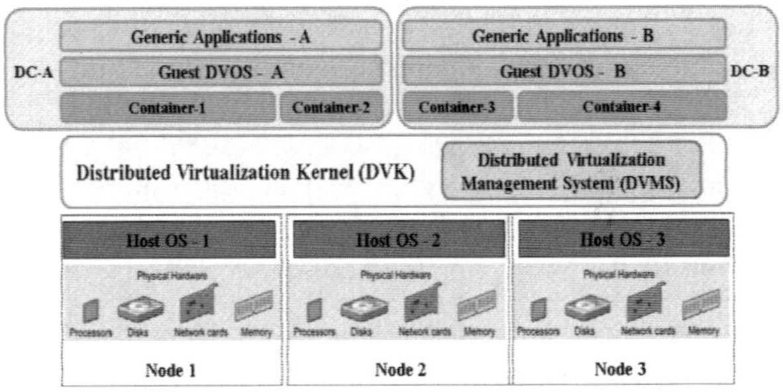

Figure 2. Distributed Virtualization System architecture model

2) Distributed Virtualization Management System (DVMS): It is the software layer that allows the DVS administrator to both manage the resources of the cluster, providing a DC for each VOS, and perform DVS monitoring.

3) Container: It is a host-OS abstraction which provides an isolated environment to run the components of a VOS. A set of Containers which belongs to the same VOS makes up a Distributed Container.

4) Distributed Container (DC): It is a set of single Containers, each one being set up by the DVMS in the host-OS of each node. There is one DC per VOS, and a DC can span from one to all nodes.

5) Virtual Operating System (VOS): Although any kind of VOS can be developed or modified to meet DVS architecture requirements, a DVOS can obtain greater benefits because it is able to distribute its processes in several nodes. Each VOS (single or distributed) runs within a DC. The task of modifying an existing OS to turn it into a VOS is simplified because it does not need to deal with real hardware resources but with virtual ones. Moreover, a VOS needs to manage neither virtual memory nor CPU scheduling because it is done by the host-OS.

6) VOS applications: They are applications (single or distributed) running within the same DC, using VOS-provided services.

The resource allocation unit for a DOS is the node as a whole; but for a DVOS (running within a DC) it is each single virtual resource provided by the host-OS on each node. This higher degree of granularity of the infrastructure unit allows a better use of resources and provides greater elasticity and efficiency.

B. DVS Prototype

Since the project startup (2013), a DVS prototype was implemented which runs on a cluster of x86 computers and Linux as OS-host. The DVS prototype considers the following abstractions, and the relations between them are presented in Fig. 3.

1) DVS: It is the top level layer that assembles all cluster nodes and it embraces all DCs.

2) Node: It is a computer that belongs to the DVS where processes of several DCs are able to be run. All nodes are connected by a network infrastructure.

3) DC: It is the group or set of related processes that might be scattered on several nodes. M3-IPC only allows communications among processes that belong to the same DC. The boundary of each DC can be based on administrative boundaries. A DC hides its internals from the outside world and hides network communication issues from its processes.

4) Proxies: They are special processes used to transfer messages and data blocks between nodes. M3-IPC does not impose a network/transport protocol to be used for inter-node communications. This feature allows programmers to choose the protocol that best fit their needs. Nodes communicate among them through proxies.

5) Process: Every process registered in a DC has an *endpoint* which identifies it. Process endpoints are unique and global within a DC, but could be repeated within other DCs.

With the exception of the process endpoints, the other DVS abstractions are hidden from the VOS and its processes. They are managed by the DVS administrator, such as adding or removing hosts as nodes of the DVS, allocating nodes to DCs, or setting proxies to communicate nodes.

Two simple VOS were developed to be executed as guests on the prototype as proof of concept. One of them is a multiserver VOS named MoL, and the other is a unikernel [30] VOS named ukVOS; both are able to provide Internet services (web server). MoL is made up of loosely coupled servers and tasks integrated as VOS components. Alternatively, they can be run alone serving Linux ordinary client processes by using some kind of kernel-user interface as FUSE or BUSE.

C. Distributed Virtualization Kernel

A DVK was implemented in the DVS prototype as a Linux kernel module and a patch, complemented by a set of libraries, commands and tools. The DVK module of each node (which includes M3-IPC) is implemented as a Linux co-kernel.

DVK APIs allow configuring and managing all DVS abstractions (DVS, DCs, nodes, and proxies), and mapping processes to DCs, DCs to nodes, and proxies to nodes.

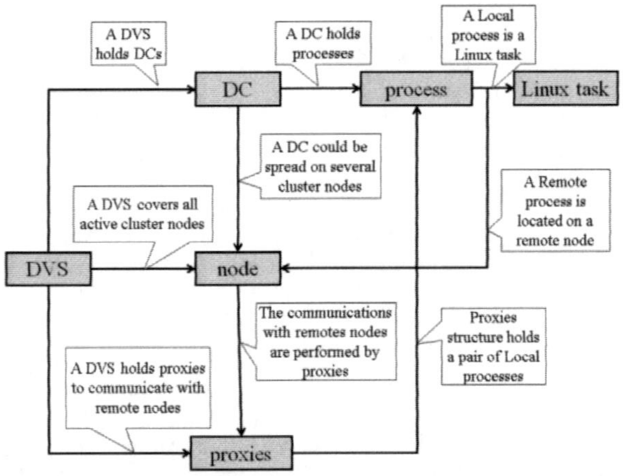

Figure 3. DVS abstractions and their relationships.

Through DVK APIs, a program can set the new node where an endpoint is located as a result of a process migration. DVK APIs also allow changing the endpoint type from Backup to Primary after the primary process has finished by a fault in a replicated service. These APIs were tested in a Virtual Disk Driver, which was developed for the prototype.

D. M3-IPC

A critical component of every distributed system is the software communication infrastructure. To simplify the development of VOS for the DVS prototype, an IPC infrastructure was developed and is named M3-IPC [14][15]. It allows building VOS components, such as clients, servers and tasks with a uniform semantics without considering process location. Provider-class features were considered in the design stage, such as process replication, process migration, communications confinement, and performance for both intra-node and inter-node communications. M3-IPC is a pluggable module embedded in the Linux kernel, supplying the IPC primitives of a microkernel OS.

Messages and data exchange among nodes is carried out by proxies. A proxy transports messages and data between two nodes without considering source/destination processes or the DC they belong to. Proxies can run either in user-mode to provide versatility or in kernel-mode for efficiency reasons, according to the DVS administrator's choice. Running proxies in user-mode may result in an efficiency loss, but it has the benefit of granting flexibility to freely choose protocols, and to easily add facilities, such as compression and encryption. At present, several kinds of proxies were developed for the DVS prototype using different protocols (TCP, TIPC [31], UDP, UDT [32], custom Raw Ethernet), some of them in user-mode and others in kernel-mode.

E. MoL-FS

One of the main processes of MoL is Filesystem Server (FS). It handles requests from user-level applications using POSIX system calls related to filesystems, files, directories, etc.

MoL-FS [33] is a modified version of Minix FS which uses M3-IPC as a message transfer mechanism. On Minix, clients, FS server and Disk task are independent user-space processes which reside on the same host. Since MoL-FS uses M3-IPC, which it does not limit communications within the same host, clients, MoL-FS, and a storage server named MoL-VDD [34] could be on different nodes of a cluster like a distributed OS.

As MoL-FS was designed to be used as a component of a VOS, only those applications developed using M3-IPC and MoL-FS protocol could use its services. A FUSE gateway was developed to extend its use to ordinary Linux applications, taking advantage of the ability to adapt granted by FUSE. Another advantage of having the FUSE gateway is that it allows performance evaluation by using standard Linux tools.

Currently, a replicated MoL-FS server is at development stage using Spread Toolkit [35] as Group Communications System (GCS) for multicast message services, failure detection, and group membership management.

F. MoL-VDD

MoL-FS supports several storage devices: ram disks, image files, raw Linux devices, and a Virtual Disk Driver (MoL-VDD).

MoL-VDD runs as a server process within a DC, and it provides its clients with the same storage devices as MoL-FS. A fault-tolerance support through data and processing replication techniques was added to it to test the behavior of the DVS infrastructure in failure scenarios. Fault-tolerance is achieved transparently for the application through the use of the facilities offered by the DVS, M3-IPC and Spread Toolkit.

MoL-VDD supports this kind of distributed environment in a dynamic and transparent way in which user processes, servers, and drivers can migrate due to availability or performance issues. These characteristics are highly appreciated by IaaS providers because they increase the elasticity, high availability, and robustness of their offered services, and because they optimize the use of their computational and storage resources.

A BUSE [36] driver was developed so as to allow Linux to mount a MoL-VDD device. Currently, an NBD [37] gateway is at development stage, which allows MoL-VDD to mount an NBD volume.

G. Other MoL Servers and Drivers

MoL is made up of several servers and tasks, which are communicated using M3-IPC. In addition to MoL-FS and MoL-VDD, other servers and tasks were developed and implemented:

- *System Task (Systask):* It handles low level requests from other servers and tasks, and it makes its own requests to its host-OS. It is also a replicated process which must run in every node of the DC.
- *Process Manager (PM):* It handles process and memory related system calls.
- *Information Server (IS):* It allows gathering information about the state of every server and task in the DC. A Web Information Server is also available to present VOS status information to a web browser.
- *Reincarnation Server (RS):* It allows for starting processes in any node of the DC and handles process migration.
- *Data Server (DS):* It is a key-value server.
- *Ethernet Task (ETH):* It is the interface to virtual (TUN/TAP) or real host's Ethernet devices.
- *Internet Server (INET):* It is a user-space implementation of the TCP/IP protocol.

As aforementioned, all MoL components must run within a DC, and all of them could run spread on several nodes of the DVS.

H. Unikernel-like VOS

Unikernel is a recent technology, which takes up library OS concepts, but instead of working on the bare-metal it runs over some hypervisor. It has many benefits that make it attractive to provide Cloud services.

A unikernel-like VOS was developed to test the DVS prototype named ukVOS. It is a single executable image, which uses low-level services provided by the host-OS and by the DVS infrastructure instead of being provided by a hypervisor.

ukVOS is based on *LwIP* [38] code because it includes a user-space implementation of the TCP/IP protocol and a simple web server with a fixed in-memory web page. A FAT Filesystem code and M3-IPC support were added to allow several unikernel VOS images and the web server was modified to support files.

Several images of ukVOS with different configurations were developed to test the DVS. One of them is a ukVOS image with FAT filesystem support, which uses the disk image file from a Linux regular file. Another image with M3-IPC allows using an external MoL-VDD. In the other ukVOS image, the web server gets the files from an external MoL-FS.

I. DVS Management

Management is a fundamental requirement of a virtualization system designed to offer Cloud services. At present, the DVS prototype is managed by a Command Line Interface (CLI). A *Webmin* [39] module is at development stage, which will allow for a web-based management interface (Fig. 4).

IV. EVALUATION

A DVS is a complex system in which several metrics may be considered as CPU, network and memory usage of cluster nodes, the time to restore a replicated service after a failure, IPC recovery time after the destination process of a message has been migrated to another node, to name a few.

The following metrics were established to be presented in this section:

1) IPC performance (Fig. 5): It is a critical issue because communications among different components of a VOS or DVOS are performed using RPC based on IPC. User-space applications use IPC to (transparently) make local or remote system calls.

2) Virtual Disk Driver performance: The throughput of storage services is critical, with or without replication.

3) Filesystem Server performance: Other components of an infrastructure are filesystem services. They provide high-level applications with files and directory services. Their throughput to store and retrieve data directly impact on applications.

4) Web server performance: File transfer throughput was considered an important metric (response time is another one) to provide web services.

For performance evaluation in distributed systems, such as a DVS, benchmarks and micro-benchmarks should be made between co-located processes and processes running on different nodes.

Benchmarks and micro-benchmarks were performed on the prototype deployed in a cluster made up of 20 PCs (Intel(R) Core(TM) i7-4790 3.60GHz), a 1-Gbps network, and Linux as the host-OS.

A. IPC performance evaluation

I. Tests between Co-located Processes

Tests between co-located processes allow the comparison of M3-IPC performance versus other IPC mechanisms available on Linux.

One of the design goals states that the expected performance should be as good as the fastest IPC mechanisms available on Linux. The following IPC mechanisms were tested using custom and [40, 41] provided micro-benchmarks: Message Queues, RPC, TIPC, FIFOs, pipes, Unix Sockets, TCP Sockets, SRR [42], SIMPL [43].

The presented results (Fig. 5-A) summarize message transfer throughput achieved by the IPC mechanisms running a single pair of client/server processes. Linux IPC mechanisms with the highest performance were pipes and named pipes (or FIFOs) followed by M3-IPC (925,314 [msg/s]).

Another micro-benchmark of message transfers between multiple pairs of client/server processes was run to evaluate performance in concurrency. The highest average throughput was 1,753,206 [msg/s], which was reached with 4 pairs of client/server processes (4 cores).

Figure 4. Webmin module menu for DVS management.

Fig. 5-B presents data transfer throughput, M3-IPC performance surpasses other IPC mechanisms on Linux. The reasons for this behavior are: 1) M3-IPC performs a single copy of data between address spaces while the others perform at least two copies (Source to Kernel, Kernel to Destination); 2) it requires a lower number of context switches; 3) it uses the Linux kernel provided *page_copy()* function, which uses MMX instructions.

II. Tests between Processes Located on Different Nodes

This section presents performance results of M3-IPC against RPC and TIPC.

M3-IPC does not consider flow control, error control, or congestion control. Those issues are delegated to proxies and the protocol they use. Reference implementations of M3-IPC proxies use TCP and TIPC as transport protocols.

As it can be seen in Fig. 5-C, a proxy using RAW Ethernet sockets has the highest message transfer throughput followed by TIPC. M3-IPC, using TCP on proxies, has a throughput similar to that of RPC. A custom RAW Ethernet protocol was designed to be used in M3-IPC proxies. In this protocol, not all frames are acknowledged because the upper layer protocol between proxies acknowledges messages and data transfers.

The remarkable performance of TIPC suggested that it could be well used by M3-IPC proxies as transport protocol. M3-IPC versatility and flexibility in proxy programming allowed authors to modify the source code of proxies in a few hours so as to use TIPC instead of TCP. These changes result in an improvement of performance, emphasizing the impact of the transport protocol on its throughput.

As shown in Fig.5-D, TIPC presents the highest throughput for transferring blocks of data lower than 16 [Kbytes]. The proxy using the custom RAW ethernet protocol has the highest throughput for transferring blocks of data greater than 16 [Kbytes].

Fig.5-D also shows that there is no noticeable difference in performance when using TIPC instead of TCP as transport protocol on M3-IPC proxies to copy data blocks.

B. Mol-VDD Performance Evaluation

Two types of micro-benchmarks were developed to assess the performance of MoL-VDD and its BUSE driver:

1) Local Tests: Client process and *MoL-VDD* run on the same node (Fig. 6).

2) Remote or Cluster Tests: Client process and *MoL-VDD* run on different nodes (Fig. 7).

The performance evaluation was carried out in conjunction with NBD [37] for comparison purposes. Micro-benchmarks used ***time*** and ***dd*** commands to perform data transfers and take measurements.

We used image files located on a Linux RAM disk to avoid the latency of hard disks.

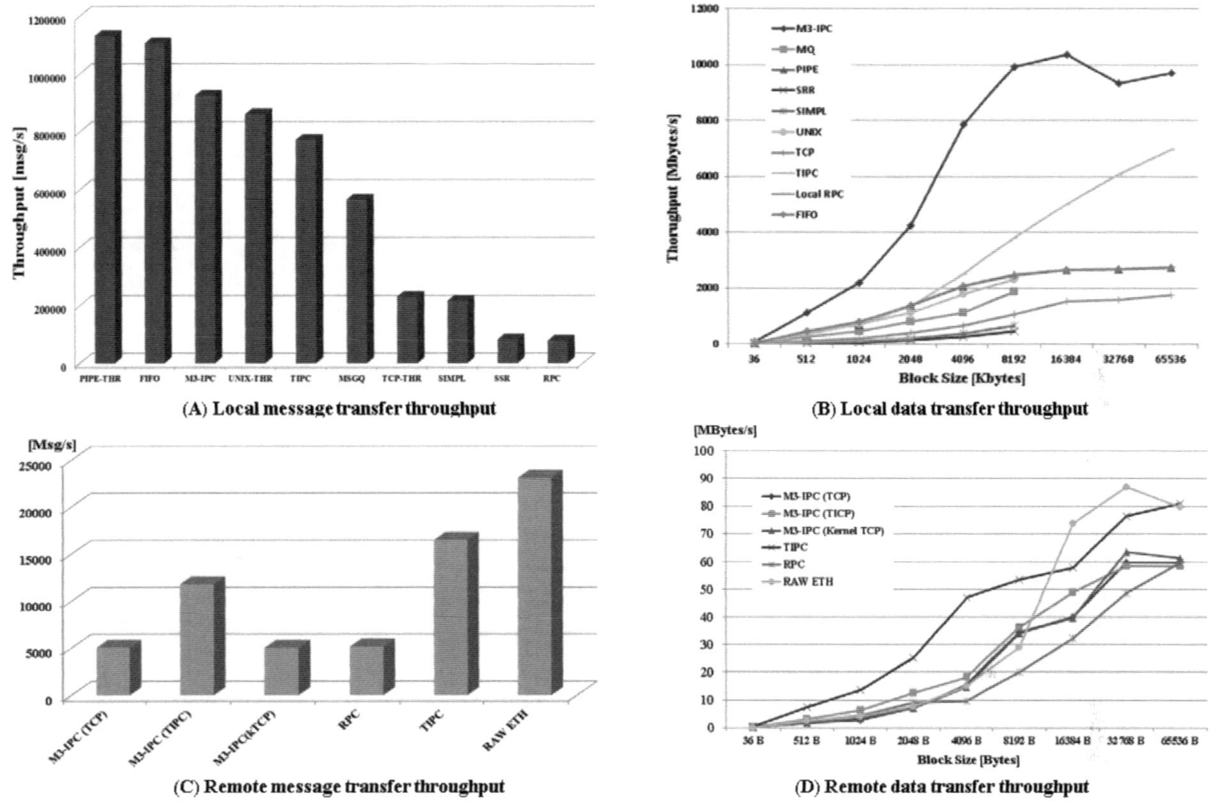

Figure 5. Results of IPC performance tests.

When MoL-VDD is mentioned in Fig. 6 and Fig. 7, it means that the transfer was performed between a client process and the disk driver by using M3-IPC.

When BUSE is mentioned, it means that the transfer was performed by the client process through the BUSE driver.

Since the BUSE driver was built using Linux threads and user-space mutexes, they negatively impact on its performance.

If the word *single* is mentioned, it means that the server is not replicated. If the word *replicated* is mentioned, it means that there is one backup MoL-VDD driver running on another node.

A TCP user-space proxy was used to exchange data and messages between nodes, while Spread Toolkit was used as GCS between replicas.

C. Mol-FS Performance Evaluation

As MoL-FS is implemented in user-space, its performance was compared against other user-space filesystems. An NFS Server (UNFS [44]) and an NFS Client (HSFS [45]), both implemented in user-space, were chosen for that purpose.

A FUSE driver was developed for MoL-FS, which allows mounting it and using every Linux command on its files and directories. For micro-benchmarks, a simple ***cp*** Linux command was used to evaluate the performance. The source and destination files were on a RAM disk image to avoid the delay of a hard disk. By space limitations, only tests where processes run on different nodes are presented in Table I.

Several operational scenarios were tested, but before starting micro-benchmarks, network performance was measured with other tools:

- SSH ***scp*** reports 43 Mbytes/s.
- TIPC custom application reports 81 Mbytes/s.
- M3-IPC custom application reports 58 Mbytes/s.

In *Config-A,* client process (Node0) gets/puts files from/to MoL-FS (Node1) which gets/puts raw data from an image file.

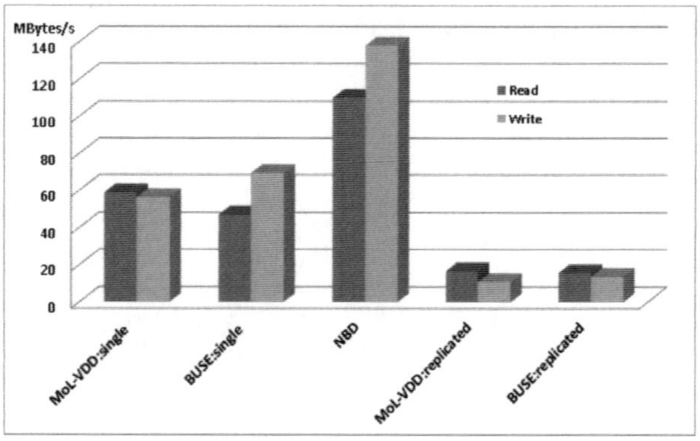

Figure 6. Mole-VDD throughput (client process in another node).

In *Config-B,* client process (Node0) gets/puts files from/to MoL-FS (Node1) which gets/puts raw data from MoL-VDD (Node1).

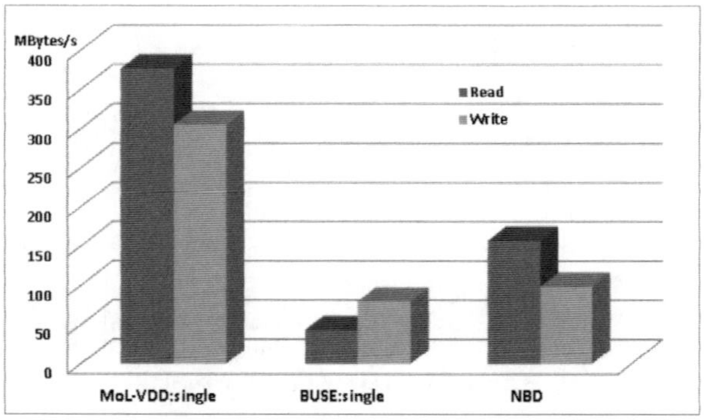

Figure 7. Mol-VDD throughput (client process in the same node).

Although the results are not attractive to adopt Mol-FS as a remote filesystem, it must be considered that they were obtained using the FUSE Gateway.

TABLE I. MOL-FS FILE TRANSFER THROUGHPUT (TWO NODES)

	Read	Mol-FS Read		Mol-FS Write	
File size [Mbytes]	UNFS/HSFS [Mbytes/s]	Config. A [Mbytes/s]	Config. B [Mbytes/s]	Config. A [Mbytes/s]	Config. B [Mbytes/s]
1	4.17	8.00	7.04	1.98	2.34
10	56.82	9.52	10.54	2.30	2.40
100	59.84	10.15	11.83	2.04	2.13

Other raw tests performed on MoL-FS without using the FUSE gateway showed a single transfer throughput of 47 Mbytes/s, but further performance optimizations must be made.

D. *Web Server Performance Evaluation*

Table II shows the performance results of benchmarks performed on a web server (*nweb*) running on ukVOS, and in MoL considering different file sizes and configurations. The web client program (*wget*) was located in the same DC and in the same node. The disk image files used in benchmarks were located on RAM disks to avoid hard disk latencies.

In *Config-A,* the web server gets its files from the host-OS filesystem on a RAM disk, and it represents a baseline measurement. In *Config-B,* the web server gets the files from MoL-FS which uses a disk image file. In *Config-C,* the web server gets the files from MoL-FS, which uses a MoL-VDD as a storage server to get raw data from an image file. The three processes run in the same DC and in the same node, using M3-IPC between them.

TABLE II. WEB SERVER FILE TRANSFER THROUGHPUT (SAME NODE)

	Unikernel (ukVOS)			*Multi-server (MoL)*		
File size [Mbytes]	Config-A [Mbytes/s]	Config-B [Mbytes/s]	Config-C [Mbytes/s]	Config-A [Mbytes/s]	Config-B [Mbytes/s]	Config-C [Mbytes/s]
10	7.44	7.03	7.04	74.62	70.00	67.54
50	6.86	6.76	6.85	81.43	79.10	79.52
100	7.96	6.82	6.72	97.11	92.13	92.31

There is an evident performance difference between running the web server in *ukVOS* versus running it in *MoL.* This suggests that this user-mode TCP/IP protocol stack implementation with Linux threads is not efficient.

MoL performance for those configurations in which process components are located on the same node (Config-B and Config-C) is somewhat lower than if running the web server directly in Linux (Config-A). This confirms the results presented in [23].

Table III shows the performance results of benchmarks performed on a web server and other related processes on the same DC but on different nodes.

In *Config-D,* the web server (Node0) gets the files from MoL-FS (Node0), which gets raw data from MoL-VDD (Node1), which uses a disk image file.

In *Config-E,* the web server (Node0) gets the files from MoL-FS (Node1) which gets raw data from a disk image file.

In *Config-F,* the web server (Node0) gets the files from MoL-FS (Node1) which gets raw data from MoL-VDD (Node1).

TABLE III. WEB SERVER FILE TRANSFER THROUGHPUT (TWO NODES)

	Unikernel (ukVOS)			*Multi-server (MoL)*		
File size [Mbytes]	Config-D [Mbytes/s]	Config-E [Mbytes/s]	Config-F [Mbytes/s]	Config-D [Mbytes/s]	Config-E [Mbytes/s]	Config-F [Mbytes/s]
10	2.62	2,90	2.75	4.08	3.,81	3.51
50	2.72	2.89	2.88	4.32	3.75	3.57
100	2.70	2.94	2.74	4.32	3.79	3.55

Since TCP user-space proxies were used in Node0 and Node1 for the benchmarks, better results are expected by using TIPC or RAW ethernet proxies according to the M3-IPC performance evaluation.

V. Conclusions and Future Works

The proposed DVS model combines and integrates Virtualization and DOS technologies to provide the benefits of both worlds, making it suitable to deliver provider-class Cloud services. With a DVS, the limits for an isolated execution environment for running applications are expanded to all cluster nodes (aggregation). Moreover, its utilization is improved by enabling the same cluster to be shared (partitioning) among several DCs. A DVS prototype was developed to check the design and implementation correctness; and after several testing environments, the feasibility of the proposed model was proved.

Migrating legacy applications from on-premises servers to a DVS is facilitated since POSIX APIs and RPC (supplied by a VOS) could be used, allowing code reuse. In this way, implementation costs and time are improved by reducing the encoding effort. On the other hand, new applications based on the MSA can execute their set of microservices in several nodes of the cluster by using RPC for communications.

Future research and development stages will focus on making improvements to provide scalable, elastic, high-performance and high-availability virtualization services; and integrating DVS management to Openstack [46].

Acknowledgments

Toni Cortes' involvement in this work was financially supported by the Spanish National Government (financial grant SEV2015-0493 of Severo Ochoa program), the Spanish Ministry of Science and Innovation (contract TIN2015-65316), and the Government of Catalonia (contract 2014-SGR-1051).

Fernando G. Tinetti's involvement in this work was financially supported by Universidad de La Plata (Faculty of Informatics) and the Scientific Research Board (CIC, for its Spanish initials) of Buenos Aires, Argentina.

References

[1] D. Hall, D. Scherrer, and J. Sventek, "A Virtual Operating System", Journal Communication of the ACM, 1980.

[2] J. Turnbull, "The Docker Book", 2014, Available online at: https://www.dockerbook.com/, accessed on 30 October 2017.

[3] C. Pautasso, O. Zimmermann, M. Amundsen, J. Lewis, and N. Josuttis. "Microservices in Practice, Part 1: Reality Check and Service Design", IEEE Softw. 34, pp 91-98, Jan. 2017, 2017.

[4] M. Chapman and G.t Heiser, "vNUMA: a virtual shared-memory multiprocessor", Proc. of the 2009 conference on USENIX Annual technical conference (USENIX'09), USENIX Association, Berkeley, CA, USA, pp. 2-2.

[5] K. Kaneda, Y. Oyama, and A. Yonezawa, "A virtual machine monitor for utilizing non-dedicated clusters", Proc. of the twentieth ACM symposium on Operating systems principles (SOSP '05), ACM, New York, NY, USA, pp. 1-11, doi: https://doi.org/10.1145/1095810.1118618.

[6] ScaleSMP, "vSMP Foundation Architecture", WhitePaper, Available online at http://www.scalemp.com/media-hub/resources/white-papers, 2013, accessed on 30 October 2017.

[7] N. Goel, A. Gupta, and S. N. Singh, "A study report on virtualization technique," 2016 International Conference on Computing, Communication and Automation (ICCCA), Noida, pp. 1250-1255, doi: 10.1109/CCAA.2016.7813908.

[8] S. Liu and W. Jia, "A Survey: Main Virtualization Methods and Key Virtualization Technologies of CPU and Memory", The Open Cybernetics & Systemics Journal, vol. 9, 2015, pp. 350-358, doi: 10.2174/1874110X01509010350.

[9] A. Whitaker, M. Shaw, and S. D. Gribble, "Denali: Lightweight Virtual Machines for Distributed and Networked Applications", Proc. of the USENIX Annual Technical Conference, 2002.

[10] J. Dike, "A user-mode port of the linux kernel", Proc. of the 4th annual Linux Showcase & Conference, vol. 4, pp. 7-7, USENIX Association, Berkeley, CA, USA , 2000.

[11] D. Aloni, "Cooperative Linux", Proc. of the Linux Symposium, 2004.

[12] P. Pessolani and O. Jara, "Minix over Linux: A User-Space Multiserver Operating System," Proc. Brazilian Symposium on Computing System Engineering, Florianopolis, 2011, pp. 158-163, doi: 10.1109/SBESC.2011.17.

[13] A. S. Tanenbaum, R. Appuswamy, H. Bos, L. Cavallaro, C. Giuffrida, T. Hrubý, J. Herder, and E. van der Kouwe, "Minix 3: Status Report and Current Research", login: The USENIX Magazine, 2010.

[14] P. Pessolani, T. Cortes, F. G. Tinetti, and S. Gonnet, "An IPC microkernel embedded in the Linux kernel" (in Spanish), XV Workshop on Computer Science Researchers, Argentina, 2012.

[15] P. Pessolani, T. Cortes, F. G. Tinetti, and S. Gonnet, "An IPC Software Layer for Building a Distributed Virtualization System", Congreso Argentino de Ciencias de la Computación (CACIC 2017) La Plata, Argentina, October 9-13, 2017.

[16] R. Buyya, T. Cortes, and H. Jin, "Single System Image", Int. J. High Perform. Comput. Appl. Vol. 15, May 2001, pp 124-135, doi: http://dx.doi.org/10.1177/109434200101500205.

[17] G. Heiser and K. Elphinstone, "L4 Microkernels: The Lessons from 20 Years of Research and Deployment", ACM Trans. Comput. Syst., vol. 34, Article 1, April 2016, doi: http://dx.doi.org/10.1145/2893177.

[18] M.Gien and L. Grob, "Micro-kernel Architecture Key to Modern Operating Systems Design", 1990.

[19] F. Armand and M. Gien, "A Practical Look at Micro-Kernels and Virtual Machine Monitors", 6th IEEE Consumer Communications and Networking Conference, Las Vegas, NV, 2009, pp. 1-7, doi: 10.1109/CCNC.2009.4784874.

[20] S. Soltesz, H. Pötzl, M. E. Fiuczynski, A. Bavier, and L. Peterson, "Container-based operating system virtualization: a scalable, high-performance alternative to hypervisors", Proc. of the 2nd ACM SIGOPS/EuroSys European Conference on Computer Systems 2007 (EuroSys '07), ACM, New York, NY, USA, pp. 275-287, doi: http://dx.doi.org/10.1145/1272996.1273025.

[21] P. B. Menage, "Adding Generic Process Containers to the Linux Kernel", Proc. of the Ottawa Linux Symposium, 2007.

[22] R. Pike, D. Presotto, K. Thompson, H. Trickey, and P. Winterbotto, "The use of name spaces in plan 9", Proc. of the 5th workshop on ACM SIGOPS European workshop: Models and paradigms for distributed systems structuring (EW 5). ACM, New York, NY, USA, pp. 1-5, doi: http://dx.doi.org/10.1145/506378.506413.

[23] W. Felter, A. Ferreira, R. Rajamony, and J. Rubio, "An updated performance comparison of virtual machines and Linux containers," 2015 IEEE International Symposium on Performance Analysis of Systems and Software (ISPASS), Philadelphia, PA, USA, 2015, pp. 171-172, doi: 10.1109/ISPASS.2015.7095802.

[24] C. Cachin, R. Guerraoui, and L. Rodrigues, "Introduction to Reliable and Secure Distributed Programming (2nd ed.)", Springer Publishing Company Incorporated, 2011.

[25] T. D. Chandra, R. Griesemer, and J. Redstone ,"Paxos made live: an engineering perspective", Proc. of the twenty-sixth annual ACM symposium on Principles of distributed computing (PODC '07), ACM, New York, NY, USA, pp. 398-407, doi: http://dx.doi.org/10.1145/1281100.1281103.

[26] K. P. Birman, "The process group approach to reliable distributed computing", Commun. ACM 36, Dec. 1993, pp. 37-53, doi:http://dx.doi.org/10.1145/163298.163303.

[27] V. Chavan and P. R. Kaveri, "Clustered virtual machines for higher availability of resources with improved scalability in cloud computing", First International Conference on Networks & Soft Computing (ICNSC2014), pp. 221--225, Guntur, 2014.

[28] B. Hindman, A. Konwinski, M. Zaharia, A. Ghodsi, A. D. Joseph, R. Katz, S. Shenker, and Ion Stoica, "Mesos: a platform for fine-grained resource sharing in the data center", Proc. of the 8th USENIX conference on Networked systems design and implementation (NSDI'11), USENIX Association, Berkeley, CA, USA, pp. 295-308.

[29] C. Wang, F. C. Lau, and W. Zhu, "JESSICA2: A Distributed Java Virtual Machine with Transparent Thread Migration Support," 2013 IEEE International Conference on Cluster Computing (CLUSTER), Chicago, Illinois, 2002, pp. 381, doi: 10.1109/CLUSTR.2002.1137770.

[30] A. Madhavapeddy, R. Mortier, C. Rotsos, D. Scott, B. Singh, T. Gazagnaire, S. Smith, S. Hand, and Jon Crowcroft, " Unikernels: library operating systems for the cloud", Proc. of the eighteenth international conference on Architectural support for programming languages and operating systems (ASPLOS '13), ACM, New York, NY, USA, pp. 461-472, doi: http://dx.doi.org/10.1145/2451116.2451167.

[31] J. P. Maloy, "TIPC: Providing Communication for Linux Clusters", Proc. of the Linux Symposium, vol. 2, pp. 347-356 2004.

[32] Y. Gu and R. L. Grossman, "UDT: UDP-based data transfer for high-speed wide area networks", Comput. Netw., vol. 51, May 2007, pp. 1777-1799, doi: http://dx.doi.org/10.1016/j.comnet.2006.11.009.

[33] D. Padula, M. Alemandi, P. Pessolani, T. Cortes, S. Gonnet, and F. Tinetti, "A User-space Virtualization-aware Filesystem", CONAIISI 2015, Buenos Aires, Argentina, 2015.

[34] M. Alemandi and O. Jara, "A fault-tolerant virtual disk driver", (in spanish) JIT 2015, Venado Tuerto, Argentina, 2015.

[35] The Spread Toolkit: http://www.spread.org, accessed on 30 October 2017.

[36] BUSE: https://github.com/acozzette/BUSE, accessed on 30 October 2017.

[37] NBD: http://nbd.sourceforge.net/, accessed on 30 October 2017.

[38] LwIP: http://savannah.nongnu.org/projects/lwip/, accessed on 30 October 2017.

[39] Webmin: http://www.webmin.com/, accessed on 30 October 2017.

[40] M. Kerrisk, "The Linux Programming Interface", No Starch Press, ISBN 978-1-59327-220-3, 2010.

[41] ipc-bench: http://www.cl.cam.ac.uk/research/srg/netos/ipc-bench/ , accessed on 30 October 2017.

[42] SRR, "QNX API compatible message passing for Linux", http://www.opcdatahub.com/Docs/booksr.html, accessed on 30 October 2017.

[43] J. Collins and R. Findlay, "Programming the SIMPL Way", ISBN 0557012708, 2008.

[44] "A User-space NFS Server", http://unfs3.sourceforge.net/, accessed on 30 October 2017.

[45] HSFS: https://github.com/openunix/hsfs, accessed on 30 October 2017.

[46] Openstack: https://www.openstack.org/, accessed on 30 October 2017.

Capturing Data Topology Using Graph-based Association Mining

Khalid Kahloot, Peter Ekler
Department of Automation and Applied Informatics (AUT)
Budapest University of Technology and Economics (BME), Hungary
{khalid.kahloot, peter.ekler}@aut.bme.hu

Abstract— **A dataset can underline a statistical plausibility and implausible characteristics. A graph can model the inter-relationship between the set variables in a dataset. On the other hand, the association mining produces causal structures for a transactional dataset in various kinds. Therefore, a better data representation can be attained by merging both of the two powerful tools together. Knowledge within a dataset is captured as a topology by combining an algorithm of association rule mining with a complex graph theory. In this paper, we present a modified graph-based version of Apriori algorithm for association mining, in which the probabilities of frequencies are represented using a graph data structure. A computational approach is reflected in the graph and all rules are composed of nodes, which are interconnected by in-degree and off-degree edges. The algorithm is using Apriori statistical rule mining to compose weighted nodes and weighted directed edges graph. The computational approach is necessary to be able to unravel complex relationships between co-occurred values due to multi-hop graph connectivity and navigability. The modified algorithm is tested based on heterogeneously composed traffic datasets.**

Keywords-Graph-based data representation; topology capturing; Apriori rule mining; Association Analysis.

I. INTRODUCTION

The graph is a multiple purpose data structure that can be navigated, clustered, shortened, and visualized. In addition, the graph can be easily transformed into other data structures. A graph can model data for any phenomenon, which enclose actors and interactions in-between. For instance, social activities can be viewed as a graph, where nodes are the people and weighted edges are for actions from an originator to a recipient. Various examples can be given for the graph modeling such as a disease infection as a study of social epidemiology, the virus spread through a LAN in network security studies, and a geographical sensor deployment for studying IoT Ad-hoc collaboration.

Data association, on the other hand, aims to discover the probability of the co-occurrence of features in a dataset. The relationships between co-occurring features are expressed as association rules. A dataset can be analyzed into numerically weight relations between variables. To break it down, a relation can be formed in two stages. First, find a statistical pattern upon a dataset and for all variables. This step will specify which features are associated with others. Secondly, calculate the numerical weights of these associations based on frequency or another statistical method. This step will build a matrix of weights cross features.

In order to build data association, a large dataset is required. The association would not be confidential and recommendable for composing rules in a certain context in a domain with a large number of features. The main objective for composing such rules is minimizing the support thresholds in a similar way as the unsupervised learning. Therefore, in order to find associations involving rare patterns, the algorithm must run with very low minimum support thresholds. However, doing so could potentially increase the number of enumerated variant datasets, especially in cases with a large number of features. This could increase the execution time significantly.

We model an aggregated real dataset as weighted multi-dimensional directed graphs to allow the discovery of correlations between heterogeneous data types. We can retain important spatial structures by using the Apriori association mining with a graph, which extracts each node degree and then using it with support and confidence as parameters.

In order to capture topology, filtering algorithms can collaborate in the process of discovering a neighborhood of variables. Several recommendation algorithms can be used as model-based techniques as long as they can learn in unsupervised way. For example, feature reduction (PCA), Self-organizing Map (SOM), and Apriori association rules mining are commonly used for feature extraction and selection. SOM and PCA are often used to reduce dimensionality, but are not necessarily the best methods as they are linear and parametric methods. The set of output variables cannot be explained or labeled. Moreover, these two algorithms are sensitive to missing values. It is recommended to feed them data after being cleaned and standardized. On the other hand, the Apriori association mining can handle text and nominal data in addition to numerical data because it is a counting method, unlike the SOM and PCA which are arithmetic computational.

In this paper, we develop a graph structure and introduce new procedures to reduce or avoid the significant costs as mentioned above in the SOM and PCA. We name the algorithm Graph-based Association Mining (GAM). In other words, we have modified the Apriori algorithm for rule mining to work with a topological weighted multi-dimensional directed graph. Apriori algorithm generates a support graph based on a support threshold. Thereafter, the algorithm uses this graph by utilizing the Kachurovskii's theorem, which states that a monotonic confidence graph can be used to dimensionalize a graph. This procedure position nodes into dimensions and magnifies their weights correspondingly.

The layout of this paper starts with related work in Section II. The formal definition of a graph, properties, procedures, is illustrated in Section III. A performance comparison between variations of Apriori algorithm is described and a practical example of application over a dataset with a discussion is presented in Section IV. Finally, a highlight of purpose, applications, and future work are stated in the conclusion in Section VI.

II. RELATED WORK

In the medical field, many types of research have considered the social effect in causality of spreading diseases or phenomena. The dataset of features is considered as a network to represent the environmental and medical confounders causes of a certain disease, which in some cases need to be adequately controlled. Researchers draw a cautious observation in health studies that conclude an attributive correlation between friends and disease spread as social network effect.

Many studies addressed obesity phenomena and the effects of social networks on its spread in countries such as England and USA or among a certain age such as elderly and children. More details can be found in [9]-[13] respectively. For instance, El-Sayed et al. [8] presented an application of simulation models for causal inference in epidemiology. They assessed whether interventions targeting highly networked individuals could help to reduce population obesity. By using network-based interventions, they recommended a useful anti-obesity strategy.

Cohen et al. in [14] used an empirical estimation to examine the network effect using common methods. They test the hypothesis against unlikely social transmission of acne and headaches. The health of the group is described in one equation with estimating social network effects within reference groups. First, that friendship selection is non-random, which leads to a correlation between the error term and friend's health. Secondly, the confounding factors affect all members of the reference group.

Other studies focus on building relationships among dataset. The behavioral data sheds a considerable light on the amount of unknown and hidden relationships. Such data is not prone to saliency cognitive filters. Studies like [5]-[7] agree that it is not enough to consider the self-reported edges and behavioral dataset especially with such as a self-reported ones with those inferred by a factor analysis of behavioral data. Moreover, these studies urge caution in combining different kinds of data. A network with multiple types of edges can obscure important nuances that should be leveraged through parallel analyses rather than flattened into a single monolithic network.

Eagle et al. [5] provide an objective way to identify, to wrestle with, and to mitigate the cognitive biases of human's expression, which often muddy the waters for scientific understanding of human phenomena. They constructed networks representing reported friends, who are communicating on phone on Saturday night, and are traveling. Nodes reflect the two groups of colleagues at the first-year of business school and the Media Laboratory students working together in the same building on campus.

Interesting research topics are concerned of graph-based visualization for the association rules, which is more suitable for visual analysis and comparison in aggregated perspective on the most important rules. Graph-based techniques can be found in [1]-[3]. Hahsler et al. in [1] introduced a new interactive Graph-based visualization method with itemsets as vertices, which allows to intuitively explore and interpret highly complex scenarios. Hahsler et al. in [1] utilized the framework for visualizing provided by Ertek et al. in [2]. As for the latter, they approached through a Market Basket Analysis (MBA) case study where the data mining results were visually explored for a supermarket dataset. Likewise, Rainsford et al. in [3] define a temporal interval data for a temporal interval algorithm of association mining. To visualize temporal relationships, a circular graph has been adapted as a set of associations that allows underlying patterns in the associations to be identified.

III. MODIFIED APRIORI ALGORITHM

This section defines a graph as a data structure and sets its properties, in addition, it explains the procedures operated by this graph. Moreover, a modified version of Apriori is illustrated to represent data as a support graph, thereafter, to reform the support graph into dimensional confidence graph.

A. A Definition for the weighted Multi-Dimensional Directed Graph

The weighted multi-dimensional directed graph is a directed graph with self-loops and parallel weighted edges, but edges are positioned in dimensions. In other words, multi-edges are multiple edges between two nodes and each edge hold a weight as data attributes to represent the capacity of that edge. Nodes are also holding a weight as data attributes for representing the magnitude of that node. Let the definition of the graph be G; a weighted multi-dimensional directed graph with size of k is defined as follows;

$$G = \left(N(G), E(G), \psi_G\right), \quad (1)$$

$$N(G) = \{N_1, N_2, \dots, N_k\}, \quad (2)$$

$$E(G) = \{e_{ij}, e_{ik}, e_{jl}, \dots, e_{lk}\}, \quad (3)$$

$$\psi_G(e_{ij}) = \{(d_1, \psi_{ij(1)}), (d_2, \psi_{ij(2)}), \ldots, (d_\lambda, \psi_{ij(\lambda)}), \ldots, (d_n, \psi_{ij(n)})\} \quad (4)$$

$$d_\lambda(E) = \left\{\left(e_{ij}, \psi_{ij(\lambda)}\right) \forall e_{ij} \subseteq E(G) \,\middle|\, d(e_{ij})\, d_\lambda\right\}, \quad (5)$$

$$d(G) = \{d_1(E), d_2(E), \ldots, d_\lambda(E), \ldots, d_n(E)\}, \quad (6)$$

In (2), N_i is a node in the G and ω_i denotes the magnitude of the node N_i. In (4), e_{ij} is a directed edge between N_i *to* N_j. In (4), $\psi_{ij(\lambda)}$ is the weight of the edge for representing the capacity and $\psi_G(e_{ij})$ is the set of all directed edges between N_i *to* N_j. While N_i & e_{ij} are denoted as identifiers but ω_i & $\psi_{ij(\lambda)}$ are numerical values, edges are directed as, $e_{ij} \neq e_{ji} \equiv (d_\lambda, \psi_{ij(\lambda)}) \neq (d_\lambda, \psi_{ji(\lambda)})$.

In (5), d_λ is the λ_{th} dimension for the edge, which is a ranking factor, and $d_\lambda(E)$ is the set of all edges, which positioned in the $d(\lambda)$ dimension for any node in the graph G. In (6), $d(G)$ is the dimensional representation of the graph G, in which $d_\lambda(E)$ is the set of the defined above.

The construction of the graph G starts by supplying N_i, ω_i the procedure *add_node*() to represent a unique identifier and a magnitude respectively. In turn, the procedure *add_node*() guarantees no duplicate identifiers for the nodes, however, in case of inserting the same identifier twice, the procedure *add_node*() will sum up the magnitudes. By comparison, the procedure *add_edge*() connects between two identifiers of two nodes N_i & N_j to create a directed edge e_{ij} with a weight $\psi_{ij(\lambda)}$ positioned in the dimension $d(\lambda)$. Nonetheless, another procedure is needed to construct paths between a set of nodes, which is procedure *add_path*(). By the supply a set of node $\{N_1, N_2, \ldots, N_k\}$ and weight $\psi_{1k(\lambda)}$ for this directed path, in turn, the procedure *add_path*() will create directed edges $\{e_{i1}, e_{i2}, \ldots, e_{kj}\}$ but in this case the weight will be divided equally for the edges, i.e. $\frac{\psi_{ik(\lambda)}}{k-1} \; \forall e_{ij}$.

Suppose that an algorithm can generate relationships between values into graph nodes and edges as described above. A procedure *combine*() is introduced to construct one graph G by combining the two graphs. As shown in Fig. 1, graph G_α and graph G_β have node N_i occur in both, also graph G_α and graph G_γ have nodes N_i, N_j and N_k occur in both. The procedure *combine*() combines the graphs together without losing the edges and sums up the magnitude of co-occurred nodes as is shown in Fig. 2.

B. Modified Apriori Algorithm

Apriori algorithm considers the data as items in a collection of baskets and statistically generates rules for consequent frequencies of items. The modified version of Apriori considers the dataset as a set of features with a variant set of values. Then, it calculates weights that express probabilistic relationships between all-to-all cross features in the dataset. For example, for a feature f_1, an association a_1 is derived from a dataset containing f_1, f_2, $f_3, \ldots, f_d$.

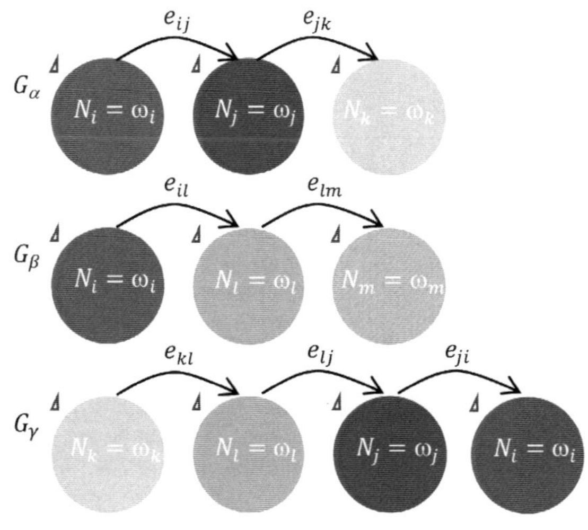

Figure 1. G_α, G_β and G_γ are Graphs with nodes coocured in all

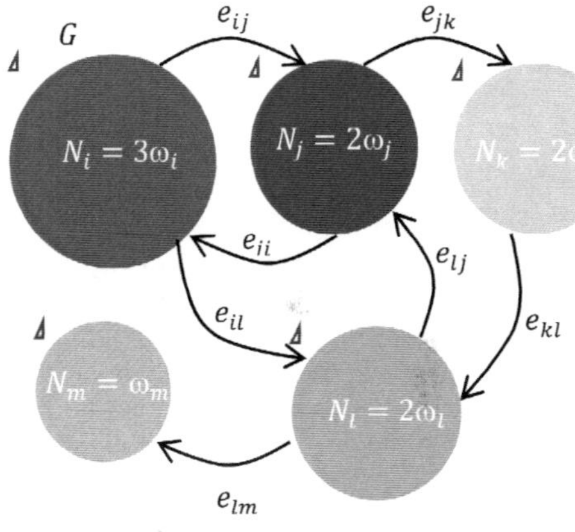

Figure 2. Graph G combined out of G_α, G_β and G_γ

This association states how often the feature f_1 changes co-concurrency to the other features of the dataset. Like decision tree rules, the algorithm derives the association from a target feature by maximizing the split and minimizing the error. The set of associations $\{a_1, a_2, \ldots, a_d\}$ is mapped to a set of graphs $\{G_1, G_2, \ldots, G_d\}$. As a matter of fact, the modified version of Apriori utilizes the graph data structures immediately by the first step. As presented below, two *algorithms* should be executed conclusively. First, the algorithm *generate_support_graph*(uses parameter *minSupport*, which is a threshold of metric *Support*. Second, the algorithm *dimensionalize*()uses parameter *minConfidence*, which is a threshold of metric *Confidence*. The formal definitions of these metrics are:

$$Support: s(N_i \rightarrow N_j) = \frac{\sigma(N_i \cup N_j)}{n} \quad (6)$$

$$Confidence: c(N_i \rightarrow N_j) = \frac{\sigma(N_i \cup N_j)}{\sigma(N_i)} \quad (7)$$

B.1. Graph Generation using Apriori Association

Let $F = \{f_1, f_2, f_3, \ldots, f_d\}$ be the set of all variables and $V = \{v_1, v_2, v_3, \ldots, v_n\}$ be the set of all values in the in a dataset D . The objective of the algorithm *generate_support_graph*() is to build a topological structure out of this dataset using association analysis. The topological structure is a weighted multi-dimensional directed graph, which contains features as nodes and directed edges out of each. An important property of an edge is its weight, which refers to the a statistically likelihood of occurrence through the dataset in a certain order. The algorithm is using the support count as a weighting scale. Mathematically, the support count, σ(N), for an ordered subset of features F can be defined as follows:

$$\sigma(N) = \sum_{i=1}^{n} |\{v_i \mid f \subseteq v_i, v_i \in V\}| \quad (8)$$

An edge is an implication expression of a directed navigation from a node to another. For instance, expressing an edge between two nodes would be; $v_{l(f_i)} \rightarrow v_{k(f_j)}$ as an association between certain the value v_l for a feature f_i co-occurred by a certain value v_k for feature f_j. Simply, it can be named as nodes $N_i \rightarrow N_j$. However, the disjoint nodes are expressed as $N_i \cap N_j = \emptyset$. The weight of an edge can be measured in term of support that determines how often a rule is applicable to a given dataset, while confidence determines how frequently a certain value $v_{l(f_i)}$ co-occurred by a certain value $v_{k(f_j)}$.

-

Algorithm 1. Graph Generation by support

-

```
G_t = {G_1, G_2, ...., G_d}
N_k = {i | i ∈ I ∧ σ({i}) ≥ N × minSup}
E_k = Aproiri(N_k, N_k) //All Edges
while N_k ≠ Φ do
    N_{k-1} = subset(N_k, minSup)
    E_{k-1} = Aproiri( N_k, N_{k-1})
    G_i = add_path(E_{k-1})
    i = i + 1
end while
output G_s = combine(G_t)
```

-

As shown in *Algorithm 1*, the objective of the algorithm *generate_support_graph*() is to eliminate the weakest edges by using procedure Apriori support association to weight the edges. Moreover, the algorithm aims to reduce the number of comparisons by getting advantage of graph data structure and graph algorithms. Let N_k denote the set of nodes and E_k denotes the set of edges. Initially, the procedure Apriori support generates temporary set of graphs G_t to represent the set of features then determines the support of each nodes. Iteratively, the algorithm generates new edges and updates the weight of the already existing edges and uses procedure *combine*() to generate the support graph G_s.

B.2. Graph Dimensionalize using Confidence Graph

The algorithm dimensionalize() is a procedure to reform the support graph G_s by directed edges generated by Apriori confidence graph G_c, which is partitioned to satisfies the confidence threshold. Unlike the support measure, confidence does not have any monotone property and generates only one edge e_{ij} for each subset. In other words, the edges generated by this procedure can only be true entirely ordered that is the reason to divided the weight $\psi_{ik(\lambda)}$ equally over between edges $e_{i1}, e_{i2}, \ldots, e_{kj}$. According to Kachurovskii's theorem, the monotonic confidence procedure can generate a topological vector space X; that is in a graph G of $X \rightarrow X^*$ is composed of monotonic analytical function such as procedure Apriori confidence.

-

Algorithm 2. Graph Dimensionalize

-

```
k = |G_s| //size of graph Gs
E_ij = {(S_i, S_j, e_ij) | e_ij ⊂ E(G_s) ∧ e_ij ∈ λ}
for each e_ij in E_ij do
    ψ_ij(λ) = conf(e_ij)
    if ψ_ij(λ) > minConf then
        //graph of subset(i)
        G_i = (N(S_i), E(S_i), 1)
        //graph of subset(j)
        G_j = (N(S_j), E(S_j), 1)
        G_ij = combine(G_i, G_j, ψ_ij(λ))
G_c = combine(G_ij ∀ λ)
output G_c
```

-

As shown in Algorithm 2, the procedure Apriori confidence is used by the algorithm *dimensionalize*() to position the edges in a dimension λ based on the confidence of each edge which extends and dimensionalizes into a confidence graph G_c. Given a supporting graph G_s, the procedure finds all the edges having $Confidence \geq minConf$, where $minConf$ is the corresponding confidence threshold. Likewise, the support graph generation, a brute-force approach is applied for mining confidence association rules. However, now it works over the given support graph G_s. This approach is much optimized and less expensive because the algorithm has to compare the edges of the graph G_s in a logarithmic time instead of exponentially comparing like in the traditional Apriori algorithm. More specifically, for a confidence graph G_c , which was extracted from a support graph G_s that contains d nodes, the possible edges are:

$$E(G_s) = 3^{\log(d)} - 2^{\log(d)} + 1 \quad (9)$$

Such approach can be less expensive because it requires $O(N \log(d) \lambda)$ comparisons, where N is the number of nodes i.e., $N(G_s) = \{N_1, N_2, \ldots, N_k\}$ number of nodes' support graph G_s to represent the set of features in $F = \{f_1, f_2, f_3, \ldots, f_d\}$, where $k = 2^d - 1$ is the number of edges in the graph G_s, and λ is the maximum number of co-occurrences, which represents the dimension.

IV. Results and Discussion

Apriori algorithm has enormous number variations which modified the data structure to outperform the original algorithm. The data structure of GAM is quite the difference of other variations of Apriori algorithm. Although GAM does not address the performance issues, it is importance to compare the performance of GAM with famous well-known variant implementations. A survey and comparison are presented in [15]. All tests were carried out on ten public "benchmark" databases, which can be downloaded from [16]. First, we compared GAM used for storing filtered transactions against a sorted list, a red-black tree (B-tree) and a trie.

TABLE I. MEMORY NEEDED AS SORTING FREQUENCIES FOR THE T40I10D100K DATASET

min_freq	GAM	Sorted list	B-tree	trie
0.05	60.1	9.3	10.8	55.4
0.02	79.7	12.7	14.1	70.3
0.0073	96.3	19.5	20.3	80.3
0.006	100.8	21.3	21.5	88.4

As shown in Table I, when it comes to memory, complex data structures are in distress. The close competitor of GAM is the trie implementation and still overcomes the GAM especially with high frequencies. However, the added structures of nodes and edges are very important and we did not mean to optimize memory although the difference is quite acceptable.

The Dataset contains accidents over the years 2012 to 2014 of traffic flow in the city of London, UK. It has been compiled from the UK government sources and it is available online for analysis. Accident events are aggregated to a square grid and stacked vertically. The number of casualties colors each event. This map was developed by a professional pythonist called Dave Fisher-Hickey and it was published on Kaggle website [17]. The available data describe the Average Annual Daily Flow, which tracks how much traffic there was on all major roads in addition to accident data from police reports.

The dataset contains 26 features. Primarily, to put down a summary, the most important features in the dataset are coordinates, number of vehicles, number of causalities, light, weather conditions and more. The values presented are 31153 records. As for Apriori parameters, the support threshold should be small for representing as many features as possible. On the contrary, the confidence threshold should be large because it is used to group sets of values into dimensions, i.e., the graph should be extended an additional dimension only for high confidence frequencies on values. We chose $minSupport$ as 17% and $minConfidence$ as 68%.

TABLE II. GRAPH NODES AND WEIGHTED

Feature	*Value*	*Weight*
Light Conditions	Daylight	3,20225
Human Control	None within 50 meters	2,98344
Casualties	None	2,94931
Accident Severity	3	2,53462
Physical Facilities	No physical crossing within 50 meters	2,43446
Weather Conditions	Fine without high winds	2,408
Number of Casualties	1	2,3346
2nd Road Number	0	2,32879
Road Type	Single carriageway	2,26773
Road Surface Conditions	Dry	2,06181
Urban/Rural Area	1	1,98775
Number of Vehicles	2	1,799987
Junction Control	Give way	1,50366
Speed limit	30	1,39708
1st Road Class	3	1,39596
2nd Road Class	6	1,22609
2nd Road Class	-1	1,17361
Urban/Rural Area	2	1,01224
Number of Vehicles	1	0,90406
Road Surface Conditions	Wet/Damp	0,85696
1st_Road_Number	0	0,79245
Light Conditions	Darkness	0,5885

The modified algorithm GAM scanned through features and values to produce 22 (feature, value) pairs with weights as shown in Table II. For instance, feature "light conditions" was chosen twice with "daylight" and "darkness" with 3,20225 and 0,5885 respectively. The interpretation can be as accidents are more likely to happen in daylight 3 times more than in darkness but still, the light condition is a most significant feature. Another example is "speed limit" that was chosen to be "30" and that implies that 52% of the accidents happened on roads with speed limit of 30. Likewise, we can state that accidents occur in "Fine without high winds" for "Weather Conditions" with a probability of 61.8%.

To study the "Number of Casualties", the highest frequent value is 1. The node of "Number of Casualties=1" has 5937 out edges for neighbors:

- 2nd Road Number = 0,
- Urban/Rural Area = 1,
- 1st Road Class = 6,
- 1st Road Number = 0,
- Human Control = None within 50 meters,
- Number of Vehicles = 2,
- 2nd Road Class = 6,
- Light Conditions = Daylight: Streetlight present,
- 1st Road Class = 3,
- Road Surface Conditions = Dry,
- Accident Severity = 3,
- Junction Control = Giveaway or uncontrolled,
- Carriageway Hazards = None,
- Road Type = Single carriageway,

The values listed above are direct co-occurred values for an accident with "Number of Casualties = 1". As a summary of GAM results, the number of possible scenarios is 7836, which is also the number of in-edges into this node. The edges are causes of accidents with parameters of "Number of Casualties = 1" and 60.5% of them when "2nd Road Number = 0". The pair (Speed limit = 30, Number of Casualties = 1) has 404 edges in between. Edges were positioned in 946 dimensions for the pair (Number of Casualties = 1, Road Type = Single carriageway).

V. CONCLUSION

We have combined Apriori association mining and graph theory to provide the weighted directed graph of a topological representation of the data. We have provided a formal description for the graph and explained the procedures operated over such graphs like a combination of two graphs. We algorithmically searched through a dataset of features and values by using Apriori, but with the help of graph data structure. The construction of the graph was done under a support threshold. Then this graph was dimensionalized using confidence threshold. We have showed indirect relationships between features and values, which appeared by navigating the path between the corresponding nodes in the graph. As a future work, we are planning to analyze the graph by applying PageRank and Hits algorithms.

ACKNOWLEDGMENT

This work was supported by the National Research, Development, and Innovation Fund of Hungary in the frame of FIEK_16-1-2016-0007 (Higher Education and Industrial Cooperation Center) project and by the ÚNKP-17-4-IV New National Excellence Program of the Ministry of Human Capacities.

REFERENCES

[1] M. Hahsler, & R. Karpienko, "Visualizing association rules in hierarchical groups", Journal of Business Economics,

[2] Apr 2017, Vol. 87, n. 3, pp 317-335, isn=1861-8928.

[3] G. Ertek & A. Demiriz, "A framework for visualizing association mining results", 21th International Symposium Proceedings, Istanbul, Turkey, pp 593–602, November 2006.

[4] C. Rainsford, J. Roddick, "Visualization of temporal interval association rules", 2nd International Conference Shatin Proceedings, Hong Kong, China, pp 91-96, December 2000.

[5] Nathan Eagle, Aaron Clauset, Alex (Sandy) Pentland, and David Lazer "Reply to Adams: Multi-dimensional edge inference", PNAS vol. 107 (9) , 2010

[6] X. Dong, P. Frossard, P. Vandergheynst, and N. Nefedov, "Clustering With Multi-Layer Graphs: A Spectral Perspective," in IEEE Transactions on Signal Processing, vol. 60, no. 11, pp. 5820-5831, Nov. 2012.

[7] A. Y. Kibangou and C. Commault, "Observability in Connected Strongly Regular Graphs and Distance-Regular Graphs," in IEEE Transactions on Control of Network Systems, vol. 1, no. 4, pp. 360-369, Dec. 2014.

[8] A. El-Sayed, L. Seemann, P. Scarborough & S. Galea; Are Network-Based Interventions a Useful Antiobesity Strategy? An Application of Simulation Models for Causal Inference in Epidemiology. Am J Epidemiol, vol. 178 (2), pp 287-295, 2013

[9] R. Bender, K. Jöckel, C. Trautner, M. Spraul, M. Berger, "Effect of Age on Excess Mortality in Obesity". JAMA.1999;281(16):1498-1504. doi:10.1001/jama.281.16.1498

[10] Amy L. Louer, Denise N. Simon, Karen M. Switkowski, Sheryl L. Rifas-Shiman, Matthew W. Gillman, Emily Oken" Assessment of Child Anthropometry in a Large Epidemiologic Study" J Vis Exp. Vol. 120, pp 54895, 2017

[11] Y Claire Wang, Klim McPherson, Tim Marsh, Steven L Gortmaker, Martin Brown, Health and economic burden of the projected obesity trends in the USA and the UK, The Lancet, Volume 378, Issue 9793, Pages 815-825, 2011,

[12] Kvaavik E, Batty GD, Ursin G, Huxley R, Gale CR. Influence of Individual and Combined Health Behaviors on Total and Cause-Specific Mortality in Men and WomenThe United Kingdom Health and Lifestyle Survey. Arch Intern Med. pp 711-718, vol. 170(8), 2010

[13] Flegal KM, Carroll MD, Ogden CL, Curtin LR. Prevalence and Trends in Obesity Among US Adults, 1999-2008. JAMA. 2010;303(3):235-241. doi:10.1001/jama.2009.2014

[14] Cohen-Cole, Ethan and Fletcher, Jason M, "Detecting implausible social network effects in acne, height, and headaches: a longitudinal analysis", vol. 337, 2008

[15] F. Bodon, "A Survey on Frequent Itemset Mining, Technical Report", Budapest University of Technology and Economic, 2006

[16] B. Goethals, M. Zaki, "FIMI 2003: Workshop on Frequent Itemset Mining Implementations". CEUR Workshop Proceedings series, vol. 90 , 2003

[17] https://www.kaggle.com/c/classify-traffic-signs/data, accessed on Feb. 7th, 2017

Analysis of Energy Saving Technique in CloudSim Using Gaming Workload

Bilal Ahmad
School of Computing,
Ulster University
Coleraine, UK
ahmad-b@ulster.ac.uk

Sally McClean
School of Computing,
Ulster University
Coleraine, UK
si.mcclean@ulster.ac.uk

Darryl Charles
School of Computing,
Ulster University
Coleraine, UK
dk.charles@ulster.ac.uk

Gerard Parr
School of Computing,
University of East Anglia
Norwich, UK
g.parr@uea.ac.uk

Abstract—**The IT industry has been totally revolutionized in the past few decades. Cloud Computing companies (Google, Yahoo, Gaikai, ONLIVE, Amazon and eBay) use large data centers which are comprised of virtual computers that are placed globally and require a lot of power cost to maintain. Demand for energy consumption is increasing day by day in IT firms. Therefore, Cloud Computing companies face challenge towards power costs. We address the solution for this energy saving problem by the enabling dynamic voltage and frequency scaling technique (DVFS) for gaming data centers. This helps service providers to meet the quality of service (QoS) and quality of experience (QoE) constraints by meeting service level agreements (SLAs). CloudSim platform is used for implementation of the scenario in which game traces are used as a workload for testing the technique. This can help gaming servers to save energy cost and maintain better quality of service for users placed globally in comparison with generally used Non-Power Aware technique. The results demonstrate that less energy is consumed by implementing a DVFS approach in comparison with Non-Power Aware technique when tested with same workload.**

Keywords- Energy Saving Technique; DVFS and Non-Power Aware Method; Gaming Workload; CloudSim Platform.

I. INTRODUCTION

Cloud Computing is one of the latest technologies that is growing across the globe rapidly. It is forming pillars for upcoming advancements in computing covering all aspects of parallel and distributed computing. Cloud computing is providing users with a substantial number of pay-per-use services, using the internet as a communication backbone. With the era of globalization, computing is also being transformed into a model where service is provided based on user requirements instead of hosting them permanently [1]. These advancements and innovations in the field of cloud technology provisions the industries to have unlimited computational power while maintaining good quality of service (QoS). Cloud industries must maintain several service level agreements (SLAs) to meet good quality of service from the user and service provider perspective. The service provider is also responsible for availability of the resources whenever and wherever they are required by the user. IT industry can save energy and power cost using service oriented architecture alongside cloud computing. Whether from the domain of parallel or distributed computing there are three major service models, namely Software as Service (SaaS), Platform as Service (PaaS), and Infrastructure as Service (IaaS) [2]. The corresponding large amount of data management and streaming leads to an increase in energy consumption. This causes a major rise in cost and threat to the environment as large amount of carbon dioxide (CO_2) is produced by these data servers [3]. Consequently, data centers are becoming unmaintainable. Therefore, a lot of work is being carried out and different kind of algorithms and techniques are being developed and implemented by researchers. Dynamic voltage and frequency scaling is one such technique that helps in reduction of power consumption. It reduces the use of underutilized resources by dynamically controlling the frequency parameter and uses different strategies to reduce static consumption by shifting load to the underutilized servers dynamically. Therefore, for the implementation of DVFS one needs to understand different factors like frequency and static power consumption. The amount of power that is being used in the data center can be managed by exploiting the trade-offs between service quality and service level agreement. Services that clouds are providing vary with time and have different workloads that require dynamic allocation of resources especially for Big Data Applications and MultiPlayer Games. Therefore, such techniques are required to be implemented in gaming with awareness of both DVFS and energy consumption while maintaining quality of service and quality of experience [4].

There are number of simulation tools which are being used for this research purpose, each having their defined use. All these tools have one thing common, namely they all use a stack based design as cloud computing is a combination of internet, grid, and distributed computing. The stack based design model provides users with the ability to add their own designed code in the model. This helps in implementation of optimization techniques and management of resources for improvement of quality of services. Better experimentation and development of algorithm can help in saving energy cost and in increasing profits. Therefore, for testing of new algorithms in IT industry researcher needs to have a secure platform. The selected platform should be fail safe and must avoid risk of customer's data privacy and data impairment [6]. Most cloud computing platforms are software based as it is very difficult and expensive to set a cloud server for test and trials purposes for each researcher. For example, it is practically difficult for researcher to use a data server consisting of 150 physical machines because of maintenance costs (e.g., energy, space, power, and cooling requirements) [5]. There is also no specific platform due to the following reasons: relocation of the virtual machine, confidentiality and data integrity, need for energy management, and cost modelling [8]. The main purpose of carrying this research is therefore to find the ways in which resource optimization can be performed in the gaming data centers. In our work we consider the following aspects of service quality: energy consumption and service level agreements, by using online gaming data in our experiments. In this paper, DVFS and Non-Power Aware technique will be tested and implemented for improvement of energy consumption and SLAs. Better results are expected to be achieved using DVFS technique as compared to Non-Power Aware technique; this hypothesis will be verified using real time gaming workload. The rest of this paper is organized as follows, Section II describes the related work; Section III describes basic details about DVFS and the platform; Section IV addresses the simulation environment; Section V discusses performance analysis and provides a discussion of our approach while, conclusions and future work close the article.

II. RELATED WORK

Recently, work has been carried in the field of cloud computing particularly relating to the cluster servers and virtualized servers. Energy saving techniques have been suggested for large amount of data using the concept of changing voltage and frequency values. It has been demonstrated that this concept can save more energy as compared to dynamic power management technique when implemented in the real world [8]. Here, the authors use a single system by implementing and comparing three different energy saving concepts i.e., DVFS (supply voltage of underloaded servers is reduced), DNS scheme (idle servers are left in sleep mode) and DNS + DVFS. The author proposes that dynamic voltage and DNS together provide better results for energy saving. However, the paper does not compare and analyze the cost comparison by maintaining quality of service metrices [9]. A solution is provided to save cost and to earn more profit on a large data scale by managing the scheduling of heterogenous machines with multiple users. This work is limited to just one quality of service metric i.e., cost from the service provider perspective [10]. Another algorithm was designed to optimize energy by using the concept of multi objective workflow and dynamic voltage scaling. However, the user was given the ability to choose between the cost or energy criterion [11]. In the field of computing, distributed computing provisions user with fault tolerance, organization, and support for resources. Typically, resources are allocated to the users based on load balancing technique where all the resources are allocated to the broker that is wholly responsible for provisioning of resources when required [12].

In [16] the authors propose several energy saving algorithms using scheduling policies. However, the work was related to virtualization mechanism only for large scale global data centers [16]. Further work was carried out relating the energy saving mechanism to different kinds of workflow on the Green Cloud Platform using bi-objective scheduling to meet the quality of service metrices for energy consumption [11]. By looking at the related work to date, it is clear that most of the work carried out related to energy saving has involved single servers and unique tasks. However, these days cloud computing platforms like Gaikai, OnLive, and Amazon EC2 have servers that are using multipurpose applications that are dispersed geographically. There is a research gap in the field of gaming especially for multiplayer games with users placed far apart from each other. On the other hand, some work in relation to energy saving has been carried using Big data with single purpose applications [6].

III. DVFS AND PLATFORM

CloudSim is one of the platforms which provides QoS parameters such as: energy, cost model, latency, virtual machine characteristics, federation policy, and analyzing the network communication model. Based on this platform, several popular models have also been designed, namely iFogSim, Cloud Analyst, Network CloudSim and iCaroCloud. Therefore, it provides enough leverage for researchers to use it to perform tests and develop new models as required. CloudSim has a layered architecture which provides user with the ability to design and implement applications. It supports core functions, such as handling of events, creation of cloud servers, hosts, brokers, and virtual machines [13]. The CloudSim simulation layer supports creation of hosts under virtual machines, application execution and application monitoring. A researcher who wants to implement an application relating energy, hosts, VM and data centers will be doing at this level. This layer supports the SaaS platform and provides users with defined quality of service levels with complex load reporting and application performance reports [14]. The topmost layer in the architecture is where a user writes a code and it allows the user to define a number of virtual machines, hosts, data centers, brokers, tasks etc. Therefore, it allows researchers to extend this layer and perform different tasks such as: generation of workload for monitoring designed experiments, designing of different cloud scenarios for robust testing and implementation of conventional applications in the cloud environment [13]. IaaS services can be simulated by extending different entities present in the cloud environments such as data centers. Such data centers consist of many hosts which are assigned to more than one virtual machines depending upon the rules defined by the service provider [15]. The data center can also manage more than one host (physical components representing the computing server) which further manages virtual machines. Host provisioning supports single and multiple core nodes. Similarly, virtual machine allocation creates virtual machine scenarios on hosts for storage and memory related tasks [16]. After modelling and designing of the application, it is allocated to a running virtual machine through a specific defined procedure. The virtual machines required to host multiple applications are provided on a First Come First Serve basis depending upon different hardware factors (storage, memory, cores etc.,). Therefore, simulation test scenarios relating to CPU cores are dependent upon factors such as time usage, space sharing policy or allocating virtual machines as and when required [7].

CloudSim has the capability to calculate the power consumption of data centers using the DVFS technique. It uses the current metric for cloud host input and returns calculated power as an output. Therefore, this provides researchers with the ability to design energy consumptions models and calculate the total power consumed during the designed experiment. CloudSim also provides developers with the capability for experimentation of dynamic scenarios i.e., different number of data centers or hosts can be created and deleted for testing unpredictable events in which users can join and leave the cloud application [17]. The DVFS scheme is limited to CPU optimization and adjusts the CPU power according to the workload that is being run on it. However, other components of the system that is memory, storage, RAM, bandwidth and network interfaces keep running on the same original frequency and no scaling is applied on them. The use of Dynamic Power Management (DPM) can turn down the power consumption for all the components of the system. The CPU has number of states for frequency and voltage which suggests that it has ability to provide better power performance as compared to basic approach [18]. Thus, powering up of system will require a large amount of energy using DPM as compared to DVFS technique [11].

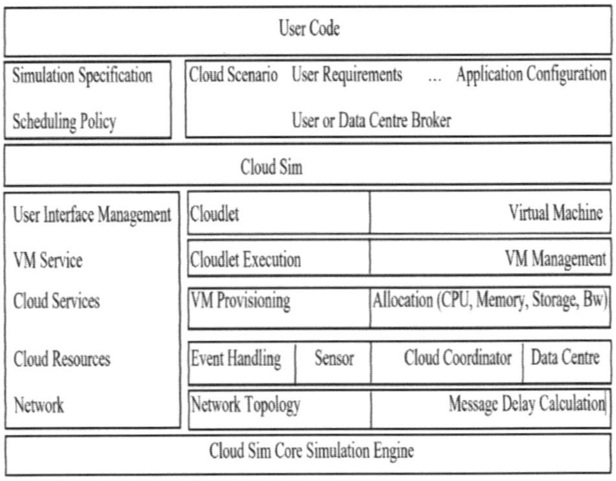

Figure 1: Layered CloudSim Architecture

IV. SIMULATION

For the implementation and evaluation of the proposed experiments the CloudSim simulation platform is used to provide users with the ability to perform the desired tests. These tests are carried out by using traces from a game as workload for the DVFS technique. The designed simulation consists of heterogeneous data centers consisting of 800 physical hosts and 1000 virtual machines which are dynamically allocated by the broker. Half of the hosts are HP ProLiant ML110G4 (Xeon3040) and other half are HP ProLiant ML110G5 (Xeon3075) servers. The systems frequency characteristics are defined based on how many instructions can be executed in one second (MIPs). Therefore, HP ProLiant ML110G4 (Xeon3040) and ML110G5 (Xeon3075) have MIPs rating of 1860 MHz and 2660 MHz, both being dual core servers. The defined system specifications are suitable to the hardware requirements for the experimental workloads envisaged. Detailed parameters are given in Table I.

TABLE I: DETAILS OF THE SYSTEM PARAMETERS

System (HP ProLiant)	MIPs Rating	Cores	RAM	Hard Disk
ML110G4 (Xeon3040)	1860 MHz	Dual	4 GB	1 GB
ML110G5 (Xeon3075)	2660 MHz	Dual	4 GB	1 GB

No dynamic allocation of virtual machines is performed in this test and host power adjustment is done based on their CPU utilization. A fixed MIPs value is provided having a value of 1000 MIP per second for a virtual machine. The simulated model has a bandwidth rate of 1 Gbits per second and RAM 4 GB for each system. A fixed defined gaming workload is provided in this experiment that consist of traces from a popular multiplayer online game, namely World of Warcraft having a data set size of 3.5 GB. The data set consists of traces from real data of the popular massively multiplayer online game, World of Warcraft (runtime of 1107 days, 91065 avatars, 667032 sessions, users located globally in 3 continents with different time zones) collected to analyze the quality of service parameters and consisting of game time, race attributes, current position, profession info, game position information, game level etc., [18]. It provides execution time of each host and energy is calculated based on power consumed by individual host. It uses time shared policy and rating of the processing elements is calculated by having millions of instructions per second. The total MIPs, i.e., total execution time is the sum of all the MIPs from each processing element (PE). Here, it is assumed that all the processing elements have same rating in the used machine. The service level agreements are also required as it is necessary to maintain the quality of service matrices [20]. The detailed parameters are summarized in Table II.

TABLE II: DETAILED DESCRIPTION OF SYSTEM PARAMETERS

Host MIPs	Host RAM	RAM	Host PE(s)
1860	4096 MBs	1Gbit/s	02
2660	4096 MBs	1Gbit/s	02

The reasoning behind the SLA violation time per active hosts is based on the observation that if there is an application that is managing the virtual machine migrations and it is busy with a host that has 100% utilization, it will not be able to address other hosts waiting for service provisioning. Therefore, virtual machines are deprived of the desired performance level causing service SLA violations [19]. The mathematical definitions and formula follow,

$$SLAV(H) = \frac{1}{H(n)} \sum_{i=1}^{n} \frac{SLAH(t)i}{AH(t)i} \quad (1)$$

The SLA level is the product of two matrices i.e., how many SLA violations there are per unit time of active hosts and how much of the performance degradation is because of virtual machine migration (Equation 3). *SLAV(H)* is the violation of per unit time for active hosts, *H(n)* is number of hosts, *SLAH(t)i* represents the time duration that leads to SLA violation by reaching CPU utilization of 100%, *AH(t)i* is the total number of *hosts(i)* in the active state.

$$P(vm) = \frac{1}{VM(n)} \sum_{i=1}^{n} \frac{Pd(k)}{Cpu(k)} \quad (2)$$

P(vm) is the effect on the performance because of virtual machines migration, *VM(n)* represents the total number of virtual machines, *Pd(k)* represents the level of degradation in the service of a particular virtual machine when it is migrated, *Cpu(k)* represents the total utilization of CPU of a particular virtual machine. Therefore, whenever a cloud server is considered for service level agreement violations it always depends on the above two factors independently described in (1) and (2). Therefore, service level violation is because of two factors: one is virtual machine migration and the other is when a host is overloaded resulting in SLA violation *(SLAV)* as follows [19],

$$SLAV = SLAV(H) \times P(vm) \quad (3)$$

SLAV(H) represents time required to have 100% CPU utilization by the active host and *P(vm)* shows performance degradation because of virtual machine migration. The overall performance of cloud servers can be analyzed by using the following equation,

$$Perf(DC) = Energy \times SLAV \quad (4)$$

The CPU time is calculated from the following formula,

$$CPU(t) = \frac{C(Le)}{PE * (1.0 - C(Lo))} \quad (5)$$

CPU(t) = CPU Time, *PE* = MIPs of one Processing Element, *C(Le)* = Length of Cloudlet, and *C(Lo)* = Load of Cloudlet. Here, MIPs represent how many instructions can be executed in one second, *PE(x)* the number of MIPs of one processing element, *PE(y)* represents MIPs of *N* number of hosts,

$$Total\ MIPs = PE(x) + PE(y)N(host) \quad (6)$$

Cost per million instructions related to a resource is calculated as follow,

$$MI = \frac{Cost(s)}{PE(MIPs)} \quad (7)$$

Cost(s) = cost per second and *PE(MIPs)* = calculating MIPs of one processing element. The execution time is calculated as follows,

$$Time = \frac{Sys(t) - Exe(t)}{1000} \quad (8)$$

Sys(t) is current time in millisecond, *Exe(t)* is system execution time and *1000* is the defined MIPs rating. Thus, energy consumed by each host, performance measure, CPU utilization, total execution time, and SLA violations count can be calculated by using the above equations. Experimentation results are shown in Section V.

V. PERFORMANCE ANALYSIS AND DISCUSSION

This test calculates the energy performance across the data center in the given simulation environment. All the tests are carried out in the simulation environment i.e., the CloudSim package which is configured using Eclipse Luna and Java IDE. The dynamic voltage and frequency scaling technique has been applied to analyze the gaming workload of the World of Warcraft multiplayer game. The workload consists of data traces from servers which are collected over time of 1107 days. An unaltered version of DVFS is used; however, a typical game workload has been provided for testing the behavior of the proposed technique. The Non-Power Aware simulation model with the same specifications is used for power analyzation of same gaming workload. The main difference between the Non-Power Aware and DVFS models lies in how resources are allocated to the hosts. All the parameters (RAM, bandwidth, storage, I/O file size etc.,) are defined however, for DVFS, resources are allocated based on dynamic voltages and frequency fluctuations of the central processing unit for the active hosts.

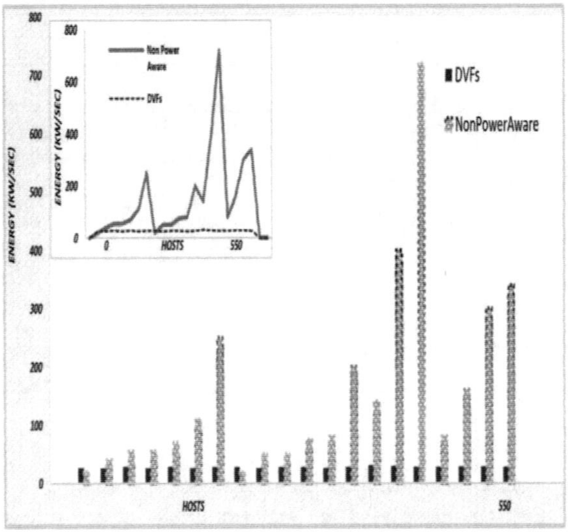

Figure. 2: DVFS vs Non-Power Aware Consumption in a Data Center

In the Non-Power Aware model hosts consume the maximum amount of power, thus increasing cost of services and causing loss of profit for service providers. Figure 2, shows power consumption in the cloud environment with a fixed number of hosts and MIPs using Non-Power Aware and

Dynamic Voltage Frequency Scaling. For DVFS, the data show a linear trend for CPU power consumption as compared to Non-Power Aware technique. The results in Figure 2 are by way of a reality check and verify the theoretical concept that in DVFS, the CPU adjusts frequency according to the workload to minimize the power consumption and thus provides a linear trend. The hosts using dynamic voltage and frequency scaling technique for the same gaming data consume less energy as compared to the Non-Power Aware technique. It can also be demonstrated (Figure 2) that in the Non-Power Aware technique hosts are loaded to maximum values and consume more energy resulting in greater values of CO_2 emissions.

The results also prove that quality of service is directly proportional to service level agreements i.e., if QoS is not observed for a certain amount of time then we have a SLA violation. Thus, by using DVFS, performance can be improved and energy consumption can be minimized resulting in a lot of cost saving from the commercial point of view (Figure 3). It can be seen that DVFS provides better trade-off for exploitation of SLAs per host for maintenance of quality of service and quality of experience. Figure 3, shows different parameters that can be analyzed towards quality of service. During the whole experiment DVFS uses less resources in the host when analyzed. Less energy consumption, mean time and number of host shutdown are performed during the experimentation. These results show that overall the best quality of service can be achieved by implementing DVFS in gaming servers placed globally.

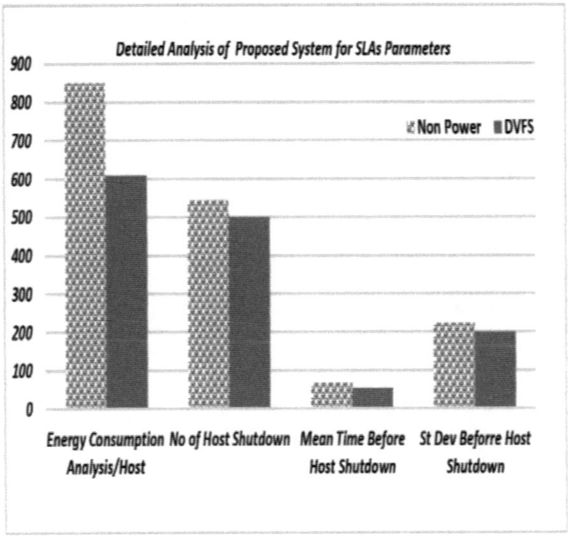

Figure 3: Detailed Analysis of the Proposed System

It can be seen from the results that minimum service level agreement degradation (SLAV) is achieved using dynamic voltage frequency scaling technique. Therefore, by using dynamic voltage and frequency scaling technique overall SLA violation can be reduced and quality of service can be improved through having less service level agreement violations in the proposed system (Figure 4).

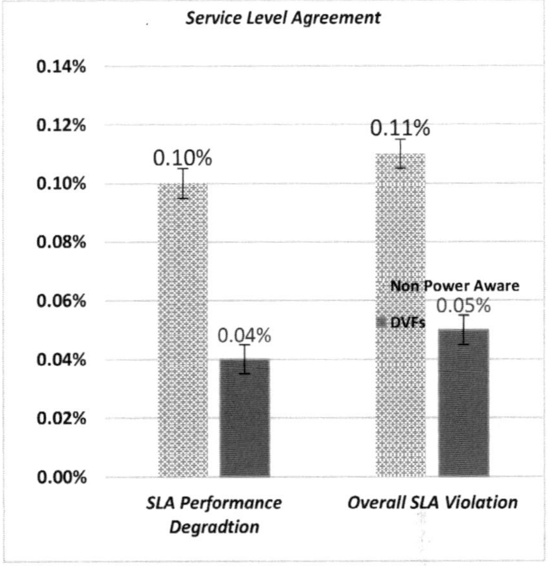

Figure 4: Service Level Agreement Violation (SLAV)

The difference in the amount of energy consumption, service level agreement and quality of service degradation can be seen through the results which is estimated on the basis of CPU utilisation. From the results, it can be seen that if the DVFS technique is used, the best results for energy utilisation are achieved and 16% of energy could be saved in comparison to Non-Power Aware technique using the same gaming workload (Figure 5).

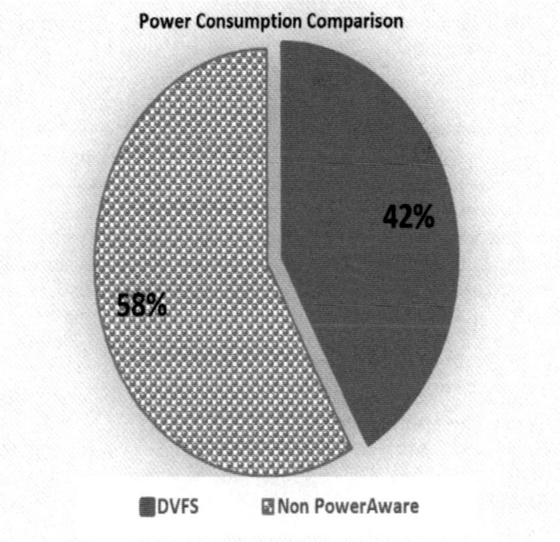

Figure 5: Detailed Analysis of the Proposed System

VI. CONCLUSION AND FUTURE WORK

The simulation tests that have been designed using CloudSim platform are based on two power consumption approaches i.e., DVFS and Non-Power Aware. The same workload (game data) and data center specifications are set for testing which technique performs better for power saving. The workload provided demonstrates that DVFS saves more energy as compared to general Non-Power Aware approach and obtains less SLAs violations which is important for maintaining QoS and QoE. CloudSim provides the ability to test the same workload scenario on two different power saving approaches. By using this simulation environment, a researcher can experiment and determine the amount of resources required (e.g., the number of Cloudlets, bandwidth, RAM, cost etc.,) for maintaining quality of service. Therefore, from the simulation results, it can be verified that cloud gaming data centers with the proposed DVFS technique can yield less energy consumption while fulfilling service level agreements for maintaining good quality of service leading to better quality of experience (QoE) for users placed globally.

In the future, this work will be enhanced and better ways and techniques to save energy will be explored for Big Data, Internet of Things and Gaming data centers.

REFRENCES

[1] S. Sidana, N. Tiwari, A. Gupta, and I. S. Kushwaha, "Nbst algorithm: A load balancing algorithm in cloud computing," in 2016 International Conference on Computing, Communication and Automation (ICCCA), Conference Proceedings, pp. 1178–1181.

[2] P. S. Rawat, P. Dimri, G. P. Saroha, and V. Barthwal, "Power consumption analysis across heterogeneous data center using cloudsim," in 2016 3rd International Conference on Computing for Sustainable Global Development (INDIACom), Conference Proceedings, pp. 1–5.

[3] H. Luo, J. Cao, Y. Wang, and X. Hu, "The dynamic migration model for cloud service resource balancing energy consumption and qos," in The 27th Chinese Control and Decision Conference (2015 CCDC), Conference Proceedings, pp. 6035–6039.

[4] P. Arroba, J. M. Moya, J. L. Ayala, and R. Buyya, "Dvfs-aware consolidation for energy-efficient clouds," in 2015 International Conference on Parallel Architecture and Compilation (PACT), Conference Proceedings, pp. 494–495.

[5] C. Prazeres and M. Serrano, "Soft-iot: Self-organizing fog of things," in 2016 30th International Conference on Advanced Information Networking and Applications Workshops (WAINA), Conference Proceedings, pp. 803–808.

[6] W. Tian, M. Xu, A. Chen, G. Li, X. Wang, and Y. Chen, "Open-source simulators for cloud computing: Comparative study and challenging issues," Simulation Modelling Practice and Theory, vol. 58, Part 2, pp. 239–254, 2015.

[7] Horvath et al. "Dynamic voltage scaling in multitier web servers with end-to-end delay control," IEEE Transactions on Computers, vol. 56, no. 4, pp. 444–458, 2007.

[8] D. Kliazovich, P. Bouvry, and S. U. Khan, "Dens: Data Center energy efficient network-aware scheduling," in Green Computing and Communications (GreenCom), 2010 IEEE/ACM Int'l Conference on & Int'l Conference on Cyber, Physical and Social Computing (CPSCom), Conference Proceedings, pp. 69–75.

[9] J. Burge, P. Ranganathan, and J. L. Wiener, "Cost-aware scheduling for heterogeneous enterprise machines," in 2007 IEEE International Conference on Cluster Computing, Conference Proceedings, pp. 481– 487.

[10] F. Cao, M. M. Zhu, and C. Q. Wu, "Energy-efficient resource management for scientific workflows in clouds," in 2014 IEEE World Congress on Services, Conference Proceedings, pp. 402–409.

[11] R. Buyya, C. S. Yeo, and S. Venugopal, "Market-oriented cloud computing: Vision, hype, and reality for delivering it services as computing utilities," in 2008 10th IEEE International Conference on High Performance Computing and Communications, Conference Proceedings, pp. 5–13.

[12] A. Beloglazov and R. Buyya, "Optimal online deterministic algorithms and adaptive heuristics for energy and performance efficient dynamic consolidation of virtual machines in cloud data centers," Concurrent. Comput: Pract. Exper., vol. 24, no. 13, pp. 1397–1420, 2012.

[13] R. N. Calheiros, R. Ranjan, A. Beloglazov, C. A. F. De Rose, and R. Buyya, "CloudSim: A toolkit for modeling and simulation of cloud computing environments and evaluation of resource provisioning algorithms," Softw. Pract. Exper., vol. 41, no. 1, pp. 23–50, Jan. 2011. [Online]. Available: http://dx.doi.org/10.1002/spe.995

[14] F. P. Tso, D. R. White, S. Jouet, J. Singer, and D. P. Pezaros, "The glasgow raspberry pi cloud: A scale model for cloud computing infrastructures," in 2013 IEEE 33rd International Conference on Distributed Computing Systems Workshops, July 2013, pp. 108–112.

[15] G. Keller, M. Tighe, H. Lutfiyya, and M. Bauer, "Dcsim: A data centre simulation tool," in 2013 IFIP/IEEE International Symposium on Integrated Network Management (IM 2013), May 2013, pp. 1090–1091.

[16] A. Varasteh and M. Goudarzi, "Server consolidation techniques in virtualized data centers: A survey," IEEE Systems Journal, vol. 11, no. 2, pp. 772–783, June 2017.

[17] S. Long and Y. Zhao, "A toolkit for modeling and simulating cloud data storage: An extension to cloudsim," in 2012 International Conference on Control Engineering and Communication Technology, Dec 2012, pp. 597–600.

[18] Y.-T. Lee, K.-T. Chen, Y.-M. Cheng, and C.-L. Lei, "World of Warcraft avatar history dataset," in 2011 " In *Proceedings of ACM Multimedia Systems 2011*, Feb 2011, pp. 123–128, 2011.

[19] J. V. Wang, K. Y. Fok, C. T. Cheng, and C. K. Tse, "A stable matching based virtual machine allocation mechanism for cloud data centers," in 2016 IEEE World Congress on Services (SERVICES), Conference Proceedings, pp. 103–106.

[20] A. Ahmed and A. S. Sabyasachi, "Cloud computing simulators: A detailed survey and future direction," in 2014 IEEE International Advance Computing Conference (IACC), Conference Proceedings, pp. 866–872.

Shade: Addressing Interoperability Gaps Among OpenStack Clouds

Samuel de Medeiros Queiroz[1], Monty Taylor[2], Thais Batista[1]
[1]DIMAp, Federal University of Rio Grande do Norte, Natal, Brazil
[2]Infrastructure Team, OpenStack Community
e-mail: samueldmq@gmail.com, mordred@inagust.com, thais@dimap.ufrn.br

***Abstract*— As much as OpenStack promised a utopian future where an application could be written once and target multiple clouds that run OpenStack, the reality was that vendor choice leaked through the abstractions to the point where the end user must know about deployment and configuration details, compromising interoperability and favoring vendor lock-in. Shade is a middleware written in Python by the OpenStack community which stands between users and clouds, abstracting vendor differences in order to allow a seamless experience in multi-cloud environments. It is widely used by OpenStack Continuous Integration systems nowadays, booting thousands of servers every day in numerous deployments distributed around the globe. This paper enumerates, categorizes and exemplifies the interoperability issues found in OpenStack deployments and then describes how Shade addresses most of them.**

Keywords-Interoperability; IaaS; OpenStack.

I. INTRODUCTION

Cloud computing is a model for enabling ubiquitous, convenient, on-demand self-service access to a shared pool of configurable computing resources over the network [1].

Infrastructure as a Service (IaaS) is the cloud computing model that allows users to consume processing, storage, and networking resources from a data center, providing users the ability to deploy and run arbitrary software. Such resources may be served in a private, public or hybrid deployment model. OpenStack [2] is the largest open source IaaS solution nowadays, empowering hundreds of companies around the globe to run production environments with no license cost.

With many options available, users may benefit from the ability of moving between providers when convenient, avoiding vendor lock-in. In order to make that possible, different OpenStack clouds must be interoperable. As an open source project, OpenStack is designed to support various use cases and configurations via highly flexible and configurable services. By allowing such a flexibility in its use cases, the responses returned by different clouds may vary significantly, compromising both syntactic and semantic interoperability.

After identifying syntactic and semantic interoperability issues, this paper presents Shade [3], a middleware standing between the clouds and end users that was proposed in the OpenStack ecosystem to abstract such issues. Shade is a library that exposes the most common cloud operations, making deployment and configuration choices transparent to end users. This paper classifies the identified issues, and then shows how Shade addresses them. Despite the fact that Shade is able to perform many use cases in OpenStack clouds, the examples in this paper focus on creation and management aspects of servers.

The next sections of this paper are organized as follows: Section II is a background section highlighting interoperability definitions, what OpenStack is and what syntactic and semantic gaps exist in it; Section III presents Shade, the technical solution abstracting those gaps in OpenStack clouds; Section IV presents related work, describing how this study is unique; and Section V presents the final remarks.

II. BACKGROUND

This section describes what interoperability and OpenStack are, and then enumerates the syntactic and semantic interoperability issues that exist in OpenStack.

A. Interoperability

Interoperability is the capability to communicate, execute programs, or transfer data among various functional units in a manner that requires the user to have little or no knowledge of the unique characteristics of those units [4]. In an interoperable environment, great user experience is achieved because users are able to communicate with all functional units seamlessly, disfavoring vendor lock-in.

There are two levels of interoperability: (i) syntactic: all functional units use the same data formats and communication protocols; and (ii) semantic: the results returned by all functional units have the same accurate interpretation, i.e., after performing requests to the units, users understand that they have executed the same functions and thus have been put into the same state.

Interoperability is a characteristic that may be achieved in different phases of the system lifecycle, in two manners: by design and post-facto. The former is when the functional units are all designed to be interoperable, and then built to comply with the well-defined interoperability syntactic and semantic specifications; while the latter is when the functional units exist and, without being prior designed to, are redesigned to become interoperable. The latter is expected to be much more complex, since there will be very well defined use cases using protocols, data formats and semantics particularities that will need to be given away for the sake of interoperability, affecting end users.

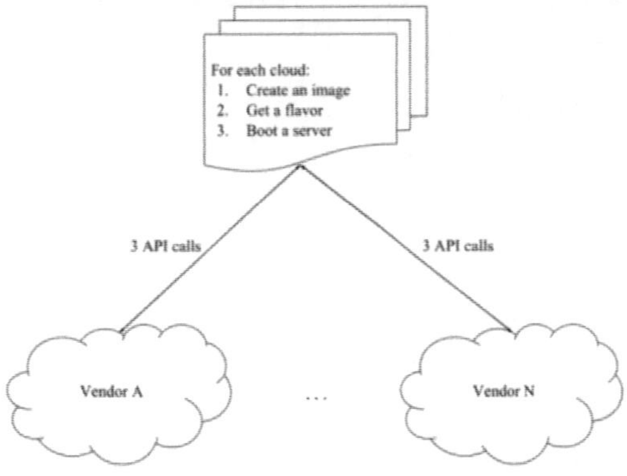

Figure 1. Users want to transparently create servers across multiple clouds via a single application.

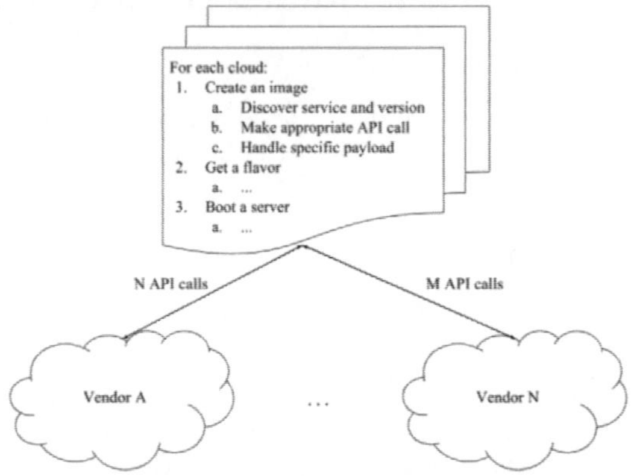

Figure 2. Users need to figure out vendor specific deployment and configuration choices to communicate to multiple clouds.

B. *OpenStack*

OpenStack is an open source IaaS platform, consisting of interrelated services exposing REST APIs to control diverse, multi-vendor hardware pools of processing, storage, and networking resources throughout a data center. In this context, interoperable functional units may represent clouds run by multiple vendors, where the user can communicate to all of them, equally; or a single cloud, where users are able to communicate seamlessly upon upgrade or downgrade. In both cases, deployment and configuration choices must be transparent.

Achieving and keeping interoperability within a single cloud is much simpler and more natural, as vendors do not want to break their customers. On the other side, however, not all vendors struggle to be interoperable with its competitors, favoring vendor lock-in.

From a cloud user point of view, interoperability translates into the utopian use case represented in Figure 1, where users create servers with 3 steps: (i) create an image, (ii) get a server configuration (flavor) and then (iii) boot the server; without any specific logic depending on what deployment and configuration choices have been made by vendors. In this model, the code would be written once and target multiple clouds that run OpenStack.

In reality, however, choosing a vendor leaks through the abstractions to the point where the end user must know about what deployment and configuration choices were made. This causes logic to require a-priori knowledge about clouds, as well as conditional complex logic even on discoverable differences, which would result in many extra API calls and conditional statements in the user application, as illustrated in Figure 2.

By analyzing multiple OpenStack clouds from different vendors, we were able to identify several syntactic and semantic interoperability issues.

1) Syntactic: when different clouds expose a functionality that is semantically equivalent, but it is exposed in a noninteroperable manner because there are differences in the communication protocols or data formats, i.e., the REST parameters or payloads, respectively.

The two patterns for the occurrence of strictly syntactic issues are listed below. Let A and B be two OpenStack clouds.

- The functionality is exposed through different APIs. Cloud A deploys the Nova Network service for networking operations. Cloud B deploys the Neutron service. As a user, how may you write an application that shows floating IPs in both clouds?
- The underlying functionality mechanism is pluggable, such as when a vendor requires password authentication and another requires a proprietary authentication mechanism. Both would return a token upon successful authentication, but each require specific REST payloads. How do you get a token in both clouds?

2) Semantic: when different clouds expose behaviors through syntactically equivalent protocols and data formats, but the results returned do not have the same accurate interpretation.

The five patterns for the occurrence of strictly semantic issues are listed below. Let A and B be two OpenStack clouds.

- Different authorization requirements for the functionality: cloud A requires a user to have member role in order to upload an object, whereas cloud B requires admin role. As a user with member role in both clouds, how may you upload an object in both A and B?
- Cloud-wide restrictions on resources: cloud A sets the maximum size of an image to 512 megabytes, while cloud B sets it to 1 gigabyte. How do you upload your 700-megabyte Linux image to both clouds?
- User account-wide restrictions on resources: you need to boot 20 servers, of which 10 go in cloud A, and 10 in cloud B. Your quota in cloud A allows you to boot up to 6 servers, and your

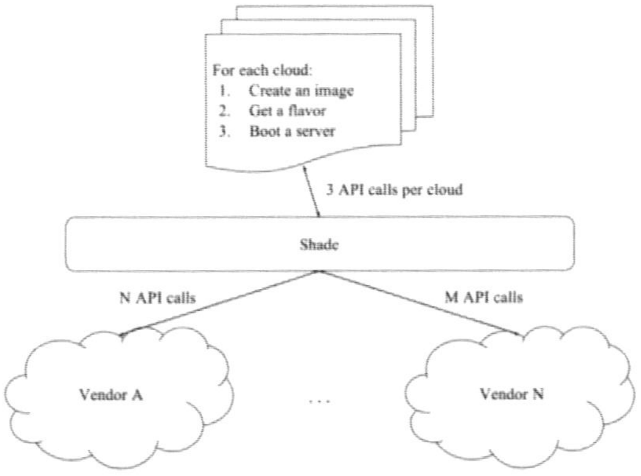

Figure 3. User executing the same program seamlessly across multiple clouds, with Shade as a middleware.

account in cloud B allows you to boot up to 12 servers. How do you boot 10 servers in each cloud?

- Inconsistent resource discovery: how do you discover the latest version of your preferred Linux image in both A and B?
- Pluggable underlying mechanism: all users in cloud A are backed by an LDAP server which is read-only by OpenStack. Cloud B uses a read-write SQL backend. How do you write an application that needs to create users in both clouds?

3) Syntactic and Semantic: there are two patterns for issues affecting both syntactic and semantic interoperability simultaneously. Let A and B be two OpenStack clouds.

- Multiple workflows for complex operations: booting a server with a floating IP attached to it is a functionality that involves many API calls and may happen in many manners, depending on how the cloud is configured, and what services are available. How do you boot a server in both cloud A and B without needing to know what deployment and configuration choices were made?
- Functionality is not provided: you write an application that uses Database as a Service (DBaaS) to create and configure a database at execution time. How do you deploy that application in both clouds A and B, given only cloud A deploys the OpenStack DBaaS solution?

III. SHADE

OpenStack has a large Continuous Integration (CI) system that launches thousands of servers every day to run tests on. It spins up servers in several clouds distributed around the globe. As a result, the CI team has learned a lot about what needs to be done to communicate with multiple clouds. Shade emerges as a promise of sharing that knowledge as a reusable library, as opposed to keeping it all inside CI scripts.

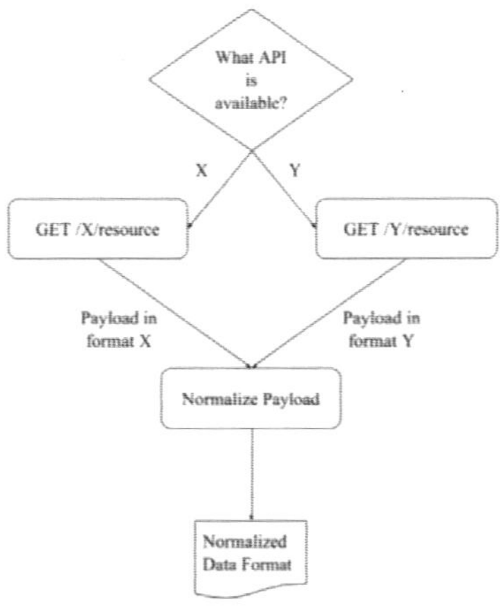

Figure 4. Discovery of the GET API for a resource and normalization of the retrieved resource.

Shade is a library written in Python standing between the user and the OpenStack clouds, abstracting most of the interoperability gaps. A consumer of Shade should never need to put in logic, such as "if my cloud supports X, then do Y, else Z". Shade will handle all the differences between clouds when possible, allowing users to seamlessly run applications across multiple OpenStack clouds, regardless what deployment choices were made. This is illustrated in Figure 3, which makes the use case in Figure 1 possible without adding complexity to the user application, as shown in Figure 2.

The next subsections will go through the issues described in Section II-B, detailing how Shade fix most of them. For the issues Shade cannot fix, we will give suggestion on how they can be addressed in the user side.

A. Syntactic

The mechanism Shade developed to abstract vendor choices on protocols and data formats to its users is by discovering what underlying APIs are available to serve the requested functionality and then standardizing resource representation through a normalization process. The normalization process consists of mapping attributes of different data representations to a common data format, which in this case is a JSON representation format that is exchanged in the REST calls, allowing users to safely rely on it. The overall process is illustrated in Figure 4.

1) Functionality is exposed through different APIs: when the functionality is exposed through different services or by the same service but in different versions, it is implemented by different OpenStack REST APIs, meaning multiple URLs and payload formats to be handled. As the URLs are not equal, the request protocol is not the same. Since the input or output payloads change, the data format is affected as well.

In order to solve this, Shade identifies what service and version are available in the service catalog, then proceed

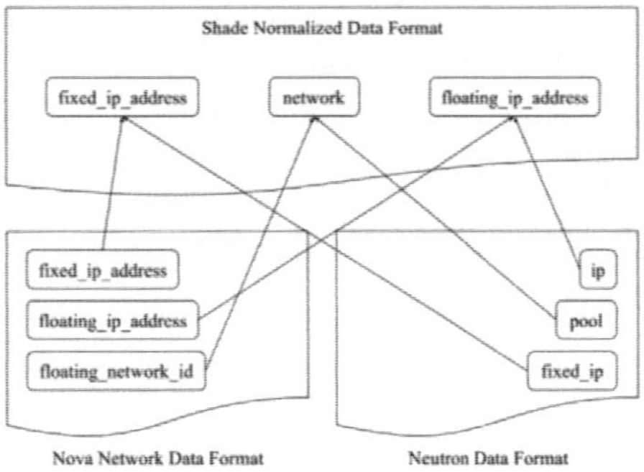

Figure 5. Normalizing a floating IP returned by Nova Network (bottom left) and another returned by Neutron (bottom right).

with the appropriate call. After getting the return from the service, it normalizes the result before returning to the user.

Networking capabilities were initially supported by Nova, the OpenStack Compute Service, via a subservice named Nova Network. Later on, Neutron, the OpenStack Networking Service, was created to centralize all those capabilities.

If an application requests Shade to show a floating IP, it identifies if Nova Network or Neutron is available, then proceed with the appropriate API call. After getting the return from the service, it normalizes the floating IP resource by mapping attributes from the heterogeneous data format to attributes in the normalized format, as shown in Figure 5 for both Nova Network and Neutron.

2) Pluggable underlying mechanism: OpenStack is designed to be flexible, supporting multiple vendors and technical solutions in most of its functionalities via plugins. While the semantic is preserved, different plugins may take different payloads to perform the requested operation. Since vendors are in charge of defining what plugins are available in a cloud, if the sets of plugins in different clouds are mutually exclusive, the user would need to use multiple payload formats to communicate to multiple clouds.

In order to communicate with OpenStack services, users must use tokens. As the authentication mechanisms are provided by plugins, there are multiple ways to authenticate and get a token.

Consider A and B are two OpenStack clouds, both will return a token upon successful authentication. Cloud A provides a password authentication plugin, that expects a request payload as in Figure 6, while cloud B provides a proprietary plugin that takes specific arguments, expecting a request payload as in Figure 7.

If the sets of plugins are mutually exclusive, there is absolutely nothing that can be done to get around and authenticate the user seamlessly across clouds with the same arguments. However, most OpenStack cloud

```
{
  "auth": {
    "identity": {
      "methods": ["password"],
      "password": {
        "user": {
          "name": "admin",
          "domain": {"name": "Default"},
          "password": "devstacker"
        }
      }
    }
  }
}
```

Figure 6. Payload for a POST /v3/auth/tokens API call to get a token using the password authentication plugin.

```
{
  "auth": {
    "identity": {
      "methods": ["xpto"],
      "xpto": {
        "id": "0a33--"
        "sequence": "2",
        "secret": "230"
      }
    }
  }
}
```

Figure 7. Payload for a create token POST /v3/auth/tokens API call to get a token using a proprietary plugin.

providers support at least the password authentication plugin, which is what Shade uses.

B. Semantic

The purely semantic issues found in OpenStack are related to how the cloud and the user account are configured, thus they cannot be solved by a technical workaround. Despite the fact Shade not being able to workaround them, there are some approaches users may take to avoid such issues when negotiating their contracts with cloud vendors and when developing their applications.

1) Different authorization requirements for the functionality: OpenStack uses Role Based Access Control (RBAC) to protect its functionalities. For each API exposed, the roles required to access it are configured by the cloud provider. When different providers configure access control differently, a user with the same set of roles in multiple clouds will get unauthorized errors when performing the same operations in the cloud with least privilege.

Let A and B be two OpenStack clouds, both support the upload and storage of objects. However, cloud A requires the admin role, while the cloud B is more permissive and requires the admin role or the member role. A user with member role trying to upload an object in both clouds will get an unauthorized error when trying to upload an image to cloud A, because they do not own the required permissions.

In this case it is up to the user to negotiate with the cloud vendor what functionalities will be available to their account.

2) Cloud-wide restrictions on resources: due to nonfunctional requirements such as reducing complexity and optimizing available storage, vendors have to configure some options that establish upper limits for resources upon creation. When clouds have different limits for a given resource, a user may get an error when trying to create resources in the cloud with the lowest limit.

When requested to create a resource, Shade makes the appropriate call to the underlying services. If different clouds have different limits for resource creation, such as the maximum disk size an uploaded image may use or how deep a project hierarchy may go, there is nothing Shade can do to work around that.

It is up to the user to understand what limits the cloud vendor sets and decide if they are acceptable. If not, try a different vendor.

3) User account-wide restrictions on resources: restrictions on resource creation in a user account basis are called quotas. They define how much resources a user may use up to, such as number of virtual machines that can be instantiated. They are assigned by the vendors to users upon request. If the limits are not consistent across different clouds, the user may get errors in a cloud with lower limits when trying to perform the same create operation across clouds.

When Shade tries to perform a create call and the user quota is not enough, Shade will simply raise to the user the error it got from the underlying service.

An example is when a user needs to boot more servers than what they are allowed. In that case, the user would need to negotiate a consistent quota for booting servers across cloud vendors.

4) Inconsistent resource discovery: some resources are created by the vendors and are cloud-wide, such as the public network, user roles and default images. The lack of standardization on what is available by default and how those cloudwide resources are labeled disfavors users to programmatically discover them in a multi-cloud environment.

How can Shade find the latest Ubuntu image available in all clouds? There is no standardization in resources names across clouds, neither helpful metadata to make it possible. Image metadata is entirely vendor-defined, thus there is no way Shade can understand it precisely in a multi-cloud environment.

Despite the fact the user cannot fully understand the default cloud-provided resources, they can create and name their own resources. Thus, a possible solution for this issue is that the users create their own resources. In the example above, the user could upload the same image to all clouds in use, ensuring both the image contents and name are the same.

5) Pluggable underlying mechanism: as stated in Section III-A2 Pluggable underlying mechanism, OpenStack supports multiple vendors and technical solutions via plugins. Plugins act as backends for the REST APIs, whose are always available, regardless the plugin implementing the operation for that API or not. An error stating the functionality is not implemented may be raised, or the API call may be silently ignored. In that case, multiple clouds using different plugins might have inconsistent behaviors when requested to execute the same API call.

It is very common to organizations to maintain a central source of truth for authentication, such as an LDAP server, when they need to have a consistent user management across the whole organization, including its applications. OpenStack provides a mechanism to integrate LDAP servers for authentication purposes. Companies do not want, however, that a deletion of an OpenStack user propagate and delete that user for all their applications. In this scenario, OpenStack would have read-only access to the LDAP server.

Consider A and B two OpenStack clouds, both will return an access token upon successful authentication. Cloud A uses a read-only LDAP backend, while cloud B communicates with a read-write SQL backend.

When performing a create user call, Shade would be successful when calling cloud B. However, it would get an exception in the call to cloud A. There is nothing Shade can do about it, since it is a functionality that is not supported by some vendors depending on how they configure their clouds.

The users need to understand what plugins the vendors support and if those meet their needs. If not, they would need to try a different vendor.

C. Syntactic and Semantic

1) Multiple workflows for complex operations: providing IaaS involves non-trivial operations, such as instantiating a virtual machine on a hypervisor and assigning a public IP address to it. By supporting many vendors and technical solutions, there are multiple manners to solve such complex tasks, each one taking a

```
import shade

for cloud_name, region_name in [
    ('cloud-a', 'region-a'),
    ('cloud-b', 'region-b')]:

    # Initialize the cloud
    cloud = shade.openstack_cloud(
        cloud=cloud_name,
        region_name=region_name)

    # Upload an image to the cloud
    image = cloud.create_image(
        'devuan-jessie', wait=True,
        filename='devuan-jessie.qcow2')

    # Find a flavor with at least 512MB
    # of RAM
    flavor = cloud.get_flavor_by_ram(512)

    # Boot a server, wait for it to boot,
    # and then do whatever is needed to
    # attach a public IP to it.
    cloud.create_server(
        'my-server', image=image,
        flavor=flavor, wait=True,
        auto_ip=True)
```

Figure 8. Using Shade to boot a server with a public IP attached to it in multiple clouds.

different workflow involving multiple API calls. Even if the final semantic result is the same, executing such operations does not consistently use the same data formats neither have the same accurate interpretation throughout the process.

In the example of booting a server and assigning a public IP to it, the first step is to figure out what is the networking service in the cloud: Nova Network or Neutron. In this example, let's assume Neutron is available. The second step is to query Neutron in order to figure out if there is a public network to boot the server on. If there is, then a single API call to Nova, the Compute Service, may be performed requesting the virtual machine to be instantiated and be put directly in that public network. If there is not, the solution will be first to create a virtual machine with a private IP and then to assign a floating IP later on via NAT mechanism.

In order to assign a floating IP via NAT mechanism, first try to pass the port ID of the private IP of the server to the floating IP create call. If that is not possible, create a floating IP and then attach it to the server. Executing all this complex functionality with Shade is as simple as shown in Figure 8.

Another complex example is the upload image functionality, managed by Glance, the Image Service. There are two mechanisms for that: (i) upload data directly to Glance via HTTP PUT, or (ii) upload the data to the Object Storage service, Swift, and then import it to Glance with an import task. Both alternatives are available in every Glance version 2 service. In some clouds, upload via PUT is disabled, and in other clouds the task import mechanism does not do anything, just ignores the requested action.

More specifically in the task import path, the accepted payloads are all vendor or plugin specific, presenting the issues described in Section III-A2 Pluggable underlying mechanism.

2) Functionality is not provided: cloud vendors may opt to not deploy or to remove some of the OpenStack services for whatever reason, such as it is not part of their market strategy. In that case, users would not be able to use the same functionality across multiple clouds.

As an example, Trove, the Database as a Service (DBaaS) service may not be available in all clouds. That would make it unfeasible to deploy an application that needs DBaaS in the clouds that do not deploy it.

Before choosing what cloud vendors to go with, the users need to understand well their service catalog to make sure all the expected functionalities are provided.

D. Validation

Shade is currently the library handling all the clouds differences for the whole Continuous Integration system of OpenStack, which spins up thousands of servers every single day across many non-interoperable clouds. It is a project developed by the OpenStack community and the authors work on this project, which is also used in a master's thesis.

In addition to the above mentioned use, Shade is also used in Ansible modules, which enable several cloud providers to orchestrate their clouds via scripts. Such modules were used to make the program The Interoperability Challenge possible, where multiple cloud vendors were challenged to run the same workloads against their clouds, live, in front of thousands of attendees at two editions of the OpenStack Summit.

In the Barcelona edition, there were 16 participating companies: Canonical, Cisco, DreamHost, Deutsche Telekom, Fujitsu, HPE, Huawei, IBM, Intel, Linaro, Mirantis, OVH, Rackspace, Red Hat, SUSE and VMware. In the Boston edition, the 15 participants were IBM, VMware, Huawei, ZTE, SUSE, EasyStack, T2Cloud, Red Hat, Rackspace, Canonical, VEXXHOST, Deutsche Telekom, Platform9, Wind River and NetApp.

All companies, in both editions, were successful on running the workloads defined by the community and implemented via orchestration scripts using the Ansible modules. Without Shade, there would be no way to communicate to all those clouds transparently without implementing the Shade logic in the Ansible modules themselves.

The patterns for the interoperability gaps detailed in this paper are enumerated in Table I, which summarizes what is solved by Shade and what requires user intervention, be it negotiate with the service provider or to use a work around when writing applications. Despite the fact that Shade solves fewer issues in terms of quantity, the ones it solves are the most impeditive for interoperability in OpenStack, because they bring a lot of complexity to the user side, while the issues solved by the users are related to understanding what functionalities are available in the clouds and how their accounts are configured.

TABLE I. PATTERNS ADDRESSED BY SHADE

Pattern	**Action**	
	Shade	***User***
3.A.1 Functionality is exposed through different APIs	X	
3.A.2 Pluggable underlying mechanism		X
3.B.1 Different authorization requirements for the functionality		X
3.B.2 Cloud-wide restrictions on resources		X
3.B.3 User account-wide restrictions on resources		X
3.B.4 Inconsistent resource discovery		X
3.B.5 Pluggable underlying mechanism		X
3.C.1 Multiple workflows for complex operations	X	
3.C.2 Functionality is not provided		X

IV. RELATED WORK

Even in 2010, when cloud computing was growing as a concept, Dillon et al. already signaled that interoperability deserved substantial further research and development [5].

In a literature review, we were able to identify studies focusing on interoperability among different IaaS cloud platforms. Zhang et al. [6] conducted a comprehensive survey on the state-of-the-art efforts for understanding and mitigating interoperability issues. Parák et al. [7] discussed challenges in achieving IaaS interoperability across multiple cloud management frameworks.

No study reporting that interoperability issues occur within a single platform was found, and that is the case being reported in this paper with OpenStack.

As opposed to defining open protocols and making the existing vendor adapt their deployments to it, the solution as presented in this paper is a post-facto high-level end-user broker for facilitating effective interoperability in the cloud, as clarified in by Parák et al. [7].

Loutas et al. [8] highlighted that creating different interoperability standards and frameworks can possibly lead to different interoperability solutions which are not interoperable between each other. However, we found that creating platform-specific interoperability frameworks such as Shade is a good strategy because another middleware could be built on the top of it and consider all OpenStack deployments interoperable, without caring about particularities of the OpenStack world, and then solve interoperability limitations between different cloud platforms. Creating multiple solutions of that higher level middleware would certainly be a problem.

V. CONCLUSION AND FUTURE WORK

As an open source platform, OpenStack is deployed by numerous vendors. By allowing great flexibility in its functionalities, it compromised interoperability, with the issues reported in this paper.

Shade is a Python library that was implemented to solve the issues when there is a programmatic way to discover how to perform the operations and how to interpret the results accurately. In the other cases where the issues are inherent to the platform, such as the lack of standardization on what is available by default, how cloud-wide resources are labeled and what is the available quota for a given resource, this paper recommended that the users should workaround themselves when possible, otherwise analyze the cloud offering and negotiate with the vendor directly.

Since interoperability was developed post-facto, being fully interoperable in OpenStack will never become a reality because that would mean giving up flexibility and, for that, backward incompatible changes would need to be introduced. One of the key attributes of OpenStack is that it strives to always be backwards compatible. Furthermore, it would require vendors to standardize their deployments, changing their market strategy and breaking their customers for the sake of being interoperable with their competitors.

This study was important because it showed that interoperability issues may emerge even within a single cloud platform. The issues were categorized, exemplified and a solution was proposed, allowing further improvements and studies to be placed on the top of it.

Future work may include creating another middleware on the top of Shade that is not language-specific, such as a Remote Procedure Calls (RPCs) or a REST API, allowing users to consume Shade in other languages than just Python.

Another important study would be to investigate other open source IaaS platforms to report what interoperability issues they present, then compare with OpenStack and analyze if a solution similar to Shade would apply. Example of platforms are Apache CloudStack, Eucalyptus and OpenNebula.

REFERENCES

[1] P. Mell and T. Grance, "The NIST definition of Cloud Computing", NIST Special Publication, USA, 2011.

[2] OpenStack, https://www.openstack.org, [Online; accessed 14 January 2018].

[3] Shade Git, https://github.com/openstack-infra/shade, [Online; accessed 14 January 2018].

[4] ISO/IEC 2382:2015, "Information technology -- Vocabulary". Switzerland: ISO/IEC JTC 1, 2015.

[5] T. Dillon, C. Wu, and E. Chang, "Cloud computing: Issues and challenges", Proceedings of the 24th IEEE International Conference on Advanced Information Networking and Applications. USA: IEEE, 2010, pp. 27-33.

[6] Z. Zhang, C. Wu, and D. W. Cheung, "A survey on cloud interoperability: Taxonomies, standards, and practice", ACM SIGMETRICS Performance Evaluation Review, vol. 40, no. 4, pp. 13-22, Mar. 2013.

[7] B. Parák and Z. Šustr, "Challenges in achieving IaaS cloud interoperability across multiple cloud management frameworks" Proceedings of the 7th IEEE/ACM International Conference on Utility and Cloud Computing. USA: IEEE, 2014, pp. 404-411.

[8] N. Loutas, E. Kamateri, F. Bosi, and K. Tarabanis, "Cloud computing interoperability: The state of play", Proceedings of the Third IEEE International Conference on Cloud Computing Technology and Science. USA: IEEE, 2011, pp. 752-757.

CloudMediate

Showcase Implementation with Google Firebase

Raimund K. Ege
Computer Science
Northern Illinois University
DeKalb, IL, USA
email: ege@niu.edu

Abstract—**CloudMediate is a peer-to-peer multimedia stream sharing platform. It provides a media aggregation framework that is flexible, powerful and scalable to identify, establish and manage connections to input media stream sources. It enables the mediation of input streams into consumable output streams, which become part of the shared content pool. Google Firebase is a cloud service. It is used to implement CloudMediate in conjunction with the Angular JavaScript web-application framework. The implementation serves as a showcase for modern, efficient and powerful realization of cloud-based distributed applications. Details of the use of hosting, user authentication and real-time database can serve as recipe for many similar efforts.**

Keywords-peer to peer; multimedia; stream sharing; stream mediation; cloud implementation.

I. INTRODUCTION

CloudMediate is a multimedia stream sharing and processing framework. Its conceptual approach and architecture is described in [1]. CloudMediate allows users to become members of a peer-to-peer (p2p) network where streams can be posted, mediated and consumed, i.e. viewed. This paper describes an implementation of CloudMediate using a modern cloud implementation framework: Google Firebase [2]. All aspects of the p2p content sharing network are handled in the cloud and are accessible everywhere.

Mobile and wearable devices are common place today and have allowed access to a multitude of disparate but often related media streams, while scaling geographical barriers. These multimedia streams are produced, stored on and accessed from various kinds of heterogeneous devices. CloudMediate allows to register and then select suitable input streams, correlate and combine them into output streams. The output streams are then made available to peers, again rendered onto suitable mobile and wearable devices. The correlation and combination of input streams into consumable output streams is achieved by active intermediary compute nodes. CloudMediate uses the term "mediator" to describe these intermediaries. We chose this term in analogy to the "Mediator" behavioral pattern that address the responsibilities of objects in an application and how they communicate [3].

Since the streams are meant to be consumed from the original source, which can be anywhere in the Internet, we choose a cloud-based implementation of stream management. We selected Google Firebase as the implementation vehicle, since it offers all the services we needed: flexible authentication, real-time database and a JavaScript based computation engine. It provides an Angular compatible API to access its features. Google Firebase also handles world-wide hosting with exceptional scaling capabilities (if we ever need them).

The rest of this paper is organized as follows. Section II gives background information on media streaming and media mediation, plus describes the features of Google Firebase and the Angular JavaScript framework. Section III describes the CloudMediate multimedia stream sharing and mediation framework. Section IV gives implementation detail and might serve as a recipe for other cloud-based implementations of similar nature. Section V summarizes our approach and effort and closes with an outlook to our future work.

II. BACKGROUND

Devices that handle multimedia are commonplace. Every smartphone has camera(s) and high-resolution screens. Every major vendor of systems and hardware has introduced mobile and wearable gadgets to support virtual and augmented reality. From simple holders for smart phones, to optical head-mounted displays from market leaders - such as Microsoft's Windows Mixed Reality headsets, Oculus Rift, HTC Vive or even the older Google Glass - software to enable these devices is becoming more commonplace. The application developer kits are becoming ever more powerful to harness the dynamic features of these devices.

Streaming of multimedia data requires significant throughput and quality of service (QoS) factors, such as latency, jitter, order of delivery, etc. Any architectures must deal with buffering and the intermittent connection associated with mobility. Connectivity capabilities are typically wireless and include high-bandwidth cellular (4G, LTE) and WLAN (IEEE 802.11) connections, plus lower-bandwidth near field connections (Bluetooth, NFC, etc.). Transmission rates in the multi megabits per second range and latency rates in the sub millisecond range are currently quite standard.

In peer-sourced augmented reality systems, the management of the multimedia source and establishment of trust is essential [4]. In our prior work [5] [6], we investigated the authentication of participants in peer-to-peer networks, the establishment and management of trust, and the use of such media sources in building content management systems. An important lesson was that while modern mobile devices are compute-capable, cloud-based components add additional heft and authority to a seamless and smooth creation of a truly immersing virtual and augmented reality experience [7][8][9].

Cloud platforms that offer integrated services are becoming more widely available. The Heroku [10] platform is probably most widely known. These platforms allow developers to compose their applications locally and then upload and deploy into cloud containers, which makes them available Internet-wide. We choose Google Firebase for the bundled services it provides, such as authentication, real-time database and compute engine, plus its comprehensive integration with the Angular [11] JavaScript web programming interface. The Angular framework offers a modern component- and object-based implementation which does not rely on server-based functionality but rather focusses on client-provided JavaScript execution. Features can be built quickly with simple, declarative templates. New components can extend a wide array of existing components.

III. CloudMediate

A. General Framework

CloudMediate is a peer-to-peer (p2p) content sharing network and aims to aggregate multimedia streams and make them available to peers. Figure 1 shows the general approach of how CloudMediate operates. The left side of the figure symbolizes the multitude of potential input streams. While audio and video streams are most common, our approach allows arbitrary streams of data from any sensor. The right side of the figure shows consumption of streams by mobile devices. The common smartphone might be one example of such a display device. Wearable devices, such as headsets and virtual glasses are the target of our approach. Both sides are connected by a cloud-hosted network of intermediaries that normalize, correlate and combine input streams into consumable output streams.

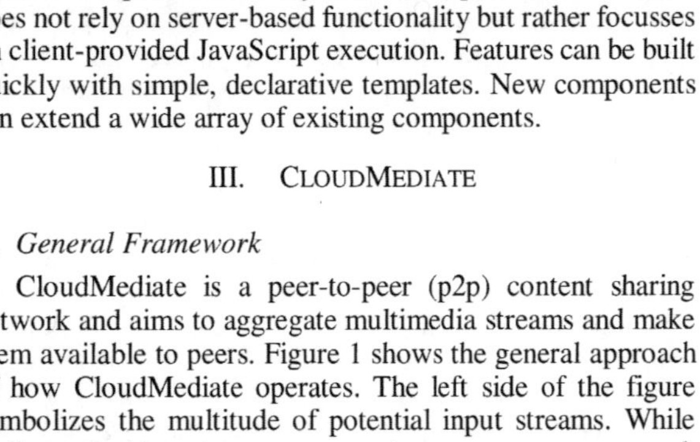

Figure 1. CloudMediate Structure

B. Mediators

CloudMediate uses the term "mediator" to describe these intermediaries. Each mediator has an input and an output side and transfers and negotiates on three kinds of information; the schema of the data stream, the data stream itself, and some QoS information specific to the stream. The nature of mediation varies from a simple combination of input streams, to correlation of virtual and augmented streams, and up to reformatting of a stream based on attitude information. Mediators can be categorized as "Combiner," "Transformer" and "Splitter." A Combiner is able to correlate multiple input streams into a single output stream; Transformer accepts one input stream and transforms it into one output stream based on a transformation schema which can be a set of static or dynamic parameters; Splitter is able to correlate an input stream into a number of output streams. Each mediator follows a schema that defines the relationship between the input and output streams. The schema can be parameterized via static values or a dynamic stream of input values. These general mediator categories are further specialized, examples of "Transformer" are the "Scaler" mediator, which changes a video streams resolution, or the "Securer" mediator, which takes an unencrypted input stream and produces an encrypted output stream. The "Securer" schema parameters determine the encryption algorithm, mode, parameters, and key.

In addition to the actual data sensed, each stream must be packaged with the exact time of recording. Multiple streams of sensor data are combined into a multimedia stream which interleaves its content streams plus provides meta-data to ensure their proper sequencing and correlation. It is important that the container format used to wrap the content streams is flexible enough to accommodate not only the stream data but also extensive amounts of reference information used to combine the streams. We are using an extension of the WebM project [12] format. The WebM container format is an open standard and allows us to collate an unlimited number of video, audio, pictures and subtitle tracks into one stream. We add the capability of identifying reference elements at identified points in time and at locations.

C. Peers

In a P2P communications model, peers participate on an equal basis. Each peer must register and gets a unique identity, which is made known to other peers. Limited information about each peer is collected and maintained. Currently, the only identifying information maintained is the peer's email address. Each peer must have a confirmed email address. The most relevant information about a peer is detailed information on a peer's participation in the network. The peer's history of relevant transactions is maintained in a container we call "trust nugget". This nugget contains detailed information on a peer's participation, such as length and quality of stream transmission, ratio of seed vs. leech behavior, judgments of other stream participants, etc. It is a matter of trust whether and to what degree the peer is allowed to partake in the shared media content.

All peers have the same capabilities: any peer can contribute a stream, any peer can consume a stream, and any peer can offer a new mediator or even a new mediator category. Peers can also preconfigure existing mediators with existing input streams and parameters to create new mediated output streams.

IV. IMPLEMENTATION

There are several components that make up our CloudMediate implementation.

In this paper, we focus on the web-based peer access portal. This portal is implemented using the Google Firebase cloud service framework. The web application is constructed from html, css, and JavaScript pieces. All processing is done in the web client using the Angular JavaScript framework. All back-end processing is provided by Firebase.

Other CloudMediate components, such as the Android and iOS application for mobile devices are not subject of this paper. They are currently under development and might be discussed in a future paper.

A. Angular

Angular is an open-source front-end web application platform. It combines declarative templates, dependency injection with end to end tooling. Angular is a framework for building client applications in HTML and either JavaScript or a language like TypeScript that compiles to JavaScript. It empowers developers to quickly and efficiently build applications that live on the web, mobile, or the desktop.

Angular web applications are constructed from components. Each component can be viewed as a class in the object-oriented sense, with instance variables and methods, even super classes. Each component has an html template and a css style file which govern its appearance. Variables and methods are accessible from within the html template. Angular also enables 2-way data binding which reduces the amount of JavaScript code necessary to keep screen data updated. Angular components that only provide services, but have no screen appearance are configured as providers. Angular providers are made available to Angular components via dependency injection.

For example, consider the Angular code in Figure 2. It declares the "AddNewMediator" component.

```
@Component({
  selector: 'addnew-mediator',
  templateUrl: './addnew.mediator.html',
  styleUrls: ['./mediator.component.css']
})
export class AddNewMediator extends MediatorComponent {

  name: string;
  url: string;
  type: string = "please select";
  streamUrl: string;
  schemaFile: File = null;

  setType(t: string) {···
  }

  setFile(event: any) {···
  }

  onSubmit() {···
  }
}
```

Figure 2. Angular Component

The "AddNewMediator" component is declared with selector "addnew-mediator", which enables this component to be inserted into html elsewhere with the <addnew-mediator> tag. The component's appearance is specified in separate css and html files. The component also defines class "AddNewMediator" as a subclass of "MediatorComponent". It inherits all instance variables and methods from its superclass. It defines additional variables to hold the name, URL, type and schema file information. These fields are filled in the html portion of the component from within a html form. The shown methods help process the input from the form, as well govern what occurs when the form is submitted, i.e., "onSubmit()".

With Angular we use module "angularfire2", which is the official library for Firebase and Angular to directly access Firebase features.

B. Firebase Hosting

The first feature of Firebase that we use has the purpose to host our portal website within Google Firebase. Firebase features a console that allows the creation of hosting space. All that it required is user authentication with a Gmail address. While Firebase provides a URL address for the hosted website, it is also possible to redirect any domain to it. Figure 3 shows the portal's home screen at mediate.ege.com:

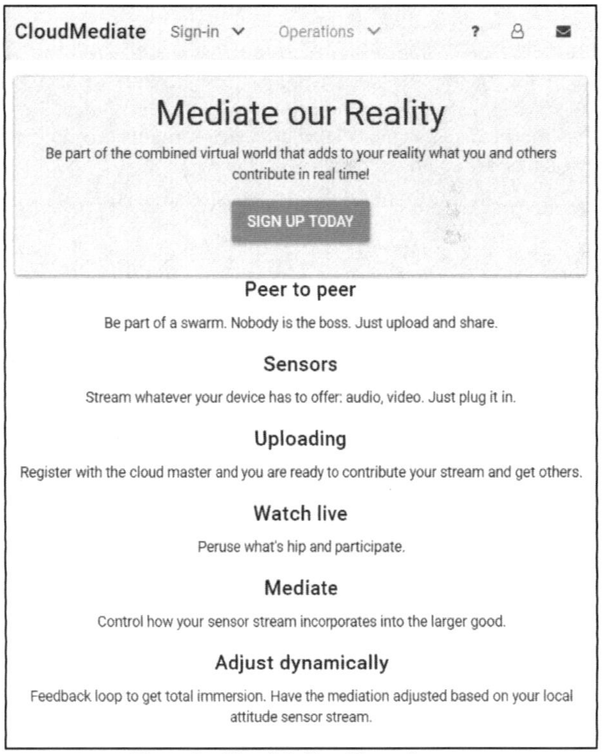

Figure 3. CloudMediate Home Screen

Firebase provides multiple levels of service. We used the "Spark" level, which is free of charge. It has limits on use and capacity. Additional levels are available at cost.

C. *Firebase Authentication*

Firebase allows websites to authenticate their users. Since we needed to authenticate our peers, we opted to use this feature. Among the multitude of options for authentication providers and features we selected "Google authentication" which allows Gmail users, and "Email authentication" which requires a peer to provide an email address. The confirmation of the email is handled automatically by Firebase. In both modes of authentication, each peer will have a confirmed email address. The management of user information is completely handled by Firebase. Once a peer has logged in CloudMediate's operation become available (see Figure 4):

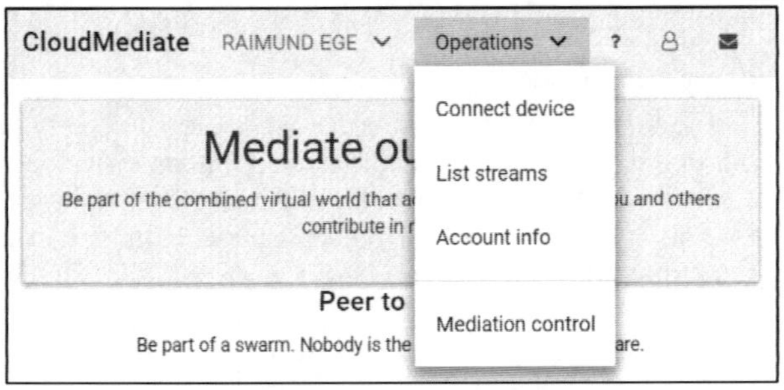

Figure 4. Peer Operations

Here, a peer can connect a stream from a device, list all available media streams, manage the account, or use the mediation features of CloudMediate.

Figure 5 shows the "Connect device" Angular component which is pulled up via menu selection:

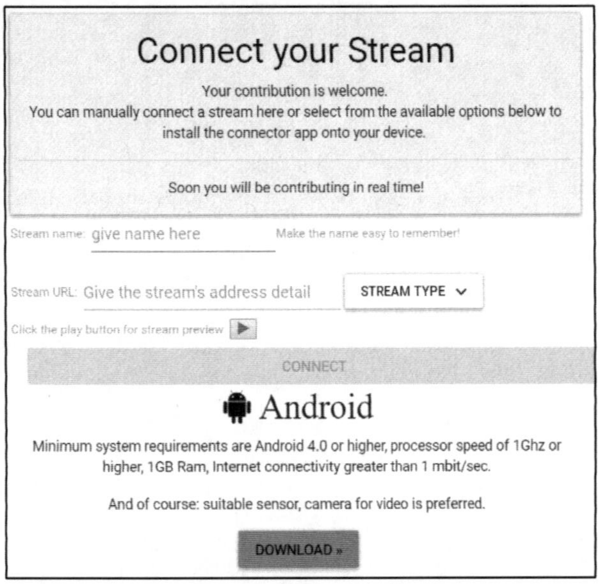

Figure 5. Stream Detail

A peer has several choices to register multimedia streams. CloudMediate calls for Android or iOS apps that can be downloaded from the presented screen. Another choice is to provide all stream detail manually here: stream name, URL, and type. Before the stream is submitted the peer can call up a preview to check the availability and suitability of the contribution. Once all fields as filled and verified, the "CONNECT" button becomes available: it submits the stream information.

D. *Firebase Real-time Database*

The central feature of Firebase is its database. Once it is enabled in the Firebase console, it is available via the Angular – Firebase interface. All database data is stored as JSON objects. The database is not constructed using tables or records. Simple JavaScript operations allow to manipulate the data. The database is a "real-time" database in the sense that any data modification done anywhere is immediately reflected in all places the data is used or displayed. All streams that were connected to CloudMediate are stored in the Firebase real-time database.

Figure 6 shows "List streams" Angular component which is pulled up via menu selection:

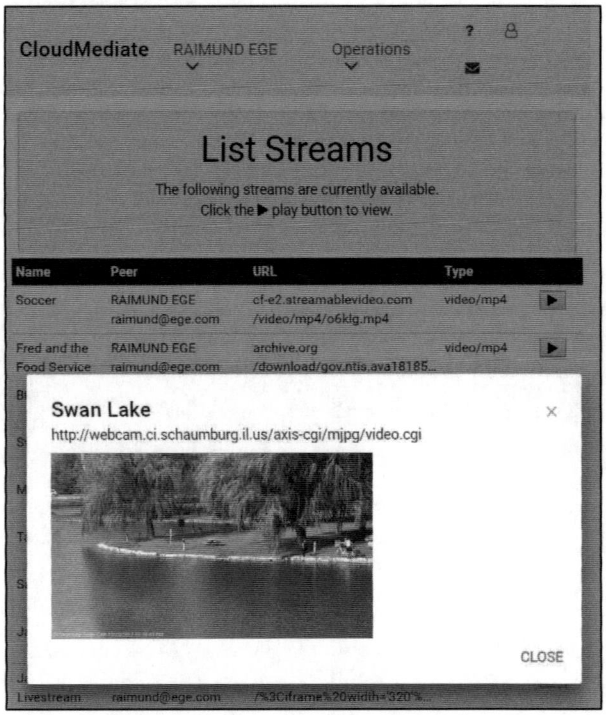

Figure 6. List streams with stream preview

All available streams are shown with their name, URL and type information, as well which peer is contributing the stream. Each stream can be viewed directly in a modal sub dialog.

The "Mediation control" selection from the operations menu opens up the central feature of CloudMediate where peers can select and configure mediators. Figure 7 shows the initial screen:

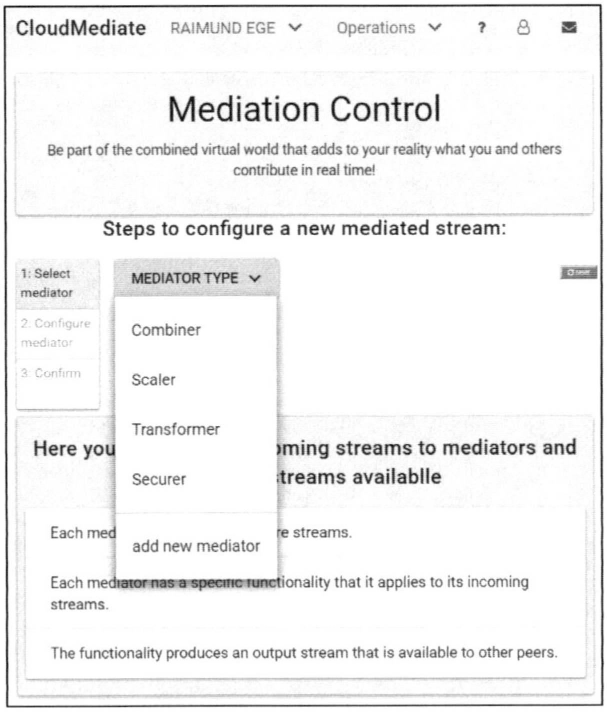

Figure 7. CloudMediate Mediation Control Component

Three steps are necessary to configure a mediator:

- Select an existing mediator: the "MEDIATOR TYPE" dropdown shows which types of mediators are currently available (the dropdown also allows to add new mediators); upon selection of the type, all available mediators are shown; the peer can select a specific mediator, which pulls up the mediator configuration component (see Figure 8).
- Configure the mediator: depending on the type it will require the specification of one or more input streams. The "Overlap" mediator shown in Figure 8 requires 2 input streams: each can be selected from the list of available streams. The parameters and the exact URL for the out stream also need to be specified.
- Confirm the submission of the configured mediator into the list of available streams in CloudMediate. The mediator's output streams are stored alongside other multimedia streams in the Firebase real-time database and appear immediately in the list of available streams for all peers connected to CloudMediate.

The dropdown menu also featured the "add new mediator" choice. It allows a peer to register a brand-new mediator type. The new mediator is configured via the "AddNewMediator" Angular component.

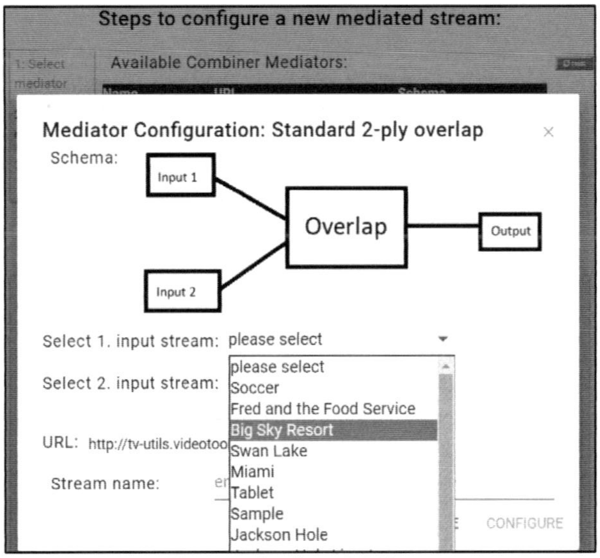

Figure 8. Configure Mediator

A new mediator is specified by giving it an expressive name, specifying the URL of the host and port where the mediation service is provided. Each new mediator needs to fall into one of the top-level mediator categories: "Combiner," "Transformer" or "Splitter." The mediation capabilities of the new mediator type are given via a mediator schema file.

Figure 2 showed the Angular component "AddNewMediator." Figure 9 shows the screen appearance of the component:

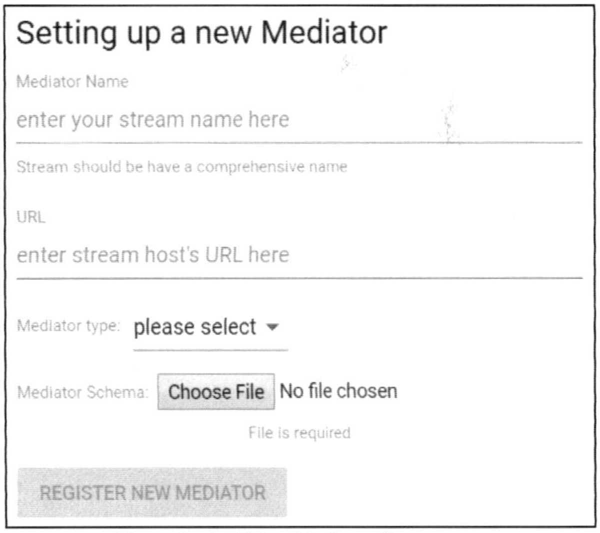

Figure 9. Add New Mediator Component

The new mediator that is configured via this component is again added to the Firebase JSON database stream list, and is instantly available to other peers.

V. Conclusion

CloudMediate is a peer-to-peer content sharing framework. In addition to sharing multimedia streams, it also allows to modify streams via mediators. Streams can be combined, split and transformed. Peers log in to CloudMediate add or select streams, configure mediators and add them to the sharing network, or just consume, i.e., view streams on their wearable devices.

In this paper, we highlighted our implementation of the CloudMediate framework using the Google Firebase cloud service. Firebase hosting, authentication and real-time database were used and allowed an efficient and scalable web portal that is available everywhere. The current CloudMediate incarnation is available at htttp//mediate.ege.com

One feature of Google Firebase that we did not use is the ability to program webservices that run within the Firebase back end. We plan to investigate the "Firebase Functions" feature (which is currently in beta status) to provide basic stream handling that would enable easier provision of more sophisticated mediator types.

References

[1] R. Ege, "CloudMediate: Peer-to-peer Media Aggregation for Augmented Reality," The Eighth International Conference on Cloud Computing, GRIDs, and Virtualization (CLOUD COMPUTING 2017), Athens, Greece, pp. 88-92, 2017.

[2] Google Firebase: Mobile and Web Application development Platform, https://firebase.google.com. [retrieved October 20, 2017]

[3] E. Gamma, R. Helm, R. Johnson, and J. Vlissides, Design Patterns: Elements of Reusable Object-Oriented Software, Addison-Wesley Professional, 1994.

[4] S. Aukstakalnis, Practical Augmented Reality, Addison-Wesley Professional, 2017.

[5] R. Ege, "Secure Trust Management for the Android Platform," International Conference on Systems (ICONS 2013), Seville, Spain, pp. 98-103, 2013.

[6] R. Ege, "Peer to Peer Media Management for Augmented Reality," International Conference on Networking and Services (ICNS 2015), Rome, Italy, pp. 95-100, 2015.

[7] R. Azuma et al., "Recent Advances in Augmented Reality," IEEE Computer Graphics and Applications (CGA) 21(6), pp. 34-47, 2001.

[8] D. Wagner, G. Reitmayr, A. Mulloni, T. Drummond, and D. Schmalstieg, "Real-Time Detection and Tracking for Augmented Reality on Mobile Phones," IEEE Transactions on Visualization and Computer Graphics, 16(3), pp. 355-368, 2010.

[9] A. Morrison et al., "Collaborative use of mobile augmented reality with paper maps," Journal on Computers & Graphics (Elsevier), 35(4), pp. 789-799, 2011.

[10] Heroku: Platform as a Service, https://www.heroku.com. [retrieved October 20, 2017]

[11] Angular: Web Application Framework, http://angular.io/. [retrieved October 20, 2017]

[12] WebM: an open web media project, http://www.webmproject.org. [retrieved October 20, 2017]

Joint Orchestration of Cloud-Based Microservices and Virtual Network Functions

Hadi Razzaghi Kouchaksaraei, Holger Karl
Computer Network Group
Paderborn University, Paderborn, Germany
email: {hadi.razzaghi, holger.karl}@uni-paderborn.de

***Abstract*—Recent studies show the increasing popularity of distributed cloud applications, which are composed of multiple microservices. Besides their known benefits, microservice architecture also enables to mix and match cloud applications and Network Function Virtualization (NFV) services (service chains), which are composed of Virtual Network Functions (VNFs). Provisioning complex services containing VNFs and microservices in a combined NFV/cloud platform can enhance service quality and optimise cost. Such a platform can be based on the multi-cloud concept. However, current multi-cloud solutions do not support NFV requirements, making them inadequate to support complex services. In this paper, we investigate these challenges and propose a solution for jointly managing and orchestrating microservices and virtual network functions.**

Keywords-Network Function Virtualization; Cloud Computing; Microservices; Virtualized Network Function.

I. INTRODUCTION

Today's cloud applications are commonly developed using a microservice architecture. In this architecture, individual software components of an application are implemented as separate lightweight functional blocks, called microservices [1]. This type of application can also smooth the road to the realisation of Distributed Cloud Computing (DCC) where microservices of a cloud application are deployed on geographically distributed micro data centres instead of on a single data centre.

Following the concept of cloud computing, Network Function Virtualization (NFV) has emerged. It aims at cloudifing network services that are conventionally provided by dedicated hardware. Similar to microservice-based or distributed cloud applications, NFV services consist of a set of distributed virtualised Network Functions (NFs) that are chained together to deliver a network service (e.g., Residential Gateway).

The distributed structure of NFV services and distributed cloud applications allows to mix and match VNFs and microservices. Such combined services, which we call *complex services*, can have remarkable benefits for actors (users, service and infrastructure providers) involved in both NFV and cloud ecosystems such as cost optimisation and service quality improvement [2]. An example of complex services (Fig. 1) is a cloud application that includes a load balancer that spreads the load among application back-end instances and also a firewall that filters incoming requests to the application front-end. Since firewall and load balancer are network functions, they can have a better performance in NFV environments.

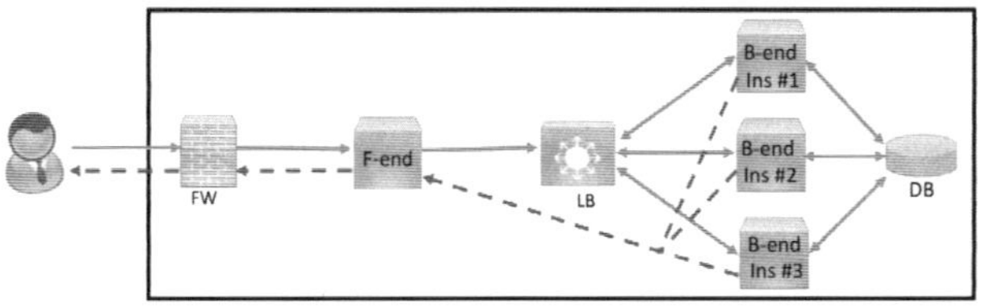

Fig. 1. An example of complex services

However, the fact that the current cloud and NFV platforms are not designed to support requirements of services from the opposite family makes the provisioning of complex services rather challenging. Some of the reasons for having different designs for cloud and NFV platforms are as follows:

- Packet processing is the main functionality of VNFs involved in NFV services, which should be performed as fast as possible using technologies such as Data Plane Development Kit (DPDK) [3]. However, the majority of cloud applications do not need to bother with packet processing as it is not their primary objective.
- Providing WAN connectivity is one of the essential tasks of an NFV manager to provide service chaining for network services that are geographically distributed. However, in cloud ecosystems, providing WAN connectivity is not crucial and is therefore typically not offered by cloud management system such as OpenStack.
- The workload composition is also different in NFV and cloud ecosystems. While service chaining is used to combine VNFs in an NFV ecosystem, choreography/orchestration is used to connect microservices in Cloud ecosystem.

A management and orchestration system that can join two ecosystems and manage all the differences can complement the shortcomings of cloud and NFV platforms in providing network functions and microservices, respectively. To this end, in this paper, we propose a multi-cloud solution that unifies NFV and Cloud ecosystems.

The paper is structured as follows. In Section II, we shortlist the candidate solutions. In Section III, the proposed solution is explained, and finally, in Section IV, we highlight our conclusion.

II. Candidate Solutions

An environment where NFV and cloud platforms can interwork with each other could mitigate the challenge of provisioning complex services. This could be realised by leveraging Multi-cloud [2] solutions, which allow VNFs and microservices to be deployed on their respective platforms. Multi-cloud is an environment that uses the resources of multiple clouds (e.g., Amazon EC2, Windows Azure) to deploy a cloud application. Some of the goals of multi-cloud are to deal with peaks in service and resource requests, minimise cost, improve quality and availability, and avoid cloud provider lock-in [2], which are similar to the objectives of providing complex services.

Although Multi-cloud can help the deployment of complex services in a combined NFV and cloud infrastructure, it cannot provide a comprehensive solution. Current multi-cloud solutions do not support NFV requirements, making them unsuitable for deployment and management of complex services.

Terraform [4], a multi-cloud solution that can handle cross-cloud dependencies, supports most of the cloud management systems such as OpenStack, K8, and AWS. However, Terraform does not provide service chaining and WAN connectivity that is required for NFV services. Cloudify [5] (another multi-cloud solution) is a composed NFV and cloud management and orchestration system. It supports the deployment of cloud and NFV services on multiple cloud infrastructures such as AWS and OpenStack. However, Cloudify does not allow the deployment of an application on multiple clouds at the same time [6], which makes it inadequate to manage and orchestrate complex services.

III. Proposed Solution

Our solution is to consolidate current multi-cloud and NFV tools to deploy, manage, and orchestrate complex services. To this end, in our architecture (Fig. 2), we combine SONATA [7], a network service development and orchestration platform, with Terraform. SONATA's orchestrator allows services to be managed based on their specific requirements. This is a valuable functionality for complex services which have management requirements other than conventional network/cloud services/applications. SONATA employs infrastructure and Open vSwitch (OVS) adaptors to provide service chaining and WAN connectivity, respectively. However, the infrastructure adaptor only supports OpenStack and deploys services based on the NFV services requirements. To solve this issue, we use Terraform to provide any cloud infrastructure for deploying microservices. Combining Terraform with SONATA infrastructure and OVS adaptors provides a unified NFV and cloud infrastructure that can be used by the orchestrator to deploy complex services.

Gathering the current tools and technologies for providing such an environment offers advantages such as reusability improvement and reducing maintenance overhead.

Our ongoing work includes the definition of a joint descriptor that can be used to describe both microservices and VNFs,

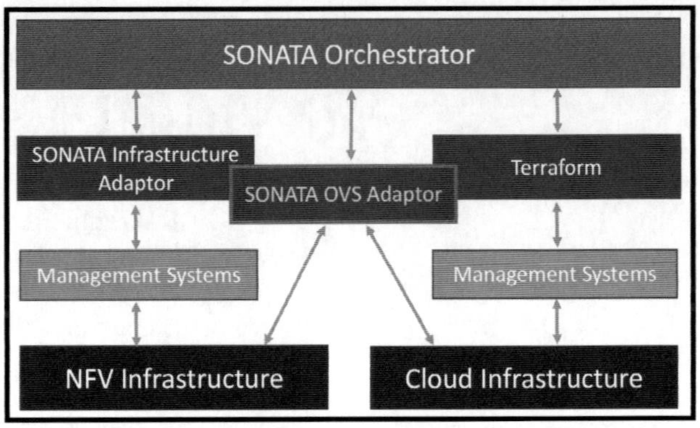

Fig. 2. Proposed solution architecture

as well as their dependencies, providing auto-scaling, and finding out the best way to distribute the life cycle management tasks between the orchestrator and management systems.

IV. Conclusion

We investigated the overlooked area of managing and orchestrating complex services composed of VNFs and microservices. Reviewing the literature, we found that running complex services in a multi-NFV/cloud environment can have remarkable benefits for actors involved in both NFV and cloud ecosystems by reducing cost and improving the service quality. Our proposed solution for providing such an environment is to leverage tools and technologies that are used to realise multi-cloud environments. To this end, we are building a service platform that combines an NFV management and orchestration tool, SONATA, with a multi-cloud tool, Terraform. This combination provides a joint NFV and Cloud environment that can be used to deploy and manage complex services.

Our future work will be extending the proposed environment to support other cloud and NFV platforms to realise the deployment of complex services on any cloud infrastructure.

Acknowledgment

This work has been partially supported by the SONATA project, funded by the European Commission under grant number 671517 through the Horizon 2020 and 5G-PPP programs and the 5G-PICTURE project, funded by the European Commission under grant number 762057 through the Horizon 2020 and 5G- PPP programs,

References

[1] J. Thönes, "Microservices," *IEEE Software*, vol. 32, no. 1, pp. 116–116, 2015.
[2] D. Petcu, "Multi-Cloud: Expectations and Current Approaches," in *Proceedings of the international workshop on Multi-cloud applications and federated clouds*. ACM, 2013, pp. 1–6.
[3] "DPDK," URL: http://dpdk.org/ [retrieved: January 2018].
[4] "Terraform," URL: https://www.terraform.io/ [retrieved: January 2018].
[5] "Cloudify," URL: http://cloudify.co/ [retrieved: January 2018].
[6] L. M. Pham et al., "Roboconf: a Hybrid Cloud Orchestrator to Deploy Complex Applications," in *IEEE 8th International Conference on Cloud Computing (CLOUD)*. IEEE, 2015, pp. 365–372.
[7] S. Dräxler et al., "SONATA: Service Programming and Orchestration for Virtualized Software Networks," in *IEEE International Conference on Communications Workshops (ICC Workshops)*. IEEE, 2017, pp. 973–978.

International Academy, Research,
and Industry Association (IARIA)
412 Derby Way
Wilmington, DE 19810

ISBN 978-1-5108-6132-9

Eighth International Conference on Sensor Device Technologies and Applications (SENSORDEVICES 2017)

Held at NetWare 2017

Rome, Italy
10 - 14 September 2017

IARIA